THE AMERICAN FILM MUSICAL

THE
AMERICAN
FILM MUSICAL

Rick Altman

Indiana University Press   Bloomington & Indianapolis

This book is a publication of

Indiana University Press
601 North Morton Street
Bloomington, IN 47404-3797 USA

http://iupress.indiana.edu

Telephone orders   800-842-6796
Fax orders   812-855-7931
Orders by e-mail   iuporder@indiana.edu

The paper used in this publication meets the minimum requirements
of American National Standard for Information Sciences—
Permanence of Paper for Printed Library Materials,
ANSI Z39.48-1984.

Manufactured in the United States of America

Cataloging information for this book is available from the
Library of Congress.

ISBN 978-0-253-30413-1 (cloth)
ISBN 978-0-253-20514-8 (paper)

5 6 7 8 9   12 11 10 09 08 07

*Front photographs courtesy of RKO Radio Pictures, Inc. and
The Museum of Modern Art, Film Stills Archive.*

*Back photographs courtesy of Wisconsin Center for Film and
Theater Research and The Museum of Modern Art/Film Stills Archive.*

For

the family piano

and those who gathered around it:

Mom

Dad

Jane

Ann

CONTENTS

As the most complex art form ever devised, the American film musical presents an unprecedented challenge to the critic and historian. Plundering every other entertainment industry and art form (painting, theater, opera, ballet, operetta, the music-hall, Tin Pan Alley, vaudeville, television), the musical also served as testing ground for many of Hollywood's most important technical innovations (sound film itself, later developments in sound technology like the playback system, special visual effects of numerous sorts), thus calling on the critic to develop expertise in an impossibly broad domain, and the historian to trace the aesthetic, social, and economic development of the better part of American artistic production in this century. Analyses of the musical will therefore continue to be partial, for no single individual can reasonably expect to master so many diverse domains, let alone delineate their interrelationships in a single book.

The American Film Musical is no exception. While I have worked for a decade now to develop the expertise necessary to understand the various individual strains which contribute to the musical's complexity and interest, I am painfully aware that I have fallen short in certain areas. In addition, my desire to make this book into a reasoned introduction to the problem of film genre study has forced me to limit my analysis of the musical itself. Many are the omissions I particularly regret: the career of Alice Faye and the important series of folk musicals produced by Fox throughout the forties; the work of individual composers (especially

Frank Loesser and Harold Arlen, whose contribution to the development of the musical has never been sufficiently proclaimed); the internal workings of individual studios, with special attention to the contributions of unsung heroes like MGM's Roger Edens; extended close analysis of numerous major dance routines; careful analysis not only of more individual songs, but of the overall structure of musical scores as well; the musical's contribution to technology (especially in special effects and sound recording technology); the complex relationship between the record industry and the musical; close attention to the musical's changing audience, especially since rock took over the genre in the late fifties; information on the musical's afterlife in informal singing groups gathered around pianos across the land. In some of these cases, I have made a conscious decision to leave out material which I have at hand. In others, sufficient information is lacking. I trust that readers will be understanding when they find that I have slighted their favorite dance or song, actor or director, composer or lyricist. Sometimes a genre's very riches present its biggest problem.

In preparing this book I have been blessed with more than my share of help and understanding. To the staffs of the archives where I have worked I give my heartfelt thanks: the British Film Institute, the Museum of Modern Art, the New York Public Library, the Library of Congress, the University of Wisconsin Center for Film and Theater Research. To the students who have kept me company into uncharted musical lands, and whose ideas have often inspired my own, I express my gratitude. In particular, I want publicly to mark my debt to Jane Feuer, with whom I discovered the byways of the genre. This is now the third book on the musical to which our many evenings of viewing and discussion have given rise. Now, a decade after our association began, it is often difficult to remember which of us first had which idea. Without the community orientation and the intellectual ferment around American genre film topics which characterized The University of Iowa during the late seventies this book would never have been written. Thanks are thus in order not only for Jane Feuer, but for Jim Collins, Tom Schatz, Alan Williams, and many others as well.

Above all, I owe thanks to my family. To my wife Janet, for believing with me that study of the musical can be a viable intellectual endeavor, and for putting up with two decades of bad piano-playing and worse singing. To my parents, for teaching me to love music—not only as something to listen to, but as something to play and sing as well. And finally, to all those who have ever gathered around a piano to sing. They are the ones for whom this book is really written, in the hope that their numbers might ever grow, along with their pleasure.

THE AMERICAN FILM MUSICAL

An Introduction to the Theory of Genre Analysis

THE AMERICAN FILM MUSICAL IS NOT ONE BOOK, BUT TWO. Most overtly, it is an account of the Hollywood musical and its place in American life. From Maurice Chevalier to John Travolta, and from Jeanette MacDonald to Barbra Streisand, no major star or director is neglected. Composers, choreographers, designers, musicians, even arrangers and montage specialists are given their due. From the twenties to the eighties (with side trips to nineteenth-century Vienna, the vaudeville circuit, and the Broadway stage), the story of the American film musical is here recounted in full. More than the musical's stars and story, however, it is the genre's recurrent structure that will receive attention in these pages. Book after book has told stories associated with the musical, but little attention has been paid to the structures and strategies which the musical shares with numerous other aspects of American life. To understand the musical is to understand the overall cultural system in which it develops and makes its meaning.

But what is the musical? How do we define it, delimit it, and analyze it? These are questions which have, alas, been too seldom asked and even less often answered. One writer after the other has been content to write the history of the musical as if the terms "musical" and "history" were entirely unproblematic, as if there were general agreement on all particulars of genre theory and genre history. Nothing could, of course, be farther from the truth. More than any other realm in the general domain of film studies, genre criticism has remained complacently untheoretical, accepting terms and categories provided by an openly self-serving industry, borrowing notions of history from fan magazines, and overall revealing shockingly little methodological self-consciousness.

In response to this situation, I have felt compelled to make this book into something more than the story of a genre. From beginning to end, *The American Film Musical* is also a treatise on how to study genre: what genre is, what it does, why it exists (and who makes it exist), what diverse roles industry, critic, and public play in generic functioning, how (and how not) to define a genre, what the responsibilities and methods of the genre historian are or might be, how to identify and delimit subgenres, and, in a broader sense, how to recognize and theorize the relationship between generic functioning and the strategies of the society that spawns a genre. In short, this is a book about the musical genre, a fascinating multi-media celebration constituting the world's most complex art form. But it is also a book about genre as such, a treatise on (and, I hope, an example of) the way in which questions of genre should be asked and answered. The reader who is less interested in the musical and more concerned to follow my theoretical argument might profitably read chapters one, five, and nine as a quasi-separate unit, while the reader primarily fascinated by questions of structure and style will find chapters two through four most rewarding, and those wanting a historical account may well skip to chapters six through eight.

General Discourse on Meaning

In order to understand the nature and function of generic categories, we must first understand the notion of meaning in general. Now, there are of course numerous ways of characterizing the process of signification, and it makes a difference for our understanding of generic functioning which one we choose. While my definition is hardly the only possible one, it will become apparent why it is a particularly appropriate one for the study of genre. Meaning, as I will define it, is never something that words or texts *have*,

but always something that is *made* in a four-party meaning-situation. An *author* (understood in the widest possible sense: individual, group, industry, etc.) circulates a *text* (which may vary from a single word, image, or gesture to multiple volumes) to an *audience* (singular or plural, present or removed) whose perception is partly dependent on the *interpretive community* to which its members belong. It is worth noting that this communication model differs in two major ways from more traditional sender-message-receiver models.[1] First, the model I am proposing has no message, that is no specific meaning that may be permanently ascribed to a given text. Instead, a text turns into a message (or different messages) only in the context of a specific audience in a specific interpretive community. When the meaning of a text seems so utterly clear as to permit no doubt, it is invariably because the author and audience are part of the same interpretive community. This common situation may seem to justify the older model, which recognizes the category of "message," but in the long run it is only another argument in favor of adding to the model a fourth category, that of interpretive community. As we shall see, the addition of the interpretive community as an active party in the process of making meaning opens up a new realm of generic activity and analysis.

An author transmits a text to an audience participating in a larger community. How is it that such a text acquires meaning? If meaning, as I believe, is fundamentally dependent on the relationships which the audience perceives in the text, then we may say that the process of making meaning is the process of constricting audience perception to certain quite specific (and limited) types of relationship. When we hear a language entirely unknown to us, say Mandarin Chinese or Bantu, we are free to play up any aspect we want, to stress whatever relationships we want, to appreciate sounds independently of the sense they might make for a native speaker. Even in our own language, this sense of "free play" remains available at certain times (dependent on our mood or the cultural circumstances), but in most situations our familiarity with the language makes it hard for us not to repress the level of sounds (signifiers) in favor of meaning (that which is signified). We could pay attention to any kind of sound relationship, but we don't, because years of familiarity with the sounds in question have taught us to stress certain connections over others. The making of meaning begins with this restriction of relationships. To put it in more technical terms, meaning can arise only in a context of finite commutability, of restricted semiosis—however temporary that restriction may be.

The process of producing meaning in literary or filmic texts is no doubt more complex, because of the existence of an additional level of meaning, but the situation is nevertheless fundamentally similar. The normal process of meaning attribution, as we have seen, involves an author, a text, an audience, and an interpretive community (one or more of each). Now, the text itself, as I have shown in more detail elsewhere,[2] may be conceived as including two levels of language: the primary language in which the text is written, and the secondary or textual language that ascribes to the words or images of the primary language meanings which they simply don't have when the primary language is used for everyday purposes. Dante's *Divine Comedy*, for example, is a text written in the Florentine dialect of Italian current around 1300. This first level of language definitely determines to a certain extent how the text will be read, i.e. what kind of meaning it will make, but this first level pre-exists the text and operates elsewhere independently of the text. At this level, words mean what they mean anywhere they might be used. The word "sun," for example, means the heavenly body that appears high in the sky during the day, passing from east to west and warming the earth. At a second level, however, dependent both on the text's own capacity for language creation and on the various traditions from which it borrows, words like "sun" can take on numerous meanings which they lack in everyday usage. In general, the extent to which such secondary, "textual," meanings are located depends largely on the interpretive community surrounding the text and the audience at a particular point in time. Thus, at various points in the history of Dante criticism, different aspects of the text have been stressed, thus constructing differing meanings: the Florentine political side, the *dolce stil novo*, the religious symbolism, the verbal patterns, the love poetry, and so forth. This variation in interpretive community has permitted the "use" of the text for an unending string of vastly different purposes: Florentine sectionalism, Italian nationalism, religious training, academic anti-utilitarianism, classical conservatism, and so forth.

It is interesting to note that nearly every one of these uses to which Dante's text is put can be neatly characterized by the *other texts* that the approach takes to be canonical. The interpretive community may thus be defined in part as a *context* in which the text is to be interpreted; the interpretive community names the *intertexts* that will control the interpretation of a given text. As in the case of listening to Bantu or English, meaning again appears as a restriction of possible perceptions to a specific, limited set of relationships.

Note that thus far there has been no mention of the text's message, or a correct interpretation, or a proper construction of meaning. What is at stake here is not *the* meaning of a text, but how *any* meaning at all arises from a text. A specific critical tradition or other cause—that is, a specific interpretive community—arrests the free play of a text's signifiers and freezes them *in a particular way*, thus producing a meaning proper to the particular community in question (by foregrounding certain patterns the recognition of which leads to the apprehension of that particular meaning). While it would perhaps be wrong to assume complete liberty on the part of a specific audience, or even of a particular interpretive community, (the primary language, after all, usually remains relatively stable, thus limiting community variation, and even the most diverse linguistic communities usually share with their larger culture certain common concerns, beliefs, or assumptions), there is nevertheless quite little to restrict possible interpretations of a text like *The Divine Comedy*. There are so many possible intertexts, and so few

truly similar texts, that almost any choice of intertexts could be justified by one interpretive community or another.

The Role of Generic Formations in Meaning Production

How does understanding of a single text differ from interpretation of a self-consciously constituted genre? In one sense, not at all. The text still has a primary language (or, in the case of film, a series of primary languages constituting both sound and image track), and a secondary language (or languages) activated by a specific intertextual context. The difference between interpretation of a single text and a generic system arises from the obvious fact that a genre already provides a specific set of intertexts (the other films identified by the industry as belonging to the same genre), and thus a self-contained equivalent of an interpretive community. The constitution of a genre thus *short-circuits* the "normal" sequence of interpretation. Text after text is generated from the same mold, thus highlighting certain textual relationships, repressing others, and eventually limiting the field of play of the interpretive community. The function of the interpretive community is usurped by the genre, thus rendering the human interpretive community all but vestigial in the meaning-making process. Seen in this light, genres appear as agents of a quite specific and effective ideological project: to control the audience's reaction to any specific film by providing the context in which that film must be interpreted.

Now, a well known truism claims that a generic text cannot be interpreted without reference to the text's generic tradition. To be sure, the categories operative in a single film can be fully perceived only through a conflation or superimposition of related films. The meaning, we often say (roughly following Lévi-Strauss or Cawelti),[3] is contained in the generic patterns rather than in the individual text. What critics have failed to realize in making such claims is the repressive power exercised by the genre. Rather than seeing genres as structures helping individual texts to produce meaning, we must see genres as restrictive, as complex methods of reducing the field of play of individual texts. Genres are not the democratically elected representatives of a group of like-minded texts. They are autocratic monarchs dictating a single standard of allegiance for all subjects. In short, genres are not neutral categories, as structuralist critics have too often implied; rather they are *ideological constructs masquerading as neutral categories*. As such they are to be identified not with some impersonal structure immanent in a text, but with the discursive activity of the producing industry. Genres are like a key addressed to the audience, a key to the codes contained in the simultaneously transmitted text. Precisely because they don't appear to be emitted by the industry, but rather to arise independently from the conflation of a series of similar texts, genres never give the impression of limiting the audience's freedom. Yet, because they make it easy to understand the text in a particular predetermined way, genres always make it less likely that a film will be construed in a different, non-generic way. By prejudicing us toward one set of intertexts rather than another (and thus toward a particular set of patterns), they provide and enforce a *pre-reading* of the text at hand.

The Role of the Critic

Genres, then, must no longer be considered solely as impersonal agents of narrative organization, but as discursive acts,[4] an active part of the industry's direct address to its audience, a rhetorical ploy destined to enforce a single pre-determined reading or at least to increase the probability that certain other interpretations will remain unexplored. What then is the role of the critic in dealing with the always already pre-interpreted generic text? It is tempting to see in the critic the denouncer of industrial ideology and the restorer of the interpretive community. Many a rewarding revisionist genre study has been based on the assumption that the critic must unmask Hollywood, that criticism is democracy's privileged form of speech, the last bastion of freedom and truth exposing the tyranny of the industry's ideologically loaded generic discourse. Now, I do not mean to condemn this attitude entirely. The critic's function as informer, as the one who fingers the self-serving strategies of this or any other entertainment enterprise, must not be neglected. The critic has a duty to see and to say what is seen. The problem lies with the notion that critics, unlike audiences and industries, have the power to see clearly and to write objectively. To demonstrate the bias implied by genres is simply, once again, for the pot to call the kettle black. Suppose I were to substitute my set of intertexts for that supplied by the genre. Would I not also be attempting to predetermine a given audience's operative interpretive community? Would I be doing anything different with my criticism than the industry with its genre? In order to answer this question properly, we must at this point take an apparent detour through the various strategies that critics (and cultures) have used to support the notion of their own objectivity while exposing the supposedly limited or tendentious nature of other, non-critical, language or endeavors.

In the long struggle to establish a privileged position for the critic and critical discourse, four opposed pairs of terms stand out as representative of alternate but related strategies. As a rule, these are not useless or spurious oppositions, they have simply been made to stand for differences which they do not in fact represent. This strategy (for it is a strategy, an argumentative rhetoric that covertly but effectively supports its author's positions) is perhaps at its most obvious and influential in the well known introduction to *The Fantastic*, where Tzvetan Todorov opposes "theoretical" to "historical" genres.[5] Seeking to dissociate himself from previous unsystematic genre study, and to stake out a firm ground on which a durable analysis might be built, Todorov distinguishes between the types which our culture traditionally recognizes (epic, short story, lyric poetry, and so forth) and the new types which the modern systematic critic will constitute. "Historical" types are thus those that are accepted by the culture, while "theoretical" types are defined by the critic. This opposition of course begs the question of the critic's position within the culture. All historical genres or types were once theo-

retical genres, defined by the critics of a former culture (who may have been known by other names—essayists, journalists, or simply men of taste and influence—but who played the role of critic nonetheless) according to a theory then current (not a self-consciously elaborated theory like that championed by Todorov, but a theory nonetheless).

In spite of the repeated pronouncements of Todorov and others, there is no place outside of history from which purely "theoretical" definitions of genre might be made. In substituting his so-called "theoretical" definition of the fantastic for a series of historical categories (fairy tale, ghost story, gothic novel, etc.), Todorov is only substituting a *current historical* understanding of literature (heavily dependent on contemporary fashions of psychoanalysis and formal analysis) for a *former historical* definition of literature (referring instead to literature's mimetic function and thus dependent on content paradigms). Reading *The Fantastic* less than a generation after its publication, we already recognize its vocabulary, its methodological tools, and its compartmentalization of literature as marked by a particular period which only recently was the present, which may once have appeared not-yet-historical, but which we now identify with structuralism. The "fantastic" as defined by Todorov is already (*was always already*) a historical genre. "Theoretical," when it is opposed to "historical," defines a utopian space, a "no place" from which the critic may seemingly justify blindness to his/her own historicity. Just as the critic is always part of a culture, thus undermining any attempt to oppose the critical to the cultural, so the theoretician always stands on the historically marked ground of a particular era. (Now, this is not to say that there is no difference between the categories of a Todorov and those which the society traditionally recognizes. Shortly, I shall be forced to ask whether and how it is possible to improve upon received typological notions. For the time being, however, it is enough to have dismissed the too easy temptation to search out a theoretical space outside of history. Later, I will try to isolate the real differences between structuralist genre analysis and the traditional categorization from which it seeks to differentiate itself.)

A second intelligent but problematic attempt to justify a particular critical terminology grows out of the strong sense that Hollywood's status as industry disqualifies it as a source of generic distinctions. Because studios are businesses, numerous critics have claimed, any terms they might devise must be taken as little more than glorified publicity for the studios' products. According to this argument, "user" vocabulary must be distinguished from "critical" terminology. In one sense it is hard to disagree with such a claim. When one follows the history of generic terms as applied to film texts, one finds that industrial labels have time and again preceded and influenced critical terminology. The first decade of this century, for example, saw a rapid growth in the tendency of film producers to identify their products by a generic title (adventure, comedy, western, etc.) which, though it may at first have been meant as a shorthand for theater owners, soon became a major factor in audience choice of films. Before long the trade papers were talking about audience taste in terms of growing or de-

clining preference for such and such a genre (with a consequent growth in scope and number of films in the more popular genres). Ever since, Hollywood's generic terminology has remained a major aspect of studio rhetoric, with the unconscious collaboration of many a film reviewer or academic film historian.

At first blush, therefore, it would seem that we self-conscious critics have every right to distinguish ourselves from those who use generic terminology for their own gain, as part of an overall strategy to make money and to garner prestige. Yet who is free of the tendency to bend whatever we write about to our own use? Just as the term "musical" was used for decades to advertise the prestigious products of MGM, so the term "fantastic" now serves to heighten the prestige of Tzvetan Todorov. We may not be users in the same way as Hollywood, but we still have an investment in our terminology and something to gain from its widespread acceptance. Like the theoretical/historical opposition, the critic/user distinction sets before us a false dichotomy. All critics are users (and all users critics) in the same way that all theories are historical (and all histories implicitly theoretical). Again, there is an important difference between what we expect of the critic and what we usually find in the industry's discourse, but that difference cannot be reached through an opposition like that of user to critic.

In attempting to specify more successfully the task of the critic, and in particular the critic's stance vis-à-vis an already existent industrial terminology, a recent group of critics interested in ideological analysis has turned toward a distinction between what might for simplicity's sake be termed "discourse" and "disclosure."[6] Falsely presenting itself as a neutral document, addressed to no one in particular, seemingly unaware that anyone might be watching, the Hollywood film in fact constitutes part of a complex circuit of discourse whereby the cinema industry speaks to its audience. The audience, however, is unaware that it is being interpellated by the industry; the spectators are convinced that the characters on the screen are acting out their lives according to principles that have nothing to do with the audience at hand. Since the audience remains unaware of the discursive circuit in which it is implicated, the critic, according to this approach, must take on the responsibility of disclosing the discourse latent in each film, each genre. Seen in this light, the industry is a magician capable of convincing an audience that black is white, while the critic is charged with unmasking Hollywood's trickery. The critic is a transparent lens through which we can observe the discourse of the text.

Yet, paradoxically, by stressing their ability to disclose discourse, to reveal the text's position, critics have effectively succeeded in hiding their own discourse. To dissimulate this discourse is one thing; to do away with it is quite another. There is no strategy, however clever, that can keep the process of criticism—and *a fortiori* genre criticism—from presenting a play of discursivities. Though Hollywood films have a discursive dimension, and though it may be important for critics to disclose that discourse, in order to do so they must employ a *discourse* of disclosure, a form of address that cannot help

but identify them with an ideological position. The critic's view of Hollywood ideology can thus hardly be taken as objective. We need to recognize in all criticism not an opposition of discourse to disclosure but a play of two discursivities, for just as the industry's more or less self-conscious constitution of a genre represents an attempt to short-circuit the activity of another interpretive community, so any critical pronouncement must necessarily be seen as a ploy to reduce the free play of text and reader, to limit both to a predetermined set of relationships.

How then do we guarantee greater objectivity in the critical process? Or do we even care to do so? Perhaps we will do well to start by changing our understanding of the term "objective." Often taken to mean "true" or "unbiased," it is better understood in its goal-oriented, military sense. A person who says that another's judgment is objective means "it shares my objectives." The term "objective" can thus be applied by a critic only to another critic working in the same paradigm—a common situation in the sciences, whence the sense that science produces positive objective knowledge, but a much less common situation in the humanities, where appeals to objectivity are commonly taken as attempts to establish the hegemony of one paradigm over another.

But if science is the proper domain of the objective (that is, in my revised sense, of shared objectives), then perhaps we can find our solution in the often invoked distinction between "everyday" and "scientific" terminology. For centuries, generic terminology has aspired toward scientific accuracy and thus often taken contemporary science as a model. While this approach has often led to abuses, as in the celebrated early twentieth-century attempts to apply Darwinian notions to the "evolution" of literary genres, there remains a great deal to be learned from the way in which positive science goes about establishing its categories. Even so, this road is not without its pitfalls.

Consider, for example, the category of "fish." Before becoming a scientific designation, "fish" was an everyday word applied to all animals that swim, from eels to whales and from sunfish to shellfish. This everyday word, when subjected to scientific scrutiny, however, revealed a serious shortcoming: the phenomena to which it was regularly applied were extremely diverse, rather than similar in basic characteristics as their presence in the same category would seem to imply. Finding little value in the everyday term, modern science constructed instead, on the basis of shared structure and function, a new term, the scientific designation "fish." Recognizing that in terms of life processes whales have more in common with cows than with mackerel, biologists were simultaneously able to justify a more careful definition of "fish" and to attribute whales to another category altogether. Thus, according to the new scientific terminology, whales *are not* fish, they *are really* mammals.

How did the whale become a mammal and why? The accepted answer to this question derives from one of science's most basic assumptions: categories are not created but discovered, they exist independently of human observation, and scientists are only the impersonal vessels of the pouring forth of truth. An alternate response is provided by Thomas Kuhn and his followers.[7] According to Kuhn, scientific truth involves not so much a faithful rendering of natural phenomena as an explanation corresponding to dominant contemporary notions of what nature is and what might constitute an explanation. While the traditional version of science holds that eighteenth-century scientists discovered certain truths (including the definition and delimitation of genera) which twentieth-century scientists are bound to respect, the revisionist version maintains that current science perpetuates eighteenth-century claims in part for institutional and cultural reasons. In order to continue to work within the dominant paradigm (i.e. in order to work at all), twentieth-century scientists must accept as discoveries many of the claims of their predecessors (much as a reader of detective fiction must accept the author's account of the circumstances surrounding the crime). According to this second hypothesis, which I will adopt here, what is at stake is not truth, but the working out of a hypothesis, albeit one not chosen by the individual scientist him/herself. The implication for film genre criticism is evident. If we use a previous definition or delimitation of genre we are not, as we might think, reiterating a truth well known to all, a truth good for all ages, we are choosing a particular paradigm associated with that genre definition. Inasmuch as this activity is a *choice*, it deserves to be analyzed as fully and as self-consciously as any other critical activity.

What difference does it make to understand the whale's generic migration as a shift in scientific paradigms rather than a discovery of the truth? For medieval fishermen, the term "fish" applied to any being living permanently in the water; those animals that swim in the water are fish, those that don't aren't. Not so terribly far from the Greek four-element world, the fisherman demanded of his terminology only that it accurately predict where he was likely to encounter a given creature—in the air, earth, fire, or water. A whale was thus a fish, not just for the medieval fisherman, but for medieval science as well (thus suggesting that the term "everyday" is often synonymous with the term "scientific," but refers to a former science rather than the current version). For modern science, however, knowledge of an animal's geographic range or habitat is insufficient as a typological indicator. Far more interested in internal functioning and in ability to mate—that is, in the intersection of social and bodily function—the Linnaean system types the whale as a mammal for reasons which any high school biology student could easily recite (mammary glands, warm blood, skin type, and so forth). Classifying the whale as a mammal permits us to analyze the whale in the terms selected by this new scientific paradigm, to establish connections that are within the limits of the system's method. Classifying the whale as a fish does not so much limit possible understanding of the whale (in fact it gives us *more* information about the whale's habitat) as it limits understanding of the whale to aspects not selected by the Linnaean system. In other words, the whale is excluded from the category of fish because of the lack of interest—from the Linnaean point of view—of considering the whale as a fish. The eel, conversely, is included because it responds to the method, i.e. gives the method ample material to work on. Thus, when the whale became a mammal it was not so much changing types as changing paradigms.

The problem that confronts us here is a delicate and seemingly paradoxical one. On the one hand, I have just suggested that scientific terminology remains discursive and historical, that the decision to call a whale a mammal involves a measure of subjectivity, an investment in a certain type of discourse. Yet on the other hand, I am sensitive to the power and usefulness of the new categories; for the biology student it is clearly more satisfying to call a whale a mammal than to call a whale a fish, given the vastly more complex and wide-ranging relationships unlocked by the former attribution. In short, it is perfectly possible for a change in categorization to be *motivated subjectively* (desire to privilege a particular paradigm and its operators) and yet *evaluated objectively* (recognition of measurable differences in the explanatory power of two terminologies).

Toward Objective Evaluation of Subjective Criticism

We find ourselves, I believe, at a critical juncture. Recent criticism has foundered on the simplistic opposition between a desire for objective criticism on the one hand and the recognition that all criticism is implicitly ideological on the other. Between the objective and the ideological, between the academic and the engagé, there is no sense of a middle ground, no theory that recognizes the always already historical, discursive position of the critic, yet which continues to strive in a systematic way for a richer and more complex, more sharable criticism. Now that we know that we are always subjective, how can we turn our self-consciousness about that very subjectivity into criticism that will be recognized as of a higher quality? How do we even define "quality" in this situation? Can we devise criteria that would authorize value judgments in an arena where every voice is marked by its own desires and prejudices? We are desperately in need, I believe, of criteria that might permit us to distinguish between better and worse genre studies.

It is in this spirit that I offer the following guidelines for choosing one generic definition or delimitation over another. All generic approaches are subjective, but I have taken as an active principle of my research and writing the need to temper my subjectivity through criteria such as these.

1) Does the genre definition treat the phenomena in question in a fashion consonant with the analyst's needs and interests?

2) Does it provide an explanation for the internal functioning of each example of the genre?

3) Does it explain a maximum number of shared attributes between examples of a type?

4) Does it consider explanations for those elements that are not shared?

5) Does it establish a terminology that permits linkage to other cultural phenomena?

6) Does the basis for systematic analysis and generic division also provide a reasonable basis for generic history?

A rapid comparison of the medieval scientific paradigm to its modern succes-

sor should help to clarify this set of guidelines. Below, evaluations of the older categorization, whereby a whale is a fish, are followed by evaluations of the Linnaean version, according to which whales are mammals:

1) *Does the typology meet the analyst's needs?*

fish—obviously (from the fisherman's point of view)

mammal—yes, but not obviously (desire for objective knowledge, interest in internal systems, economy based on breeding animals rather than hunting and fishing)

2) *Does it explain internal functioning?*

fish—in terms only of habitat and locomotion

mammal—in terms of systems as well as individual traits (reproduction, skin functioning, organ type and function, etc.)

3) *Does it attempt to maximize explanation of shared attributes?*

fish—no

mammal—yes, stresses all above, plus many others

4) *Are explanations for differences considered?*

fish—not at all

mammal—only after the problem of evolution is considered by Lamarck, Darwin, etc.

5) *Do operative criteria link easily with other cultural phenomena?*

fish—minimally

mammal—yes, through the extension of the Linnaean system to all other living beings

6) *Does the typology facilitate the development of a typological history?*

fish—not at all

mammal—yes, through Darwin, for whom the basic Linnaean criterion (inter-reproduction) becomes an historical operator (partner choice); likewise with Mendel's notion of trait transmission through bisexual reproduction

Schematic as it may be, this analysis simultaneously recognizes the subjective basis for the choice of each scientific paradigm and the objective basis for preference of the more recent approach. Neither designation is "right" or "wrong," but the identification of the whale as a mammal (as well as the entire classificatory system on which that identification depends) maximizes our ability to recognize and manipulate the information and relationships which our culture deems pertinent and important. A different culture might well have another order of priorities, but I take it as a given that one of the tasks of criticism is to teach a culture about itself. In order to be understood by one's own culture, the critic must of necessity share in that culture's subjectivity, for the only classifications that will make full sense to a culture are the ones that share its particular manner of perceiving. Even within this overall subjectivity,

however, it remains possible to separate, as I have tried to do, more productive from less productive uses of subjectivity. While I am aware that any set of supposedly objective guidelines is susceptible to becoming a veiled reiteration of the subjectivity it seeks to control, I believe that the simple criteria presented here can be helpful in our attempt to devise new and richer terminology for the description of Hollywood genres.

Establishing a Corpus

As the previous section suggests, critical work on the film musical continues to depend on a definition provided largely by the film industry itself. The musical, according to the industry, is a film with music, that is, with music that emanates from what I will call the diegesis, the fictional world created by the film (as opposed to Hollywood's typical background music, which comes instead out of nowhere). From a producer's point of view, this definition is a perfectly reasonable one, for it indicates from the very start what kind of personnel the producer will need for the production. Musicals require composers, arrangers, singers, dancers, musician-actors, specialized sound technicians, and a variety of other personnel not needed for, say, a western (which in turn will need a variety of personnel, equipment, and sets not needed by the musical). The consumer, too, finds this simple meaning of the term musical quite convenient and informative. When choosing a film, the prospective spectator knows what to expect when the film is labeled a musical. For the critic, however, the industrial definition of the genre is of extremely limited interest. Putting aside any question of possible ideological investment carried by Hollywood's term, there still remains a fundamental poverty in terms of the criteria listed above. Far from seeking to explain the genre or its texts, far from creating a vocabulary appropriate both to systematic and historical analysis, Hollywood's version of the musical serves only to locate the genre, rather than to provide a method of dealing with its functioning or even of justifying this particular delimitation of the genre. Just as the medieval fisherman called everything that swims in the water a fish, so Hollywood calls everything that shows music on film a musical. What is needed at this point is a radical reconsideration of the genre and its terminology, in order to discover whether there are more complex and far-reaching principles underlying the identification of a musical genre, and in order more systematically to define and delimit the genre. Does the musical have its whales? Are there texts commonly called musicals which in fact operate according to a logic different from the vast majority of other musicals? How can we go about bringing the analysis of the musical out of the middle ages and into the modern world?

I propose the following series of steps as a reasonable and efficient method of constituting both a critical definition of a genre and a corpus generated by that critical definition rather than by an industrial/journalistic tradition.

1) The fact that a genre has previously been posited, defined, and delimited by Hollywood is taken only as *prima facie* evidence that generic levels of meaning are operative within or across a group of texts roughly designated by the Hollywood term and its usage. The industrial/journalistic term thus founds a hypothesis about the presence of meaningful activity, but does not necessarily contribute a definition or delimitation of the genre in question.

2) The broadest possible corpus implied by the industrial/journalistic term is taken as the critic's *preliminary* corpus. In the case of the musical, this means that every conceivable film with diegetic music is at first accepted and treated as a musical, from *Gilda* to *Singin' in the Rain*, from *Hallelujah* to *The Lady and the Tramp*, from *Paramount on Parade* to *Woodstock*, from the films of Shirley Temple to those of Elvis Presley. In other words, the early stages of a generic study must be undertaken with a corpus different from the one with which the study concludes. Lacking biology's centuries of shared paradigm, we cannot begin our work simply by naming a genre and listing the corpus that such a naming implies. Instead, *the constitution of a corpus comprises one of the genre critic's most important tasks.*

3) The broad, amorphous corpus thus borrowed is then subjected to diverse modes of analysis. Here the critic's subjectivity infallibly comes into play. Nevertheless, by respecting the earlier guidelines for choosing one generic definition over another, the critic will identify and describe certain traits and systems present and operative within a large number of the texts constituted by the preliminary corpus. A major stage of any genre study thus involves the location and presentation of the shared structures and functions that justify the original hypothesis whereby generic activity is assumed to be discernible

in this particular group of texts. In the present book, chapters two, three, and four are devoted to such a presentation.

4) Once a method of analysis has been established—for the identification of specific systems implies a particular methodology, that is, a particular way of looking at the films, i.e. a way of looking for particular traits and structures in the films—it becomes possible to constitute a revised corpus. The accepted layman's notion of science involves the delimitation of a corpus followed by the development of a method sufficient to and dictated by that corpus. This is what appears to lend an objective character to science: the material dictates the approach (independently of personal, religious, national, or other ideological interests). The methodology which I am here prescribing, however, (and which is operative in the first section of this book), reverses the accepted relationship between corpus and method. Far from the corpus dictating the method, the corpus is itself in part dictated by the method chosen. Texts which correspond to a particular understanding of the genre, that is which provide ample material for a given method of analysis, will be retained within the generic corpus. Those which are not illuminated by the method developed in step three will simply be excluded from the final corpus, even though they were present in the preliminary corpus. In terms of the musical, this would mean admitting that there are some films which include a significant amount of diegetic music, and yet which we will refuse to identify as musicals in the strong sense which the final corpus implies. Just as the Linnaean system, in its desire to stress social and bodily functioning, rather than

habitat alone, removes the whale from the corpus of fish, so we must entertain the possibility that a systematic study of the musical will redistribute generic texts and borders.

5) Once a final corpus has been established, the question of genre history can no longer be avoided. Just as the initial stages of analysis must depend on the false premise constituted by a preliminary, soon-to-be-surpassed corpus, so the early stages of generic analysis must accept the fiction that a genre exists outside of time, without a history, for only by temporarily suppressing historical relationships can we perceive systematic relationships. With the final corpus and the methodology on which it is based, however, comes the opportunity to return history to its rightful place. Now, history has never been given its due in generic studies, partly because it has often been assumed that generic categories not only are developed but also continue to exist outside of time. Precisely for that reason, this study will devote a major effort to providing a model for writing genre history, along with the extended example constituted by the history of the musical. The problems involved in writing such a history will be dealt with in chapter five. Chapters six through eight apply the conclusions of chapter five to the musical's three main subgenres.

6) One final step is necessary in the elaboration of a genre study. Since genres are social as well as esthetic categories, and since the terminology used to describe them will have been devised in such a way as to permit linkage to contemporary cultural phenomena, it is important not to abandon a genre study without analyzing the way in which the genre is molded by,

functions within, and in turn informs the society of which it is a part. Such an analysis is of course not without its potential pitfalls. Nevertheless, it will be attempted in a final chapter, which begins with an essay on the ways in which cultural analysis might be done in the context of genre study.

Presented here in part as a justification for the organization of this particular genre study, the above method is not meant to be limited, however, to the present enterprise. Instead, it is introduced as the beginning of a general discourse on genre study, a discourse which continues in chapter five.

The American Film Musical
as Dual-Focus Narrative

WHEN WE LOOK AT A NARRATIVE FILM OR READ A NOVEL, WHAT do we tend to see? All our experience predisposes us toward a particular way of viewing. We expect certain character relationships and plot patterns just as surely as we expect a film to have a specific shape on the screen. The very vocabulary we use to describe narrative reveals a great deal about our presuppositions. We speak, for example, of the hero or protagonist of a film as if a film always had a single central character, around whom all other activity revolves. Indeed, all our notions about narrative structure seem to support this proposition. When we speak of a plot we usually mean the hero's (or heroine's) trajectory from the beginning of the text to the end; alternately acting and acted upon, he (she) ties the plot together by providing a psychological bridge between each action and the next. The concept of motivation is thus essential to this standard view of narrative structure. An event takes place, it motivates a second event, which in turn occasions a third, and so on until the necessary chain of causality has been extinguished and the film draws to a close.

It is of course not possible to *prove* that one event causes another, any more than we can prove that a moving billiard ball striking a stationary ball causes the stationary one to move. The traditional approach to narrative solves this problem by postulating psychological motivation as a necessary and sufficient connector. When we watch a character read a telegram, then see him grab his hat and coat, rush out the door, and head for the police station, we assume that his actions are motivated by the telegram, that something in his synapses or his brain *causes* him to react in a specific way to a specific stimulus. As spectators of commercial cinema, we have acquired the habit of linking one segment of a traditional film to another by postulating such an intermediary psychological motivation. From this point of view each plot looks more or less the same. An initial impulse sets in motion a series of causally related events, each one closely tied to the preceding and following events:

$$a \longrightarrow b \longrightarrow c \longrightarrow d \longrightarrow e \longrightarrow \ldots x$$

Why belabor these apparently obvious notions about narrative? It seems clear that most films follow the destiny of a single character, integrate other characters and happenings into his/her career, motivate the plot by reference to his/her psychology, and depend on the twin chains of chronological progression and causal sequence.[1] Attempts to analyze the musical following these principles have consistently come up short, however, for like many popular genres the musical operates only in part according to the model of psychological motivation. To be sure, the musical *looks* as if it can be properly defined by a linear, psychological model, but this impression is created by no more than a veneer, a thin layer of classical narrativity which we must learn to look beyond, discovering instead the radically different principles of organization which lie just beneath the surface.

Let us take as an extremely clear example the first two sequences of MGM's 1940 version of *New Moon*. The first few shots set the scene: the French ship Marseilles in 1789 en route to New Orleans, carrying a group of extremely well-dressed society ladies. The older ladies in the group soon pressure one of the younger members to share her operatic talents, a typical method of introducing Jeanette MacDonald's first song. As MacDonald holds forth on deck, demonstrating her appetizing physical features along with her well developed voice, her song is slowly drowned out by muffled male voices. The camera immediately cuts to the source of this second song: imprisoned in the hold, a group of disheveled young Frenchmen about to be sold into slavery sing of their plight. Their leader, played by Nelson Eddy, is introduced in the same shot sequence previously used for MacDonald's song: full shot for the first two lines, cut to medium shot at line three, then to a close-up at line seven. At the request of the ladies on deck, an emissary soon appears to order the men in the hold to cease their singing or suffer the consequences.

These first two scenes appear to correspond quite closely to the characteristics of classical narrative outlined above. An event within scene one (the voices drowning out MacDonald's song) motivates a cut to scene two, where we witness the logical consequences of the first scene (Eddy and friends are told to reduce the "noise"). What this chronological approach ignores, however, are the careful parallels set up between Jeanette MacDonald and Nelson Eddy. Tied together by similar shot scale, mise-en-scène, and domination of the sound track, the two stars are nevertheless implicitly contrasted in numerous ways. *She* sings on deck, *he* sings in the hold; *she* sings to entertain a bevy of society women, *he* sings to relieve the misery of a group of penniless men; *she* is free, *he* is behind bars. The first two scenes must be visualized not one after the other but one balanced against the other. Now classical narrative analysis would make the chronological relationship primary, relegating the simultaneity and parallelism of the scenes to the shadows of stylistic analysis or theme criticism. In order to understand

While Jeanette MacDonald warbles a well-known song on deck
Nelson Eddy and his henchmen belt out their frustrations in the hold
British Film Institute [BFI]

the musical, however, we must learn to do just the opposite; we must treat the conceptual relationships as fundamental, assuming that the rather tenuous cause-and-effect connections are in this case secondary, present only to highlight the more important parallelisms which they introduce. Instead of stressing a causal progression, the first two sequences of *New Moon* present and develop the two centers of power on which the film depends: *the female*—rich, cultured, beautiful, easily offended; *the male*—poor, practical, energetic, tenacious. Yet they share one essential attribute: they both sing.

Two centers of power, two sexes, two attitudes, two classes, two protagonists. We seem to be traveling not on the Marseilles in 1789 but on Noah's Ark many millennia earlier. Instead of focusing all its interest on a single central character, following the trajectory of her progress, the American film musical has a dual focus, built around parallel stars of opposite sex and radically divergent values.[2] This dual-focus structure requires the viewer to be sensitive not so much to chronology and progression—for the outcome of the male/female match is entirely conventional and thus quite predictable—but to simultaneity and comparison. We construe the first two sequences of *New Moon* not according to their syntagmatic ties but in the light of their paradigmatic relationship; that is, we subordinate their sequential connection to their parallelism. The principle which holds for the paired initial scenes also applies to the following scene which joins Eddy and MacDonald for the first time. In terms of traditional plot analysis we might say that this scene

serves to initiate the love plot, which will eventually culminate in the couple's final embrace. If this, however, is the sole function of the scene, then it is wasted indeed. What moviegoer in 1940 needed a preliminary infatuation scene to inform him that Eddy and MacDonald would ultimately fall in love? *New Moon* was the seventh movie in five years to pair the two as lovers. In short, the matched scenes that open *New Moon* are sufficient to suggest the course which the plot will take.

What then *is* the purpose of the stars' first meeting in *New Moon*? Having simultaneously decided to visit the captain, both Eddy and MacDonald at first seem simply to continue the thematics of the original balanced sequences. *He* is still concerned about the fate of his singing friends; *she* still wants to be able to sing without interruption. *He* is all rebellious energy, caring little for social mores as long as the cause of freedom is served; *she* is all properness, expecting the dictates of society to be obeyed even on the high seas. It is in this context that we must interpret the simple but significant clothing motif developed during this first meeting. When Eddy first sees MacDonald he forgets his revolutionary purpose for a moment in order to don the nearest coat; even then he apologizes for having appeared in shirt sleeves before a lady. By the end of the scene, MacDonald has reversed the process; she arrived bundled up, but she is so captivated by Eddy that she soon removes her shawl, and with it some of the propriety which has thus far defined her. If the initial paired scenes define Eddy as energy, MacDonald as restraint, this first joint scene moves each of

Male and female, dark and light, bondsman and aristocrat—all are brought together in *New Moon*'s romantic conclusion.

[BFI]

the prospective lovers a step toward the other, Eddy demonstrating his civility and MacDonald her desire. As this analysis suggests, the plot of *New Moon* depends not on the stars' falling in love (they do that early on) nor even on their marriage (even that takes place well before the end), but on the resolution of their differences. Each must adopt the characteristics of the other: Eddy must exercise restraint and MacDonald must learn to reveal her desire before the love story—and the film—can end.

This simple analysis is given not as an interpretation of the film, but as an example of how the American film musical must be construed. Those aspects which

form the heart of traditional narrative analysis—plot, psychology, motivation, suspense—are to such an extent conventional in the musical that they leave little room for variation: we alternate between the male focus and the female focus, working our way through a prepackaged love story whose dynamic principle remains the difference between male and female. *Each segment must be understood not in terms of the segments to which it is causally related but by comparison to the segment which it parallels.* The first three sequences of *New Moon* are thus not to be construed in traditional terms:

$$A \longrightarrow B \longrightarrow C$$

but in a radically modified fashion:

A/B, C/C'

The first two paired scenes (on deck, in the hold) are balanced; they are meant to be measured against each other. The third scene (in the captain's cabin) can be understood only when we divide it in half, comparing Eddy's conduct to MacDonald's. *New Moon* is thus seen not as a continuous chain of well-motivated events but as a series of nearly independent fragments, each a carefully constructed duet involving the two principal personages. The presence of Jeanette MacDonald and Nelson Eddy predetermines the plot of *New Moon*, forces it to conform to certain definite criteria, even makes it stoop to the most unlikely combinations in order to set up repeated confrontations or parallels between the two stars. Whereas the traditional approach to narrative assumes that structure grows out of *plot*, the dual-focus structure of the American film musical derives from *character*.

An extended example from a well-known film should help demonstrate the importance of this new method of viewing the musical. Vincente Minnelli's *Gigi* (MGM, 1958) borrows from the French novelist Colette a story about a young girl on the verge of becoming a woman. During the course of the film, Gigi (Leslie Caron) changes from an impish girl into a dazzling beauty capable of exciting the interest of Gaston Lachaille (Louis Jourdan). Very few scenes in the film actually advance this plot, however, and those that do are singularly lacking in motivation. Gaston leaves Gigi's apartment one lovely Paris night, he stops on a bridge, looks pensive, the music swells, and presto! he suddenly realizes that his young friend has changed. To judge from the point of view of the plot, *Gigi* is a remarkably unimpressive affair: it wastes time, motivates little, seems more concerned to paint representative days in the lives of its characters than to fashion the kind of tightly knit fabric that characterizes masterful narrative. But if we inspect the film from the vantage point of dual-focus structure we find that from its very first words it creates an organized and compact whole.

"Bonjour Monsieur, bonjour Madame," says Gaston's Uncle Honoré (Maurice Chevalier) as the film opens, thus dividing the world from the very beginning into two groups, the very groups that will preside over the film's structure. The film's first song, "Thank Heaven for Little Girls," demonstrates the extent to which even the youngest members of society are defined by gender. In fact, the scenes which follow make no sense at all unless we see them as outgrowths of the basic sexual parameter introduced by Chevalier. We first see Gigi at home, where she is told by her grandmother to change her clothes, comb her hair, and hurry to the lessons in femininity which her Aunt Alicia gives her once a week. Over the music of "Thank Heaven" we then dissolve to Gaston receiving a visit from his uncle; while Gaston buys two cars and admits having recently bought an entire railroad, his uncle reminds him that he is expected at an embassy tea. It is not the plot that justifies Gaston's appearance here, but the extended series of parallels linking these two scenes. We observe Gigi at home, then Gaston at home; Gigi is with an older relative, so is Gaston; Gigi has no great desire to keep her appointment, neither does Gaston; Gigi is defined by female preoccupations (looks, clothes, manners), Gaston by their turn-of-the-century male counterparts (business, politics, riches). Before they have even met on screen, Gigi and Gaston are linked in the viewer's mind by these parallel scenes, thus initiating the duality which will inform the film's structure.

The following sequences further develop this paradigm. Gaston's song "It's a Bore," which emphasizes his profound disgust with Parisian life, is matched by Gigi's "I Don't Understand the Parisians." While Gigi endeavors to learn the manners of Gaston's world, Gaston enjoys the camomile tea and cookies to which Gigi is accustomed. Each scene involving only one of the lovers is invariably matched by a parallel scene (song, shot, event) featuring the other lover. From this rather simple discovery about the *structure* of *Gigi* we can deduce certain important attributes of the *interpretation process* appropriate for *Gigi* and the American film musical in general. In any film a given scene, in order to be properly understood, must be set in its proper context. Traditional narrative analysis usually stresses other scenes involving the same character, but *in the musical the basic context is constituted by a parallel scene involving the other lover.* When Gaston wanders through the park singing "Gigi" he sits down on a park bench. Not just any bench, however; it is the very same bench used by Gigi during her earlier song. She sang "I Don't Understand the Parisians;" now he insists that

he doesn't understand Gigi. Objects, places, words, tunes, positions—everything becomes colored with the other person's actions and values.

It is this aspect of *Gigi's* structure that Raymond Bellour misses in his influential analysis of *Gigi*.[3] Building his interpretation around segments which "rhyme"— i.e., which rework the same material— Bellour limits his examples to situations where a character repeats in modified fashion an action which he/she performed earlier. Bellour is unable to capture the text's dialectic, paradigmatic structure because he does not recognize that the musical uses one character's actions to establish the context for the other character's parallel activities. His presuppositions about the linear, cause-and-effect, psychological nature of classical narrative have blinded him to the structural patterns particular to the musical.

When Gaston returns home from Honfleur, where he punishes his mistress's infidelity, his uncle informs him that he must not leave Paris. "Male patriotism" requires that he give a series of parties to celebrate his triumph. The episodic sequence that follows reveals Gaston performing his masculine duty, hosting party after party. How do we interpret this short but effective sequence? From a psychological point of view it is all but useless, since it tells us nothing about Gaston which we do not already know; it motivates nothing which is not already motivated in a number of other ways. If we wait a few minutes, however, we soon find this episodic sequence matched by another, this time on Gigi's side. When Gigi returns from Trouville (the next resort down the coast from Honfleur), Aunt

a&b—Female occupations: Gigi primping
  Male occupations: Gaston buying
c&d—While Gigi learns the manners of Gaston's world
  Gaston helps himself to another of Mamita's cookies
e&f—Two songs culminate on the same park bench:
  Gigi sings "I don't understand the Parisians"
  In front of a family of swans Gaston sings that Gigi
    is no longer an ugly duckling ("Gigi")
g&h—Juxtaposition of similar mirror shots highlights
  Gigi's and Gaston's divergent attitudes toward love

Alicia insists that her education be speeded up. Gigi is no more enchanted by her aunt's lessons than Gaston by his uncle's parties, but follow the dictates of the older generation they must, and so we are given the only other episodic sequence in the entire film, in which Gigi is forced to serve tea, to sip wine, to choose cigars, to select a dress. Throughout these parallel sequences we recall the worldly wisdom of Gigi's aunt and Gaston's uncle: if the function of men in society is to collect women, the role of women is to collect jewels. A role for men, a symmetrical role for women—such is the vision of the world which Minnelli's dual-focus editing constantly produces. Each pairing of shots reinforces the notion that men and women alike play predetermined parts in an already written scenario. Individuals have responsibilities to their sex; the older generation must remind the younger of these responsibilities. Older characters serve not so much as go-betweens but as symbols of the conduct expected of their younger charges. This symbolic function reaches its height when Gigi's grandmother and Gaston's uncle sing "I Remember It Well" against the setting sun. This dialogue-song recapitulates in miniature the film's characteristic alternation between the sexes, demonstrating the extent to which love is an eternal and unchanging part of the human scene, ever the same from generation unto generation.

We have seen thus far how every aspect of Gigi obeys a principle of duality. Instead of the traditional pattern whereby a cause calls forth an effect, we have a less linear configuration whereby each male aspect seems to call for a parallel female one, and vice-versa. This rule is by no means limited to actual events. It includes paired songs ("It's a Bore"/"I Don't Understand the Parisians"), paired montage segments (the episodic sequences), paired roles (collecting women/collecting jewels), paired trips (to Honfleur/to Trouville), paired locations (Gigi's and Alicia's apartments/Gaston's and Honoré's rooms), as well as paired activities (Gigi's lessons/Gaston's embassy tea), paired feelings (Gigi's exasperation with her aunt/Gaston's boredom), and paired scenes (Gigi at home with her grandmother/Gaston at home with his uncle). The technique even extends to paired shots and objects: just before the couple's first "date" we are given a single shot of Gaston in front of his mirror (choosing a jewel) from which we cut directly to Gigi in front of her mirror (dressing and primping).

What conclusions can we reach about Gigi based on comparison of these various pairings? The question is an essential one; on our answer rests the very variety of the American film musical. If we can say only that Gigi's pairings divide the world into male and female in order ultimately to bring the two sexes together again in matrimony, then all musicals will seem identical, for nearly every American film musical sets up a series of male/female oppositions, eventually resolving them to harmonious unity through the device of marriage. On careful inspection, however, we can distinguish in any musical a secondary but essential opposition alongside the primary sexual division: each sex is identified with a particular attitude, value, desire, location, age, or other characteristic attribute. These secondary attributes always begin diametrically opposed and mutually exclusive.

If sexual differentiation represents *Gigi*'s major duality, then what will its minor opposition be? What characteristics constantly inform the opposition of Gaston to Gigi? Two answers to this question are immediately apparent. First, we have learned that both sexes are collectors, men collecting women and women amassing jewels. This simple opposition remains important throughout the history of the American film musical, from the Gold Diggers series of the thirties (where man is seen as an endless source of gold, while woman is identified by her beauty) to the tongue-in-cheek extravaganzas of the fifties (e.g., Howard Hawks's 1953 *Gentlemen Prefer Blondes*, which turns on this simple principle: "Don't you know that a man being rich is like a girl being pretty?"). Marriage is seen, according to this view, as the only way to join beauty and riches, to effect not a compromise but a merger between the *dulce* and the *utile*. And no wonder, for in the sexually differentiated climate of the three decades in which the musical flourished a woman could by and large become rich in only one way: marry for money. Similarly, a man could not fully enjoy the charms of feminine beauty without marrying. Sexual stereotyping and a strict moral code went hand in hand, leaving only one solution for young men and women alike: marriage. In this sense *Gigi,* like many other musicals, is an apology for traditional mores, an ode to marriage as the only way to combine riches and beauty.

The beauty/riches motif is a common one, however; we must search further if we are to understand the specificity of *Gigi* as a functional mechanism, one which overcomes the very contradictions on which society is founded. When we first see Gigi and then Gaston, she is preparing for her "femininity" lessons with Aunt Alicia, while he is about to leave with his uncle for an embassy tea; she must change clothes and brush her hair, while he is buying cars and railroads. At first I characterized these activities as typically female and male: she is concerned with beauty, he with riches. On second glance, however, a minor premise of some importance becomes apparent. *She* skips and hops, plays tag and eats candy; *he* is reserved, serious, moody. *She* wears a brightly colored pinafore; *he* has formal attire and a cane. In short, *she* is a child and *he* is a man. The initial paired sequences clearly stress the stars' respective female and male qualities, yet simultaneously create a generation gap between Gigi and Gaston. This impression is reinforced at their first meeting, when Gigi speaks to Gaston as a naive child would speak to a favorite uncle; Gaston returns the compliment, treating Gigi as he would a daughter, even threatening to spank her. When they go off to the ice palace together he orders champagne for himself and the turn-of-the-century French equivalent of a milkshake for her.

Now there is nothing problematic about an intergenerational relationship—unless, that is, the members of different generations suddenly develop a romantic interest in each other. And that, of course, is just what happens in *Gigi.* We even find out that Gigi's grandmother and Gaston's uncle are former lovers who might have been married were it not for his infidelity. There is something vaguely incestuous about the Gigi-Gaston relationship (since they could, indeed, be related by blood). One minute she is sitting in his lap, cheating at cards and munching on caramels, the next she is being eyed, invited, and embraced as a potential sexual partner. The point here is not that Gaston and Gigi violate society's prohibition against incest. In fact, quite to the contrary, their love affair serves to gloss over the very oppositions on which the incest taboo is based.

In many societies a specific ceremony or ritual process marks the passage of the child into adulthood. In American society more than any other, however, such rites of passage have been minimized, thus depriving society of a convenient way in which to handle the child/adult opposition. We act as if the dichotomy were a mutually exclusive one (for movie ratings, air fares, drinking and driving ages, and so forth). Children and adults are conceived as two diametrically opposed groups that allow no overlapping. Yet in order to reach maturity every individual within our society must violate the seemingly airtight partition separating the two categories. Children are not adults, yet at some indefinite point they become adults. It is this problematic relationship between childhood and adulthood that *Gigi* mediates, with the marriage model providing the resolution: the distinction between the generations is leveled by a merging of adult and childlike qualities within the couple. As Gigi for the first time gains the right to engage in adult activities, Gaston progressively refuses

to carry out the petty duties to which adulthood condemns him. Now *he* eats the caramels he brings to Gigi, dances wildly around the room with Gigi and her grandmother, plays leap-frog on the beach at Trouville. While she is becoming an adult, he is recapturing some of the excitement of youth. Instead of simply making Gigi into an adult and thus creating an adult couple, the film operates a merger of the generations through the couple's marriage. In this sense Maurice Chevalier is a perfect symbol of the film's attempt to bridge the generation gap: he is both young and old, both living in the past and constantly creating new memories, glad that he's "Not Young Any More" and yet able to "Thank Heaven for Little Girls."

Gigi thus appears as a series of paired segments built around a fundamental duality, that of sexual differentiation, and two minor oppositions, beauty/riches and child/adult, both of which represent problematic dichotomies for society. Beauty and riches are treated like sex-linked chromosomes, with each quality allotted to a single sex. Yet both qualities are desirable; society's ideal individual has both. The child/adult pairing causes difficulties because it treats a dynamic, diachronic process as a stable, synchronic opposition. These problematic dichotomies are eventually resolved only when the resolution of the sexual duality (marriage) is used as a non-rational mediatory model for the attendant thematic oppositions, bringing together categories and individuals that seemed irreconcilably opposed. The only way for the same individual to enjoy both riches and beauty is to marry. The only way to save both childlike and adult qualities is through a merger, thus blurring the barrier between the generations, thereby erasing the spectre of incest.

Though extremely simple, this method must radically change our understanding of the American film musical. No longer can we point to the musical's conventional plot, call it gauche and episodic, and walk away satisfied. Once we have understood the dual-focus approach we easily grasp the importance of the many set pieces or production numbers which some see as cluttering the musical's program and interrupting its plot. The plot, we now recognize, has little importance to begin with; the oppositions developed in the seemingly gratuitous song-and-dance number, however, are instrumental in establishing the structure and meaning of the film. Only when we identify the film's constitutive dualities can we discover the film's function.

Seen as a cultural problem-solving device, the musical takes on a new and fascinating identity. Society is defined by a fundamental paradox: both terms of the oppositions on which it is built (order/liberty, progress/stability, work/entertainment, and so forth) are seen as desirable, yet the terms are perceived as mutually exclusive. Every society possesses texts which obscure this paradox, prevent it from appearing threatening, and thus assure the society's stability. The musical is one of the most important types of text to serve this function in American life. By reconciling terms previously seen as mutually exclusive, the musical succeeds in reducing an unsatisfactory paradox to a more workable configuration, a concordance of opposites. Traditionally, this is the function which society assigns to myth. Indeed, we will not be far off the mark if we consider that the musical fashions a myth out of the American courtship ritual.

The Structure of the American Film Musical

NO SINGLE INTERPRETIVE PROCEDURE CAN ENSURE PROPER analysis of every individual work throughout an entire genre. Unless we have a general sense of a genre's characteristic configurations, however, we are likely to misconstrue the structure and meaning of individual texts. This is particularly true in the case of the American film musical, which has suffered from a singular lack of careful and methodologically self-conscious criticism. At the risk of oversimplification, therefore, I will in this chapter provide a detailed analysis of the musical's fundamental dualistic structure. A set of four propositions will serve not only to define the components and relationships characteristic of the American film musical, but also implicitly to describe a four-step interpretive procedure.

The film progresses through a series of paired segments matching the male and female leads

The musical invites us to forget familiar notions of plot, psychological motivation, and causal relationships; we must learn instead to view the film sideways, as it were—arresting the temporal flow and sensing the constant parallels between the principals' activities. The sequence of scenes is determined not out of plot necessity, but in response to a more fundamental need: the spectator must sense the eventual lovers as a couple even when they are not together, even before they have met. Traditional notions of narrative structure assume that chronological presentation implies causal relationship (*post hoc ergo propter hoc*); in the musical, chronological presentation and causal relationships alike are at climactic moments eschewed in favor of simultaneity and similarity.

In the most conventional musicals, such as those starring Jeanette MacDonald and Nelson Eddy in the late thirties, the parallelism between paired scenes is unmistakable. Sets and situations, costumes and movement, even dialogue and shots are replicated in such a way as to telegraph the film's structure to even the sleepiest viewer. *Sweethearts*, for example, opens on MacDonald and Eddy giving the sixth anniversary performance of their celebrated Broadway operetta. For all the couple's harmony on stage, however, the subsequent scenes suggest that something is amiss. We first see MacDonald in her dressing room, admitting that she squelches her own ideas in order to do what others want. Cut to Eddy in a rigorously parallel dressing room. Not only is the set similar, but the camera is positioned the same way for both scenes. Now back to MacDonald, who receives a phone call from her aunt, a scene soon matched by Eddy's phone call from his mother. And so on throughout the film: if she is seen with a black dachshund, he must immediately be seen with a white bulldog; if she wears white and sings to string accompaniment, he must be shown in red and sing with brass accompaniment. Neither dressing room scene *causes* the other; instead, their parallelism serves to identify the MacDonald-Eddy relationship as primary, to draw our attention to the alternation between the two and away from the rather conventional break-up/make-up plot. Even the partners' separation provides an excuse for still more parallel scenes. As each goes off with an understudy of the other, Slavko Vorkapich's montage stresses the similarity of their careers even while they remain apart: identical activities, clothes, colors, and angles, culminating in parallel scenes in small hotels, each star reading *Variety* about the other. When their quarrel is finally ended, it is of course by parallel phone calls. At no point is the spectator allowed to lose sight of the relationship between the two principals, for neither can move a muscle without inducing the camera to record the other's corresponding muscle movement.

Few musicals are as blatant as *Sweethearts* in their establishment of male/female alternation and parallelism. Most are content to submerge the similarities beneath a veneer of difference, thus reserving for the viewer the pleasure of discovering the hidden links. *An American in Paris*, for example, uses an unusual but effective method of introducing the female lead, Leslie Caron. We have already watched Gene Kelly awaken in his Paris flat; with customary style and grace he manipulates the room's many Keaton-like devices as he cleans up and prepares breakfast. In the next scene Oscar Levant sits in the café below with Georges Guétary, who proceeds to describe his fiancée; as he outlines her many qualities and moods, Leslie Caron appears in the café's mirror and acts them out, demonstrating her versatility and grace. Now, at this point Kelly and Caron have not even met, yet director Minnelli has already begun linking them in our minds by devoting the first two extended scenes to sequences which demonstrate their shared grace, style, and versatility. Subsequent scenes continue this practice—characteristic in Minnelli's work—of disguising or displacing parallelism. In the café scene just described we learn that Caron is engaged to Guétary; in the sequence which follows, we watch as Kelly meets a potential romantic partner (Nina Foch). Rather than pointing up the parallelism of the two love affairs through similar camera work or carbon-copy sets, Minnelli depends entirely on the positioning of the scenes, the age difference between Caron/Kelly and Guétary/Foch, and eventually, the younger lovers' increased resistance to the advances of their older suitors. In the same way, the scenes leading to and following the first declaration of love between Caron and Kelly conceal rather than advertise the fact that each must disregard a date with the older suitor in order to keep the rendezvous with the younger one. Indeed, the entire "plot" is built on submerged parallelism: Guétary constantly pushes Caron toward marriage while Foch encourages Kelly to prepare for an exhibition. Each of the two young lovers owes a great deal to the older partner (Guétary protected Caron during the war, Foch is financing Kelly's show), but each desperately tries to put off the event that threatens to confuse gratitude with love. The situation is saved only when the older suitors learn about their young charges' true feelings. Here again Minnelli disguises the parallelism, preferring a carefully planned but seemingly chance juxtaposition to the more immediately recognizable formal opposition characteristic of MGM's MacDon-

Parallel shots, parallel actions, parallel messages, and symmetrically split images—the musical perpetually reveals its capacity for creating and reinforcing duality. Here Gene Raymond and Dolores del Rio cable home in *Flying Down to Rio*.

[pers]

ald/Eddy films or Berkeley's Warner extravaganzas: Guétary overhears the young couple's declarations of love immediately after the scene in which Levant tells Foch how Kelly really feels.

The difficulty of establishing such formal similarities is often complicated by a variety of historical or incidental factors. A scene-for-scene analysis of *An American in Paris* reveals that Kelly receives more than double the screen time of Caron, a virtual unknown in 1951. When the two principals have radically different personalities or talents, a similar problem occurs, especially when their roles seem to include few shared attributes. *The Music Man* solves this problem in a number of interesting ways. Robert Preston plays a con artist who hawks expensive instruments and band uniforms on the false pretense that he will teach the town's children to play music and form a band. Shirley Jones works as a librarian whose prime purpose seems to be keeping noise out of the library. To complicate matters, Preston is an accomplished song-and-dance man, while Jones is primarily a sweet-voiced singer, entirely lacking in dance talent. Even here, however, the film is easily conceived as a series of parallel scenes. The main characters are both given academic names, each used as the title and primary motif of a song ("*Professor* Harold Hill" and "Marian the *Librarian*"). A scene in which Marian oversees her little sister's piano practice provides an opportunity to oppose her regimented methods to Hill's lack of method. Each character begins by severely criticizing the other's principles, but slowly, in a series of paired scenes, each comes to appreciate the other's values.

An even more radical problem is created by the presence of performers who are not suited to a love-interest plot, either because they are too young or too wacky. In this situation one of two methods is commonly used to set the musical back on its couple-conscious course: 1) the young girl is paired with an older man (or men) who becomes her co-conspirator(s) rather than an amorous partner (e.g., Shirley Temple in *The Little Colonel*, Deanna Durbin in *One Hundred Men and a Girl*, or Judy Garland in *The Wizard of Oz*); or 2) a secondary pair are in love, the principals serving as catalysts (e.g., Shirley Temple in *Little Miss Broadway* or Abbott and Costello in *Ride 'Em Cowboy*).

An interesting variation on the traditional paired-scene arrangement involves the introduction of one or more "wrong" couples. At the beginning of the film the alternation seems to designate a particular male for a specific female, yet as the film progresses we recognize that these are not the two who are "Fated to Be Mated," as Fred Astaire puts it in *Silk Stockings*. "It's fate, baby, it's fate," sings Betty Garrett to Frank Sinatra in *Take Me Out to the Ball Game*—couples are by convention not made during the course of a musical film, they are pre-ordained (made in heaven, maintains the popular audience; yes, but according to the current constellation of stars, responds the critic.)

Proliferation of couples provides the most important method of ensuring a steady alternation between male and female elements without at the same time producing too great a sense of repetition and sameness. Many musicals set up a secondary couple in order to relieve the monotony and—just as important—to provide work for their older stars or create an image for a new face. The Kelly-Sinatra musicals (*Anchors Aweigh, Take Me Out to the Ball Game, On the Town*), for example, provide an opportunity to treat the male principals as a couple as well as to create a second male-female couple (a strategy used again years later in *Paint Your Wagon*). The same approach in *Anything Goes* permits Paramount to play Bing Crosby and Donald O'Connor off against each other as well as against their respective girls. *Gentlemen Prefer Blondes* does the same thing with Marilyn Monroe and Jane Russell. In *Thousands Cheer*, on the other hand, MGM doubles the main couple (Kelly and Grayson) with older actors (John Boles and Mary Astor) fondly remembered by the previous generation of musical devotees. Other films raise the ante to three independent couples, usually spanning generations or representing different styles of life, dance, or song (*Bye Bye Birdie, Meet Me in St. Louis, Born to Dance, Ziegfeld Girl*, many others). But why stop at three? If there are seven boys in the family, there must be *Seven Brides for Seven Brothers*. In fact, hardly a musical exists that does not at some point literally cover the screen with dancing couples. The American film musical seems to suggest that the natural state of the adult human being is in the arms of an adult human being of the opposite sex. Pairing-off is the natural impulse of the musical, whether it be in the presentation of the plot, the splitting of the screen, the choreography of the dance, or even the repetition of a melody. Image follows image according to the nearly iron-clad law

requiring each sequence to uphold interest in male-female coupling by including parallel scenes and shared activities.

Each separate part of the film recapitulates the film's overall duality

By definition, popular art appeals to a large and varied audience. As one of Hollywood's most popular genres, the musical has traditionally drawn its spectators from the widest possible spectrum of the public. For every spectator interested in the structure and meaning of the musical, there are thousands of others who are out only for a good time. Seeking entertainment and not a message, the average spectator of musicals cannot be expected to analyze the film he or she is enjoying. According to many critics, the musical has refused to meet this implicit challenge, simply abandoning any claims to meaning in favor of a wholehearted surrender to entertainment. This position, however, simply begs the question of entertainment's meaningful role in American life. A more fruitful approach assumes that the musical inscribes its message in such a way as to reach even those spectators unwilling to engage in a process of conscious interpretation. The key technique in the musical's approach to meaning is *repetition*, across the genre as well as within individual films.[1] The same configurations are ceaselessly repeated, with only the context changing. Even before anything approaching meaning can be ascertained or established, this process of repetition has created the pattern within which meaning will be inscribed. By transferring the male-female duality to every aspect of the film experience, the musical sets up a redundant pattern that eventually serves as a model for the film's thematic oppositions. This section will detail the various ways in which the sexual duality is reinforced throughout the film. The following section will deal with the transformation of the sexual opposition into a more clearly thematic duality.

Almost any category can be used to underscore the musical's basic male-female duality: *color* (dark-haired Gordon Macrae in black opposite blond Shirley Jones in white throughout the opening scenes of *Carousel*), *costume* (Nelson Eddy's valet livery contrasting with Jeanette MacDonald's fancy gown in *New Moon*), *age* and *background* ("We're from two different worlds, two eras"—Fred Astaire and Cyd Charisse in *The Band Wagon*), *national origin* (Richard Beymer and Natalie Wood in *West Side Story*), and *size* (the man towering over the woman in almost every case, except those of Fred Astaire and Mickey Rooney, who both often worry out loud about this departure from accepted practice). Other areas include attitude, profession, competence, manners, and so forth, but viewed in perspective these all constitute secondary categories contributing to five major realms: setting, shot selection, music, dance, and personal style.

1) *setting*. The American film industry has always had a genius for constructing parallel sets. Ever since D. W. Griffith first placed the good guys and the villains in similarly shaped and furnished rooms, set-builders have understood the value of matching backgrounds. In the musical, parallel settings have run an enormous gamut. The backstage plot has often provided male and female stars with similar dressing rooms (*Sweethearts, Broadway Melody of 1940, The Barkleys of Broadway, A Star Is Born* [1976]). The adolescent stars of the late thirties often retired to parallel houses at the end of the day (e.g., Mickey Rooney and Judy Garland in *Strike Up the Band*), while their older counterparts had similar apartments or hotel rooms (as in *Chocolate Soldier, For Me and My Gal, Easter Parade, Take Me Out to the Ball Game*). Long parallel sequences are often constructed around symmetrical sets, specially conceived to underscore the similarity of the principals' positions. In *The Band Wagon*, for example, Jack Buchanan (the director) attempts to persuade the potential backers to support his show while Cyd Charisse and Fred Astaire (the performers) observe from mirror-image rooms opening on to the living room where Buchanan is selling the show. The symmetrical nature of the set, as well as the similarity of the stars' activities and the repeated use of parallel shots, serves to prepare the confrontation between Astaire and Charisse, which takes place, predictably, in the neutral ground between the two waiting rooms.

When the musical went on location in the fifties, the problem of providing parallel backgrounds became somewhat different. Instead of constructing similar sets, Hollywood now turned to associating each of the main characters with a specific and highly differentiated locale and activity. The most common solution was to borrow a chapter from American tradition, identifying the woman with the house and showing the man riding the range, working the mine, or simply en-

joying himself away from home (as in *Oklahoma!*, *Paint Your Wagon*, *The Music Man*, and *Carousel*). Perhaps the most effective use of American scenery occurs in a musical that was not shot on location, however. The set for *The Harvey Girls* represents the main street of a western town along the main line of the Atchison, Topeka, and the Santa Fe. On the left is John Hodiak's Casino, hangout of all the town rowdies; on the right is the Harvey House restaurant, where Judy Garland works with a company of prim and proper Harvey House waitresses. Sets like this one hardly need a plot to expound their latent symbolism.

2) *shot selection*. Three basic strategies guide the musical's attempt to keep the male-female duality constantly in view. The first and most obvious we might call the *duet*, a shot in which all the performers are paired off. This can be a simple two-shot of the lovers, a four-shot (like the split-screen parallel-rehearsal number in the 1956 version of *Anything Goes*), or a mammoth fresco shot covering the entire screen with couples (as in the "Pettin' in the Park" number from *Gold Diggers of 1933*). The duet is complete in itself and thus nearly always serves as the film's concluding shot. The *solo*, on the other hand, is only half of a diptych, for it presents only one sex (either a single individual or more than one person of the same sex). Whether in close-up, medium shot, or large group long-shot, the solo

needs to be paired with another solo of the opposite sex in order to achieve its ultimate function. Sailor musicals (*Born to Dance, Follow the Fleet, Anchors Aweigh, On the Town*, and more) traditionally begin with a mixture of individual and group solo shots. Until these shots are matched by corresponding female solo shots, however, the film can go nowhere. (It's not that a plot cannot be devised without them, but that a couple cannot be created without them, and in the musical *the couple is the plot*.) The group solo calls for either a corresponding group solo or for an individual solo of a representative member of the opposite sex (Kathryn Grayson or Judy Garland with an all-male orchestra or band, Eleanor Powell or Ann Miller with a male dance chorus); the close-up solo, particularly in a love scene, all but requires a matching close-up solo. Good dance directors like Charles Walters or Stanley Donen are adept at mixing paired solos with duets in order to achieve an overall balance both of the sexes and of shot types. The third type of shot might be called *unmarked*, since it includes both men and women without marking any particular pairings. In general this rather unbalanced shot involves secondary characters and is more closely related to traditional notions of plot than are the other two types. Even here, however, where the love interest may seem absent, the viewer remains aware of the importance of any given shot or scene for the ultimate coupling.

A quick look at Ernst Lubitsch's *Love Parade* (1929) will reveal how one early masterpiece succeeds in varying its sexual iconography without ever letting sexual

The duet shot—Fred Astaire and Lucille Bremer are backed up by a screen full of couples in Vincente Minnelli's "This Heart of Mine" number from *Ziegfeld Follies*.

[MOMA]

interplay disappear from the screen. This tongue-in-cheek story of Maurice Chevalier's marriage with the Queen of Sylvania, Jeanette MacDonald, begins in Paris, where Chevalier is quarreling with one of his mistresses. These early shots have nothing to do with the plot, such as it is, but they do serve to define the subject from the very start: whatever the subject, it has to do with a man and a woman sharing the screen. Before Chevalier and his valet (Lupino Lane) leave Paris, Lubitsch gives us a delightful throw-away sequence—or rather, it would have been thrown away if the plot rather than the couple were central. Chevalier is seen on his balcony. The next shot appears to represent Chevalier's view of a group of girls on the balcony across the way. Such pretense at realism soon gives way, however, since throughout Chevalier's song ("Oh Paris Please Stay the Same") Lubitsch regularly intercuts to a different group of women. Are all these beauties within Chevalier's line of vision? Are they figments of his imagination? His memory? No matter, for one thing is sure: Lubitsch has cleverly provided us with a series of matching solo shots, reinforcing the previous duets and clearing the way for a second and third series of paired solo shots involving the valet and then—the dog! The introduction of Jeanette MacDonald is handled in equally astute fashion. Before MacDonald appears in female solo shot with her ladies-in-waiting, a male solo shot depicts the army marching outside the palace. After her awakening, MacDonald goes directly to a duet with her all-male cabinet. These carefully engineered duets and paired solos featuring one principal and a horde of secondary characters provide the necessary *sexual* preparation for the meeting between Chevalier and MacDonald, which is constructed out of a judicious combination of duets and paired solo shots.

That night the couple dines together. The entire court watches from various positions of vantage. Does Lubitsch waste this opportunity on a series of unmarked shots? Not likely. He uses the newly formed couple of Chevalier's valet and MacDonald's maid (Lillian Roth) to provide a peeping-tom duet, while in paired solo shots he balances the cabinet members outside the palace against the ladies-in-waiting spying at the door. By the end of the evening Chevalier and MacDonald are in love, but more important from the point of view of iconography, the Queen's ladies have now paired off with the palace men in order to cover the screen with couples. Throughout the rest of the film, this pattern never falters: when the Queen walks to the wedding altar her white train is carried by eight boys clad in black; when we leave the royal couple it is often to witness the antics of their comic servant reflections; when we

see all the servants around the kitchen table they are paired off. Lubitsch has found numerous methods, many of which will be copied by later directors, to turn every unmarked shot into a pair of solos and every solo into a duet—and duets are the name of the musical game.

3) *music*. In music as in iconography, the duet is the musical's center of gravity, its method of summarizing in a single scene the film's entire structure. Because it has such power, however, the duet is usually reserved for moments of maximum tension or exultation. The solo must carry the film's major musical burden. True to the principles already outlined here, however, the solo song longs to be paired, as does its cousin, the solo shot. The first song in *The Pirate*, for example, is Gene Kelly's acrobatic "Niña," a tribute to the many women of his dreams. Almost immediately afterward Kelly hypnotizes a pretty señorita from the provinces and induces her to pour out her heart. The young lady is of course Judy Garland, and so her emotions come out in song: "Mack the Black," the famous pirate, is the man of *her* dreams. A simpler solution simply has one sex continue a song which the other has started, as in *Carousel's* seaside rendition of "June is Bustin' Out All Over" and innumerable thirties' production numbers. An important variation on this approach gives the reprise of a song to the mate of the singer who introduced it. Still another solution involves using one star's solo as background music for a scene involving the other member of the couple.

The duet serves the important function of crystallizing the couple's attitudes and emotions. Among duets, none is more ef-

Matched solo shots—Barbra Streisand and Kris Kristofferson in mirror-image shots with similar backgrounds, chosen by MGM to publicize the 1976 version of *A Star Is Born*.

[MOMA]

fective in setting up the male-female duality than the many songs which are delivered in echo fashion: one line for him, one line for her, and so on alternately until the voices merge in a final embrace. Songs like "People Will Say We're in Love" (*Oklahoma!*), "If I Loved You" (*Carousel*), "Every Little Movement" (*Presenting Lily Mars*), and "Make Believe," "Why Do I Love You?," and "You Are Love" (*Show Boat*) represent the minimal form of the echo duet, for here the lovers alternate verses rather than individual lines, as in true echo duets like "Anything You Can Do" (*Annie Get Your Gun*), "No Two People" (*Hans Christian Andersen*), "I Love You More" (*Pajama Game*), "Paris Loves Lovers" (*Silk Stockings*), "I Remember It Well" (*Gigi*), and "Bess You Is My Woman Now" (*Porgy and Bess*).

The last song, one of George Gershwin's many outstanding contributions to the American film musical, provides a particularly clear example of the multiple and subtle ways in which music contributes to the audience's overall impression of the film's sexual structure. Porgy begins with twelve bars in B major (a), followed by eight bars in F# major (b). Bess

then takes up the words and melody which Porgy sang in (a), but she sings it in D major and reverses all the sexual designations (c); she too now modulates into F♯ major but this time keeps neither Porgy's words, his rhythm, his tempo, nor his accompaniment (d). Her final measures in F♯ major nevertheless are echoed by Porgy in the same tune and the same key (e). At this point Bess begins again, repeating her sections (c) and (d), while Porgy harmonizes, singing new words and rhythms (f,g). The final sixteen bars (all in F♯ major) have Porgy humming while Bess sings for two bars, then Porgy echoing Bess's song while she hums. An embrace covers two bars leading to a short unison sequence and a harmonic climax.

Now on the surface, this short analysis seems to present a strikingly symmetrical arrangement. Porgy's sections (a) and (b) are reflected in Bess's sections (c) and (d), with (e) serving as a first meeting point. Then (f) and (g) repeat the same material, this time as a harmonic rather than an alternating duet, leading ultimately to a conclusion which matches emotional and musical harmony. The intriguing aspect of this duet, however, is not the rather pat antiphonal setup, but the tension beneath. The song's alternation serves to set up a sexual duality, thus creating a context in which each phrase is sensed not just for itself but as a function of its counterpart, sung by the other member of the couple. Because we alternate between Porgy and Bess, we feel each as a function of his/her differences from the other. When Bess changes Porgy's words (e.g., from "Bess" to "Porgy") we unconsciously sense the difference in gender. Far more important, when Bess suddenly speeds up (*subito più mosso*) in part (d), abandoning not only Porgy's words but his lilting self-assurance, we take notice, even if only subconsciously. At the same time Bess's melodic line becomes syncopated and chromatic, whereas Porgy's was regular and full of elated ascending jumps; the accompaniment turns eery, becoming more insistent and dissonant, repeating eighth notes in a downward chromatic slide (whereas Porgy was accompanied by light, ascending arpeggios). Excitement, fear, and a sense of forced emotion emerge from these measures. No matter that the duet should end on a musical and physical embrace, Gershwin has admirably succeeded in telegraphing Bess's misgivings, her mistrust of herself, her fear of the future. Like all artists who work within the musical genre, Gershwin has achieved his effect through a structure of sexual duality which alone permits us to measure the distance separating the principals. That Bess should run off and leave Porgy in the final sequence comes as no surprise to those who have listened carefully to the music along the way.

The antiphonal style of "Bess, You Is My Woman Now" calls to mind the musical's distant ancestry in pastoral poetry. From Theocritus to Virgil and on to the Italian Renaissance, a type of verse termed "amoebic" (or "amoebean") characterizes pastoral composition. Whether between two shepherds in a singing match or two lovers competing in fun against each other, the basic principle of this type of verse is contained in its name: *amoibe* or change. Creating a mirror effect, the formal similarities of succeeding verses invite the listener to conceive the world as fundamentally dual and to contrast the male and female principles underlying that duality. Now, it would be an exaggeration to suggest that musicals adhere to amoebic principles from beginning to end. In fact, it is interesting to note just how carefully most musicals are designed to move from a preponderance of sexually unmarked novelty or comic numbers in the opening reels to a heavy concentration of paired or antiphonal songs toward the end. Quite apart from questions of plot, then, the tendency of the music is toward the amoebic, toward sexual definition of the film's fundamental principles.

4) *dance.* The beauty of dance is that it needs no words—indeed, it escapes words, surpassing any description which we might devise. Filmed dance is doubly difficult to evoke in words, for Hollywood's directors have become unusually adept at making the camera dance along with the actors. The filming of dance has come a long way since the early days of filmed vaudeville, when the camera remained bolted to the center seat of the

Fred Astaire and Cyd Charisse seem to have been created out of the same mold in *The Band Wagon*'s rendition of "Dancing in the Dark."

[MOMA]

fifth row of the orchestra. In the *Gay Divorcee*'s classic version of "Night and Day" (1934), Fred Astaire induces an unwilling Ginger Rogers to join him in dance on an empty ballroom floor. The camera is placed along the center line of this symmetrically organized space, panning left and right to follow the dancing couple, but always returning to center. Astaire and Rogers appear to be on stage, with the camera-spectator sitting in that proverbial fifth row. This simple procedure lays a heavy responsibility on the

performers—they must establish on their own both the male-female duality and its amorous resolution.[2] Astaire and Rogers are of course up to this task, using the ballroom style to perfection as she molds herself to his lead, replicating with perfection his every gesture.

Lesser performers, different technique. Busby Berkeley is largely responsible for discovering an alternate method more easily suited to the average hoofer. Instead of tying a stationary camera to the fluid movements of a single duet, Berkeley relegates individual dancers to the status of constitutive elements in an overall pattern, whose changes he captures from the vantage point of a mobile camera on a crane or a track located above the stage. This technique calls for constant substitution of one symmetrically organized duet shot for another. In *Strike Up the Band*, a characteristic example of Berkeley's later work, he applies this stage technique to a ballroom number, "La Conga." From Judy Garland and Mickey Rooney singing and dancing together we move to a high-angle (crane) long shot of the whirling couples filling the floor. As the camera remains stationary the couples separate and form two rows, men and women facing each other across the screen's center line. This switch from multiple single-couple duets to a single group duet is followed by a sweeping movement ending in a low-angle medium shot of the lead couple—Garland and Rooney—who then go through a vaudeville-inspired kicking routine as the camera moves back to frame them in the midst of the other dancers, who soon form into concentric male and female circles, and finally pair off once more into the original couples. This long number demonstrates both the various types of duet available to the creative director (single couple, multiple couple, paired lines, concentric circles, and so forth), but also the different possible relationships between dancers and camera (dancers regroup for stationary camera, camera moves to pick out new duets). With Astaire and Rogers individual steps were highlighted; here it is the male-female patterning that stands out, almost independently of the dance steps employed.

Another approach to dance, characteristic of MGM in the forties, combines solo and group dancing, realistic sets and empty stages, as well as narrative and ballroom dancing. Minnelli's "This Heart of Mine" number, from *Ziegfeld Follies*, is an outstanding example of this technique. In this mimed story Fred Astaire is a jewel thief intent on stealing the expensive bracelet worn by the radiant Lucille Bremer, whose white gown contrasts with his black tails. Their first steps together take them from a crowded ballroom floor to a specially prepared empty set. After Astaire's song, Bremer tries to escape on a conveyor belt; then Astaire hops on a second conveyor belt, replicating Bremer's movement. They continue to alternate on the conveyor belts, trading steps until the two belts, now moving in opposite directions, give them an opportunity to dance their paired steps simultaneously—but in opposite directions. They are soon joined by a circle of couples who dance around and behind them, highlighting the male-female duality. The sequence ends as Astaire and Bremer return to the more realistic ballroom set, where he takes both a kiss and the bracelet; she then matches his actions and his desire by *giving* him her necklace along with a kiss. As in *Yolanda and the Thief*, of which "This Heart of Mine" is like a mimed summary, Astaire wants Bremer's jewels and will gladly pay a kiss in order to get them; Bremer, on the other hand, wants the kiss and happily pays for it with her jewels. The resolution—in which we find out that their goals are less divergent than we might have thought—has been fully prepared by the dance's movement from separate activity to alternating paired

The narrative frame of *Ziegfeld Follies*' "This Heart of Mine" number, in which Fred Astaire eyes Lucille Bremer's jewels, lends a narrative component to an otherwise ethereal, non-representational dance.

[MOMA]

movement and finally to shared movement reinforced by the background of sixteen other harmonious couples. This little-known dance deserves to take its place with "Slaughter on Tenth Avenue" (*Words and Music*) and "The Girl Hunt Ballet" (*Band Wagon*) as one of the musical's most elegant narrative dances. It owes its class not only to the superb artistry of Bremer and Astaire, but also to Minnelli's ability to vary the methods which he uses to keep the idea of a couple foremost in the audience's mind—and eye. Paired solo close-ups are mixed with duet long shots, lavish multiple-couple shots with simple takes of a single couple against a neutral background, moments when the camera simply follows the main couple with instances where the camera's choice of scale or angle intensifies our notion that the two dancers are best sensed as a couple.

5) *personal style*. This final major category derives its importance from its all-pervasiveness. Just as setting, iconography, music, and dance function to keep the male-female duality constantly in the forefront of the spectator's mind, ear, and eye, so the actors' personal styles serve to reinforce the film's fundamental sexual dichotomy. The most common use of stylistic juxtaposition occurs, predictably, in the omnipresent song-and-dance numbers. In the numerous films which Maurice Chevalier made with Jeanette MacDonald, for example (*Love Parade, One Hour with You, Love Me Tonight, The Merry Widow*), the entire story might be summarized by the stars' singing voices: she has a sophisticated opera voice, versatile and mellifluous; he, on the other hand, has the rasping

but personable voice of a Paris *chansonnier*—pleasantly natural rather than sophisticated, carefree and happy-go-lucky rather than trained. This opposition constantly presents the potential lovers' differing backgrounds to our ears, even when the camera shows them to our eyes only one at a time. Even when the musical style is not so prominently displayed, it makes its presence felt, sometimes as a simple accompaniment (e.g., strings for MacDonald, brass for Eddy in *Sweethearts*) or as a source of comic relief (when Buster Keaton becomes a Hollywood king in his first musical, *Easy Go*, his whispered words to the queen come out as low notes on the tuba, while her responses are heard as muted high notes on the trumpet, thus exaggerating the normally different speaking registers of men and women). The same opportunities for differentiating stylistically between the sexes occur in dance as well. A typical juxtaposition sets popular tap-dance or ballroom styles against the ballet routines of high art (e.g., Kelly and Caron in *An American in Paris*, Astaire and Charisse in *Band Wagon*, Travolta and Gorney in *Saturday Night Fever*).

Personal style is by no means limited to the rhythmic forms of song and dance, however. Talented directors play multiple aspects of each actor's performance against the style of the corresponding actress. Often this stylistic pairing is a necessary part of the script: what would *My Fair Lady* be without the disparity between the language spoken by Rex Harrison and that muttered by his young charge? What would be left of *The Music Man*'s plot and theme if Robert Preston were not a faker and Shirley Jones not a very serious young woman? Still more often, however, an actor underscores through his own personal style an opposition only latent in the script. The outstanding practitioner of this approach is surely Gene Kelly, who can't seem to help exuding confidence and charm, a style easily paired with the reserve of Esther Williams (*Take Me Out to the Ball Game*), the nervous naïveté of Judy Garland (*The Pirate*), the responsible work ethic of Kathryn Grayson (*Anchors Aweigh*), the shy and retiring manner of Leslie Caron (*An American in Paris*), or in a unique—and largely unsuccessful—experiment, the even greater self-confidence and self-ishness of Marie MacDonald (*Living in a Big Way*). The same configuration can be found, slightly altered, in Mickey Rooney's many movies, where his natural egotism spills over into his screen persona, often juxtaposed to Judy Garland's selflessness and practicality.

The point to retain is not that head-liners of the American film musical have "style." All good actors have some kind of style, whether in Hollywood, on Broadway, or at Stratford-on-Avon. What distinguishes the musical is its ability to pair personal styles, providing yet another way to keep the male-female duality constantly before us. What good is a bashful Frank Sinatra without an over-eager Betty Garrett (*Take Me Out to the Ball Game, On the Town*)? What would Julie Andrews's vivacity mean if it were not opposed to Christopher Plummer's reserve (*The Sound of Music*)? Where would Shirley Temple's childish excitement have gotten her without the sour

disposition of some parent figure to oppose it (e.g., Lionel Barrymore in *The Little Colonel*)? Style is style, no doubt, but in the American film musical, style comes in matched pairs.

The basic sexual duality overlays a secondary dichotomy.

Writing a serious book about a form which appeals precisely because it does not seem serious can create problems. I have just spent the better part of a chapter analyzing the components of the American film musical, demonstrating the multiple methods used to inscribe sexual duality on the film's surface. In sum, I have been engaged in the paradoxical activity of proving the uselessness of my analysis: if sexual duality is so prominent in the musical then any spectator—deaf, blind, or color-blind—will without the least bit of difficulty sense the couple's structural significance. The whole point in overdetermining the musical's dualistic structure is precisely to make sure that the spectator will sense the film's overall patterns without analysis. The analysis presented here has nevertheless allowed us to perceive an increasing complexity in the development of dual-focus structure. From setting and iconography I moved to the considerably more complex realms of song and dance, finishing with a type of stylistic juxtaposition that borders on thematics. As I dealt in turn with each category, I spoke as if each separate parameter served to reinforce a sense of sexual duality. The time has come to admit the limitations of that approach. In fact, it is quite the opposite process that actually takes place: informed of the impor-

Cyd Charisse's silk stockings—and the dances with Fred Astaire that help her discover her own innermost desires.

[MOMA]

tance of sexual duality by every possible indicator, we soon begin to notice other parameters suggested by their relationship to the already perceived sexual duality. In other words, as soon as we have become firmly aware of the coupling motif—which occurs extremely early in a musical—the pattern of sexual duality leads us to the secondary dichotomies determining the film's thematics and defining the categories which the film ritualizes.

By way of example, *Silk Stockings* (Mamoulian's 1957 musical remake of *Ninotchka*) pits the happy-go-lucky Hollywood director Fred Astaire against a serious Cyd Charisse, khaki-clad, businesslike, and devoted above all to her country—the U.S.S.R. Now we could establish a long list of paired qualities associated with the two stars—he is frivolous, she is serious; he seems to have nothing to do, she is always on her way somewhere; he makes his own decisions, she takes orders from Moscow. At one level, Cyd Charisse's cold and calculating manner represents the Russian mentality, as seen from the vantage point of the Cold War, while Fred Astaire's debonair joyfulness figures America's vision of itself during the carefree Eisenhower years. With its never-ending five-year plans, its ironclad chain of command, and its women dressed in men's clothing, the U.S.S.R. has always appeared to the American populace as an aberrant colossus, characterized by the cold of Siberia and the ruthlessness of the Party. To that stereotyped portrayal, Mamoulian opposes an equally simplistic view of Western life, dominated by shapely women, noisy parties, and vulgar entertainment. Indeed, it is the film's fascination with popular entertainment that catapults its thematic concerns beyond a rather pat and oversimplified opposition between Russian and Western practices. Wherever she goes, whatever she does, Charisse remains fundamentally businesslike. Everything is business, right down to the lights of Paris. For Astaire, nothing is business, not even his job. Instead, his characteristic light touch transforms everything into entertainment. On the one side business (use value defined from the point of view of the reality principle), on the other side entertainment (use value seen from the standpoint of the pleasure principle). Every scene, every character, every dialogue contributes to this overall thematic dichotomy which is grafted, as it were, onto the basic male/female duality. Resolution comes when Hollywood's sleight of hand dissipates the dichotomy altogether, proving with the establishment by Charisse's henchmen of a night club ("La Vieille Russie") that good entertainment *is* good business.

A similar motif provides the secondary thematic context in *The Sound of Music* as well. Here, however, the roles are reversed: Christopher Plummer is the discipline-conscious ex-Navy officer who has lost all contact with his children, while Julie Andrews is the joyous one, the ex-nun always ready to burst into song and thus to bring some excitement into the lives of her employer's children. Whereas he wears the uniform of the aristocracy, has friends from Vienna, and values order over all other qualities, she dresses in the simple garb of the folk, prefers mountain pastures to rich city dwellers, and would rather sing than sip cocktails. In other words, not only are the primary qualities of these two characters matched (one is male, the other female), but their secondary attributes are paired as well, permitting the establishment of a complex of thematic motifs running parallel to the love plot.

Yolanda and the Thief introduces another variation on the same basic serious/fun motif. Yolanda Acquaviva (Lucille Bremer) is the only heiress to the multimillion-dollar fortune of Patria's richest family. She lives in a palace, owns half the country, possesses a beautiful face and figure. She has one problem, however: she suffers from an overabundance of money. Her responsibilities force her to abandon her own desires. As a con-artist who preys on unsuspecting young lovelies, wooing them with his clever wit, his debonair manner, and his expertise on the dance floor, Johnny Riggs (Fred Astaire) has fled to Patria because it has no extradition treaty with his own country. The pattern is quickly established: whereas Bremer is trusting and rich, Astaire is entertaining but conniving. As in the "This Heart of Mine" sequence from *Ziegfeld Follies*, Astaire and Bremer represent polar opposites, each one having something which the other cannot do without. The same pattern operates again in *Let's Dance*, where Betty Hutton's Boston Brahmin family tries to keep her away from the theater and her former partner, the ever-present Astaire, whom she had abandoned because of his unreliability. Now that Hutton is associated with money and Astaire with mad get-rich-quick schemes which never succeed, she recognizes the extent to which she is incomplete without his spontaneity. Astaire, on the other hand, has in the meantime become painfully aware of his need to settle down and hold a steady job.

At first glance it might seem that these thematic oppositions have little in common. *Silk Stockings* opposes a Russian worker to an American playboy, *The Sound of Music* sets a pixie against a martinet, *Yolanda and the Thief* juxtaposes an heiress and a crook, *Let's Dance* confronts a woman who has just married into a good family with a bachelor who can't even keep a job. *Carousel* brings together a loose-living carnival barker and a virtuous young working girl who dreams of a husband, a home, and a family. *Stormy Weather* reverses this relationship, making Lena Horne the one who lives for her career on stage, while Bill Robinson yearns for a more permanent home. *Meet Me in St. Louis* identifies all the happy-go-lucky women folk with the Midwest, while their ambitious men yearn for college or a job in the East. *Funny Face*'s female star (Audrey Hepburn) works in a bookstore and studies French philosophy, thus opposing her to the male lead (Fred Astaire) who spends his time in the comparatively frivolous world of fashion photography. *My Fair Lady* sets Eliza's Cockney energy against Professor Higgins's suave concern for order, rules, and proper pronunciation.

The list can go on endlessly. Each musical finds its own specific thematic pairing to support the main male-female coupling. In spite of the tremendous variety in this thematic material, however, one constant remains. In every case, *one side of the thematic dichotomy is closely associated with the work ethic and its values, while the other is devoted to those activities and qualities traditionally identified with entertainment.* Self-conscious of its status as "only" entertainment in a world where work alone merits full value, the American film musical has adopted society's work/entertainment dichotomy as its own thematic center. Now, American entertainment involves a curious tension between cultural and counter-cultural values. In the musical this tension is worked out through the thematic material identified with the members of the couple, one partner representing the thoroughly cultural values identified with work and a stable family structure, the other embodying the counter-cultural values associated with entertainment. It goes without saying that these two categories are not in fact mutually exclusive: working or raising a family can be fun, just as dancing is hard work. The musical's strategy requires the suppression of such nuances, however, in favor of an initial clearcut dichotomy (which, as we will see in the next section, is set up only to be resolved later).

Two further examples should help to illustrate this rather radical hypothesis. I have chosen two films sharing several superficial similarities—their Broadway location in particular—in order to show how much variation is possible within the basic work/entertainment framework. *Little Miss Broadway* stars an almost grown Shirley Temple (she was ten in 1938) at her very best. As an orphan adopted by the proprietor of the Variety Hotel—inexpensive haven for actors and vaudeville performers of all sizes, shapes, and incomes—Shirley helps to organize a show designed to save the hotel's occupants from the eviction threatened by the hotel's neighbor and owner, Edna Mae Oliver. Shirley's crusade leads her into the landlady's palatial residence, where she befriends Oliver's good-looking young nephew, George Murphy (who soon falls in love with the daughter of the hotel proprietor). The two parallel sets (fancy apartment and rundown hotel) help to establish the film's primary thematic duality setting money and good business practice against the arts and the unforgettable pleasure provided by good entertainment. The long final courtroom scene brings this opposition to a head. The performers succeed in turning the courtroom into a stage, constantly drowning out the judge's requests for order in the groundswell of laughter emanating at first from the audience and, finally, from the judge himself. Against a funny joke or a thrilling performance, even an alliance of money, law, and order is powerless. Yet as Edna Mae Oliver recognizes in the scene's final words, good entertainment *is* good business—and so she herself buys the show, thus saving the hotel from ruin at her own hands. The entire film is built around a simple variation on the basic work/entertainment duality. Work produces riches, which must be defended by law; this complex of values is opposed to vaudeville and its radically different concomitants: talent, fun, togetherness. In the end, of course, the two sets of values no longer seem so distant; like George Murphy and his girl, they have achieved a matrimonial pact catalyzed by little Shirley Temple, "Little Miss Broadway."

The Barkleys of Broadway need no such Cupid. From the very first close-up of their dancing feet, Ginger Rogers and Fred Astaire are married, dancing their third successful show together (in real life, their tenth film). Nevertheless, they still quarrel and indulge in occasional flights of jealousy: she is in a huff about the shapely understudy with whom Fred must practice daily, he is concerned about the suave French playwright who seems to have captured Ginger's imagination. Eventually Rogers, piqued by Astaire's criticism and flattered by the Frenchman's praise, leaves the world of musical comedy for the dramatic stage (breaking up the team for the same reason she had in real life separated from Astaire a decade earlier). Up to this point we had been alternating between Rogers and Astaire, setting up the couple's respective spheres of influence; now that Rogers has aligned herself with serious theater, abandoning Astaire's song-and-dance fare, we begin to alternate instead between the two theaters, implicitly comparing Astaire's numbers, his audience, and his genre, to Rogers's high-brow counterpart. As the young Sarah Bernhardt, Rogers has every opportunity to portray the very aspects of the stage world that are foreign to Astaire: a conservatory education, an aristocratic public, and absolute dependence on a text made up primarily of words.

This opposition between "high" and "low" forms of art is of course dealt with in anything but an objective fashion. We see the rather poor rehearsals of Ginger's play, whereas we are given a polished performance of Fred's heavily edited dance "Shoes with Wings On"; Ginger acts in street clothes, while Fred has a costume; Ginger's set has not been built yet, Fred benefits not only from a set but from many special effects as well. In general, everything is done to make *Young Sarah* seem like a lot of work, while the Astaire show just naturally happens, with even the most complex steps coming spontaneously. Now, the opposition of serious theater to musical comedy is a far cry from the business/art duality central to *Little Miss Broadway*. If anything, musical comedy is run as a business, while serious theater is considered an art, yet *Barkleys* manages, by a slick rhetorical effort common to all the Comden and Green scripts, to make the high-brow/low-brow distinction seem just as much a part of the work/entertainment paradigm as was the riches/pleasure opposition in *Little Miss Broadway*. From film to film the specific incarnation of the work/entertainment duality may change, but in one way or another every musical somehow manages to build its thematic complex around its very status as a form of entertainment.

The marriage which resolves the primary (sexual) dichotomy also mediates between the two terms of the secondary (thematic) opposition

When people go to a film to be entertained, they don't want to be told that they are wasting their time. Justifying the entire entertainment enterprise, the musical demonstrates that people who are insensitive to entertainment somehow miss the best part of life. In an important sense, the American film musical constitutes an apology for its own existence: by setting up the work/entertainment polarity in such a way as to demonstrate the incomplete and potentially destructive nature of work ("All work and no play makes Jack a dull boy") as well as the desirable qualities of entertainment, the musical justifies its own existence. Instead of simply supplanting the work ethic, however, entertainment values complement it, providing an able and energetic partner for the work ethic's more sober and conservative approach. The musical's typical romantic resolution, which depends on the harmony of a couple originally at odds, is thus matched by a thematic resolution in which opposite life styles or values merge. In most cases, to be sure, we are not permitted to verify whether this apparent solution is actually a workable one: the couple is united, the film ends, and we must accept on faith the implied assertion that they lived happily ever after. By convention, time stops when the couple kisses, and change is forevermore banished from their life together. The conventional American willingness to make courtship the paradigm of life itself is used to good effect by the musical's thematic component. Just as romantic problems are considered definitively solved once they result in marriage, so the resolution of the musical's thematic dichotomies is presented as permanently efficacious. The ecstatic, uplifting quality of the musical's final scene permits no doubt about the permanence both of the couple and of the cultural values which the couple simultaneously guarantees and incarnates.

Thematic resolution in the musical takes place in as many different ways as there are variations on the fundamental work/entertainment opposition. In *Little Miss Broadway* the representatives of law, order, and money reveal during the long courtroom scene their sensitivity to a good show; by the same token, the Variety Hotel's performers demonstrate the financial possibilities of their entertainment. The tycoons and judges become an audience, the performers become business men. This crossover represents a characteristic configuration of the musical's closing moments: the values once associated with one of the partners are finally adopted by the other. The *Barkleys of Broadway*, for example, avoids the easy solution of simply debunking high-brow art. Instead, Fred Astaire admits that Ginger Rogers can act well in any type of play—as long as she has the proper direction. This is just what Astaire proceeds to give to his estranged wife (over the phone and in a disguised voice). With Astaire as director, Rogers's performance is a hit—but only because Astaire directs serious theater the way he handles musical comedy. Astaire's concession to Rogers's career on the legitimate stage is immediately met by her decision to return to the world of song and dance. Now that each knows that the other respects his/her talents and tastes, they are free to kiss and make up—and continue producing their peculiar mixture of good theater and joyous entertainment. In both these films, the final peace treaty is symbolically represented by a song or dance which combines two different styles. In *Little Miss Broadway* the pact between the old fogey aristocrats and the performers led by

Shirley Temple is symbolically sealed by a performance of "Swing Me an Old Fashioned Song," a combination of old and new, of classical and modern, just like the *Barkleys*'s "Swing Trot" (a technique also used for the "Girl Hunt" jazz ballet in *The Band Wagon*, the final opera/pop number of *This Time for Keeps*, the combination ballet/tap finale of *An American in Paris*, and the chansonnier/opera duets of Chevalier and MacDonald).

The musical's thematic resolution is often symbolically figured by a trading of styles on the part of the principal characters. In *My Fair Lady*, Professor Higgins's very profession and class define him as a man who can control his voice and his movements; Eliza, on the other hand, has too much energy and too little education to control much of anything. The final scenes, however, demonstrate the strong effect which each of these well-defined personages has had on the other. Professor Higgins has taught Eliza the restraint of polite society; at the same time, some of her impetuousness has rubbed off on him. Eliza Doolittle, in perfect control of her voice and body, now confronts an easily perturbed Higgins, who rants and raves at every provocation. Not until the film's thematic dividing line is thus crossed can the film hurry to its conclusion. Now that they not only understand each other's values but actually adopt each other's attitudes and characteristic patterns of action, Higgins and Doolittle are finally ready for romantic resolution as well. Precisely the same pattern presides over *The Sound of Music*, where a sedate older man is lured out of his shell by an energetic young woman, while she, out of a desire to appeal to him, takes on

new responsibilities along with the sobriety of the older generation. As an outward sign of this new attitude, Baron von Trapp finally joins his young wife and children in song. *Gigi* adopts exactly the same configuration: Gaston suddenly breaks into song and dances through the streets of Paris (as Gigi had done earlier) while Gigi becomes subdued and proper, nearly motionless (as Gaston was in the opening carriage ride with his uncle). All three of these films successfully translate into movement or sound the thematic reversal of position that accompanies the successful conclusion of the love plot.

The Music Man provides a particularly clear example of the process whereby the couple's romance becomes synonymous with the film's thematic resolution. Harold Hill is a traveling salesman; Marian is a librarian, surely the world's most sedentary occupation. He represents noise for the sake of noise (the instruments he sells make sounds but not music); as a librarian, Marian represents quiet for the sake of quiet. He teaches music according to the "belief" method (just think the note and play), thus encouraging creativity at the expense of precision; she advises her sister Amarylis to limit her piano playing to rote repetition and sheer imitation, thus enforcing precision by stifling creativity. Morally speaking, Harold has a history of loose women and pool halls, while Marian plays to perfection the part of the archetypal virgin. He wants to seduce her and move on to another town and another woman; she wants to convert him to sedentary life devoted to home and family. The pattern is a familiar one, about which more will be said in the chapter devoted to the American folk musical. The man, with his wandering ways, preference for entertainment over work and promiscuity over fidelity, appears as a fitting representative of wilderness values, while the woman exhibits all the trappings of civilization. Taking place in turn-of-the-century Iowa—an Easterner's version of the frontier between the civilized East and the barbarian West—*The Music Man* encapsulates one of the most important and persistent themes of American history.

In typical musical fashion, *The Music Man* refuses to decide between the diametrically opposed values represented by Robert Preston and Shirley Jones. Instead of permitting either partner to control the relationship, director Da Costa reveals in turn each character's doubts about his/her own moral code. When Jones discovers that Preston has lied about his graduation in Gary Conservatory's "Gold Medal Class of Ought-Five," she hides the evidence from the town's mayor. Has she been hooked by the handsome Preston? Or is she beginning to sense the joy and energy which he has brought to River City? When he is warned that his crooked schemes have been discovered, he hesitates instead of taking his customary flight. Is he tired of running? Or has he recognized the many pleasures—figured by Jones and the dream of a family which she represents—which his errant life precludes? Whatever the psychological motivations may be in these parallel cases, the thematic effect is apparent: each set of values is shown to be incomplete, to be in desperate need of other virtues which its present structure forbids. Just as man needs woman and woman needs man, so sound and silence are interdependent, so

civilization cannot do without its wilderness, so a town needs *both* a library and a brass band.

In order to achieve this marriage of values, both characters must abandon or at least temper their previous code of conduct. As soon as this compromise takes place, the results are instantaneous. Marian's little brother could not talk without stuttering (no doubt the outward sign of the repressive atmosphere in which he was raised), but now his relationship with the Music Man has restored his normal voice. Even the band itself makes something approximating music, thus delighting parents all over town. Shirley Jones suddenly becomes radiant now that she is fighting *for* a man rather than running *from* one. She wanted him to trade liberty for stability, he wanted to replace her seriousness with passion. Now, however, we see that no such trade is necessary. Marian can still continue to be serious about her work and yet reveal passion and enjoy its fruits; the only liberty which Harold must relinquish is the freedom to leave town on the run with a posse in hot pursuit. He is no longer seen as a threat to her serious purpose, she no longer seems the grasping woman bent on putting an end to his liberty.

As Jones and Preston embrace, their value structures merge as well, thus resolving one of America's most persistent problems: how at the same time to ensure both freedom and order. The Founding Fathers balanced the Declaration of Independence with the Constitution. Our federal democracy ensures a certain balance of power between the federal government and the states. Recent land-use laws, inspired by the ecology movement, attempt to establish a proper balance between land development and preservation of wilderness areas. In no way, of course, does *The Music Man* actually solve these dilemmas, as our legal system attempts to do, yet in a very real sense, the film does provide a solution to the age-old either/or dichotomy opposing the values of freedom to those of order (as well as those of entertainment to those of work). The solution proposed by *The Music Man* is a ritual one, a hypothetical case which furnishes the spectator both a model for the coexistence of these seemingly mutually exclusive values, and an actual experience of that coexistence. By sharing the process by which Jones and Preston recognize the necessity of *both* values, the spectator not only recognizes the shortsightedness of neglecting one or the other value, but he/she also rehearses the merging of those values, thus experiencing, albeit in a ritual manner, the actual possibility of resolving what seemed like an unsolvable problem.

Just as individual musicals may be characterized by the dualities which they resolve, so certain performers have, by the careful development of a characteristic screen persona, become identified with particular dualities. Perhaps the most interesting case in point is Gene Kelly, certainly one of the most important influences in MGM's revitalization of the film musical form in the post-war years. Kelly's peculiar charm has often been commented upon by musical fans, most of whom see him as a self-confident and energetic individual whose talent and style turn the entire world into a realm of gaiety and dance. Watching him dance makes us want to dance, seeing him express his joy makes us joyous in turn. In short, Kelly does what every performer does, just more so and better, and in a particularly American way. No doubt this is an apt characterization of the quality of Kelly's dancing, but it says little about the thematic dimension of Kelly's character. After all, Kelly does more than dance in his movies. A closer look should permit us to discover the more specific polarities first established and then mediated by the presence of Gene Kelly within the musical world.

One fact seems immediately striking: unlike other male dancers, Gene Kelly never had a stable female partner with whom he could establish a standard duet style, as Astaire did with Ginger Rogers. Indeed, it is hard to think of a single female partner with whom Kelly danced more than a few numbers. He danced with Vera-Ellen in *Words and Music* as well as *On the Town*, but the former appearance was limited to the well known set piece "Slaughter on Tenth Avenue." In *For Me and My Gal* he does the title number with Judy Garland, yet he never danced with her again until the closing number of *The Pirate* (as well as later in *Summer Stock*). In *Cover Girl* he danced with Rita Hayworth, with Debbie Reynolds in *Singin' in the Rain*, with Cyd Charisse in *Brigadoon* and *It's Always Fair Weather*—yet for all of these numbers we don't remember Gene Kelly for the dances which he did with women. In fact, in numerous major movies Kelly dances continually, yet never does an extended number with a woman (*Thousands Cheer, Anchors Aweigh, Living in a Big Way, Take Me Out to the Ball Game*). In *An American in Paris* Kelly dances with Leslie Caron, to be sure, but he also finds the time to do numbers with Georges

Gene Kelly in his element—singing "I Got Rhythm" to (and with) a bunch of kids. Compare this ode to intergenerational unity in *An American in Paris* with the original film version in *Girl Crazy*, which serves to further the romance between Judy Garland and Mickey Rooney.

[MOMA]

Guétary, a bunch of kids, and an old woman, as well as a solo number on Oscar Levant's piano—not to mention the non-stop clowning in the final ballet sequence.

The Gene Kelly who stands out, performing numbers which only he could bring off, is not a Gene Kelly *making love*, but a Gene Kelly *showing off*. Always confident of his own abilities, Kelly seems at his best when he is clowning: with Sinatra in *Anchors Aweigh, Take Me Out to the Ball Game,* and *On the Town,* with Phil Silvers in *Cover Girl* and *It's Always Fair Weather,* with children in *Anchors Aweigh, Living in a Big Way,* and *An American in Paris,* with a mop in *Thousands Cheer,* with a statue in *Living in a Big Way,* on roller skates in *It's Always Fair Weather,* as a circus performer in *Thousands Cheer,* under stormy skies in *Singin' in the Rain,* with cartoon characters in *Anchors Aweigh* and *Invitation to the Dance.* The list could go on and on: in *Cover Girl* Kelly even dances with his own reflection.

These many examples suggest that for Kelly dance is not primarily a sexual activity, as it is for Fred Astaire, Ann Miller, Eleanor Powell, Cyd Charisse, and most of the musical's finest dancers.

Gene Kelly romancing a lone newspaper and a squeaky floor board in *Summer Stock.*

[MOMA]

When Gene Kelly puts on skates he is demonstrating his youth, exercising his liberty, and showing off for a crowd *(It's Always Fair Weather)*. When Fred Astaire skates, he is elegantly competing with and courting Ginger Rogers ("Let's Call the Whole Thing Off" from *Shall We Dance*).

[MOMA]

For Kelly dance is instead a silly, clowning, childish activity, an expression of the eternal youth which seems even today to be fixed in Kelly's smile. From film to film Kelly's partners and his style may change, but his adolescent energy and ego never disappear. Like a child, Kelly seems always to be looking out for himself. In *For Me and My Gal* he plays a spoiled brat who puts his own success above patriotic duty. In *Thousands Cheer* he tries every trick to escape his service obligations, even using romance as a road to personal advancement. In *Anchors Aweigh* he is lulled to sleep by Frank Sinatra's lullaby; the next morning he awakens late in an obvious replica of the fetal position. He clowns from one end of *The Pirate* to the other, even walking the tightrope and posing as a pirate. He recovers his job in *Take Me Out to the Ball Game* by getting the local kids to clamor for his return. He attracts Leslie Caron's attention in *An American in Paris* by constantly showing off, as he does throughout the "Niña" number in *The Pirate*.

Now the presentation of a major film character as a childish figure who needs to grow up is nothing new. Kelly does in fact "grow up" in a number of his films. Taking on new responsibility, he learns to limit his affections to one chosen partner whom he now considers as an equal and no longer as simply a stepping stone for his personal advancement. The Kelly who needs to become a man, however, is only half the story. No matter how childish Kelly's behavior sometimes appears, it is always joyous and somehow appealing in spite of its egotism. In short, Kelly's peculiar combination of childlike qualities and childish self-centeredness poses a special problem which is hardly peculiar to Kelly but which he represents in a particularly clear fashion: we want children to grow up and thus lose their childish faults and limitations, but by the same token we want to preserve youth's childlike naiveté and enthusiasm. It is this very quandary that Kelly's various love relationships must solve. In general, he is paired with a woman endowed with reserve and a sense of responsibility. During the course of the film her mature concerns rub off on him while his energy and enthusiasm are eventually invested in her. In this way Kelly's childlike qualities are preserved, while his childish egotism is dispersed. He achieves the impossible feat of becoming a man without ceasing to be a child, just as his female counterpart recovers some of her girlish vitality without ceasing to be a woman. Their union celebrates and symbolically represents this marriage of two ages.

The key notion in this view of Kelly's screen persona is the idea of *clowning*. What is a clown but a grown man playing a child? The clown somehow manages to overcome the age-old dichotomy between childhood and adulthood—he is neither and both. In *Take Me Out to the Ball Game* Esther Williams tells Kelly she doesn't like his clowning. When Kelly finally returns to the team he is mad at Sinatra, who is on base; the only way Kelly can reach him is to get a hit and chase him home. It turns out Kelly was right—only by clowning can the team win the pennant and Kelly steal the hearts of his viewers. Even with women, clowning is Kelly's most successful approach—a technique immortalized by the final number of *The Pirate*:

Be a clown, be a clown
All the world loves a clown
Be a crazy buffoon
And the demoiselles'll all swoon
Dress in huge baggy pants
And you'll ride the road to romance
A butcher or a baker ladies never
    embrace
A barber for a beau would be a social
    disgrace
They'll all come to call if you can
    fall on your face
Be a clown, be a clown, be a clown.

The song's suggestion aptly summarizes Kelly's *passepartout* solution to life's many problems.

It is not difficult to understand why Kelly's approach should be especially appealing to the American public. No country on earth so prizes childlike qualities as the United States. The child star is a peculiarly American phenomenon: when Europe had the war we had Mary Pickford, when Europe had Hitler we had Shirley Temple, when the war returned to Europe we had Mickey Rooney and Judy Garland. Across the Atlantic the femme fatale, on this side the child-woman; France had Jean Gabin, we have Gene Kelly. American ideals, styles, and morality all glorify the cult of youth, all testify to our desire to retain the qualities of childhood past the age of maturity. The screen persona of Gene Kelly demonstrates that the task is not an impossible one. As Gene says to Jerry, his cartoon partner in *Anchors Aweigh*, anyone who is happy can dance. There lies the secret of eternal youth, as embodied by Kelly himself. Be happy, dance, and clown— and somehow the impossible can be achieved. Man and child *can* coexist in the same body. Unwilling to accept the flow of time which changes us from children into adults, we long to recapture certain qualities of childhood. Gene Kelly shows us the way.

The interpretive process proposed here by no means pretends to unlock the multiple meanings of all Hollywood musicals. In particular, the above analysis acknowledges duality alone as an organizing principle, providing no space for plot, motivation, and chronology, which common sense recognizes as important components of numerous musicals. While traditional concepts no doubt deserve some room in the analysis of a genre as wide-ranging and diverse as the musical, we should, however, guard against a too rapid return to familiar notions, even as partial components of an interpretation. To take but a single example, the presence of psychological development by no means undermines the precepts developed here, for the musical's dual-focus organization regularly removes psychological development from the realm of the chronological and the causal simply by doubling that development. While the tools of traditional narrative analysis no doubt help us to recognize the signs of psychological change, only the duality-oriented approach presented above can properly locate and interpret that change—by setting it in the context constituted by the other lover's parallel and inverse change. When one change is thus balanced against another, questions of plot, motivation, and chronology tend to disappear in favor of the musical's characteristic formal and thematic concerns.

The Style of the American Film Musical

THE STRUCTURE OF THE AMERICAN FILM MUSICAL IS CLOSELY tied to cinema's role in American culture during the musical's heyday. In Europe, cinema has always been accepted as an important art form, worthy of the concerted efforts of the most talented, intelligent, and sophisticated directors, performers, and technicians. Many of Europe's most renowned authors wrote for the screen or participated in the actual production of films. Prokofiev saw no contradiction in composing a serious orchestral score for Eisenstein's *Alexander Nevsky*. Cocteau alternated regularly between the legitimate theatre and the Seventh Art, as the French long ago dubbed cinema. Intellectual currents from surrealism to structuralism and from expressionism to existential phenomenology have made some of their most important statements through film and film criticism. In short, cinema and the experience of film viewing have never been as divorced from "high-art" and "culture" as they were in America from the coming of sound to the influx of so-called European "art" cinema in the late fifties and early sixties. For many European filmgoers, no qualitative difference exists between cinema and other art forms. To go to a movie theater is only slightly different from attending a play, reading a novel, visiting a museum, or going to the opera. In Europe today, the study of cinema approximates equal status with the study of other visual and verbal art forms, while in America film is often relegated to the never-never land of "popular culture," a catch-all title for mass-produced artifacts deemed undeserving of treatment as autonomous aesthetic creations.

In Europe, therefore, the movie house often enjoys a privileged situation. Like the theater, the opera house, the museum, it represents the summit of cultural achievement, the end result of centuries of hard work and serious thought. In America, on the other hand, the movie theater constitutes a refuge from the high seriousness of Art, it gives 'em what they can't get in the legitimate arts. Instead of representing culture,

59

like its European counterpart, the American movie theater is a haven from culture, a darkened dream-world in which spectators can finally release their repressed desires, fears, angers, and frustrations. This radical division between American culture and the movies' countercultural tendencies sets up an important relationship:

movie theatre : culture in general
: : entertainment : work

The musical's fundamental opposition between work values and entertainment values thus concretizes the general status of cinema in American society. Through its dual-focus structure the musical succeeds in commenting on the very duality out of which the genre arises.

Once inside the theater, spectators find themselves implicated in a further duality. Between the screen and the audience there is an empty space, a sort of no-man's-land into which no one dares to venture. Up there, the screen, alone and bright; back here, row upon row of darkened seats. Up there an imaginary but fascinating realm, a light show which takes on an aspect of reality; back here a dimly perceived world of flesh and blood, a darkened crowd which seems to lose its reality as the film takes on a reality of its own. It is this very opposition that characterizes the *style* of the American film musical:

audience : screen : :
real : imaginary : :
dark : bright : :
ordinary : exotic : :
humdrum : fascinating

Transferred into the film itself, the opposition between the audience and the projected image sets up a fundamental tension between a world given as real and another realm portrayed as ideal. This second, ideal world shares many of the qualities of the projected image: it is bright, colorful, and fascinating, but ultimately chimerical, the product of a dream, a light show, a magician's legerdemain. Still, it easily captures the imagination of characters imprisoned within the drab existence offered by the film's "real" world. Just as the audience disregards its own corporeal existence in order to immerse itself in the imaginary world portrayed on the screen, so the film's characters remain aware of another world, a world that is "Over the Rainbow" and to which they long to fly.

Out of this confrontation of two radically divergent realms grows the musical's peculiar style. Seductive unreality runs side by side with unseductive reality until such time as the stylistic conflict, like the thematic conflicts mentioned in the previous chapter, can be resolved by a merging of the two strains. If the structural configurations of the musical serve to mediate the opposition between the movie theater and the world, between entertainment and work, the musical's stylistic patterns mediate the dichotomy between image and audience, between imaginary and real.

Two major paradigms govern the musical's presentation of the real/ideal or real/imaginary dichotomy. The notion of "reality" is in fact quite a complex notion, allowing many possible contraries (sham, fantasy, imagination, ideal, memory, fiction, literature, and so forth). Two such contraries stand out, however, because of their positive connotations and their power to subsume other related notions. *Art* is opposed to reality by its fictitious, imaginative nature, yet we commonly assume that art, by virtue of its very imaginary status, has the power to express higher realities, truths which would otherwise remain invisible. By the same logic, *dream* involves fantasy and imagination, both directly opposed to reality, yet in some vague fashion, we sense that our dreams have the power to render reality more meaningful than it could ever be by itself.

The opposition between art and reality is perhaps most clearly evidenced in the "backstage" musical. A child of the depression, the backstage musical reveals daily life as a constant fight against joblessness and hunger. This lackluster existence is balanced, however, by the joy and harmony of the film's production numbers. While the narrative is characterized by locations remarkably similar to the theater we are sitting in, characters who look and dress pretty much like us, and problems which remind us of our own, the stage numbers feature surreal sets, sumptuous costumes, uplifting song, and an entire cast moving to the same rhythm. The musical's internal stylistic dichotomy (world/stage, real/ideal) thus corresponds exactly to the audience/image opposition implicit in the cinema viewing situation: the production number on stage compensates for the world's drabness in the same way that the screen image permits the audience momentarily to forget its real situation. The use of the stage for production numbers makes this relationship particularly obvious, but it

should not be allowed to obscure the similar functioning of any space which is marked off, separated from the normal world, and reserved for an idealized, artistic presentation: a magazine cover (*Lady in the Dark, Cover Girl*), a fashion show (*Roberta, Funny Face*), a night club (*Anything Goes, Can-Can*), a Paris street (*An American in Paris, Gigi*), the deck of a ship (*Shall We Dance, Ship Ahoy*), a park (*Top Hat, Born to Dance, Summer Holiday*), or even a football field (*Pigskin Parade*). In each of these cases, the characters break out of the normal world into a realm of performance and art, a world where stylization and rhythm provide a sense of community and beauty absent from the real world.

A similar relationship governs the introduction of dream or fantasy material into the musical. The character who is dreaming sees his/her dream as if it were projected onto a screen, setting up the following homology:

$$\frac{\text{the character}}{\text{the dream double}} : : \frac{\text{the spectator}}{\text{the film character}}$$

The character thus shares with the spectator a fixed, limited reality, while the dream and the film both enjoy a freedom from the normal physical laws of time, space, and causality.

The dream device is an important one in the history of the musical, particularly during the forties, when the extended dream sequence reached the status of accepted alternative to the backstage musical's production number. *Lady in the Dark, Cabin in the Sky, Anchors Aweigh,*

Yolanda and the Thief, The Pirate, and many other films of the period reserve their most flamboyant numbers for presentation as dream. In one sense, however, the dream device is only a special case of the musical's common tendency to present material which is so clearly divorced from reality that we feel it to be like dream. In the thirties this penchant usually takes the form of an exotic set, so stylized and spectacular that it can only have come from fairy tales by way of dream. Nearly all the films of MacDonald and Chevalier fall into this category, as does the Astaire-Rogers series. Other films of the same period justify dream-like material through memory (*Maytime*), a moonlight ride (*Ride 'Em Cowboy*), or a utopian community (*New Moon*). Beginning with the late forties, the musical is beset by a newly felt desire for realistic presentation, and thus discovers ever new ways of motivating and thus justifying the inclusion of dream-like sequences: hypnosis (*The Pirate*), intoxication (*Summer Holiday*), escapism (*South Pacific*'s Bali Ha'i), even reincarnation (*On a Clear Day You Can See Forever*). In an important sense, each of these many ways of introducing fantasy simply objectifies the musical's fundamental concern for making believe—the same concern that brings the spectator to the movie theater.

The use of art forms and dream sequences within the musical contributes strongly to the genre's tendency to blend the real and the ideal or imaginary, yet we will be able to say little about the style of any given film as a whole if we must treat it simply as an alternation between set pieces each employing a radically different set of conventions, techniques, and concerns. Too much criticism of the musical has begun—and ended—with the ever-present opposition of narrative to number. Yet the production number and the dream sequence, in their opposition to a framing narrative, do not alone constitute or even directly suggest the stylistic makeup of the American film musical; they only help to define the major components out of which the musical's style is fabricated. The real and the imaginary, life and art, waking life and dream life are not the fabric of the musical's style, but they are the warp and the woof out of which that style is woven.

Audio Dissolve

Even in the silent movie theater, the film viewing experience is defined by the competition between two types of sound. In the back of the theater a whirring sound, a mechanical grinding constantly reminds us that the film itself is not a reality but only the product of projection. In the front of the theater a piano player tickles the ivories, desperately trying to cover up the noise of projection, to disguise the artificiality of the image:

$$\text{projector} : \text{piano} : : $$
$$\text{reality} : \text{cinema}$$

This opposition is transposed into the talking picture as the opposition between two separable sound tracks: the diegetic track, bearer of realistic sounds (e.g. traffic noises in a city street scene), and the music track, bearer of an instrumental accompaniment (e.g. the theme song played over the lovers' kiss). By convention, these two audio tracks have taken on a quite specific sense: the diegetic track reflects reality (or at least supports cinema's referential nature), while the music track lifts the image into a romantic realm far above this world of flesh and blood.

Almost any non-experimental sound film might be given as an example, but David Lean's *Brief Encounter* (1946, scripted by Noel Coward) provides a particularly clear use of this convention. This typically British psychological drama of middle-class infidelity takes place largely in the railroad station of a provincial town in postwar England. We hear the clink of glasses, the bumping of chairs, the shuffling of feet as people await the arrival of their train; then suddenly the bell rings, the engine appears with a huff and a snort, compartment doors slam, and the train roars off. There are times, however, when these diegetic noises recede into the background, in favor of the romantic strains of Rachmaninoff's Second Piano Concerto. Symbol of a world beyond middle-class morality and its earth-bound limitations, Rachmaninoff's music lifts us out of the here-and-now into a special realm which is the private province of romantic love—and the cinema which portrays it.

Within this generalized separation and opposition of audio tracks, the musical holds a unique position, for its very definition depends on a merging of the two tracks. Nearly all films employ music on a separate music track; the musical records music on the diegetic track (i.e., music is represented as being performed by characters in the film rather than by the invisible instrumentalists who record the music track of other films). In the non-musical film the music and diegetic tracks remain entirely separate; in the musical film there is a constant crossing-over. Music appears on the diegetic track, diegetic noises are transformed into music. This intermixing is at the very heart of the style characteristic of the American film musical. By breaking down the barrier separating the two tracks, the musical blurs the borders between the real and the ideal.

The key to this merger is a technique which I will call the *audio dissolve*. Like a video dissolve, which uses superimposition to pass from one distinct image to another, the audio dissolve superimposes sounds in order to pass from one sound track to another. The most common form of audio dissolve involves a passage from the diegetic track (e.g., conversation) to the music track (e.g., orchestral accompaniment) through the intermediary of diegetic music. This simple expedient, perhaps more characteristic of the musical than any other stylistic trait, has long been sensed as a typical—and somewhat unrealistic—musical technique. Here, for example, is Otis Ferguson's description of what he sees as the chief problem in the musical, how to bring in the first number: "Somehow, before the film has gone many feet, somebody has got to take off from perfectly normal conversation into full voice, something about he won't take the train he'll walk in the rain (there is suddenly a twenty-piece band in the room), leaving everybody else in the piece to look attentive and as though they like it, and as though such a business were the most normal of procedures" (*New Republic*, October 2, 1935). What Ferguson has neglected to point out is that all those attentive people, however they might move about, no longer make any sound, for the diegetic track has now been stripped of everything but the song.

But can we say that the song is part of the diegetic track? It seems to belong to the character whose lip movements are synchronized with the words, and thus *appears* to constitute diegetic sound. Yet more than any other type of film the musical has resorted to dubbing, rerecording, looping, postsynchronization, and other techniques which involve separate recording of the image and diegetic music. It is of course common practice to record the music track separately, but in this country only the musical regularly records major portions of the diegetic track separately as well. This practice of postsynchronization has many functions within the musical's overall strategy. Beyond its obvious function of providing a cleaner, more technically perfect recording, it disguises breathing and other signs of effort, covers up missed notes, and in general creates an eerie, far-off effect, an injection of the ideal world into the real. More important still, the practice of postsynchronization reflects the importance of diegetic music as the mediating factor around which the

musical's style is created. On one side we have purely diegetic sound, defined by an apparently logical relationship connecting image to sound (a door slams, we hear the sound of a door slamming); in the majority of cases this relationship is established simply by recording image and sound simultaneously (thus assuring, for example, that an actor's words will be synchronized with his lips). On the other side we have pure musical accompaniment, defined by its lack of diegetic relationship to the image (though a thematic relationship may exist); in general this music track is recorded separately and then postsynchronized.

What then do we do with diegetic music? It is just as diegetically motivated as the sound of the door slamming yet it is music and not just noise, often postsynchronized and not simultaneously recorded. Diegetic music thus has extremely close ties to both tracks. Looked at from the point of view of source and motivation it belongs to the diegetic track, but seen from the standpoint of actual production and general effect it seems to belong to the musical track. This bivalent character of diegetic music leads to its pivotal position in the audio dissolve. This mediating function can best be seen in the following diagram:

Diegetic track	Diegetic music	Music track
simultaneous recording of sound and image	recording seems simultaneous but is actually postsynchronized	separate recording and postsynchronization

image and sound logically related	image and sound are both logically (lip sync) and rhythmically (body movement) related	image and sound thematically, emotionally, or rhythmically related
natural sounds	music appears natural	music
referentiality	image and sound refer to someone singing but as in a dream (reduced diaphragm effort)	dream
reality	real and ideal are merged	ideal

Diegetic music is that space where two worlds meet—a realm of unrelenting reality where slamming doors always make the sound of doors slamming (*action produces sound*), and a never-never-land in which doors only slam if they can be made to do so in time to the music (*music produces action*). In life and on the diegetic track of most movies, people go about their lives making sounds as a function of their activities. The privileged moments of the musical reverse that relationship, inviting people to move in time to prerecorded music. Lubitsch had the wedding scene of *Love Parade* played to a beat, in order to assure the primacy of the musical accompaniment (recorded to the same beat) over natural activity and sound. Every dance by definition involves the same primacy of rhythm. Looked at from this point of view, every musical involves two separate and seemingly mutually exclusive approaches to life: the real world, in which the diegetic track alone is heard, and the ideal world, represented by the film's production numbers, in which only the music track is heard, all diegetic noise having been removed (except for rhythmical sounds like taps). In one case sound is produced by activity; in the other, movement obeys the rhythm of the music. In between, diegetic music provides a bridge, for it obeys the laws both of *natural causality* (moving the mouth produces sounds) and of *rhythmical causality* (music produces rhythmical movement).

A few examples are in order. The difficulties involved in scripting a composer's biography prove instructive here. Typically, an account of some aspect of the composer's life provides the major source of the film's diegetic track. The biopic's very *raison d'être*, however, is the composer's memorable songs, which provide the music track. The obvious technical problem that faces scriptwriter and director alike is this: how to get from one level to the other without constantly resorting to the device of filming a stage production. In MGM's tribute to Jerome Kern, *Till the Clouds Roll By*, Kern's career begins with a visit to the arranger who would become his life-long friend, Hessler. As Hessler's daughter plays Kern's composition "Kahlua" on the piano, Hessler himself outlines the way he would orchestrate the song. As he names each instrument he would use, that instrument begins to play its part. We end up watching little Sally playing Kern's song on the piano, while we hear an orchestral version instead. The diegetic piano music has served as a bridge connecting the scene in Hessler's house to a realm beyond, where Kern's music will be recognized as deserving of the finest orchestras. If the diegetic track (which bears the piano version) represents Kern's past, the music track (which bears the orchestral version) represents Kern's promising future, catalyzed by Hessler's arranging. This standard progression (conversation —→ diegetic music —→ non-diegetic orchestration) appears continually throughout the history of the musical. In another biopic, MGM's *Words and Music*, Richard Rodgers (Tom Drake) plays his first composition "Manhattan" twice. The first time, the piano music stands ungloriously alone. The second time, however, Lorenz Hart's lyrics (sung by Mickey Rooney) add the magic touch that calls forth an audio dissolve to orchestral accompaniment. In this short sequence, "Manhattan" passes out of the limited context of a story about Rodgers and Hart and into that mythical realm of the classic song, with its power to jar our memories and remind us of good times past.

Parenthetically, we might note the extent to which the film musical's use of the audio dissolve separates its technical concerns from those of its Broadway cousin. With rare exceptions, the live, stage musical so consistently ties vocal music to orchestral music as to make the two seem redundant. When a character gets ready to sing, it is by convention acceptable for the director to stand up, wave his baton and bring the orchestra to life simultaneously with, or just before the actor's first notes. Broadway thus has only two musical levels to offer: not-singing and singing. The more complex nature of the film sound track, on the other hand, adds a third musical level, an all-important "place" whose very existence is constitutive of the genre. Consider the following example. Near the beginning of *Blue Hawaii*, Elvis Presley gives an Austrian music box to his girl friend's grandmother. The music may be Austrian, he says, but the message is the same in any language. When the music box is opened and begins to play, Elvis joins it in an extremely pleasant rendition of "I Can't Help Falling in Love with You." Before he has finished a verse, however, the music box has been joined by a full orchestra. Soon, in fact, the tinny Middle-European sound of the music box disappears entirely as a large chorus is added to the orchestra. Imperceptibly we have slid away from a backyard barbecue in Hawaii to a realm beyond language, beyond space, beyond time. With the disappearance of the music box sound we have moved into a world of pure music, divorced from this or any other specific plot. We have reached a "place" of transcendence where time stands still, where contingent concerns are stripped away to reveal the essence of things. This privileged moment cannot last forever, however. Just as careful audio mixing created a continuous bridge from the world of diegetic sound to the transcendent realm of pure timeless, spaceless music, so an audio dissolve returns us gently to the narrative. From non-diegetic orchestra and chorus we slide to non-diegetic orchestral accompaniment for Elvis and the diegetic music box; then, as the orchestra disappears, we are left where we began with the music box and Elvis at a backyard barbecue. If this had been a stage production, Elvis and the orchestra no doubt would have started up together, with the chorus spelling the lead singer for appropriate refrains and repeats. Song as a special domain would be opposed to the humdrum world of dialogue, but this would constitute a naked opposition, an all-or-nothing alternative between two antithetical realms. The film introduces a diegetic source of music—the music box—to break down the absoluteness of that opposition. Like so many sources of diegetic music introduced into musical films with the specific function of creating a bridge between time-bound narrative and the timeless transcendence of supra-diegetic music, the music box exists only to be silenced, surpassed, and left behind like some latter-day Virgil handing the spectator on to a heavenly Beatrice. As compared to theatrical usage, therefore, the film counts on the flexibility of complex sound mixing to lead the spectator slowly and imperceptibly past the simple notion of song as special to the still greater transcendence of sourceless, supra-diegetic sound.

Though the movement from diegetic sound without music through diegetic music to non-diegetic music without diegetic sound is undoubtedly the most common version of the audio dissolve, there are nevertheless many other variations. Perhaps the most characteristic of these involves Fred Astaire's use of rhythmic walking as a bridge. Throughout Astaire's career, this technique remains one of his hallmarks, either alone or in the company of his talented partners (particularly Ginger Rogers and Cyd Charisse). In the first song/dance of *Top Hat* ("Fancy Free"), Astaire slides from conversation with Edward Everett Horton into song simply by rhythmifying and melodizing his voice patterns. There is no point at which we can say "here is where he starts singing." The movement from diegetic conversation to diegetic song is continuous and imperceptible. The entrance of the orchestra is rendered equally imperceptible by the simple expedient of fading the accompaniment in behind Astaire's voice. Now that Astaire has slipped quite naturally from speech to song, he repeats the exercise by subordinating all his movements to the song's rhythm—at an undetermined point we suddenly recognize that he is dancing, yet we never saw him begin to dance. Just as his slow slipping from speech to song justifies a further sliding from song to orchestral accompaniment, so his transition from walking to dancing turns the space around him into a stage. The same technique leads into Astaire's next song ("A Lovely Day to Be Caught in the Rain"), this time with Ginger Rogers. He walks into a dance, trying to impress her, but she is having none of it. Yet she cannot help beating time with her cane, which soon becomes beating time with her feet as she walks around the band shell mocking Astaire's every move. But to mock his movements she must imitate them, and so, imperceptibly once again, rhythmical movement has led to dance. The band shell, which was once just a band shell, has now become a stage, so much so that the number concludes with a bow to the camera. By this point all diegetic sound has been either excluded or assimilated to the music's rhythm. The thundering storm which brought on the rain has now abandoned its realistic function in order to serve as accompaniment for the couple's song-and-dance number.

As Robert Preston affirms in *The Music Man*, "Singing is just sustained talking." It is this continuity between diegetic sound (talking) and diegetic music (singing) that both reinforces (and is reinforced by) the audio dissolve. So important is the establishment of continuity between talking and singing that the musical must accord a very special place to the vocal activity which most clearly bridges speech and song: humming. An untold number of songs in the Hollywood musical begin with a character humming a catchy tune, thus calling into existence an orchestral accompaniment and eventually turning the character— our name for inhabitants of the narrative world—into a singer, a citizen of songland. Along with humming and its freedom from strict linguistic rules go all of those related moments when the free play of the signifier and the voice's liberation from familiar, codified patterns combine in a dum-de-dum, a la-di-da, or the most famous lead-in of all: Gene Kelly's "doodle-do" bridge between sober, straight talk and the far more exhilarating singin' in the rain.

As with sound, so with movement. Dancing is just rhythmical walking, the musical seems to affirm. This hypothesis is elegantly demonstrated in the dog-walking sequence of *Shall We Dance*, where Astaire and Rogers turn a humdrum responsibility into a festive activity simply by walking in time to the music. Still more to the point, however, are

dances like the "Kansas City" number in *Oklahoma!*, which demonstrate the continuity that exists between normal diegetic activity and the dance, with its power to lift the characters out of the real world and onto the stage, and the sound track out of diegetic noise and into the realm of music. Will Parker has just returned from Kansas City. At the Claremore depot he begins to recount his experiences in the big city. As he talks, his speech grows more and more rhythmical, thus calling forth and justifying, as it were, the entrance of an orchestral accompaniment. At the same time, his audience begins to move in time to the music—first the two young girls who appear repeatedly throughout the film, then, after Will's demonstration of the two-step and ragtime, the entire group. As in the band shell example from *Top Hat*, the progression from diegetic movement to dance begins with a contagious rhythm: the bystanders cannot help tapping their feet in time to the rhythm. Unison foot-tapping soon progresses to walking in time, and from there the transition to choral dance is seamless. Just as humming performs an essential transitional function for the sound track, so foot-tapping, swaying to music, and other ways of visibly beating time serve to transform a narratively organized space into a rhythmically organized image.

Once a beat has been established, we have the impression that the direction of causality reverses. Within the film's diegesis it is assumed that one thing happens after another, and previous events cause (motivate, justify) subsequent ones. Will Parker has been to Kansas City *and so* he arrives at Claremore depot with a story to tell *and so* a group of interested listeners gathers around him. This mode of causality fades away (along with diegetic sound) as soon as the rhythm becomes contagious. Can we say that the audience moves rhythmically *because* Will Parker is telling a story? No, because rhythmic movement does not accompany all stories told in the film. Is it because he is singing his story? Strictly speaking, it cannot be for this reason either, since Will's audience continues to tap and dance even when Will is not singing. We must conclude, I think, that the order of priorities of audio and image track has now been reversed. At first the image track calls forth musical accompaniment by means of an audio dissolve (sound is motivated, naturally and thematically, by the diegesis/image). Once this progression is complete, the reversal can take place: *the movement which we see on screen is now an accompaniment to the music track.* A new mode of causality now appears, a simultaneous mode wherein the image is "caused" by the music rather than by some previous image. In short, the normally dominant image track now keeps time to the music track, instead of simply being accompanied by it. The music and its rhythm now initiate movement rather than vice versa.

In leaving normal day-to-day causality behind, the music creates a utopian space in which all singers and dancers achieve a unity unimaginable in the now superseded world of temporal, psychological causality. The dominance of sound over image serves to unify groups by synchronizing their movements, just as Hollywood itself had to discover special methods of synchronizing independently recorded image and sound in order to develop the musical genre. In

daily life people hear different drummers and thus live their lives out of sync; when music begins to initiate the movements of a couple, they start to move in time to each other because they are hearing the same beat.

Schematically, we might express this reversal in the following manner. The standard Hollywood arrangement is as follows:

That is, diegetic event *a* causes diegetic event *b* and that relationship motivates the musical accompaniment. Thus, if *a* is *entering a dark, deserted house,* and we fear that *b* will be *unexpected attack by dangerous enemies,* then the music, reflecting this relationship, will be ominous and discordant. If *a* is *declaration of love* and *b* is expected to be *joyous embrace,* the music will be uplifting and romantic. In these cases we quite properly speak of musical *accompaniment,* because the music track does indeed accompany and support the diegetic material (both image and diegetic sound). The more complex setup in the musical looks something like this:

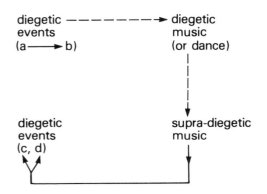

That is, diegetic events, which seemed to be progressing according to an entirely causal scheme, slide imperceptibly, through an audio dissolve, toward the reduction of diegetic sound and the introduction of transcendent, supra-diegetic music. At this point, the events of the diegesis change motivation. Diegetic sound disappears; the only diegetic sounds which remain at normal volume are those which keep time to, i.e., are subordinated to, the music (e.g., taps, slaps, rhythmic natural sounds). The image now shows movements which depend more on the music than on one another. The rhythm calls forth each element independently. Why does each foot-tap follow the preceding one at the same interval? Does each one cause the next? Hardly. Each one responds to the music's beat just as each step of the dance, each note of the song must fit into a prescribed pattern. If the tempo of the music changes, so must that of the dance.

The extent to which a change in rhythm is doubled by a change in linguistic patterns is instructive here. With very few exceptions (e.g., *Love Me Tonight*), the film musical depends on dialogue that is resolutely prosaic, resorting to rhyme only for those special moments when language is transformed by music. As we move from diegetic sound to supra-diegetic sound, we are thus commonly moving toward a more poetic type of linguistic relationship as well. In normal discourse, June might well call forth a variety of other words, according to the meaning that each respondent attributes to the word. Summer, July, hot, my birthday, end of school, baseball—all of these might be legitimate associations. But, as Ira Gershwin has permanently impressed upon us, no such logic applies once we have gone down the rabbit hole of an audio dissolve into the wonderland of song. "June" calls forth "moon," just as "above" implies "love," and "cottage for two" can only be mated to "darling with you."[1] The bonds of linguistic meaning are loosened, as words once again return to their primal characteristics of rhythm and rhyme. Instead of thought, words become sound, and thus rediscover their rightful place in a world dominated by song.

If the music's rhythmic consistency lends order and regularity to diegetic time, the irregularities of diegetic space are made to conform to a pattern in the same way. Fred and Ginger move in parallel or symmetrically; the dancers at the Claremore depot turn a neutral irregular space into an ordered stage, with each camera placement reinforcing the balanced patterns achieved by the dancers' positions. The logical consequence of this progression is a treatment of the image itself as pure pattern. Freed from the realistic and causal constraints of the diegesis, the image can now reflect the music in its overall pictorial quality just as it does in the rhythmical movement of any single performer. In technical terms, the subordination of the diegesis to the music track parallels and justifies the subordination of the object plane to the picture plane.

This transfer is closely associated in the musical with the name of Busby Berkeley, for he alone among the early practitioners of the musical understood the extent to which the audio dissolve liberates the picture plane of all diegetic responsibilities. By placing the camera directly above his performers, Berkeley was able to destroy perspective and thus concentrate attention on the picture plane. When Gene Kelly dances, his movements are controlled by the music (in a sense he is just as animated as his cartoon character partners), but they are still Gene Kelly's movements, i.e. they are still connected to the diegesis by the representational character of the image, which permits us to identify the dancer as the same character who was just feeling so happy that he felt like dancing. When we reach the climax of a Berkeley production number, however, we have entirely abandoned the representational mode. *Everything—even the image—is now subordinated to the music track.* Even when we can identify the elements of Berkeley's patterns as women, our attention is drawn away from the image's referential nature by shots which organize hundreds of hats, legs, feet, arms, or torsos into a single pattern. In the flower patterns typical of his thirties extravaganzas (*Gold Diggers of 1933, Footlight Parade, Dames, Wonder Bar*), the simultaneous movement of the dancers produces a kaleidoscopic effect in which the overall configuration always obliterates individual referential aspects. It is as if the screen were transformed into an electronically generated visual accompaniment to the music.

This reversal of the image/sound hierarchy lies at the very center of the musical genre, so much so that any definition of the genre must take it into account. One reason why we hesitate to classify certain films as musicals—even though they include many songs—is that those songs never lead to a reversal of the image/sound hierarchy, but are used only as accompaniment or interludes (the typical case would be the fifties' theme song movies). So many definitions of the musical have stressed the presence of diegetic music (in order to distinguish the musical from the hundreds of narrative films which resort to non-diegetic musical accompaniment), that the special status achieved by music in the musical has gone nearly unnoticed. In the last decade or so the popularity of the concert film has increasingly revealed that the presence of diegetic music alone is simply not enough to produce a musical. Far more than diegetic music, it is the tendency to transform diegetic music into supra-diegetic music—with a consequent reversal of the traditional image/sound hierarchy—that distinguishes the musical as a genre from its documentary cousins.

Constituting the *locus classicus* of the musical's tendency to subordinate image to sound, Berkeley's films have too often been treated as eccentric and atypical. Though their technique may be extreme, the general patterns they establish are representative, indeed symbolic of the musical's most fundamental configurations. Berkeley's characteristic style revolves on alternation between eye-level shots and top shots, between dominance of diegetic material and independent musical material, between the screen as window (privileging the object plane) and the screen as frame (privileging the picture plane). This alternation produces a constant and strongly felt opposition between a sense of pattern and a sense of randomness. In one mode we see from above and thus are able to grasp the interrelationships which govern the characters' movements; in the other mode we

a-f—The early years of the musical saw numerous experiments with high-angle photography as a simple device to turn men and women into patterns, thus tending toward destruction of the cinema's familiar three-dimensional illusion. On the left, the startling birth sequence from Mamoulian's 1929 *Applause*. Above, a naturalized high-angle shot from *The Gay Divorcee* (1933), apparently shot from a hotel room balcony. Below, a Berkeley top-shot turns women into a flower. Note the effect of shooting against a black studio floor, which completes the flattening effect of extreme high-angle photography.

a-d [pers]
e [MOMA]
f Center for Film and Theater Research,
University of Wisconsin [UW]

see from the point of view of an observer within the diegesis, to whom all is random, chaotic, unclear. Like the opposition between image dominance and music dominance, the distinction between top shot and eye-level shot reflects a dichotomy fundamental to the musical. Any viewing of a musical sets up an alternation in the spectator between *doubt* that everything will turn out all right (he is too hard-headed, she is too prudish, the train may leave without him, and so forth), and *knowledge* that everything must turn out all right (musicals "always" end with an embrace). In the first case, we identify with the characters, sharing their misgivings as well as their limited perception; in the second, generic coding has raised us to the level of the director, who always knows how the plot is structured. In other words, the spectator's alternation is always between eye-level shot (the world as whirling chaos) and top shot (the world as pattern). Berkeley's style is the perfect stylistic correlative of the musical's particular brand of ritual suspense, wherein we alternate between foreknowledge and a conventional willingness to ignore that knowledge. Just as the musical harbors two types of causality (sequential or natural and simultaneous or rhythmic), so it proposes two modes of being and knowing—one which treats the film as an ongoing reality, whose future is no more known than the real future, and another which recognizes in the musical an artistic product of a highly conventionalized generic system, in which the future is always well-known because plot formulas remain from film to film substantially the same.

The transition from eye-level shot to top shot is often rather brusque in the Berkeley style. It remained for Vincente Minnelli, with his extremely fluid use of the boom shot, to transform into a dissolve what for Berkeley had always been a cut. Whereas Berkeley alternates between and thus opposes the human and Olympian points of view, Minnelli creates a continuity between them. A single example should suffice. During the party at the Smith home in *Meet Me in St. Louis*, the camera begins to sail over the heads of the dancing couples, as if it were looking for something, as if somehow it were seeking to comprehend the pattern underlying all this dizzying movement. Without warning, as the camera is tracking up and back, it stops stock still, as if it had found an answer to its question. Indeed, the camera's freeze coincides exactly with the separation of the whirling couples into two lines facing each other— girls on one side, boys on the other. Peering from above down the center line of this row dance, the camera has at last isolated the sexual symmetry on which all activity in the room depends. From its vantage point above the crowd, the camera can see—and point out by its sudden stop—what the dancers only vaguely sense. Minnelli's crane shot captures stylistically the spectator's constant sliding from a participant's limited perspective to that of a director who manipulates both performers and audience from his vantage point. Like Berkeley with his top shots, Minnelli and his boom succeed admirably in demonstrating the flexibility of the film medium, as well as the exhilarating sense of superiority which cinema offers to its spectator. Not content simply to overcome the spectator's perceptual limitations, the musical makes of those limitations and the desire to overcome them the very object of its discourse.

Video Dissolve

In the "audio dissolve," continuity is created between two distinct categories of sound; the use of diegetic music (or rhythm) provides a bridge connecting the (realistic) diegetic track to the (romantic) music track. In the more familiar visual dissolve, a similar pattern operates: two distinct images are made to seem continuous through superimposition. In the following discussion, however, the notion of "video dissolve" will apply in a somewhat broader fashion to any visual device bridging two separate places, times, or levels of reality. In particular, I will show how these visual devices are used to connect diegetic space of a realistic nature to an idealized space—diegetic or not—which represents its diametrical opposite. As I have suggested, the characteristic style of the American film musical involves a merging of the real and the ideal; the video dissolve contributes to this style by superimposing in the viewer's mind two radically different landscapes.

Perhaps the most representative use of the video dissolve involves the superimposition of time levels: the diegetic present—banal, limited, ruled by necessity—is opposed to, but fades into the distant past or future—exciting, limitless, controlled by a romanticizing memory or tendency toward dream. In one sense this usage of the technique is only an extension of Hollywood's conventional use of the dissolve to suggest lapse of time. It is important, however, to recognize the extent to which the musical uses the dissolve thematically, ascribing radically different reality levels to the two different images which are superimposed. In *Maytime,* for example, we begin at a Maypole dance somewhere in nineteenth-century America. The day, the songs, a young couple—everything reminds the elderly Miss Morrison (Jeanette MacDonald) of her youth. From this quiet, uneventful scene we slowly dissolve to the splendor of Napoleon's court, where Miss Morrison sang as the famous singer Marsha Mornay. More than a transition to the past, this dissolve takes us into the wonderland of memory. There it was that this proper New England spinster first knew love. Even within that world the dissolve serves to separate—or rather connect—daily events and those special occasions which we never forget. Marsha Mornay first meets her lover (Nelson Eddy) after a dissolve expressing the length of her moonlit ride through the streets of Paris. The moment when he first confesses his love is separated from the rest of the film by two long Slavko Vorkapich dissolve montages, the first including traditional symbols of spring (blossoms, birds, sunbursts), the second an impressionistic account of their successful but separate careers. In the end, her love affair brings only tragedy; her jealous husband eventually kills the lover who brought spring to her heart. Yet the past is still a golden memory for Miss Morrison. The film ends with a stabilized dissolve, past and present overlaying one another as they do in our memory. Just as the framing May Day echoes a May Day long before, so the video dissolve recaptures both the separation and the simultaneity essential to the musical film experience. Real and ideal, present and past remain distinct, but for one fleeting moment the spectator, like Miss Morrison, is allowed to perceive them in a single complex image.

This use of the dissolve to introduce idealized memories is commonplace in the musical. *Cover Girl, Till the Clouds Roll By,* and *On a Clear Day*—to name but a few examples—use it to introduce material from a distant past. *Paint Your Wagon* and *The Unsinkable Molly Brown* introduce in this fashion one lover's memories of the other. *Les Girls* demonstrates an alternative method: the first flashback is introduced by a pan right which takes us out of an English courtroom and into a Parisian flat. Through its ability to construct sets in which London and Paris are contiguous, Hollywood has the power to build the "dissolve" right into the set. *It's Always Fair Weather* creates one of the most unusual "dissolves" by providing Cyd Charisse with two seemingly identical skirts. The first, symbolic of her business-like manner, is tight and constricting, but the second, as we discover at the boxing club, has a hidden split which permits her to reveal her balletic energy. Not just two different skirts, but different versions of the same skirt, and thus one type of behavior superimposed on another. In still other films the final shots are given a special status by the dissolve which separates/links them to the rest of the film *(San Francisco, Harvey Girls, Belle of New York, Singin' in the Rain)*. These dissolves seem to set the lovers in an ideal future, a realm of increasing joy somehow out of time and thus separate from this workaday world. Just as the dissolve can be used to suggest that behind the present lies an infinite realm of pleasant memories, so the dissolve can reinforce the notion that properly matched lovers live happily *ever* after.

Shining through the present, thanks to a video dissolve, the memory of a harmonious past and the promise of a glorious future lend the present moment a certain depth, a warm glow of happy associations. But if this dissolve technique attributes special value to the characters' memories and hopes, it implicitly does so for the spectator as well. New York as we see it in *The Belle of New York* is part of our idealized past. The pre-World War I small town (*Meet Me in St. Louis, Summer Holiday, The Music Man*) is part of our cultural heritage. Memories of vaudeville or the Follies (*The Great Ziegfeld, Ziegfeld Girl, Broadway Melody of 1940, For Me and My Gal*) recall better times gone by. By the fifties we could already look back on those golden days when people actually went to see musicals (*Singin' in the Rain, The Band Wagon, The Boyfriend*). In each of these cases there is a dissolve which takes place *within* the spectator, reestablishing his/her roots in a cultural past. Just as Miss Morrison's Maytimes past are projected on a mental screen and thus superimposed on her Maytime present, so our memories—called forth by the nostalgic image before us—join, reinforce, and deepen our present-day experiences. This visual merging of past into present is aided by the reuse of songs which we have all known and loved.

What spectator in 1951 had not hummed, sung, or danced to *Singin' in the Rain*'s "You Are My Lucky Star?" Anyone who had not heard it introduced in *Broadway Melody* would certainly have had thousands of opportunities to listen to it on the radio or swing to it on the dance floor. Hearing it again in 1951 (or again in 1971 in *The Boyfriend*) any spectator would be hearing his/her own past, reliving personal memories come to join and complement the present. Visions out of our common past, recollections of childhood and youth, tunes of yesteryear—all invite the spectator to enter into contact with the past, to dissolve the temporal barriers which govern our lives, and to invest the all-too-real present with a fondly remembered past.

This artificial regression common to all cinematic experiences reaches its high point in the musical. Constantly sliding from present to past, from reality to dream, from life to art, the American film musical regularly serves what Freud terms "psychic economy," the natural human tendency to reduce the amount of stimulation present in the mental apparatus. By collapsing categories and overcoming oppositions, the musical succeeds in avoiding psychic expenditure. Characters like *Maytime*'s Miss Morrison who might well have dwelled on their regrets are permitted to live the present as past through the technical—and psychological—wonder of the dissolve. By the same token, performers who might have stressed the work which separates conception from performance instead give the impression that neither time nor effort stands be-

tween an idea and its realization. In *San Francisco*, only a dissolve separates Jeanette MacDonald's first rehearsal of the title number from her full costumed performance. In *The Band Wagon*, we see all the fruitless rehearsals of the first, moribund show, but the second moves directly from its community conception through its successful road trip to its New York triumph, with dissolves connecting all the stages. In *Cover Girl*, as in many another musical, only a dissolve separates the photographing of a pretty girl from the appearance of her picture on the cover of a magazine. No negative, no development, no printing presses. Planes of reality lose their distinctness, outlines are blurred, and categories flow into one another.

This is of course the very mode of dream, where separate experiences are displaced and condensed in such a way as to provide a single fluid vision. Normal notions of causality are replaced by a free-floating network of memories, desires, and fears, each dissolving into the next by a principle which is psychic rather than physical. The musical's characteristic style approximates this dream world, constantly calling us out of diegetic reality to the past, a performance, a dream sequence. Scenes from reality suddenly metamorphose into well-known art works (*Summer Holiday, An American in Paris, The Belle of New York, The Music Man*). The roar of the city disappears—along with its hectic pace, frantic sense of time, and concern for social advancement—as we slide into a park. In New York, Central Park serves this pastoral purpose (*Hallelujah I'm a Bum, Born to Dance, Shall We Dance, The*

Band Wagon), but every city, however small or large, has its public park (*Top Hat, Maytime, Summer Holiday, Gigi*), circus, or amusement park (*Damsel in Distress, State Fair, Centennial Summer, On the Town, Let's Dance, Grease*), in which time stands still, causality holds no sway, and true emotions can be freely expressed. Just as the park provides an internal refuge within the city walls, so the country serves as an external escape from the perversities of modernism (*Love Me Tonight, Damsel in Distress, The Gang's All Here, Brigadoon, Gigi*). In the same way, a glamorous far-off city can serve as a pendant to humdrum small-town American life (*Roberta, The Pirate, An American in Paris, Let's Be Happy*). In *This Time for Keeps*, everything that seemed so confused in the hectic big city world of show business is clarified by a trip to Mackinac Island, site of the famous Grand Hotel, where cars and other modern appurtenances are forbidden. Like the characters in *This Time for Keeps*, the musical spectator has embarked upon a journey to a utopian space where values are somehow made plain, where difficult decisions are simplified, where geography is that of the mind rather than that of the globe. Thus in *The Sound of Music*, the Trapp family can escape over the mountain from Nazi Salzburg to neutral Switzerland *in spite of the fact that Switzerland is hundreds of miles away* (Salzburg is on the border between Austria and Germany, not Switzerland). Anomalous as this situation may seem, it clearly expresses the fundamental configuration underlying the musical's imaginative geography: an ideal realm is never more than a dissolve away, a world

where men and women are free to live as they do in their imagination. Not a musical exists which does not have its Camelot, its "Switzerland of the mind," be it a moment of past joy, an instant of theatrical perfection, a romantic interlude, a dream of greatness, or a privileged space free from life's cares.

The musical's special character does not derive from these utopias alone, of course, for they are a general characteristic of American film. What distinguishes the musical is its tendency to dissolve one realm into another. At the beginning of *The Pirate*, Judy Garland makes a much desired trip from her humdrum country town to a romantic coastal city. Typically, however, this opposition is not allowed to stand, for the actor whom she meets there (Gene Kelly) follows her back to her provincial village, thus bringing romance to reality and dissolving one into the other. The musical does not just oppose reality to dreams, it merges the two, just as the experience of watching a musical overcomes the dichotomy between screen and spectator, slowly dissolving away the barrier which separates a world of flesh and blood from a realm of light and shadow.

The self-consciousness with which certain directors have employed the video dissolve is particularly apparent in the opening sequences of Vincente Minnelli's musicals. At the end of the credits in *Meet Me in St. Louis* we see an old-fashioned black-and-white tintype image of the Smith mansion. As we track in toward the house this ornately framed vision from the past, brown with age, slowly takes on the bright colors of summer and the activity of small-town life. This simple device sets up a number of relationships which guide our viewing of the film. Taken, as it were, from the family album of the American heritage, the discolored picture defines the entire film as a memory, a recollection of those wonderful days when life was still a family affair. When we dissolve to a Technicolor shot of the mansion, however, that past suddenly becomes a virtual present, a reality characterized by clarity, color, and movement, rather than by the washed-out static quality of an old postcard. Minnelli's introductory device thus defines his film as both memory and present reality, both artistic stylization of experience and realistic reproduction of that experience. The film's style thus depends on a merging of memory and observation, of art and reality: each scene, each shot presents an aspect of daily life at the turn of the century, but all is too perfect. Every sequence blends the reality of observation and the idealization of memory in such a way that *Meet Me in St. Louis* takes on the character of a perpetual dissolve: the past fades into the present, art coincides with but overlays reality.

Throughout Minnelli's career he continues to employ the opening shots of his films as a short course in hermeneutics, as a lesson in the theory of interpretation. The credits of *Yolanda and the Thief* are superimposed on a garish, painted backdrop. Obviously two-dimensional, this backdrop looks as shallow and unrealistic as the musical genre itself has appeared to more than one critic. Even before the end of the titles, however, our perception— and thus our opinion—is challenged by the entrance of a man leading a llama.

Entering the frame from the left, he crosses to the center and moves toward the camera. Where once we saw an entirely artificial, two-dimensional backdrop, now we see an equally artificial, but fully three-dimensional space. The entrance of a human being into the contrived world of the musical somehow lends it an added dimension, an increased reality. If the initial dissolve in *Meet Me in St. Louis* defines that film as a mediation between remembered and lived experience, the perceptual redefinition of *Yolanda*'s first sequence announces this film's main thematic concern and its stylistic counterpart: the depth of the artificial. We are too quick to assume that the musical is shallow and meaningless, *Yolanda* seems to say; look again and discover the truth which the human dimension lends to the artificial.

Yolanda's credits are no isolated case within the Minnelli canon; throughout his career he sets up the reality/art theme from the very start by sliding from two- to three-dimensionality. *Cabin in the Sky* cuts from a billboard drawing to an almost deep-focus shot of the people entering a rural church. *Ziegfeld Follies* expresses Florenz Ziegfeld's memories as pictures on the wall of his heavenly abode, pictures which, once animated, will become a final incarnation of the Follies. *An American in Paris* shows us no human beings until it has characterized Paris as a city of statues, beautiful but inanimate, lacking the energy which Kelly and Caron will provide. *Gigi* sets its credits against drawings by Sem, suggesting that the very meaning of three-dimensional Paris is governed by its glorification, indeed its mythicization in the two-dimensional work of its painters. Through time-lapse photography of blooming flowers, *On a Clear Day*'s credit sequence calls attention to cinema's ability to alter our normal sense of time. Each film is thus defined from the start as a tension between art and reality, between the film's status as stylized artifact and its referential function. The screen is both a frame and a window, a self-enclosed two-dimensional aesthetic phenomenon and a transparent pane opening onto a world beyond. Minnelli's opening sequences serve warning that his musicals are about this fundamental duality of cinematic ontology.

The Pirate and *The Band Wagon* extend this configuration to the notion of legend. Instead of directly confronting the art/reality or frame/window dichotomies, they begin by opposing legend to life. The credits for *The Pirate* are superimposed over an old map of the Caribbean, which soon dissolves into a book recounting the story of Macoco, the famous pirate whose deeds have become so legendary that they deserve literary consecration. The next shot reveals Judy Garland reading the book, savoring its every word like some tropical Emma Bovary dreaming of Parisian elegance. This simple beginning clearly defines the film's two worlds: a dream world inspired by the Macoco legend and the normal everyday world to which Judy is soon called by her aunt. But, as we soon find out, no ultimate separation between the legendary and the everyday is possible, for Judy's fat fiancé—to her the very symbol of the practical, colorless, quotidian world—turns out to be none other than Macoco him-

self in disguise. While the opening sequence establishes the opposed realms between which the text oscillates, it does so only to collapse that opposition, as first one and then the other of Judy's partners resorts to disguise (and thus to simultaneous representation of both worlds).

The Band Wagon operates in similar fashion, but borrows its legend directly from the cinema world. The credits are superimposed on what looks like a photograph of a top hat, white gloves, and a cane—probably the most famous icons in the history of the American film musical. Suggesting the entire career of Fred Astaire, and with it a bygone era, these nostalgic items serve to recall an entire genre and its former glory (and, in particular, the credits of *Top Hat*). Such nostalgia is definitively banished by the opening scene, however, in which the top hat is transformed from symbol into commodity: Astaire's famous head gear is up for auction to the highest bidder. But who wants a top hat in 1953? Hollywood's most famous headcovering will not bring a single dollar. This alienation effect clearly delineates one of the film's constitutive antinomies: unlike legend, which can exist in the mind alone, life is judged by the criterion of function. If it's not useful it has no value. In Marxist terms, legend is pure exchange value, life depends on use value. This opposition sets Fred Astaire squarely in the middle. We see him both as Fred Astaire, the legendary song-and-dance man, and as Tony Hunter, the character trying to make a musical comeback on the Broadway stage. Within the film this duality defines a fundamental question: can Astaire/

Hunter be of any use in making the show a success or is he just a figurehead kept around to attract his faithful following?

In each of these films the initial dichotomy which opposes reality to art, dream, or legend sets a certain tone, but it by no means suggests the finality of that division. Quite to the contrary, the function of style in the Minnelli *œuvre* seems to be the leveling of the original dichotomy. If *Meet Me in St. Louis* begins by opposing the screen as frame to the screen as window, it ends by picturing St. Louis in both ways simultaneously. The fairy-tale splendor of the World's Fair combines the unreal stylization of the art work with the fully physical nature of the real world; the World's Fair is at the same time a dream image and a hometown reality for the Smith family. *Yolanda*'s opposition of the two- to three-dimensional is resolved in the person of Fred Astaire, who is both Lucille Bremer's guardian angel (a spiritual, two-dimensional being) and her lover (a quite corporeal, three-dimensional being). In *The Pirate* it is Gene Kelly who manages to unite the two aspects of Macoco. As an actor, he is adept at being both man and legend, whereas the real Macoco has lost all contact with the legend suggested by his deeds. The stage—and by extension the film—is the only place where legend and life can become one. The same strategy presides over the resolution of *The Band Wagon*. Astaire's image and his performance coincide as do the show's success and the romance of its stars. By the end of the film Tony Hunter's performance in "The Band Wagon" (the show within the film) has made *The Band Wagon* (the film) a part of the Astaire legend. Use and exchange values are brought together once more as the star and the character, the legend and the life, fade into one.

Whether the video dissolve is handled technically or thematically, it remains at the service of psychic economy, constantly reducing oppositions and dissolving contradictions. Indeed, the ultimate version of the video dissolve—condensation of actor and character into the same image—always contributes in the musical to a leveling of representational levels. More than in any other genre, the musical calls on actors to play themselves. Thus Chevalier plays the song-and-dance-man Chevalier, Astaire plays the elegant top-hat-white-tie-and-tails Astaire, and Kelly plays the familiar happy-go-lucky self-confident Kelly. As viewers, we rarely have to deal with a contradiction between actor and character, thus reducing the gap separating fiction and reality, and with it the spectator's psychic expenditure. All is organized in such a way as to dissolve all tension and absorb the audience directly into the image.

Personality Dissolve

We have seen thus far how the stylistic qualities of the American film musical depend on an ambiguous relationship: the ideal is opposed to the real, yet during the course of the film that opposition is bracketed, reduced, and at a few crucial points actually erased. The dissolve constitutes the perfect stylistic correlative of this process, for by its very nature the dissolve preserves the *conceptual separation* between two categories (shots, sound tracks, levels of reality) while at the very same time establishing *perceptual conti-*

nuity between them. A similar notion governs the constitution and presentation of character within the musical. There are "two sides to every girl," sings Kathryn Grayson in *Two Sisters from Boston*. In fact, the typical Hollywood musical character is not only double, he/she is something of a hermaphrodite, internalizing the basic dichotomy that characterizes the male/female opposition within the musical. In *The Music Man*, for example, Robert Preston clearly represents certain values given as typically masculine (entertainment, freedom, energy, irresponsibility), while Shirley Jones exemplifies their feminine counterparts (work, security, stability, responsibility). Yet as the film progresses it becomes more and more clear that the values and drives associated with each one are present in the other, but in a hidden, repressed state. Preston's happy-go-lucky, girl-in-every-town, here-today-and-gone-tomorrow values are clearly a defense, a smoke-screen designed to hide his inability to find the right girl, the right purpose to make him settle down. When Jones finally forgets her librarian's propriety we recognize the extent to which she too uses her primary identification (culture, morals, the classics) to cover up her inability to actualize an equally important secondary identification (with love, excitement, and music as expression).

As a preliminary formulation, we can thus state not only that each character is double, made up of both a surface and a repressed personality, but that *the surface personality of each member of the couple corresponds to the repressed personality of the other*. In other words, the relationship between the members of the couple is a complementary one, each representing the hidden, neglected aspect of the other. In *Silk Stockings*, Fred Astaire's debonaire manner and romantic inclinations coincide exactly with the side of Cyd Charisse which Russian regimentation has made her repress. Julie Andrews in *The Sound of Music* represents precisely that excitement and warmth which Christopher Plummer has been afraid to exhibit in front of his children, while he constitutes the stability and firmness of character which she has lacked. Even the X-rated *Alice in Wonderland* sets up a similar correspondence between male overtly sexual intentions and Alice's repressed libido.

Sometimes it is the very circumstances of performance that establish a hierarchical relationship between the two sides of a character's personality. A single still is enough to affirm the dual nature of the Fred Astaire role in *Shall We Dance*. As Petrov, Astaire is a world-famous ballet dancer, but Petrov is really Pete Peters, a disguised American whose real sympathies are for tap dancing. To the dismay of impresario Edward Everett Horton, Astaire's toe shoes are thus equipped with taps, suggesting the inseparability of Astaire's two *personae*. It is only when Astaire sails for the States, however, that we understand the psychic relationship which ties these two roles together. On deck Horton supervises a ballet practice, while in the engine room Astaire taps out "Slap that Bass" to the spirited accompaniment of the crew. The ship-as-allegory is not a new notion, but it is here used to good purpose. Ballet and the Petrov personality correspond to the part which shows above the water line; beneath the surface the ship—and by extension Astaire—is driven forward by the machine-room tap dancing of Pete Peters. What Astaire aspires to, but must repress because of his role, is the energy and enjoyment of jazz dance. Ginger Rogers, on the other hand, is tired of her tap dance career and aspires to something "higher." It is no wonder that their marriage is hailed in the press as a merger of jazz and ballet, and on stage by a dance ("They All Laughed") which fades balletic pirouettes into tap breaks through the intermediary of ballroom steps and swings.

Such a merger perfectly exemplifies the mythology of the couple as it is promulgated by the American film musical. Each partner is seen as potentially complete but unable to actualize one side of his/her personality; marriage serves to provide each lover with the perfect complement, the one person capable of giving life to the repressed component in a dualistic psychic configuration. Any individual character is thus unstable and asymmetrical (since one component is on the surface and the other submerged), but the couple as a unit achieves balance, permanent in its symmetry. Until boy meets girl, an important aspect of human experience is lost for each character. When two lovers meet, however, each sees his/her repressed self in the other as if he/she were looking in a psychic mirror. At first, this reflection only makes the character aware of hidden desires

without actually bringing them to the surface. It is usually at this point that the submerged personality component appears in the unreality of dream (*Cabin in the Sky, Lady in the Dark, Yolanda and the Thief*), the pretending of performance (*Top Hat, Easter Parade, The Band Wagon, Les Girls*), the protection of "make believe" (*Showboat, Carousel, Can-Can*), or the loss of self-consciousness engendered by a seductive scene (the female leads in *Maytime, The Pirate, Silk Stockings,* and *The Music Man* all give in to their romantic longings only to snap suddenly out of their swoon, as if from a trance). Only by passing through this intermediary stage, in which the character expresses desires without having to take full responsibility for them, can the musical character ever recover his/her repressed personality and with it his/her balance.

We are now in a better position to understand why the musical's characteristic style involves what I have termed a "personality dissolve" rather than simply a dichotomized personality. As in the case of audio and video aspects, the notion of "dissolve" is here used to suggest a technique which preserves conceptual distinctions while establishing perceptual continuity. This continuity is created much as it is in the audio and video registers: two antithetical entities are made to overlap by the creation of a third term which shares certain qualities of both:

surface component	"make-believe"	submerged component
responsibility	no responsibility	no responsibility
conscious state	conscious state	unconscious state

Falling in love in spite of themselves, Gene Raymond and Dolores del Rio find themselves listening to an alter ego. To fall in love, the images suggest, is to listen to one's other self, one's hidden personality *(Flying Down to Rio)*.

[pers]

We are conscious of our overt behavior and thus must take responsibility for it. Our repressed desires, quite to the contrary, are unconscious and thus can hardly be held against us. The problem with this configuration is that the submerged personality component cannot surface without carrying with it a measure of responsibility. As long as consciousness and accountability are tied together no change is possible. This dilemma is resolved by the introduction of a mode in which certain types of conscious behavior are accorded a special status which frees them from the frightening spectre of accountability. In all of these "make-believe" modes—dream, performance, and role-playing are the most common—an individual gains the right to "play out" personal fantasies without submitting to the judgments normally associated with conscious behavior. The character can say and do what he/she pleases and yet in the eyes of his/her psychic censor it is as if nothing had either been said or done. Like a child

playing "dress-up"—like the spectator watching the film—a character can try on a role without actually assuming it. This strategy ultimately permits the recovery of repressed material and thus the merger of submerged and surface components of the personality. By way of make-believe one dissolves into the other.

In *The Pirate*, hypnosis serves as a bridge linking the two levels of Judy Garland's character. "I realize that there's a practical world and a dream world," she claims near the beginning. "I know which is which. I shan't mix them." When she meets up with Gene Kelly, however, his hypnotic powers ("animal magnetism," as he calls it) cause her to slide out of her practical world and into dream. Three times she repeats a formula—"Beneath this prim exterior there are depths of emotion and romantic longings"—thus suggesting a fundamental parallel in the musical. To go beneath the surface, to recover one's hidden desires, is rigorously homologous to the fulfillment of

In *The Pirate*, Gene Kelly's hypnotic powers induce Judy Garland into a new world of emotion, illusion, and song.

[BFI]

one's dreams. In *The Pirate* three different levels therefore coincide: ideal world, submerged personality, and partner in love all represent, each in its own way, the *ideal* complement of Judy's *persona*. Or, to put it in another way, Judy's *persona* represents the *real* in three separate manners, each matched by and eventually fused with a counterpart figuring the ideal.

Judy Garland

Judy Garland	matched by	
-as woman (representative of culture, monetary concerns, worldly problems)	*matched by*	-partner in love (representative of theatrical sub-culture, fun, entertainment)
-as surface personality component ("prim exterior")		-submerged personality ("romantic longings")
-as resident of the "practical world"		-ideal world (legend of the pirate Mack the Black)

The "make-believe" motif is often used to provide prospective lovers an opportunity to "try on" a relationship. As such, it often informs song lyrics, particularly in an initial duet. MGM's 1951 version of *Showboat*, for example, uses an interesting visual alternation to underline the meaning of Jerome Kern and Oscar Hammerstein's "Make Believe." As Howard Keel sings, he turns alternately to Kathryn Grayson and to a dress hanging out to dry. The images tell us that he is singing to her, yet not singing to her (but to the dress). The words tell us both that he loves her and that he's just pretending. The same situation occurs near the beginning of *Carousel* as Gordon Macrae and Shirley Jones sing "If I Loved You." Just as the film itself creates an ideal world free from the constraints of reality, into which the spectator can escape, "trying on" the identities of imaginary characters, so the song creates an ideal present into which the would-be lovers can slip.

In fact, the very practice of dancing in couples creates a similar atmosphere of make-believe. Lovers embrace and mean something by it; people who are not in love do not embrace because they mean nothing to each other. Ballroom dancing mediates this opposition by providing an activity where people embrace but mean nothing by it. Dancing thus serves as a privileged interlude when potential lovers, friends, or even strangers can act as if they were lovers without having to bear responsibility for their actions. While they dance they can find out just how they feel about each other. Many a musical character can say, as Astaire does in *Easter Parade*, "It only happens when I

dance with you." Time and again we watch Astaire and his various partners fall in love only when they step into that privileged land of make-believe created by dance. If lovers' hearts beat in time to each other, then the dance provides an opportunity to rehearse that rhythm, to slide imperceptibly from indifference to passion.

One of the most interesting and innovative variations on the make-believe motif occurs in MGM's *Harvey Girls*. In response to romantic letters, Judy Garland goes West to marry a man whom she has never seen (Chill Wills). When she arrives in the frontier town of Sandrock, however, she finds that he is both uncivilized and uninterested in marriage. In fact, the man who sent the letters is not even the one who wrote them; they were written, as a joke, by John Hodiak, the owner of the Alhambra saloon. As the town of Sandrock unfolds before us, its structure becomes quite clear: on the left the Biblical house built on the *sand* (the saloon, presided over by bar girl Angela Lansbury), on the right the house built on a *rock* (the Harvey House Hotel, dominated by Judy Garland, who takes a job there when her marriage falls through). On one side loose women, heavy drinking, and bawdy shows; on the other side proper young ladies, hearty meals, and sophisticated dances.

Within this overall configuration, one pairing in particular stands out: the fight waged by Lansbury and Garland for the love of John Hodiak. This type of doubling is a common motif in the musical because it provides a proper correlative for the psychic structure of the man in the middle. Hodiak's surface personality identifies him with the saloon and thus with easy entertainment and the girl who provides it, Angela Lansbury. When Garland comes to town, however, something begins to happen. Desires long hidden in the inner recesses of Hodiak's psyche slowly leak out: there is a valley, not far from Sandrock, where Hodiak dreams of settling down one day. These are the dreams which he wrote about in his letters to Chill Wills' unknown correspondent, not as a joke but as a release, as a means of giving expression—even if only in make-believe—to his deeper desires. Clearly, then, Judy Garland corresponds to this submerged personality. Not surprisingly, Lansbury never understands the far away look in Hodiak's eye, nor his letter-writing, nor the solitary pilgrimages to "his" valley. She cannot grasp, as we do, the coincidence which exists between Hodiak's submerged personality, his valley, and Judy Garland (the same three counterparts to a given reality that we saw in *The Pirate*: repressed desires, ideal vision, and ideal partner). When he encounters Garland contemplating the same valley, obviously sharing his dreams, it is only natural that he should embrace her, for she, like the valley, represents the fulfillment of his dreams. In fact, in one sense we might say that she *is* his valley; he cannot acquire one without the other.[2]

The notion of a valley where life is truer pervades the American film musical. Derived from the archetypes of conservative Christianity, the iconography of European pastoral, and the utopian dreams of American settlers, the "valley" takes on many forms in the musical, from the comfortable womb of the family mansion (*Meet Me in St. Louis, Living in a Big Way, This Time for Keeps*) to the exotic halls of a European castle or hotel (*Love Me Tonight, Top Hat, Damsel in Distress*), from a real dreamland within sight (the hill in *High, Wide and Handsome*, the utopian island in *New Moon*, Bali Ha'i in *South Pacific*) to an entirely imaginary realm beyond time (*Snow White, Wizard of Oz, Camelot*), from the stage (*Dames, Stormy Weather, Call Me Mister*) to the Hollywood lot itself (*Easy Go, Anchors Aweigh, Singin' in the Rain, A Star Is Born*). It is to this *axis mundi*, this center of the world, that each protagonist must gain entrance, thereby achieving access to the hidden center of his/her personality. The method of access is typically neo-platonic: each character must give up his/her own (surface) desires and become the other, adopting the other's desires, in order to fulfill his/her own dreams. In *The Harvey Girls* this process begins when Hodiak and Garland finally accept the other's presence and all that it represents. He begins this partial capitulation: "If they want a church to let steam off in instead of the Alhambra, I guess the Alhambra can hold its own." She is not far behind; recognizing that their differences are really only a matter of style, she acknowledges that "maybe it's good for the men to have a little entertainment." At the end both renounce their own plans in order to enter into the world of the other. This renunciation of self both creates and corresponds to the Valley. Entering into the world of make-believe through the fiction of his letter-writing, Hodiak eventually successfully carries out the "personality dissolve" by which his divergent desires become merged into a single coherent—and stable—character.

No film more clearly than *Funny Face* exemplifies the profoundly neo-platonic character of the Hollywood musical. Ex-

The three sites of *The Harvey Girls*:

The Harvey House, a female world where John Hodiak clearly appears as an outsider

The saloon, a world of poker and beer which clearly makes Judy Garland uncomfortable

The "valley," a neutral no-place, a utopia where Hodiak and Garland can finally be united

[MOMA]

The drive-in as "valley"—the only place where Olivia Newton-John and John Travolta can speak their most sincere thoughts in *Grease*.

[MOMA]

pounding a philosophy of "empathicalism"—clearly a homespun American counterpart to fifties' French existentialism—*Funny Face* posits two couples based on apparent similarity of interest and personality, only to dissolve them in favor of a single couple formed through the attraction of opposites. At first, fashion editor Kay Thompson and her photographer Fred Astaire seem properly matched, while bookworm Audrey Hepburn yearns for the intellectual company of her Parisian philosopher idol "Flostre." While in Paris, Astaire, who has now fallen for the heady Hepburn, is repeatedly cornered into her intellectual world, while she is busy learning to be a model. When one look at her last costume—a wedding dress—causes Hepburn to bolt, it is only by resorting to empathicalism that she can be found. Empathy—the ability to put oneself in another's place—leads Astaire to the church where a similar process has taken her. There, with him throwing down his camera and she jettisoning her bouquet, each becomes the other, thus creating a stable unit of two mirror-image individuals now bonded together by understanding of the other's position. The style may be camp and the delivery somewhat tongue-in-cheek, but the simultaneous achievement of personal wholeness and couple unity through empathy and reversal of attributes clearly reiterates a strongly familiar pattern throughout the musical tradition.

This process has its parallel in the split viewer. He/she comes to the theatre fresh from experiences which reveal both daily reality and the surface personality which has evolved to deal with that reality. Lin-gering beneath that surface, however, is a dream, a vision of a Valley, a submerged personality which only an experience of make-believe can bring to the surface. By giving up oneself, that is by giving up one's surface self, by entering fully into the world of the Other—the film—the spectator accedes, if only for a moment, into the realm of vision, into his/her Valley. Like Garland and Hodiak, the specta-tor must surrender to another's vision in order to actualize his/her own.

The Problem of Genre History

THE FIRST FOUR CHAPTERS OF THIS BOOK HAVE PLACED US IN A seemingly embarrassing position. Without defining the musical, without delimiting it, without so much as establishing a provisional corpus, I have developed a methodology for analyzing "the musical." We know how to analyze it, but we don't even know what "it" is. What's more, I have described "its" structure without so much as a nod in the direction of historical awareness. We think we know what "it" looks like, yet our portrait has assumed—preposterously—the fundamental identity and timeless unity of texts which the flow of time has rendered extremely diverse. Worse still, examples have been adduced with no respect for established categories. Auteur directors like Vincente Minnelli share the spotlight with studio stagers like Mark Sandrich; the primitive, artificial efforts of the early years are treated alongside the integrated musicals of the fifties; Astaire is mixed in with Presley, rock musicals with operettas, and backstage plots with biopics. Decades of definition, categorization, and analysis of the musical have been abandoned in favor of a return to chaos.

Far from constituting an irremediable defect, this seemingly unsophisticated approach is the only one appropriate to the early stages of the study of a genre. As I suggested at the end of chapter one, the constitution of a generic corpus is not independent of and logically prior to the development of a methodology for dealing with that corpus. On the contrary, *every* corpus is in part the reflection of a particular methodology. This fact is most obviously reflected in the index of the typical genre study. Whereas the definition proposed near the beginning of the book is broad and inclusive, the list of texts *actually* mentioned clearly suggests a far narrower definition; while the first, broad definition typically stems from a particular tradition of literary or film criticism, the second definition usually corresponds to the new methodology proposed by the writer, who often refuses to recognize this *definitional drift*.

In recent criticism the *locus classicus* of this tendency is surely the offhand manner with which Northrop Frye's *Anatomy of Criticism*[1] slides from a general understanding of the term "comedy" (which he identifies with phenomena as diverse as theater, vaudeville, comic strips, and television programs, and authors from Aristophanes and Menander to Chaplin and O'Casey) to a far more restrictive definition which is nevertheless given as a simple equivalent of the original broad notion.

The art with which Frye accomplishes this slippage is worth admiring. In "The Argument of Comedy,"[2] he slides in a single sentence from a broad, traditional definition of comedy—which, he says, may be broken down into the Old Comedy popularized by Aristophanes and the New Comedy identified with Menander, Plautus, and Terence—to a limited definition, one that serves his purposes: "Old Comedy, however, was out of date before Aristophanes himself was dead; and today, when we speak of comedy, we normally think of something that derives from the Menandrine tradition". This simple redefinition is, however, directly contradicted in no less a location than the parallel passage in *The Anatomy of Criticism*, where, in an effort to establish the continuity of comic structures, Frye points out that "the audiences of vaudeville, comic strips, and television programs still laugh at the jokes that were declared to be outworn at the opening of [Aristophanes'] *The Frogs*" (*Anatomy* 163). Even such open recognition of the continued importance of Old Comedy does not keep Frye, however, from claiming that "The plot structure of Greek New Comedy, as transmitted by Plautus and Terence, in itself less a form than a formula, has become the basis for most comedy, especially in its more highly conventionalized dramatic form, down to our own day" (*Anatomy* 163).

Like nearly all other genre critics, Frye reveals two complementary needs: to remain faithful to a traditional definition, yet to deal primarily with those texts which correspond most clearly to the methodology and the overall theory which he propounds. Far from criticizing Frye for establishing his own specialized corpus, I am claiming that genre critics always do so. What is needed is not another way of arriving at a corpus, but only sufficient openness to recognize that genre critics rarely work with the traditional corpus. Our understanding of the notion of generic corpus—and thus our theories of how a corpus is established—must openly contend with the gap separating traditional notions from individual critical practice. With a properly constituted theory of corpus formation, there will no longer be any need for the Northrop Fryes of the world to proclaim the breadth of the genre in one sentence and then limit the genre in the next. Our first task will thus be to develop a methodology and an attendant critical vocabulary consonant with the dual corpus which we now recognize as operative in all genre study.

Problems with Current Terminology

No matter what area of current genre studies we look to—the constitution of the generic corpus, the writing of genre history, or the elaboration of genre theory—we find available terminology particularly confusing and poorly defined. Individual critics regularly hesitate between different definitions of a key term. Often, what appears as hesitation in the terminology of a single critic will turn into a clear contradiction when studies by two or more critics are compared. Now, it would be one thing if these contradictions were simply a matter of fact. On the contrary, however, I suggest that these are not temporary problems, bound to disappear as soon as we have more information or better analysts. Instead, these uncertainties reflect constitutive weaknesses of current notions of genre. Three contradictions in particular seem worthy of consideration.

When critics establish the corpus of a genre they generally tend to do two things at once, and thus establish two alternate groups of texts, each corresponding to a different notion of corpus. On the one hand, we find an unwieldy list of texts corresponding to a simple, tautological definition of the genre (e.g. western = film that takes place in the American West, or musical = film with diegetic music). This *inclusive* list is the kind that gets consecrated by generic encyclopedias or checklists. On the other hand, we find critics, theoreticians, and other arbiters of taste sticking to a familiar canon which has little to do with the broad, tautological definition. Here, the same films are mentioned again and again, not only because they are well known or particularly well made, but because they somehow seem to represent the genre more fully and faithfully than other apparently more tangential films. This *exclusive* list of films generally occurs not in a dictionary context, but instead in connection with attempts to arrive at the overall meaning or structure of a genre. The relative status of these alternate approaches to the constitution of a generic corpus may easily be sensed from the following typical conversation:

—I mean, what do you do with Elvis Presley films? You can hardly call them musicals.

—Why not? They're loaded with songs and they've got a narrative that ties the numbers together, don't they?

—Yeah, I suppose. I guess you'd have to call *Fun in Acapulco* a musical, but it's sure no *Singin' in the Rain*. Now there's a real musical.

When is a musical not a musical? When it has Elvis Presley in it. What may at first have seemed no more than an uncertainty on the part of the critical community now clearly appears as a contradiction. Because there are two competing notions of generic corpus on our critical scene, it is perfectly possible for a film to be simultaneously included in a particular generic corpus and excluded from that same corpus.

A second uncertainty is associated with the relative status of theory and history in genre studies. Before semiotics came along, generic titles and definitions were largely borrowed from the industry itself; what little generic theory there was tended therefore to be confused with historical analysis. With the heavy influence of semiotics on generic theory over the last two decades, self-conscious *critical* vocabulary came to be systematically preferred to the now suspect *user* vocabulary. The contribution of Propp, Lévi-Strauss, Frye, and Todorov[3] to genre studies has not been uniformly productive, however, because of the special place reserved for genre study within the semiotic project. If structuralist critics systematically chose as object of their analysis large groups of popular texts, it was in order to cover over a basic flaw in the semiotic understanding of textual analysis. Now, one of the most striking aspects of Saussure's theory of language is his emphasis on the inability of any single individual to effect change within that language. The fixity of the linguistic community thus serves as justification for Saussure's fundamentally synchronic approach to language. When literary semioticians applied this linguistic model to problems of textual analysis, they never fully addressed the notion of interpretive community implied by Saussure's notion of linguistic community. Preferring narrative to narration, system to process, and *histoire* to *discours*, the first semioticians ran headlong into a set of restrictions and contradictions that eventually spawned the more process-oriented second semiotics. It is in this context that we must see the resolutely synchronic attempts of Propp, Lévi-Strauss, Todorov, and many another influential genre analyst. Unwilling to compromise their systems by the historical notion of linguistic community, *these theoreticians instead substituted the generic context for the linguistic community,* as if the weight of numerous "similar" texts were sufficient to locate the meaning of a text independently of a specific audience. Far from being sensitive to concerns of history, semiotic genre analysis was by definition and from the start devoted to bypassing history. Treating genres as neutral constructs, semioti-

cians of the sixties and early seventies blinded us to the discursive power of generic formations. Because they treated genres *as the interpretive community,* they were unable to perceive the important role of genres in exercising influence *on the interpretive community.* Instead of reflecting openly on the way in which Hollywood uses its genres to short-circuit the normal interpretive process, structuralist critics plunged headlong into the trap, taking Hollywood's ideological effect for a natural ahistorical cause.

Genres were always—and continue to be—treated as if they spring full-blown from the head of Zeus. It is thus not surprising to find that even the most advanced of current genre theories, those that see generic texts as negotiating a relationship between a specific production system and a given audience, still hold to a notion of genre that is fundamentally ahistorical in nature. More and more, however, as scholars come to know the full range of individual Hollywood genres, we are finding that genres are far from exhibiting the homogeneity which this synchronic approach posits. Whereas one Hollywood genre may be borrowed with little change from another medium, a second genre may develop slowly, change constantly, and surge recognizably before settling into a familiar pattern, while a third may go through an extended series of paradigms, none of which may be claimed as dominant. As long as Hollywood genres are conceived as Platonic categories, existing outside the flow of time, it will be impossible to reconcile *genre theory*, which has always accepted as given the timelessness of a characteristic structure, and *genre history*, which has concentrated on chronicling the development, deployment, and disappearance of this same structure.

A third contradiction looms larger still, for it involves the two general directions taken by genre criticism as a whole over the last decade or two. Following Lévi-Strauss, a growing number of critics throughout the seventies dwelled on the mythical qualities of Hollywood genres, and thus on the audience's ritual relationship to genre film. The film industry's desire to please and its need to attract consumers were viewed as the mechanism whereby spectators were actually able to designate the kind of films they wanted to see. By choosing the films it would patronize, the audience revealed its preferences and its beliefs, thus inducing Hollywood studios to produce films reflecting its desires. Participation in the genre film experience thus reinforces spectator expectations and desires. Far from being limited to mere entertainment, film-going offers a satisfaction more akin to that associated with established religion. Most openly championed by John Cawelti, this ritual approach appears as well in books by Leo Braudy, Frank McConnell, Michael Wood, Will Wright, and Tom Schatz.[4] It has the merit not only of accounting for the intensity of identification typical of American genre film audiences, but it also encourages the placing of genre film narratives into an appropriately wider context of narrative analysis.

Curiously, however, while the ritual approach was attributing ultimate authorship to the audience, with the studios simply serving, for a price, the national will, a parallel ideological approach was demonstrating how audiences are manipulated by the business and political interests of Hollywood. Starting with *Cahiers du cinéma* and moving rapidly to *Screen*, *Jump Cut*,[5] and a growing number of journals, this view has recently joined hands with a more general critique of the mass media offered by the Frankfurt School. Looked at in this way, genres are simply the generalized, identifiable structures through which Hollywood's rhetoric flows. Far more attentive to discursive concerns than the ritual approach, which remains faithful to Lévi-Strauss in emphasizing narrative systems, the ideological approach stresses questions of representation and identification previously left aside. Simplifying a bit, we might say that it characterizes each individual genre as a specific type of lie, an untruth whose most characteristic feature is its ability to masquerade as truth. Whereas the ritual approach sees Hollywood as responding to societal pressure and thus expressing audience desires, the ideological approach claims that Hollywood takes advantage of spectator energy and psychic investment in order to lure the audience into Hollywood's own positions. The two are irreducibly opposed, yet these irreconcilable arguments continue to represent the most interesting and well defended of recent approaches to Hollywood genre film.

Toward a New Terminology

Here we have three problems which I take not to be limited to a single school of criticism or to a single genre, but to be implicit in every major field of current genre analysis. In nearly every argument about the limits of a generic corpus, the opposition of an inclusive list to an exclusive canon surfaces. Wherever genres are discussed, the divergent concerns of theorists and historians are increasingly obvious. And even when the topic is limited to genre theory alone, no agreement can be found between those who propose a ritual function for film genres and those who champion an ideological purpose. We find ourselves desperately in need of a theory which, without dismissing any of these widely held positions, would explain the circumstances underlying their existence, thus paving the way for a critical methodology which encompasses and indeed thrives on their inherent contradictions. If we have learned anything from post-structuralist criticism, we have learned not to fear logical contradictions but instead to respect the extraordinary energy generated by the play of contradictory forces within a field. What we need now is a new critical strategy enabling us simultaneously to understand and to capitalize on the tensions existing in current generic criticism.

In assessing theories of genre, critics have often labeled them according to a particular theory's most salient features or the type of activity to which it devotes its most concentrated attention. Paul Hernadi, for example, recognizes four general classes of genre theory: expressive, pragmatic, structural, and mimetic.[6] In his extremely influential introduction to *The Fantastic*, Tzvetan Todorov opposes historical to theoretical genres, as well as elementary genres to their complex counterparts.[7] Others, like Frederic Jameson, have followed French semiotics in distinguishing between semantic and syntactic approaches[8] to the genre.* While there is anything but general agreement on the exact frontier separating semantic from syntactic views, we can as a whole distinguish between generic definitions which depend on a list of common traits, attitudes, characters, shots, locations, sets, and the like—thus stressing the semantic elements which make up the genre—and definitions which play up instead certain constitutive relationships between undesignated and variable placeholders—relationships which might be called the genre's fundamental syntax. The semantic approach thus stresses the genre's building blocks, while the syntactic view privileges the structures into which they are arranged.

The difference between semantic and syntactic definitions is perhaps at its most apparent in familiar approaches to the western. Jean Mitry provides us with a clear example of the most common definition. The western, Mitry proposes, is a "film whose action, situated in the American West, is consistent with the atmosphere, the values, and the conditions of existence in the Far West between 1840 and 1900."[9] Based on the presence or absence of easily identifiable elements, Mitry's nearly tautological definition implies a broad, undifferentiated generic corpus. Marc Vernet's more detailed list is more sensitive to cinematic concerns, yet overall it follows the same semantic model. Vernet outlines general atmosphere ("em-

---

*It should be noted here that my use of the term "semantic" differs from Jameson's. Whereas he stresses the overall semantic impact of a text, I am dealing with the individual semantic units of the text. His term thus approximates the sense of "global meaning," while mine is closer to "lexical choices."

phasis on basic elements, such as earth, dust, water, and leather"), stock characters ("the tough/soft cowboy, the lonely sheriff, the faithful or treacherous Indian, and the strong tender woman"), as well as technical elements ("use of fast tracking and crane shots").[10] An entirely different solution is suggested by Jim Kitses, who emphasizes not the vocabulary of the western but the relationships linking lexical elements. For Kitses the western grows out of a dialectic between the West as Garden and as Desert (between culture and nature, community and individual, future and past).[11] The western's vocabulary is thus generated by this syntactic relationship, and not vice-versa. John Cawelti attempts to systematize the western in a similar fashion: the western is always set on or near a frontier, where man encounters his uncivilized double.[12] The western thus takes place on the border between two lands, between two eras, and with a hero who remains divided between two value systems (for he combines the town's morals with the outlaws' skills).

Now, in passing we might well note the divergent qualities associated with these two approaches. While the semantic approach has little explanatory power, it is applicable to a larger number of films. Conversely, the syntactic approach surrenders broad applicability in return for the ability to isolate a genre's specific meaning-bearing structures. This alternative seemingly leaves the genre analyst in a quandary: choose the semantic view and you give up *explanatory power,* choose the syntactic approach and you do without *broad applicability.* In terms of the western, the problem of the so-called "Pennsylvania western" is instructive

here. To most observers it seems quite clear that films like *High, Wide and Handsome* (Mamoulian, 1937), *Drums Along the Mohawk* (Ford, 1939), and *Unconquered* (DeMille, 1947) have definite affinities with the western. Employing familiar characters set in relationships similar to their counterparts west of the Mississippi, these films construct plots and develop a frontier structure clearly derived from decades of western novels and films. But they do it in Pennsylvania, and in the wrong century. Are these films westerns because they share the syntax of hundreds of films we call westerns? Or are they not westerns, because they don't fit Mitry's definition?

In fact, the "Pennsylvania western" (like the urban, spaghetti, and sci-fi varieties) represents a quandary only because critics have insisted on dismissing one type of definition and approach in favor of another. As a rule, semantic and syntactic approaches to genre have been proposed, analyzed, evaluated, and disseminated separately, in spite of the complementarity implied by their names. Indeed, many arguments centering on generic problems have arisen only when semantic and syntactic theoreticians have simply talked past each other, each unaware of the other's divergent orientation. I maintain that these two categories of generic analysis are complementary, that they can be combined, and in fact that some of the most important questions of genre study can be asked only when they *are* combined. In short, I propose a semantic/syntactic approach to genre study.

Now let us return to the three contradictions delineated earlier, in order to discover whether the proposed semantic/syntactic approach provides any new understanding. First, the split corpus that characterizes current genre study—on the one side an inclusive list, on the other an exclusive pantheon. It should now be quite clear that each corpus corresponds to a different approach to generic analysis and definition. Tautological semantic definitions, with their goal of broad applicability, outline a large genre of semantically similar texts, while syntactic definitions, intent as they are on explaining the genre, stress a narrow range of texts that privilege specific syntactic relationships. To insist on one of these approaches to the exclusion of the other is to turn a blind eye on *the necessarily dual nature of any generic corpus.* For every film that participates actively in the elaboration of a genre's syntax there are numerous others content to deploy in no particular relationship the elements traditionally associated with the genre. We need to recognize that not all genre films relate to their genre in the same way or to the same extent. By simultaneously accepting semantic and syntactic notions of genre we avail ourselves of a possible way to deal critically with differing levels of genericity. In addition, a dual approach permits a far more accurate description of the numerous inter-generic connections typically suppressed by single-minded approaches. It is simply not possible to describe Hollywood cinema accurately without the ability to account for the numerous films that innovate by combining the syntax of one genre with the semantics of another. In fact, it is only when we begin to take up problems of genre history that the full value of the semantic/syntactic approach becomes obvious.

As I pointed out earlier, most genre theoreticians have followed the semiotic model and steered clear of historical considerations. Even in the relatively few cases where problems of generic history have been addressed, as in the attempts of Metz and Wright to periodize the western,[13] history has been conceptualized as nothing more than a discontinuous succession of discrete moments, each characterized by a different basic version of the genre, that is by a different syntactic pattern which the genre adopts. In short, genre theory has up to now aimed almost exclusively at the elaboration of a synchronic model approximating the syntactic operation of a specific genre. Now, quite obviously, no major genre remains unchanged over the many decades of its existence. In order to mask the scandal of applying synchronic analysis to an evolving form, critics have been extremely clever in their creation of categories designed to negate the notion of change and to imply the perpetual self-identity of each genre. Westerns and horror films are often referred to as "classic," the musical is defined in terms of the so-called "Platonic ideal" of integration, the critical corpus of the melodrama has largely been restricted to the post-war efforts of Sirk and Minnelli, and so on. Lacking a workable hypothesis regarding the historical dimension of generic syntax, we have insulated that syntax, along with the genre theory that studies it, from the flow of time.

When genres are redefined in terms of their semantic and syntactic dimensions, however, new life is breathed into the notion of genre history. Instead of simply enumerating the minor variations developed by various studios or directors within a general, fundamentally stable generic framework, genre history based on a semantic/syntactic hypothesis would take as its object three interrelated concerns: 1) the introduction and disappearance of basic semantic elements (e.g., the musical's deployment of a succession of musical styles—from operetta and chansonnier to crooning and opera to swing and folk to rock and nostalgia); 2) the development and abandoning of specific syntactic solutions (e.g., the move from the early sound period identification of music with sadness, usually in three-person plots assuring a sad, solitary oddman-out, to the post-1933 emphasis on music as celebration of a joyous union of opposites, in the culture as well as the couple); 3) the ever-changing relationship between the semantic and syntactic aspects of the genre (e.g., the way in which diegetic music, the musical's semantic element *par excellence,* is transformed from a flashy but unintegrated element of spectacle into a signifier of success and a device for reversal of the traditional image-over-sound hierarchy). Far from being exiled from history, the musical's characteristic syntax can be shown by the generic historian to grow out of the linking of specific semantic elements at identifiable points. A measure of continuity is thus developed between the task of the historian and that of the theoretician, for the tasks of both are now redefined as the study of the interrelationships between semantic elements and syntactic bonds.

But what is it that energizes the transformation of a borrowed semantics into a uniquely Hollywood syntax? Or what is it that justifies the intrusion of a new semantics into a well-defined syntactic situation? Far from postulating a uniquely internal, formal progression, I would propose that the relationship between the semantic and the syntactic constitutes the very site of negotiation between Hollywood and its audience, and thus between ritual and ideological uses of genre.[14] Often, when critics of opposing persuasions disagree over a major issue, it is because they have established, within the same general corpus, two separate and opposed canons, each supporting one point of view. Thus, when Catholics and Protestants or liberals and conservatives quote the Bible, they are rarely quoting the same passages. The striking fact about ritual and ideological genre theoreticians, however, is that they regularly stress the same canon, that small group of texts most clearly reflecting a genre's stable syntax. The films of John Ford, for example, have played a major role in the development of ritual and ideological approaches alike. From Sarris and Bogdanovich to Schatz and Wright, champions of Ford's understanding and transparent expression of American values have stressed the communitarian side of his films, while others, starting with the influential *Cahiers du Cinéma* study of *Young Mr. Lincoln,* have shown how a call to community can be used to lure spectators into a carefully chosen, ideologically determined subject position. A similar situation obtains in the musical, where a growing body of ritual analyses of the Astaire/Rogers and post-war MGM Freed unit films is matched by an increasing number of studies demonstrating the ideological investment of those very same films. The corpus of nearly every major genre has developed in the same way, with critics of both camps gravitating toward and eventually basing their arguments on the same narrow range of films. Just as Minnelli and Sirk dominate the criticism of melodrama, Hitchcock has become nearly synonymous with the thriller. Of all major genres, only the *film noir* has failed to attract critics of both sides to a shared corpus of major texts—no doubt because of the general inability of ritual critics to accommodate the genre's anti-communitarian stance.

This general agreement on a canon stems, I would claim, from the fundamentally bivalent nature of any relatively stable generic syntax. If it takes a long time to establish a generic syntax, and if many seemingly promising formulas or successful films never spawn a genre, it is because only certain types of structure, within a particular semantic environment, are suited to the special bilingualism required of a durable genre. The structures of Hollywood cinema, like those of American popular mythology as a whole, serve to mask the very distinction between ritual and ideological functions. Hollywood does not simply lend its voice to the public's desires, nor does it simply manipulate the audience. On the contrary, most genres go through a period of accommodation during which the public's desires are fitted to Hollywood's priorities (and vice-versa). Because the public doesn't want to know that it's being manipulated, the successful ritual/ideological "fit" is almost always one that disguises Hollywood's potential for manipulation while playing up its capacity for entertainment.

Whenever a lasting fit is obtained—which it is whenever a semantic genre becomes a syntactic one—it is because a common ground has been found, a region where the audience's ritual values coincide with Hollywood's ideological ones. The development of a specific syntax within a given semantic context thus serves a double function: it binds element to element in a logical order, at the same time accommodating audience desires to studio concerns. The successful genre owes its success not alone to its reflection of an audience ideal, nor solely to its status as apology for the Hollywood enterprise, but to its ability to carry out both functions simultaneously. It is this sleight of hand, this strategic overdetermination, that most clearly characterizes American film production during the studio years.

The approach to genre sketched out in this chapter of course raises some questions of its own. Just where, for example, do we locate the exact border between the semantic and the syntactic? And how are these two categories related? Each of these questions constitutes an essential area of inquiry, one that is far too complex to permit full treatment here. Nevertheless, a few remarks may be in order. A reasonable observer might well ask why my approach attributes such importance to the seemingly banal distinction between a text's materials and the structures into which they are arranged. Why this distinction rather than, for example, the more cinematic division between diegetic elements and the technical means deployed in representing them? The answer to these questions lies in a general theory of textual signification which I have expounded elsewhere.[15] Briefly, that theory distinguishes between the primary, linguistic meaning of a text's component parts and the secondary, or textual meaning which those parts acquire through a structuring process internal to the text. Within a single text, therefore, the same phenomenon may have more than one meaning depending on whether we consider it at the linguistic or textual level. In the western, for example, the horse is an animal that serves as a method of locomotion. This primary level of meaning, corresponding to the normal extent of the concept "horse" within the language, is matched by a series of other meanings derived from the structures into which the western sets the horse. Opposition of the horse to the automobile or locomotive ("iron horse") reinforces the organic, non-mechanical sense of the term "horse" already implicit in the language, thus transferring that concept from the paradigm "method of locomotion" to the paradigm "soon-to-be-outmoded pre-industrial carry-over."

In the same way, horror films borrow from a nineteenth-century literary tradition their dependence on the presence of a monster. In doing so, they clearly perpetuate the linguistic meaning of the term monster ("threatening inhuman being"), but at the same time, by developing new syntactic ties, they generate an important new set of textual meanings. For the nineteenth century, the appearance of the monster is invariably tied to a Romantic over-reaching, the attempt of some human scientist to tamper with the divine order. In texts like Mary Shelley's *Frankenstein*, Balzac's *La Recherche de l'absolu*, or Stevenson's *Dr. Jekyll and Mr. Hyde*, a studied syntax equates man and monster, attribut-

ing to both the monstrosity of being outside nature, as defined by established religion and science. With the horror film, a different syntax rapidly equates monstrosity not with the overactive nineteenth-century mind, but with an equally overactive twentieth-century body. Again and again, the monster is identified with his human counterpart's unsatisfied sexual appetite, thus establishing with the same primary "linguistic" materials (the monster, fear, the chase, death) entirely new textual meanings, phallic rather than scientific in nature.

The distinction between the semantic and the syntactic, in the way I have defined it here, thus corresponds to a distinction between the primary, linguistic elements of which all texts are made, and the secondary, textual meanings which are sometimes constructed by virtue of the syntactic bonds established between primary elements. This distinction is stressed in the approach to genre presented here not because it is convenient nor because it corresponds to a modish theory of the relation between language and narrative, but because the semantic/syntactic distinction is fundamental to a theory of how meaning of one kind contributes to and eventually establishes meaning of another. Just as individual texts establish new meanings for familiar terms only by subjecting well-known semantic units to a syntactic redetermination, so generic meaning comes into being only through the repeated deployment of substantially the same syntactic strategies. It is in this way, for example, that making music—

at the linguistic level primarily a way of making a living—becomes in the musical a figure for making love—a textual meaning essential to the constitution of that syntactic genre.

We must of course remember that, while each individual text clearly has a syntax of its own, the syntax implied here is that of the genre, which does not appear as *generic* syntax unless it is reinforced numerous times by the syntactic patterns of individual texts. The Hollywood genres that have proven the most durable are precisely those that have established the most coherent syntax (the western, the musical); those that disappear the quickest depend entirely on recurring semantic elements, never developing a stable syntax (reporter, catastrophe, and big caper films, to name but a few). If I locate the border between the semantic and the syntactic at the dividing line between the linguistic and the textual, it is thus in response not just to the theoretical, but also to the historical dimension of generic functioning.

In proposing such a model, however, I may leave too much room for one particular type of misunderstanding. It has been a cliché of the last two decades to insist that structure carries meaning, while the choice of structured elements is largely negligible in the process of signification. This position, most openly championed by Lévi-Strauss in his cross-cultural methodology for studying myth, may seem to be implied by my model, but is in fact not borne out by my research. Spectator response, I believe, is heavily conditioned by the choice of semantic elements and atmosphere, because a given semantics used in a specific cultural situation will recall to an actual in-

terpretive community the particular syntax with which that semantics has traditionally been associated in other texts. This *syntactic expectation*, set up by a *semantic signal*, is matched by a parallel tendency to expect specific syntactic signals to lead to pre-determined semantic fields (e.g., in western texts, regular alternation between male and female characters creates expectation of the semantic elements implied by romance, while—at least until recently—alternation between two males throughout a text has implied confrontation and the semantics of the duel). This interpenetration of the semantic and the syntactic through the agency of the spectator clearly deserves further study. Suffice it to say for the present that linguistic meanings (and thus the import of semantic elements) are in large part derived from the textual meanings of previous texts. There is thus a constant circulation in both directions between the semantic and the syntactic, between the linguistic and the textual.

Still other questions, such as the general problem of the "evolution" of genres through semantic or syntactic shifts, deserve far more attention than I have given them here. In time, I believe, this new model for the understanding of genre will provide answers for many of the questions traditional to genre study. Perhaps more important still, as I hope I have shown here, the semantic/syntactic approach to genre raises numerous questions for which other theories have created no space. The remainder of this chapter will be devoted to an exploration of the way in which this approach might affect the traditional concerns of defining and delimiting a generic corpus, formulating notions of genre history, and dividing the genre into pertinent subgeneric categories.

Defining the Corpus

In keeping with the semantic/syntactic approach propounded above, the definition developed here will be double, stressing semantic and syntactic concerns separately and thus producing two different but related versions of the musical corpus. In developing this dual definition I have not so much ignored traditional definitions as paid careful attention to the shared characteristics whose presence makes possible the kind of analysis stressed in chapters two through four. Having developed a specific type of analysis correlated to texts of a specific type, I now must tease out a clear definition of the traits indicative of that type. The following paragraphs provide the elements of that definition, accompanied by comments on the generic limits implicit in each defining characteristic—five semantic and five syntactic.

Format. Even at the most brute semantic level, the musical must be seen as a narrative genre. Only within a narrative framework does the musical number become the timeless interlude, the brake, indeed the break that eventually sets up a signifying relationship between narrative flow and musical stasis. The revue film thus provides an interesting limiting case here. Made by the same directors using the same artistic and technical personnel as narrative musical films, the revue has thus nearly always been assimilated to musical films more clearly indebted to a narrative tradition. Yet the function, meaning, and "feel" of music in, say, *Paramount on Parade* and *Ziegfeld Follies* differentiate these revues

radically from films like *Love Parade* and *Anchors Aweigh*. Instead of being sensed in contradistinction to the narrative progression that they interrupt, the musical numbers of a revue are instead seen as opposed to the comedy routines with which, as in the vaudeville tradition, they commonly alternate. As whole films, therefore, revues will be seen as having an important industrial relationship with the musical (as do the musical shorts and cartoons of the thirties), but in terms of generic identity they will be treated as no more than second cousins. It does happen, however, that an individual number within a revue may recapitulate in miniature the narrative and musical patterns of the full-length musical. If "This Heart of Mine," from *Ziegfeld Follies*, seems more deserving of inclusion in the corpus than most short musical revue numbers, it is because this number is not just musical—its dream-like dance grows out of the Bremer/Astaire mimed narrative which opens the selection.

It should perhaps be pointed out here that the importance of narrative to this definition in no way implies narrative fiction. A film providing the record of a rock concert will be excluded from the corpus not because it is a documentary, but because the film lacks narrative. (The musical numbers are thus not positioned vis-à-vis some narrative drive and logic, but only in terms of a rote numerical ordering.) Of course it takes very little to create a narrative sense in a film which otherwise concentrates on creating a straight documentary record of a performance. Take *Woodstock*, for example. This most famous of concert documentaries becomes a fully narrative film when it is read in terms of the rural romance with flower children: motivated by love for music and peace, half-a-million youths overcome local resistance and eventually demonstrate love for the land. Looked at in this way, *Woodstock* clearly fits my definition. The *Woodstock* that fits my definition, however, is not the *Woodstock* that most people see. To most people, the film is one long non-stop rock concert. Viewed as a musical, in my sense of the term, the film instead establishes a parallel between male-female coupling and the romance between the wandering hippies and the stable populace. *Woodstock* thus serves as a perfect example of the marginal film which is drawn into the musical corpus, as I am defining it, only to the extent that the methodology implied by (constitutive of) that corpus can illuminate the film in question. The difference between *Woodstock* (which I include in my corpus, thanks to the narrative reading sketched above) and the many films which *only* record a rock concert demonstrates the extent to which my definition (in keeping with the methodology which it reflects) depends on multiple characteristics—the presence of diegetic music alone is insufficient to classify a film as a musical.

Length. Without the leisure to move in and out of song numerous times, a film lacks the opportunity to develop the relationships characteristic of the musical as a narrative genre. As a rule, this means that musicals must approximate what the industry terms "feature length." In a way, however, this designation is misleading. Though few numbers in revues or musical shorts actually do so, it is still perfectly conceivable to imagine a musical which would miniaturize its segments to the point where it would be fully qualifiable as a musical and yet far shorter than feature length. In other words, the requirement that a musical be a feature-length film is in truth the bold semantic expression of a far more subtle and elusive syntactic requirement for a minimum number of segments developing a specific set of relationships. Length is thus not an absolute guarantee; it constitutes only the sort of *prima facie* case usually associated with semantic characteristics. Thus Vitaphone's 1934 musical short *Masks and Memories*, with Lillian Roth's haunting rendition of Duke Ellington's "Sophisticated Lady," or the "My Bridal Veil" wedding fantasy number in the 1930 revue of *King of Jazz*, will be excluded from the musical corpus solely on account of length, in spite of their clear affinities with the genre. To include them would invite overemphasis on musical style and spectacle, whereas the method that nourishes this corpus depends on a strong sense of narrative situation and development. Such an exclusion of course does not preclude identifying shorter films or revue numbers with the particular location and function in a full-length musical from which they are implicitly derived.

Characters. The analytical methodology developed in chapters two through four of this book clearly applies most fully to films built around a romantic couple whose coupling takes place within a recognizably human society. On this notion hangs the totality of this book. No couple, no musical. Now, such a claim, while reasonable in the context constituted by the earlier chapters of this book, remains quite problematic when seen in the overall context of the history of the genre and its major texts. From the saccharine sweetness of Shirley Temple to the cartoon extravagances of *Dumbo* and *Pete's Dragon*, the musical has long been associated with children, both as characters and as audience. How do we reconcile the notion of a genre built around a romantic couple with the numerous films built around child stars and addressed to a juvenile audience? Or, to put it in another, more succinct way, can a definition which excludes *The Wizard of Oz* from the musical corpus be worth a second thought? This question represents no small threat to the methodology elaborated here. It is thus deserving not only of careful and complete consideration, but of two separate responses, the first corresponding to theoretical concerns and the second to problems of a more analytical nature.

Now, the theoretical problem of the "children's" musical is quite similar to that of the fairy tale, which addresses alternately the problems of childhood and those of adolescence. While some tales, like "Hansel and Gretel," "Jack and the Beanstalk," and "Goldilocks," clearly place the child in the protagonist's role, with parent surrogates playing the fearsome antagonists, another set of tales, including "Beauty and the Beast," "Cinderella," and "The Frog King," depicts the desires and hesitations of the adolescent facing sex, marriage, and adult responsibilities. In both cycles, monstrous characters abound; in order to know how the monstrous character functions in the tale, whether it represents a parent or a potential marriage partner, we must know to which cycle the tale belongs. The musical operates in much the same way. By and large, music accompanies and celebrates the making of a couple, while in a few films of vastly different inspiration music marks the passage of a child into the adult world. Just as our understanding of fairy tale monsters must depend on a generic distinction which we make within the fairy tale category, so our understanding of the musical depends on our ability to separate the children's musical from the genre's major tradition. To identify the pre-puberty musical film as a "musical" would compromise our ability to locate and describe generic functioning just as would the inclusion of the non-narrative rock concert documentary. Theoretically, then, we are justified in excluding numerous children's films from our corpus, on the grounds that they fit music into an entirely different framework, one which does not correspond to the methodology developed in the first section of this book.

In practice, however, we find a situation that is in every way surprising. Just as the biopic somehow always manages to bend a biographical account to dual-focus presentation, just as many rock concert films redefine the concert's function by inserting it into a narrative framework, by far the majority of so-called "children's" films reorder their priorities along courtship lines. Perhaps the most familiar method of mating a child-star with a couple-oriented film is the one borrowed from Roman mythology and perfected by Shirley Temple: have the moppet play Cupid to a more mature pair. In recent years this strategy has been taken into the cartoon world by movies like *Pete's Dragon*. Other recent successes have simply transferred courtship concerns to cartoon, animal, and/or fantasy realms, as in *Song of the South* (1946), *Cinderella* (1950), *The Lady and the Tramp* (1955), *Sleeping Beauty* (1959), *Babes in Toyland* (1961), *The Aristocats* (1970), *Shinbone Alley* (1971), *The Rescuers* (1977), and *The Muppet Movie* (1979). Still others set up a series of male-female pairs, but displace narrative energy away from the im-

While clearly destined for children, *The Lady and the Tramp* nevertheless turns on an archetypal musical plot, with a mongrel from the wrong side of the tracks successfully romancing the purebred spaniel from a good family. The holiday family portrait shown here recalls many others throughout the folk musical tradition.

[MOMA]

plicit romantic paradigm, thus calling on the genre analyst to restore through interpretation the connection to the courtship model implicit in films like *Snow White* (1938), *The Wizard of Oz* (1939), and *Mary Poppins* (1964). In other words, there are in fact precious few musical films that do not stress romantic coupling, even when they are aimed openly and directly at a pre-puberty audience. The only major group of films that systematically avoids courtship while adopting music is the celebrated series of Walt Disney initiatory films: *Pinocchio* (1940), *Dumbo* (1941), *Bambi* (1942), *Alice in Wonderland* (1951), and *Peter Pan* (1953). Even these films share with the musical as I am defining it numerous thematic concerns (especially the elements of fantasy and wish fulfillment), but in the long run it will be more revealing, I believe, to see these films as belonging to an entirely different genre, a childhood initiation genre that borrows heavily from a widely shared European fairy tale tradition and thus cuts across many of the more established film genres. What is striking—and ultimately constitutes strong support for my decision to predicate a genre-delimiting methodology on courtship concerns—is the fact that such a high percentage of films obviously aimed at juvenile audiences should nevertheless bend so far in the direction of romance. It is a sure mark of the health—and existence—of a courtship-oriented genre that so much "foreign" material should so easily and so regularly be domesticated for integration into the courtship musical.

Acting. Only when a film combines rhythmic movement with a certain sense of realism can we call that film a musical. Perhaps the most elegant demonstration of this fact can be obtained by tuning through twenty or thirty cable television channels on an average weekend night. Chances are that two or three stations will offer performances of some sort, with a great deal of effort expended on bringing out their characteristic rhythm. Hold on the station for a few minutes. If the rhythm continues unabated, with all cameras focused on the performance, we soon become convinced that it is a concert we have tuned to, and not a musical at all. But cut away to the wings for a sigh or a wisecrack, or to the intense glance of a carefully selected audience member and presto! it seems we have suddenly entered the special realm of the musical. No matter what the performance—even straight ballet (*The Band Wagon*), orchestra (nearly all the films produced by Joe Pasternak), or opera (especially in the latter half of the thirties)—the world of the film musical begins where reality and the fantasy, rhythmic world of the show merge. A similar but reverse proof is also available for those stations which reveal straight "realistic" narratives. As long as people go about their business according to purely practical principles, and as long as the camera follows them in a straightforward utilitarian manner, then we have

no sense of entering the world of the musical. But just let someone start to tap to the background music, or let the ladies of the steno pool pick up their pencils all at the same time, or let the camera start drawing patterns with its movements, and there it is, the door to the realm of the musical suddenly seems to open before us. The musical thus shows a natural affinity for those forms of music which traditionally combine a sense of narrative realism on the one hand and a timeless notion of formal patterning on the other. It takes the hamming of an Oscar Levant to break a concerto out of the staid patterns to which it is normally limited, but nearly any jazz concert reveals musicians who are alternately rhythm machines and bearers of emotion. Indeed, the entire realm of American popular music might be defined by this tendency to combine the artistic with the expressive. In dance the situation is quite similar: given its need for a merger of recognizable realism and rhythmic patterning, the musical more willingly borrows from the tradition of American folk ballet than from the classical repertoire (just as it is more comfortable with the mixed world of the operetta than with the uniformly rhythmified realm of opera).

Sound Track. Just as the musical mixes rhythm (activity dictated by the music) with realism (activity not dictated by music), so it must combine sounds which together constitute music, and others which remain independent of musical expression. Curiously, then, the absence of non-musical sound can just as easily disqualify a film as a musical as can the absence of music. Jacques Demy's *Umbrellas of Cherbourg* cannot possibly be seen as a musical, from my point of view, for it doesn't provide any non-musical context against which music is to be measured. In the same way, a full-length ballet film would have to be excluded, even if it presented a narrative similar to those characteristic of the musical, for it is not the presence of music, dance, or rhythm that constitutes the genre, but the opposition of those patterned activities to less patterned moments and endeavors. In fact, one might justifiably claim that a film which mixes song and dialogue, rhythm and reality, but which does so with two utterly unrelated casts (e.g., one on stage singing and dancing, the other in the audience simply spectating), is not in any meaningful sense a musical. Unless the principal actors combine the roles of rhythm and reality, or song and dialogue, then we never achieve the sensation of a radically bifurcated musical world—the only one suited to the equally radical merger which the musical's syntax requires.

As we pass on to the syntactic definition, it will perhaps be wise to take a minute out to comment on the line of demarcation between semantic and syntactic concerns. Earlier, as I argued for a courtship-oriented notion of the musical, and thus against the inclusion of childhood initiation films, it no doubt became clear to many readers that my semantic definition requiring the presence of a romantic couple in fact implied a certain syntactic undercurrent. Defining the presence or absence of the romantic couple as a semantic element, I necessarily disqualified some children's "musicals." I might just as well, however, have treated that romantic relationship as a syntactic concern, a particular tie between two semantic elements (the man and woman). Looked at in this way, the musical might be defined as having all the characters of the family, with

one type of musical stressing male-female relationships and another playing up intergenerational concerns. While this solution is not the one I have chosen, it does have some merit and might well serve as a working hypothesis for some future study. For the limits between the semantic and the syntactic are never clearly set; the decisions of each critic on this score will have repercussions on everything from elaboration of a corpus to functional analysis to aesthetic evaluation. Thus, when I call for a definition requiring the presence of actor-singers (or actor-dancers), I am raising the semantic requirements within sight of their syntactic counterparts. I could have listed actors and singers or dancers as semantic requirements, with the integration of both functions in the same character as a syntactic development. In accepting a relatively high level of implicit syntactic content within semantic definitions, I am taking a chance on becoming too exclusive in order to assure the highest possible level of systematic analysis. A critic with another purpose might equally legitimately stress the semantic by providing syntactic definitions more closely tied to the semantic level than mine tend to be. The following five requirements constitute the major concerns of a syntactic definition.

Narrative Strategy. The musical borrows its narrative structure from the dual-focus tradition. The text thus proceeds by alternation, confrontation, and parallelism between male and female leads (or groups), with each sex not just representing its own immediate and local interests, but also identified with a specific cultural value or set of values. Chapters two and three exemplify in detail this process. Now, the careful reader will no doubt have decorated the margins of those chapters with notes like "not in biopics" or "in Shirley Temple films?" or "not when a big star is matched with a newcomer." The easy way out of this seeming dilemma would be simply to call these films exceptions, or to remark that they do not follow the genre's syntactic model. More than that is at stake here, however, not only in terms of the musical, but in terms of generic analysis in general. The fundamental principle justifying genre study is this: the single text is no more interpretable by itself than an ancient document representing the sole surviving text in its language. Only in relation to other texts does any text (and *a fortiori* a genre film) deliver up a meaning. The categories operative in a given text can be made visible only by the conflation of numerous films of the same genre. In a single film certain characteristics may seem attributable to a given actor or character; when set in the context of the entire genre, however, these characteristics appear instead as a type of activity on which the individual draws, but which must ultimately be attributed to generic semantics or syntax, and not to any particular individual. When we watch *Little Miss Broadway*, we might be tempted to claim that the rhetoric of the text privileges Shirley Temple, that it invites us to concentrate our attention on her, thus belying the supposed dual-focus organization of the musical. Such a conclusion, however, is justified neither by Fox's handling of their diminutive star nor by my notion of generic syntax. Confident of spectators who would be sufficiently versed in the importance of courtship to the musical, Fox could afford to imbed the dual-focus love plot within a narrative otherwise dominated by Temple's Cupid.

From the point of view of generic syntax, a similar assumption holds true: even when the rhetoric of an individual film seems to imply something other than strict alternation between members of a romantic couple, the relationship of a particular film to the genre as a whole asks us to privilege, within the text, those elements that *do* reveal alternation and parallelism between the members of the couple. In other words, to construe a film as a musical is to show heightened sensitivity to certain aspects of the text, aspects which will be more or less present in each individual text. Dozens of circumstances may contribute to the privileging of one character over another, from the pairing of a non-singer or non-dancer with a singer or dancer to a mid-shooting budget cut, but none of these has any more status in terms of genre syntax than the single text uninterpretable by itself. Of course there are films which alternate between the sexes less formulaically than *Sweethearts* or *Grease,* but only by reading these films from the point of view of courtship and male/female parallelism can we discover their operation as musicals.

Couple/plot. The formation of the couple is linked either causally or through parallelism to success in the ventures which constitute the plot. Indeed, so prevalent and clearcut is this trait that I will predicate an entire subgeneric division of the musical genre on it alone. Whether it is the kingdom's health that depends on the couple's relationship (as in *Love Parade*), the show's success that contributes to and depends on love's progress (as in *Gold Diggers of 1933*), or the settling of an entire territory that implicitly depends on and is celebrated by the young couple's marriage (*Oklahoma!*), the relationship between male and female is never treated as simply an add-on, a throwaway portion of the musical's overall plot. Time and again, to solve the couple's problems becomes synonymous with, and thus a figure for, a solution of the plot's other enterprises.

Music/plot. Just as the couple is not simply tacked on to a plot that could have done without, so music takes on a specific role within the musical's discourse. Far from simply providing an alternative to silence—as does background music in other Hollywood films—the musical's music (as well as its dance) enters into a process of signification whereby it comes to stand for personal and communal joy; expressing a romantic triumph over the limitations of nature, of time, of society, and of economics, music becomes the signifier *par excellence* of the value of the couple and of courtship. It is thus not just the presence of music that counts here, but music's tendency to enter into structured relationships. Thus the all-black musical commonly sets up an opposition between church music and jazz (e.g., *Hallelujah, Cabin in the Sky*), while Astaire films often establish an opposition between those who appreciate music and those who loathe it (*Top Hat, Shall We Dance, The Band Wagon*). As long as music stays in the background, figuratively or otherwise, then the musical's characteristic syntax remains to be tapped. When music becomes an active force in the production of meaning then the musical's other traits cannot be far behind.

Narrative/number. The musical does not just combine realism and rhythmic movement, dialogue and diegetic movement, as the semantic definition implies, it creates continuity between these radically different areas. As explained in chapter four, the musical's style turns on a series of dissolves, each exploiting the interpenetration of different spaces, characters, images, sounds. While this continuity is not directly related in every film to the male-female coupling process, it clearly derives its basic model from the interpenetration of space, psychology, and name implied by the biological act of sexual intercourse and the social institution of marriage which consecrates it. In societies heavily dependent on mythical thinking, marriage is openly conceived as a mystical phenomenon, a magic moment permitting the union of the two into one. Even in the more practical traditions of western capitalism, however, the basic arrangement remains the same. Where strong laws prohibit individuals from changing their names and regulate the transfer of goods or the enjoyment of particular acts, the status of marriage remains quasi-miraculous, creating opportunities where there were none and family ties where none existed before. It is on the model of this mystic union of opposites that the musical assures continuity between all its contradictory tendencies.

Image/Sound. As I demonstrated at length in chapter four, the traditional classical narrative hierarchy of image over sound is reversed at the climactic moments of the musical. In fact, this reversal is commonly the agent which permits the establishment of continuity between sequences stressing realistic movement and sound and those which tie movement and sound to a rhythmic source. The audio dissolve, as defined in chapter four, is thus a fundamental technique here, for it not only establishes perceptual continuity between conceptually distinct phenomena, but it also commonly introduces those sections of the film which most clearly privilege sound over image.

These five semantic and five syntactic elements of a definition of the musical are summarized in the accompanying table.

Reformulating Genre History

As it is commonly written, the history of the Hollywood musical is more the product of American publishing practices than of historiographic theory and historical scholarship. Bending to a requirement for neat chapters of roughly similar size, historians of the musical have consistently started by seeking to identify neat, workable categories, usually bor-

DEFINING THE MUSICAL CORPUS

SEMANTICS	Format	Narrative
	Length	Extended (feature-length)
	Characters	Romantic couple in society
	Acting	Combination of rhythmic movement and realism
	Sound	Mixture of diegetic music and dialogue
SYNTAX	Narrative Strategy	Dual-focus: alternation, confrontation, parallelism between male and female; each sex identified with specific cultural value
	Couple/Plot	Parallelism (and/or causal link) between formation of couple and success in plot ventures
	Music/Plot	Music and dance as expression of personal and communal joy, as signifiers of romantic triumph over all limitations
	Narrative/Number	Continuity established between realism and rhythm, dialogue and diegetic music, on model of mystic marriage
	Image/Sound	Classical narrative hierarchy (image over sound) reversed at climactic moments (audio dissolve)

rowed from the industry itself. Only when this division of the subject into neat categories/chapters is concluded will an order be selected and thus the genre's historical dimension be determined. Corresponding primarily to short-lived studio formulas, these categories permit rapid coverage of the genre's highlights (as in the general studies of Stern, Springer, and Masson), but their lack of historical (or, for that matter, theoretical) foundations makes them extremely suspect as building blocks of genre history. A short outline of the standard account will make it easier to pinpoint specific drawbacks.

The most widely accepted version of the musical manages to reduce the enormous variety of early offerings to the names of three studios and the practices supposedly associated with them. If all accounts start with Warner Brothers and the legendary figure of Al Jolson, they move on to stress the backstage plot initiated by MGM's *Broadway Melody,* and from there to the technical innovations and European savoir-faire of Paramount's two highly acclaimed operetta directors, Ernst Lubitsch and Rouben Mamoulian, and their appealing stars, Jeanette MacDonald and Maurice Chevalier. During the early thirties, critics point out, the public tired of mass-produced musical spectacles, making the musical genre a nearly forgotten and highly unprofitable affair. Not until after 1933, with the dazzling success of Busby Berkeley's extravaganzas at Warners, did the musical push through a New Deal and recover from its crash. The mid-thirties, then, are seen as the private province of Berkeley and Warners on the one hand, and of the Astaire/Rogers team at RKO

on the other, with only minor attention given to MGM's lucrative but maudlin pairing of Jeanette MacDonald and Nelson Eddy. Turning the corner into the forties, we usually find a chapter devoted to the children, with emphasis on Judy Garland and Mickey Rooney at MGM. At this point, a catch-all chapter sometimes attempts rapid coverage of the films excluded by strict emphasis on Warner, Paramount, MGM, and RKO throughout the thirties. Predictably, even these minor strains are organized by studio/star: Fox/ the blondes, Columbia/Rita Hayworth, Paramount/Bing Crosby, and Universal/ Deanna Durbin. Another optional chapter may be fit in here, chronicling the biopic (biographical study of a musical figure's career), the first development since the invention of sound itself to be conceived in terms broader than a single studio. The longest chapter of all is here devoted to the so-called "golden years" of the "Metro musical," with its established production teams (the Freed and Pasternak units), its superstar directors (Vincente Minnelli, Stanley Donen, Charles Walters), and its extraordinary musical talent (in particular Garland, Kelly, and Astaire). Most of the prose given over to what many critics consider the heyday of the Hollywood musical (mid-forties to mid-fifties) stresses the excellence of the work done at MGM, demonstrating how Metro at last introduced location photography, "integrated" the musical numbers into the plot, and thus reduced the awkward sense of unreality often associated with earlier musicals. With the integrated musical of the early fifties treated as the genre's *telos,* it is not surprising that all remaining musicals are often squeezed into two chapters which denigrate, respectively, Hollywood adaptations from Broadway and rock musicals (often defined more by their supposed adolescent audience than by a shared rock-and-roll musical style). The only acclaimed musicals of the last thirty years are commonly grouped in a final section on reflexivity and the anti-musical, from *A Star Is Born* and *The Country Girl* to *All That Jazz,* with emphasis on nostalgia, intertextuality, and attempts to undermine the received ideas of a long musical tradition.

As an overview of the genre, this summary has its value, for it provides an evaluation of the high points of the genre on which most critics agree. As a history, however, such an account leaves much to be desired: hopping from category to category, from one "successful" formula to another, this mode of history borrows its critical terminology from the films themselves and from the industrial practices that produced them, rather than from the signifying practices that they enter into. The categories generated by this approach are thus located on the same level. While the tradition of borrowing labels from the films' own studios, actors, and artistic personnel simplifies the categorization of films, it has three extraordinarily debilitating effects on history and criticism alike. These three problems might be termed, for the sake of simplicity, the proper noun problem, the inter-generic/intra-generic problem, and the problem of history vs. enumeration.

Categories labeled with a proper noun have always been something of an embarrassment for the historian. On the one

hand, they tend to imply more than the proper noun label actually states. We speak of "Hollywood" films, but we regularly include in that category films made by Paramount in New York City in 1929 and the films made all over the world by American production companies during the last decade. Histories of the musical lionize the Warner/Berkeley films, but if MGM's 1933 *The Dancing Lady* gets mentioned at all, it is in the chapter devoted to Warner Brothers and Berkeley, evidently because *The Dancing Lady* corresponds to a style implied by—but invisible in—the proper noun label. The use of proper nouns as a metonymy for something else (a style, a pattern, an approach) thus creates all manner of confusion, because it tends to hide the principles of categorization which are in fact operative. On the other hand, categories defined by proper nouns tend to exclude from consideration all those films not associated with a canonized proper noun. Gone from the standard account are the many early operettas not directed by Lubitsch or Mamoulian for Paramount; nowhere to be seen is that standard World War II device, the troop show (except when a Kelly or a Garland is involved); literally hundreds of films fall into the interstices of such a history. In addition, the use of proper nouns as historical category labels renders nearly impossible the successful interfacing of genre history with genre theory. While a category like RKO (a common figure of speech meaning the upbeat films of Astaire and Rogers made by RKO) may locate a series of films within a historical grid, such a proper noun category provides no key at all to the func-

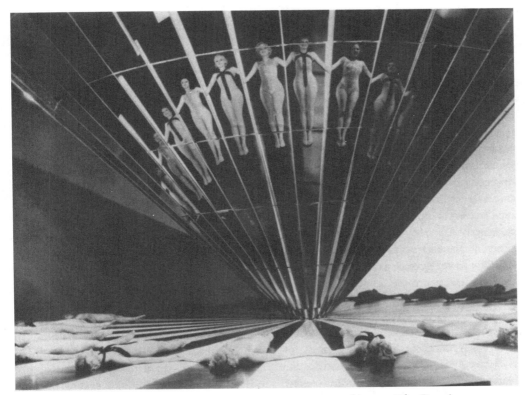

The very type of film dissimulated by a proper-noun history, *The Dancing Lady* was MGM's 1933 entry into the growing show musical extravaganza sweepstakes. As the above still shows, Berkeley was not alone in his ability to turn women into patterns with the aid of mirrors, odd angles, and careful floor painting.

[MOMA]

tioning of the films in question, no indication of their relation to other films (either theoretically or historically).

A second problem involves the range and type of relationships included in current genre histories. Discussions of the musical commonly limit themselves exclusively to the musical; accounts of the western labor hard to subdivide and periodize the genre, often resulting in a rigid, evolutionary framework, but these analyses rarely go beyond the genre's borders. While presenting a plausible account of a single genre's trajectory, current developmental schemas studiedly avoid any data which might tie the genre to external phenomena, concentrating instead on an internal progression. Borrowing from established theorists like Focillon[16] (experimental—classic—refinement—baroque) and Meyer[17] (preclassical—classical—mannerist), genre analysts like Metz[18] (classical western—parody—contestation—critique) and Wright[19] (classical—professional western) have supported a technique of historical analysis that totally privileges the intra-generic over the inter-generic. While in one sense it seems utterly reasonable to write the history of separate genres separately, it is nevertheless essential that our theory of history (and the methodology it generates) be capable of reflecting the influence of one genre on another. Now, a history of the musical that uses proper names to designate major categories has enough trouble relating one group of musical films to another; it provides no model whatsoever for handling inter-generic relationships. From the low budget offerings of the thirties' singing cowboys (Gene Autry, Roy Rogers) to the technicolor superproductions of the fifties and sixties (*Seven Brides for Seven Brothers, Oklahoma!, The Unsinkable Molly Brown, Paint Your Wagon*), the musical clearly owes a massive debt to the western (and vice-versa), but nowhere is such an influence traceable within a history restricted to the musical alone. The list of inter-generic relationships could go on and on, from the highly verbal sophisticated sex comedies of the early thirties (matched by Paramount's European musicals) and the somewhat more repressed screwball comedy (closely related to the Astaire-Rogers films) to the gangster film of the forties and fifties (called up, for example, by *Ziegfeld Girl, Guys and Dolls, It's Always Fair Weather, The Joker Is Wild,* and *Party Girl*), and the non-filmic rock concert craze of the sixties and seventies (as absorbed by films as diverse as *Woodstock, Monterey Pop, A Star Is Born, The Blues Brothers,* and *The Rose*). While I hardly propose to write the history of these and all other such inter-generic relation-

ships, I will insist on developing an approach to genre history that does not cut one genre off from another. Inter-generic influences are too widespread and too important in Hollywood to be written out of generic history, as they too often have been.

Still a third problem involves the very definition of the term "history," as it has been elaborated in practice by film historians. The early years of any discipline tend to be dominated by a definition of history almost totally devoted to the establishment of "facts," i.e., those referential statements on which the discipline agrees to base all further discourse. Now, facts are notoriously discontinuous and extremely diverse in nature; the style of writing appropriate to the presentation of facts typically privileges discrete utterances, giving no emphasis at all to the relationships which might tie one claim to another. It is thus not surprising to find the style of a discipline's second form of history—the chronicle—treating continuous phenomena as if they were in fact discrete occurrences. The standard "history" of the musical, as outlined above, thus appears more as an enumeration of successive but discontinuous moments than as a unified, motivated account of strategic shifts in the genre's structure and function. In order to move the history of cinema into its third phase, we need systematically to leave behind the definition equating "history" to the chronicle or enumeration, and adopt instead a notion of history that includes the necessary presence of explanatory principles motivating change. In other words, we need to adopt a notion of history that includes a theory of history. As long as "history" is limited to proper noun categories, intra-generic relationships, and enumerative concerns, however, such a move will remain impossible.

Alone among the critical terms commonly used to chart the history of the musical, the notion of "integration" provides an opportunity for coordinated treatment of theory and history. As a historical category, the "integrated musical" is the product of numerous attempts to develop closer ties between narrative and musical numbers; as a theoretical category, the notion of integration provides a method for describing the structure and style of individual texts.[20] Though the notion of integration has no doubt been abused in the study of the musical (producing such debatable claims as Jerome Delamater's treatment of integration as the genre's Platonic ideal),[21] and though the very notion itself champions a standard of realism which I believe to be antithetical to the spirit of the genre as a whole, the notion of integration nevertheless constitutes the *type* of term which genre history/theory/criticism cries out for. The terminology which we use must be such that the different aspects of genre study establish a secure continuity. One of genre study's major problems has been its inability to conceive its different tasks in such a way that the discoveries in one area might contribute to the elaboration of another. Until we have a common critical vocabulary, each aspect of genre study must remain locked away, separate from the others.

This is where the versatility of the semantic/syntactic terminology introduced above proves its worth. In their purely theoretical sense, these terms permit us to distinguish between the two basic corpuses to which genre critics refer (a semantic genre, or large category including all those texts which display a limited number of specified semantic elements, and a syntactic genre, or narrow category including only those texts which function according to a prescribed syntactic pattern). As critical terms, the same pair provides a model for the understanding of individual texts, and, by extension, a standard for the comparison of texts within or marginal to the genre. As historical terms, the semantic/syntactic pair can have yet another function: they organize our thinking about the way in which a genre becomes a genre, and thus provide a model for the writing of generic history.

In the sense that I am using the word genre, a group of texts may be recognized as constituting a genre if and only if they constitute a semantic type *and* if that semantic type is matched by a corresponding syntactic type as well. In other words, a group of films with a common syntax but lacking a shared semantics (or vice-versa) would not be recognized as constituting a genre. A genre, then, in the strong sense which I will hold to, is neither an artificially derived but historically unattested theoretical type nor a theoretically unacceptable historical type. A genre does not exist fully until a method is found of building its semantics into a stable syntax. In other words—and this obvious notion has rarely been recognized by genre critics—genres are made and not born. A genre is not something which exists prior to the production of specific texts (and this is true even when a similar non-film genre does already exist, such as the Broadway musical, the pulp western, or the hard-boiled detective novel). A genre is always developed by and through texts. First and foremost, then, genre history is an originary account, a tale of the coming into being of the genre as genre, the story of the stabilization of a particular semantic field and its progressive association with a specific syntax. When genre history is written with the aid of proper-noun categories, it is at best difficult to reveal the shifting relationship of semantic and syntactic concerns and the resultant growth or demise of the genre. When genre history is conceived from a semantic/syntactic point of view, however, there is no difficulty integrating the contributions of various studios, directors, or performers into an overall understanding of the genre's development. Because a genre's fundamental stability, as well as its ability to signify, are dependent on the relationship between the genre's semantic and syntactic dimensions, the history of genre is properly organized around changes in the semantic/syntactic relationship.

Implied in the terms semantic/syntactic as I use them is a hypothesis about the way in which Hollywood genres commonly come into being. As a rule, the meaning of the term "genre" most easily accepted by studio personnel was a semantic one. If a film made it big, the similar follow-up films which attempted to cash in on the popularity of the first film always resembled the initial film semantically, but only sometimes syntactically. From *The Sheik* to *Son of the Sheik*, from *Frankenstein* to *The Bride of Frankenstein*, from one beach-blanket movie to another, the spectator could always count on (because Hollywood's publicity promised) many of the same actors, similar sets, repeated plot motifs, and so forth.

Not that Hollywood was entirely blind to continuity of syntax, but the decisions instrumental in establishing the existence of a type tended to be semantic in nature. Thus the constitution of a semantic "genre," i.e. the consecration of a particular grouping of semantic elements as acceptable, desirable, even normal, tends to precede the establishment of any specific manner of interconnecting those elements. Historically speaking, generic syntax thus most often appears as a series of experiments carried out on an already accepted semantics.

In general, then, we may postulate a simple but elegant relationship between semantics and syntax, between the semantic genre and its syntactic mate: the semantic genre is transformed into a syntactic genre by the successive privileging of specific links between semantic elements. The stability of an established syntax, however, is never more than relative. If there were no stability, we would have no cause to distinguish the phenomenon with a generic label (for the term "genre" implies, after all, a certain stability and continuity in the face of the flux of time), but if the stability were not relative, then the syntax could never have developed in the first place. An initial stable syntax can thus perfectly well dissolve or be critiqued in such a way as to return the syntactic genre back to its origins, whence a new and different syntax might or might not be developed. The history of a genre will thus be defined not in terms of the varying proper name categories which traverse or constitute it, but in terms of the process of accretion whereby semantic elements develop the stability and coherence which authorize the identification of a semantic genre, and in terms of the process of construction whereby those semantic elements are built into differing patterns until one eventually achieves a high level of general acceptance and banishes the others.

As widespread as this process of genre creation may be, however, it is decidedly not the only one available to Hollywood. Indeed, one of the clear benefits of a semantic/syntactic account over a proper-noun approach is the ability to deal effectively with the numerous inter-generic aspects of Hollywood history that express themselves through the borrowing of an already constituted syntax. It is especially with regard to wartime semantic shifts that this capacity is most welcome. On the whole, critics tend to have recourse to extra-filmic events in order to explain the large variety of wartime films that portray the Japanese or Germans as villains. While such explanations clarify questions of timing, they totally miss the extent to which films like *All Through the Night*, *Sherlock Holmes and the Voice of Terror*, or the serial *Don Winslow of the Navy* simply transfer to a new set of semantic elements the syntax of the righteous cops-punish-criminals genre which the gangster genre of the early thirties had become starting with *G-Men* in 1935. Or take the development of the science-fiction film. Again it is the interplay of syntax and semantics that provides grist for both the historical and the theoretical mills. At first defined only by a relatively stable science-fiction semantics, the genre first began borrowing the syntactic relationships previously established by the horror film, only to move in recent years increasingly toward the syntax of the western. By maintaining simultaneous descriptions according to both parameters, we are not likely to fall into the trap of equating *Star Wars* with the western (as numerous recent critics come dangerously close to doing), even though it shares certain syntactic patterns with that genre.

Before we turn to the musical, and to the account that such an approach to genre history might produce, one further question commands our attention. I have suggested that most Hollywood genres begin as semantic clusters and achieve true generic status only when characteristic semantic elements are built into a stable syntax. Thus the western, endowed from the dime-novel days with a picturesque semantics of adventure and violence, only in the thirties develops the characteristic syntax whereby a divided hero is opposed both to the savage and to the civilized, to the original inhabitants of the West (Indians, bears, buffalo) as well as to the current representatives of the East (schoolmarms, bankers, and so forth). Once a genre has established a syntactic base, it may develop by semantic shifts, as in the sliding of the horror genre from one scientific paradigm to another, or it may develop by further syntactic reformulation, as in the western's shift, as described by Wright, from a "classical" to a "professional" syntax. What this model has not provided yet, however, is an understanding of the often acknowledged pattern whereby virtually all genres eventually become reflexive, self-critical, and often even self-destructive. Why is it that the western, from the fifties on, becomes fascinated with the very violence that earlier constituted its unquestioned appeal? Why is it that musicals increasingly seem to question the "happily-ever-after" of married life implied by the final freeze-frame of the couple? The answer to these questions, I believe, as well as an understanding of the familiar experimental/classical/baroque or mannerist/parody/contestation/critique patterns, depends on proper understanding of the term "syntax." While it is convenient to think of syntax in terms of patterns of meaning, that is in terms of the types of relationship favored by a particular genre in order to make a particular type of meaning, I believe that we do better in this context to think of a syntax as carefully *excluding* certain relationships and thus meanings. In other words, while establishing certain meaningful links, a syntax is simultaneously seeing to it that others will never be made. A syntax is thus more than a neutral pattern of meaning; it is also a pattern of repression and as such is constitutive of significant tensions. In the western, for example, a very early syntactic pattern establishes violent confrontation as a method of punishing the unjust. Now, while this syntax successfully reinforces previously latent notions of justice, all the while glorifying the just, it precludes rational consideration of violence itself, so imbedded is violence within a narratively valorized system of justice. As I suggested in the opening chapter, genres serve as an ideological interference in the process of interpretation. We now see just where that ideological activity lies—in the ability to make certain readings all but impossible.

Generic syntax removes consideration of violence itself from the realm of western signification, using its effects instead as a signifier of value, as a method of

reinforcing the primary civilization vs. savagery signification network. But the question of violence is not eradicated by this process, it is only repressed; that is, it remains in the system as a force whose intensity grows the longer it is held beneath the surface. The same is true of the treatment of married life in the musical. Projecting an image of the happy couple into eternity, the typical musical of the thirties or forties seems to deny time, as if its plot were somehow sufficient to overcome time. The successful lovers are traditionally placed for eternity in some extra-terrestrial utopia (usually enjoying a typological relationship with heaven). Time is displaced, destroyed, repressed. To ask about time would be to misunderstand the genre's syntax. But if the musical's repression of time creates pressure to release time from the eternal prison where the music hides it, then it is hardly surprising to find the fifties musical dwelling on the problems of married couples and no longer on the first kiss of the adolescent pair. This reflexive, seemingly self-destructive development does not appear out of obedience to some formalist notion of the necessary development of a mannerist stage in any style, nor does the modish term "reflexive" fully describe what is taking place. Because any syntax, any structure, for that matter any meaning is achieved only at the expense of a corresponding repression—and this is just as true of generic meaning as it is of the meaning of any natural language—meaning-making systems carry within them the seeds of their own destruction. Thus understood not only as "structure," but also as "repression," the notion of syntax proposed here leads to a general and more unified understanding of the often noted pattern whereby Hollywood genres tend not to fade away unnoticed but to go out in a blaze of self-critical, openly reflexive glory. While this approach does not by itself provide the necessary explanation of the timing governing the return of any particular repressed meanings, it does assure a coherent account attuned to the pressures and energies associated with history.

The History of the American Film Musical: A New Approach

Earlier sections of this chapter have suggested a new model for the writing of genre history. According to this approach, historical accounts must avoid limiting themselves to a single definition of the genre in question (e.g., iconographic definition of the western, structural definition of the horror film), but must work simultaneously with multiple aspects of the genre, thus concentrating on the development of and interrelationship between semantic and syntactic aspects of the genre. Now, if I were to write the history of the Hollywood musical as a whole according to this model, the account would run something like this.

Sound came to Hollywood at the low point of European operetta influence on the Broadway stage. The majority of early musicals thus borrowed their materials from a more indigenous, lower-middle class urban theatrical model. Following the backstage or night-club devices already popular in twenties theater, the musical tends to motivate music professionally (stage show, night-club act, etc.) rather than personally. In fact, by 1929

the Jolson *persona* so dominated the genre as to enforce acceptance of a syntactic solution borrowed from melodrama: plots built around a romantic rivalry, with closest attention paid to the odd-man-out (often retaining a child to remind him of his lost love), are enhanced by music whose main function is to reflect the sorrow of death or parting. Dominant until the end of 1930, when the bottom fell out of the musical market, this syntax disappears almost entirely during the slack years of 1931–32. From 1933 on, substantially the same semantic materials are recast into an entirely new syntax (thanks largely to work done at Warners). Music-making, whether professionally or personally motivated, is now equated with the joy of adolescent coupling (whereas the earlier solution usually preferred older, more worldly wise partners), the strength of the community (whereas Jolson and his contemporaries often conclude the film alone), and the pleasures of entertainment (often undermined in the 1929–30 heyday). With this new syntax, a variety of new semantic elements begins to appear more regularly. The youth of the protagonists leaves more room for parent figures (and thus for their function as the *senex* figure of New Comedy), the emphasis on community makes the dancing (or singing) chorus a staple, and the emphasis on joyful, popular entertainment calls for a branching out into every conceivable form of current and previous musical entertainment (the Follies, vaudeville, the specialized world of musical prologues, even light opera, beer halls, and sing-alongs). The balance of the thirties can easily be seen as the dissemination of this syntactic solution into every corner of the musical world. Little by little, nearly every other studio adopts this general solution (especially after MGM won the Best Picture Oscar for its 1936 Warners look-alike, *The Great Ziegfeld*). Performers from all walks of life are pressed into a middle-class mold, from Astaire playing the American commoner abroad, to diverse opera singers trying their best to look and act like normal people while practicing a profession where such normality is far from the rule. While different individuals and teams established their own styles and semantic clusters (Astaire and Rogers = American entertainers in Europe; Eddy and MacDonald = classical singers against a historical costume-drama backdrop; Crosby = crooning in modern-dress America; Garland and Rooney = putting on a kiddie show in small-town America), the overall syntax and stage semantics remained remarkably stable until the war, when new, historically conditioned semantic situations enter the picture (the troop show, the servicemen's canteen, the process of filmmaking itself, and eventually television as well) along with an increase in episodic plots with the forties' characteristic form, the biopic. With the forties comes as well, spearheaded by Fox in relatively low-budget pictures and by MGM in a series of more prestigious offerings, a tendency away from the stagey solutions of the thirties' entertainer-oriented fare. Stressing folk motifs, music, dances, and decors, these new films delve systematically into America's past to produce fables of nationalism for a country at war. With this "folk" semantics comes a slight modification of the genre's familiar syntax. Now the joy of music and coupling are set not in parallel to or at the service of putting on a show, but a patriotic function is instead fulfilled. Singing, like working, is now an anthem of allegiance to the nation's past glory, present strength, and future hope. In retrospect, the introduction of the troop show as a new semantic element appears as a harbinger of the syntactic developments which cause the "folk" solution of the forties to replace the thirties' "show" solution. Indeed, the extent of integration achieved with the folk syntax (folk music growing more "naturally" out of characteristic plot situations than the disruptive stage show) becomes a model for the films of the late forties and fifties, especially at MGM, where the Freed unit constituted a sort of ensemble company concerned to integrate not only music and plot, but the best of recent modern dance as well.

At this point the account necessarily splits, with one fork leading to Hollywood's enormous financial problems resulting from divestiture and competition from television. This way lies Broadway and the film industry's increasing tendency to depend on the Great White Way for prepackaged products, which, thanks to the wonders of modern technology (original cast recordings, color photojournalism, television), were so well known to audiences the country over that Hollywood was afraid to effect the major changes it made with all the shows it adapted in the thirties. This way lies an increasing connection of Hollywood not only to Broadway but to the other—and increasingly successful—entertainment realm, the record industry. From the films of Elvis Presley and the teenie-bopper beach blanket shows starring Frankie Avalon and Annette Funicello to the rock concert documentaries of the seventies and the current tendency toward single-star concert-oriented films where the number of minutes on stage outweigh the rather flimsy plot, the musical has slowly destroyed itself by losing its balance between narrative and music, indeed by abandoning the classic syntax whereby narrative is not just an excuse for music, but stands in a particular, structured relationship to that music. This way, in short, lies the musical as illustrated record album. This way lies MTV.

The other way lie Comden and Green, *A Star Is Born*, and Bob Fosse. Along this path, ushered in by the recycling of the genre's stars (Astaire and Rogers in *Barkleys of Broadway*, Crosby in *The Country Girl*, and Garland in *A Star Is Born*), its composers (Gershwin, Freed and Brown, Dietz and Schwartz in *An American in Paris*, *Singin' in the Rain*, and *The Band Wagon*, respectively), and the entire range of the genre's favorite clichés, we find increasing attention to all those potential concerns so effectively repressed by a quarter-century of generic syntax. At first, however, the repressed material returns only to demonstrate once again how it was that it came to be repressed in the first place. Throughout the early fifties, musicals reach a high point of respectability by both providing entertainment and showing the processes and ideology by which that entertainment is assured. We get to consider the genre's shortcomings as if we were serious fellows and yet walk away sure in the knowledge that a song and a kiss still

have the power to save us from the ravages of time. Not until much later, with the films of Fosse and Altman (*Sweet Charity, Cabaret, Nashville, All That Jazz*) are the genre's shortcomings properly confronted—to the point where whatever function the genre once played now becomes obliterated. Down one path lies the death of the musical by subservience first to Broadway and then to the recording industry; down the other lies the death of the musical by self-inflicted wounds. Today we retain only a limited production of children's musicals (usually cartoons), adolescent musicals (usually dance fad or concert-oriented), and old folks musicals (nostalgia compilations or throwbacks), with only an occasional attempt along Fosse-Altman lines.

Though it is but a faint shadow of a proper historical account (in particular, too little attempt is made to explain why any particular syntactic development or semantic shift occurs), the above sketch represents the kind of genre history called for earlier in this chapter. Individual styles and formulas, studios and performers, directors and designers, choreographers and composers might easily be integrated into such an account, which concentrates on the development of an interaction between semantic and syntactic concerns. Nevertheless, it is not this story that the remaining chapters of this book will tell. Instead, I propose to write the history, one by one, of the three subgenres which together make up the near totality of the musical genre as a whole. To write the history of a genre presupposes that the genre not only makes sense primarily as a genre, but also that its major developments occur on a genre-wide level. External influences, even though they may be more strongly felt in one area than another, by and large touch the genre as a whole; internal developments take place not in a specifiable, limited arena, but apropos of the entire genre. This, I would submit, is precisely what does not happen, except at certain key points, in the history of the American film musical. Far from developing as a single genre, the musical has such well developed, independent subgenres that almost every major shift involves only one of the subgenres, except in the not uncommon case where one of the subgenres exercises a recognizable influence on another. This tendency toward internal influence is alone sufficient to make a case for a subgeneric approach to any historical account of the musical. Other concerns are hardly lacking, however. A treatment of the musical's early years which privileges Jolson and the melodramatic strain, for example, has the unfortunate tendency of suppressing the extremely important European operetta influence not only in 1929–30, but throughout the thirties. It is true that the Broadway operetta was on the decline in the late twenties, but the silver screen provided new life for it, a new life which resurrects opera stars for two decades, and which assures Jeanette MacDonald and Nelson Eddy their extraordinary success. Indeed, to treat MacDonald and Eddy as a subset of backstage semantics and syntax has further unfortunate circumstances: while one or the other is commonly identified as a singer by trade, the syntax developed in their films is usually far from that of the Berkeley chorus line. The same is true of Astaire and Rogers, who, in spite of their professional en-

tertainer status, owe more to the complementary traditions of operetta and screwball comedy than the general account tendered above makes it possible to reveal. By insisting on treating the genre as a whole, we may gain a sense of certain general patterns, but more often than not we lose the important ability to distinguish between those periods when the genre does in fact evolve as a single signifying system and those more frequent periods when there is a major divergence among—or even conflict between—the methods of signification employed by differing subgenres.

Before identifying those subgenres, I want to consider for a moment the notion of subgenre itself, particularly since previous theoretical discussions have tended to ignore any categories smaller than that of the genre as a whole. In such important and carefully reasoned studies of narrative structure as Propp's *Morphology of the Folktale* and Tzvetan Todorov's "Narrative Transformations,"[22] for example, great care is taken not only to name the basic units of the narrative text, but to establish criteria for division of the text into those units. When the same authors reach the point of naming subtypes, however, method is thrown out the window and the memory of plain language resurfaces, producing categories that are totally unjustified theoretically. Establishing a method for dividing texts into primary units constitutes, it is clear, the fundamental goal of these two influential studies, and so nearly all of the respective authors' theoretical energy is expended on this effort, with none left for careful consideration of the isolation and naming of secondary units or types. Now, this is precisely the situation which I seek to avoid. I will thus disregard the unequal rhetorical effects of the terms "genre" and "subgenre," the former sounding strong and important, the latter meek and subservient. In fact, the two terms are part of a chain of category labels in which, by chance, they are the only two derived from the same root, thus making their relationship appear more privileged than is in fact the case. The following sequence describes an ever narrowing progression from larger to smaller categories:

film/
   representational film/
    narrative film/
     Hollywood narrative film/
      genre film/
       film of a particular subgenre

While it might appear that this list depends on an embarrassing mixture of historical and theoretical considerations, the fact is that while the categories are indiscriminately *named* according to differing concerns, the principle of isolation of each category is the same—and quite familiar, at that. While "Hollywood narrative film," for example, appears to represent a historical or geographical category, its recognition as a category in actuality stems from the fact that films of this type build a recognizable semantics into an identifiable syntax. An independent "structuralist" film made in Hollywood is thus not a "Hollywood narrative film," whereas a 1929 film made at Paramount's Astoria Studios on Long Island (e.g. Mamoulian's *Applause*) would be considered within that category. Each level, each category, is related to the pre-

ceding level or category by its ability to stake out, within the general territory of the larger category, an identifiable (and thus meaningful) sphere and type of activity. All such categories are thus theoretically similar in status and not, as everyday language implies, borrowed from different realms and thus dependent on different theoretical systems. The major justification for splitting off a category may come from any realm at all, but the process of recognizing a new, meaningful category is always the same, and always dependent on the constitution of a relatively stable semantics and syntax.

The status of subgenres is thus, at least in one sense (qualitatively, we might say) exactly that of the broader genre. And yet, as the term "broader" suggests, there is a quantitative difference, one which is obviously of paramount importance for any approach which sees genres as culturally significant. Clearly, individual films or minor, limited sub-subgenres cannot lay claim to the same cultural role that a major genre like the western can. In the process of identifying significant subgenres, i.e. those which have a broad enough impact and a sufficiently stable identity to support the assumption that they mediate general cultural values and not just limited local or personal concerns, two independent principles must then be combined. First, the qualitative dimension, which involves replicating on a smaller scale the same operations which permitted identification of the original genre; this approach assures subgeneric categories that are similar in nature to the genre on which they depend. Second, a quantitative concern, which places a particular subgenre along a continuous spectrum stretching from public to private, from potential involvement in a specific cultural pattern to participation in a solipsistic, personal code. Only those subgenres located toward the public end of the spectrum interest me here, for they alone reveal sufficient continuity and dissemination of specific semantic/syntactic ties to guarantee a relationship with the society at large.

In other words, I will identify subgenres by the same method that led me to my original definition and delimitation of the musical. This method, if I may briefly recall, had nothing to do with the accepted notion and corpus of the musical, or rather, though it began with accepted notions, the method quickly established its own criteria based on the establishment of a common semantics and syntax; that is, on the elaboration of a common signifying system. In the same way, subgenres will be identified without regard to categories recognized by the industry (e.g., studios), without regard to personnel (performers, directors, producers, librettists, composers, choreographers, etc.), and even without regard to semantic choices alone (e.g., location, iconography, musical style, etc.), unless those differences coincide with the development of a durable syntax elaborated in the context of a stable semantic field.

Without in any way negating the musical's status as a locus of cultural meaning and as constitutive of a corridor of historical influence, we can recognize within that genre three different ways of making meaning, three divergent and semi-independent spheres of historical influence. From a semantic point of view, we readily identify three quite different visual, so-

cial, and economic realms from which the genre's material is drawn:

—palaces, resorts, fancy hotels, ocean liners, and other locales frequented by the aristocracy;
—the middle-class world of theater and magazine publication (centering on New York City);
—the America of yesteryear, from small town to frontier.

In spelling out these semantic fields in this particular way, I am of course relying only in part on direct observation of the films themselves; I also depend in large measure on knowledge of the specific syntactic patterns associated with given semantic configurations. How do I know to separate the theater from the hotel (two worlds which resemble each other in many ways)? Largely on the basis of the differing syntactic treatment of the two milieux. How do I know that a frontier hotel belongs in a different category from the Ritz? I don't at first; I can't until I see how these similar (but different) semantic units are made to function, and only after I have seen many seemingly similar films will I be able with any assurance to make a specific attribution and thus to delimit my categories reasonably. How do I know that palaces and ocean liners belong in the same category? Again, because they tend to fulfill the same function in a repeated, relatively stable syntax.

In other words, making semantic distinctions always involves a potentially vicious circle with the diametrically opposed necessity to formulate syntactic distinctions. Constituting a problem only when unacknowledged, this fact has unfortunately rarely been recognized even by (*especially* by, alas) the critics who claim to be explaining a systematic methodology and who, all too often, end up substituting the results of their investigation for an explanation of the method that facilitated it. I think particularly of Lévi-Strauss' famous essay on "The Structure of Myths,"[23] in which a sample analysis of the Oedipus myth, given as an example of how we should go about analyzing a large corpus of related narrative texts, takes for granted that we know how to distribute the material of the texts into the categories/columns from which Lévi-Strauss will eventually extract a fascinating but utterly unreplicatable interpretation. In fact, the process of distributing any group of items into meaningful categories is always dialectical in nature. Initially, we choose categories based on prior experience, distribute our material into those categories (say, categories of semantic elements), then check that distribution against the function fulfilled by the material in the process of signification (e.g., syntactic arrangements). This procedure necessarily causes a redefinition of the original categories and thus a redistribution of the initial material. Checking this new distribution against the syntactic patterns which engender signification produces still another redefinition of the semantic categories. And so on, until we are reasonably satisfied either that our material carries no meaning (i.e., sets up no stable relationships), in which case we drop the process altogether, or that we have isolated meaningful types, in which case we may, at least provisionally, feel justified in treating the categories as established and no longer requiring constant redefinition.

What does this process mean in practice? It means, for example, that I, like everyone else who has worked on the Hollywood musical, started out with a notion that all films with professional performers belong in a single semantic category which has often been labeled the "backstage" musical (even though this term is often used only figuratively). Founding an assumption about syntactic activity, this preliminary semantic analysis soon was revised as I discovered that certain types of performance take on a syntactic function different from that commonly associated with the Broadway stage show and its star-crossed young lovers. Fred Astaire's status as professional performer, for example, along with his numerous dance solos in front of a theater audience, seem outweighed by his penchant for a type of romantic ballroom dancing which actually lures him away from his professional responsibilities, away from the theater's admiring crowds. Conversely, several films which deal with the production of a fashion magazine, while devoid of professional performers as such, nevertheless share numerous plot patterns and syntactic concerns with the more traditional Broadway show production. The operative semantic category thus becomes no longer the presence of the performer him/herself but emphasis on the production of a show, with that term now defined more broadly. Only an infinity of tiny redefinitions such as this one can spell the difference between a categorization that is just one more set of waste baskets in which texts will be filed and lost, and a categorization which will reflect signifying activity and thus facilitate access to the genre's overall methods of making meaning. Most genre studies cover their traces, erasing all evidence of the constitution of a corpus, the choice of categories, and the development of terminology, thus leaving the reader methodologically where he/she started, able only to borrow other people's conclusions. I hope that paragraphs such as this one will help make this a book that enfranchises the reader, rather than enslaving him/her to my conclusions.

We now see why a semantic typology is something of a lie, a magic trick, an informed decision masquerading as a naive observation, until it is accompanied by the syntactic typology which grounds it (and which, reciprocally, it simultaneously grounds). That typology is based on the primary relationships between the musical's love plot and the cultural plots which it supports (and which are reflected in the different semantic fields constituting the semantic typology):

—restoring order to the couple accompanies and parallels (and frequently causes or is caused by) restoration of order to an imaginary kindgom, suggesting the metaphor "to marry is to govern";
—creating the couple is associated with the creation of a work of art (Broadway show, Hollywood film, fashion magazine, concert, etc.), recalling the traditional metaphor according to which "to marry is to create";
—integrating two disparate individuals into a single couple heralds the entire group's communion with each other and with the land which sustains them, suggesting the well known metaphor whereby "marriage is community."

Each of these approaches to the couple/culture relationship of the musical defines a different signifying practice and thus a different subgenre, each supported by and in part identifiable through the corresponding cluster of semantic elements.

Indeed, each of these subgenres overtly celebrates one particular value associated with the genre as a whole. In the *fairy tale musical* (so named because of its tendency to predicate the future of a kingdom on the romance of a "princess" and her suitor), the creation of an imaginary kingdom creates ample opportunity to stress the transcendence of the real that characterizes the musical as a whole in comparison to other Hollywood genres. The *show musical* (so named for the type of production set in parallel to the couple's success), maximizes the genre's general expression of joy through music and dance. The *folk musical* (after the characters, music, and general atmosphere), plays up the togetherness and communitarianism characteristic of the genre's general choral tendencies. Each subgenre, then, is built around one of the fundamental tenets of the genre as a whole. For this reason, we will often be able to discover relationships between the subgenres quite as important as the differences which distinguish them. In general, however, we will find that by virtue of their divergent ways of making meaning, these three subgenres operate differently and enjoy separable if not entirely separate histories.

The ritual/ideological role played by individual subgenres cannot be fully appreciated until the history and functioning of all three subgenres have been described at length. Nevertheless, it may be useful at this point to provide a preliminary sketch of that role to guide the reader through the chapters that follow. As subgenres, the fairy tale musical, show musical, and folk musical all champion values which are consonant with those of the genre as a whole. At the same time and by the same token, of course, these subgenres owe their continued existence to their ability to speak for Hollywood while speaking to the public, and thus to play an active role in the reaffirmation of the industry/audience entertainment ideology. Thus the fairy tale musical plays on the popular need for identification with royalty and riches in order to valorize its own ability to create and maintain the glamour and modern royalty known as stardom. The show musical similarly uses the popular tendency to confuse art with life in order to disguise Hollywood's own dependency on illusionism. In a like manner, the folk musical appeals to the popular desire for community in order to make it seem that Hollywood is capable of providing the community banished from the modern post-folk world. Yet we all know that Hollywood is not life, that its glamour is false, that its product is mass-produced and mediated. In short, Hollywood's own self-preservation is achieved through each subgenre's ability to stimulate the fulfillment of our most unfulfillable desires. Each subgenre thus concretizes a particular kind of make-believe:

—*fairy tale:* to be in another place (whence the worldwide, aristocratic, travelogue semantics);

—*show:* to be in another body (whence the emphasis on everything related to the stage illusion);
—*folk:* to be in another time (whence the semantic emphasis on America of yesteryear).

To be somewhere else, someone else, at some other time—these are the fundamental audience desires to which the Hollywood musical so cleverly panders, with the syntax of each subgenre built around one of them.

Such statements of course make it sound as if subgeneric categories were to be considered watertight, with a text "belonging" to one and one only. Such a filing-cabinet approach to genre will net us only frustration. Let us adopt instead a more fluid approach which recognizes the possibility that a single text may very well combine two modes in a new and meaningful way, graft an unexpected syntax on a familiar semantics, or even promiscuously mix one subgenre with another in such a way as to impede the operation of both. Indeed, the most often remade musical film, and perhaps the single most important source of Broadway influence, never seems to settle on a single subgenre. Sharing its time among three classes of river boat dwellers (gambling aristocrats, performing actors, and downtrodden black crew and servants), *Show Boat* moves from one semantic field to another, from syntax to syntax, settling down no more than the river on which it steams. Nor, on the other hand, must we assume that all musicals will adhere closely to one or the other of these subgenres any more than all Hollywood films must fit neatly into a specific genre. In particular, because subgenres are made and not born, the films of the early years of the musical often seem to float in a world unaware of any such categories, as do some of the most creative offerings of recent years, when subgeneric sensitivity has all but disappeared.

Our task in the chapters ahead, then, will be to follow the development of semantics and syntax not of the entire genre, but of each subgenre independently, thus revealing a specificity of materials, of technique, and of meaning unavailable through an analysis of the genre as an undifferentiated whole.

The Fairy Tale Musical

WHERE DOES THE HISTORY OF THE FILM MUSICAL BEGIN? AND where does it end? The day when song was first added to narrative? With the latest television musical special? More perhaps than any other genre, the musical has a history which explodes into every conceivable realm. Not only are the artists who make film musicals often stolen from other arts or media (dance, opera, the Broadway stage, Tin Pan Alley, rock groups, and so forth) but nearly every Hollywood musical is more or less overtly influenced by some other film genre (romantic comedy, screwball comedy, the western, even family melodrama and the *film noir*). What's more, the average film musical borrows at least part of its material directly from the theater (title, plot, songs). How then can we separate the Hollywood musical from its Broadway counterpart? Or for that matter from its TV successor?

These questions have received surprisingly little attention in the dozens of books and scores of articles devoted to the musical. As a general rule, authors treat either the film musical or the stage musical, with only an occasional allusion to the interpenetration of the two arts. The assumption seems to be that a difference in medium implies a difference in content, presentation, and value so radical as to separate the musical into two nearly watertight categories. An alternative method confronts the problem seemingly head on, with Broadway musicals and their Hollywood "adaptations" compared and contrasted.[1] If the separate-but-equal system sins by omission, this alternative approach succumbs to a multitude of critical prejudices. Generally limiting discussion to the period after 1950 (the only era when Hollywood regularly borrowed material from Broadway without making radical changes), these treatments fail to consider Hollywood's dependence on earlier stage shows (European as well as American), as well as Hollywood's important contribution to the development of the stage musical. That such an approach should lead to a critique of Hollywood's sterility and servility is hardly surprising. When the standard of quality is inventiveness and the texts chosen are by definition tributary, then a negative judgment of those texts is a given.

A still more serious, but far less visible problem plagues both of these approaches. Most critics of the Hollywood musical subdivide the genre in such a way as to render comparisons with other media nearly impossible. Categories like Astaire/Rogers, Freed unit, coming of sound, studio golden years, Minnelli, or Warners are hardly conducive to establishing any kind of rational link with other media. The history of the musical having been written nearly entirely on the basis of studio terminology, thus stressing concerns external to the operation of the films themselves, structural ties between film musicals and other texts lie largely outside the scope of critical thought. As a precondition to a structural history of the musical, we must possess a terminology and a methodology based on the text's internal workings, applicable not only to films but also to related forms, and appropriate for the description of historical concerns as well as critical ones. To provide such a terminology, such a methodology, is the goal of semantic/syntactic description, coupled with subgeneric division based both on semantic and syntactic elements. This system should permit us 1) to conceive the continuity between stage, film, and TV as more than a question of borrowing and adaptation; 2) to distinguish among the varying relationships between the Hollywood musical and its predecessors.

The latter, essential point will inform much of the second half of this book.

Far from assuming that the film musical is entirely independent of the Broadway musical, or that Hollywood always depends equally and in the same way on Broadway, I will distinguish between the various Broadway-Hollywood relationships corresponding to the different subgenres. In general we may say that the show musical regularly borrows the material conditions of Broadway theater as its subject matter—stage economics, politics, conventions, and the life stories of stage actors, composers, and directors—but with very few exceptions, the show musical borrows little directly from the *texts* of Broadway musicals. (Though, as we shall see, it does owe a great deal to non-musical Broadway plays of the twenties. Even when the show musical appears to be borrowing from its stage counterparts, it is usually because the show musical is largely *about* the stage and related worlds of show-making. The chapter on the show musical thus regularly delves into the world of non-film musicals, but not to outline the continuity between the film musical and the non-filmic text. Rather it is to discover in the performing life the source of show musical semantics.

The folk musical exhibits a radically different relationship to the Broadway stage. To an extent unrecognized even by those who know the musical best, the folk musical is a joint product of Broadway and Hollywood. No account of one medium is complete without the other. The chapter on the folk musical thus moves back and forth regularly between California and New York, often following the pivotal figure of Rouben Mamoulian, the individual most responsible for the interdependent growth of a single subgenre in two media.

The fairy tale musical, first of the three subgenres to reach maturity in film, did so thanks to massive borrowing from a long tradition of European and American operettas. While the history of the Hollywood fairy tale musical reveals numerous attempts to "Americanize" the pattern established in nineteenth-century European operetta, it must nevertheless be admitted that the fairy tale musical on film is part of a tradition which begins long before cinema. Whereas the show musical takes advantage of the invention of a new medium—sound cinema—to create new structures and new meanings, while film and theatre together give birth to the folk musical, the film fairy tale musical simply takes up where the stage operetta (all but) left off. As surely as Friml, Herbert, and Romberg carry the torch passed on to them by Lehar, Straus, and Fall from Offenbach, Strauss, and Sullivan, that same torch is passed directly to the composers Richard Rodgers, Irving Berlin, and Frederick Loewe and to the personnel who bring them to us on film: Jeanette MacDonald and Maurice Chevalier, Fred Astaire and Ginger Rogers, Vincente Minnelli and Elvis Presley.

Three chapters and thus three radically different approaches, three totally different relationships to the stages of Broadway and Vienna. The history of the fairy tale musical is continuous across media much as the history of cubist composition is continuous from oil painting into collage and beyond. The show musical, on the other hand, is the McLuhanesque subgenre par excellence. Whereas the fairy tale musical is nearly media-blind, in the show subgenre the medium of the stage musical becomes the message of its film counterpart. Paradoxically, the folk musical exactly inverts this situation. Displaying folk material largely derived from a world where cinema is unknown, the folk musical is nevertheless the one subgenre on which the live arts (from hootenanny to vaudeville and sing-along to stage) actively collaborate with a canned art (in Hollywood, if it's finished, it's "in the can"). Perhaps this differential treatment of the Broadway-Hollywood relationship will help to put away forever the simplistic and holistic argument according to which (nearly) all Hollywood musicals are seen as poor cousins who keep their heads above water thanks only to repeated loans made by the rich uncle in New York. There is much to be learned from an honest evaluation of Hollywood's borrowing from its Broadway partner—and even more to be gained from full recognition of the complex interaction tying the two cultural centers together.

Prehistory

When film first learned to speak, it sang instead. It is a matter of record that the earliest synchronized sound tracks for moving pictures first reproduced orchestral atmospheric music (like that previously provided for all silent films) and "live" music performed by characters portrayed within the film. As in the early history of literature, where poetry regularly precedes prose and song antedates speech, the early days of sound film clearly belong to music. According to a persistent legend, speech owes its very presence in the first feature-length synchronized-sound narrative film to song. "Wait a minute. You ain't heard nothin' yet!" Al Jolson is reported to have said apropos of the songs he recorded for *The Jazz Singer* (1927). Present in the films of the late twenties largely as a support mechanism for song, speech introduces, justifies, explains, and completes song in the same way that pretty gift wrapping makes a Christmas surprise somehow more pleasing still. Yet when New Year's Day rolls around, the wrapping has gone the way of the tree, the turkey, and the trimmings. For film producers of the late twenties, the equation of sound with song created a new and unaccustomed dilemma: though studios had stables of script-writers and every local theater had its pianist, Hollywood was very nearly devoid of composer-librettists accustomed to working in an extended narrative medium. Musical material was needed and it was needed fast, faster than it could possibly be written by as yet unhired personnel.

In an important sense, the range of solutions offered to this dilemma predetermined the various directions in which the film musical would grow, and thus the subgenres representing its differing modes of organization. In some ways the most obvious solution was simply to record the singing of well known performers in live performance. When used undiluted, this method produced the "revue" format, which achieved enormous popularity during sound film's first five-year plan. When imbedded into a narrative line devised by already proficient studio writers, scenes from vaude-ville, minstrel shows, or the musical theater turned into the native American backstage form. A second solution involved the borrowing of music from the folk tradition. Of course, folk material grew more slowly into a separate, identifiable subgenre because its performance is less identified with a stable group of performers in predictable situations. What's more, Hollywood was not alone in seeking to exploit folk tunes during this period. The growth of the folk musical is thus a jerky one, slower and less isolatedly cinematic. The third solution was perhaps the most obvious of all. To many students and practitioners, silent film was the ideal form. Far from constituting a handicap, the lack of a voice made silent film relatively immune to the influence of established genres, literary and otherwise, whose major vehicle is language. For over a quarter of a century, film thus grew at its own pace and in its own direction, influenced by the history of literature to be sure, but protected from a crippling all-out attack by its very infirmity, its inability to speak. With the coming of sound this protectionist policy suddenly turned into the most open laissez-faire attitude. Previously stripped of their verbal texts at the border of filmland, the popular hits of European and American literature now found an open market. With Hollywood looking for musical material, what could seem more inviting than a long tradition of stage musical successes: musical plays, operettas, opéras comiques, opéras bouffes, and other musical entertainments? Foremost among these were more than a half-century of European productions whose popularity in the United States made New York, their port of entry, the American center of musical theater.

Even before the Civil War, Americans had shown more than just a passing interest in "serious" musical theater, i.e. staged, costumed drama with a plot, orchestral music, and trained voices (as opposed to the informality of the minstrel show, vaudeville, or camp meeting). It is a cliché of American musical comedy criticism that the genre began with the 1866 Niblo's Garden performance of *The Black Crook,* yet long before the end of the Civil War American audiences had shown a penchant for a combination of theater and song. The first half of the nineteenth century brought numerous English productions—usually predictable narratives written to accompany a series of well known ballads.[2] The first American composer to achieve substantial success in the operetta form was Julius Eichberg, a German violinist trained in Brussels and Geneva who came to the U.S. only five years before the triumph of his *Doctor of Alcantara* in 1862. Delving into an unbroken tradition alive in Europe since the halcyon days of Renaissance pastoral, Eichberg packed his play with cliché after cliché: two fathers who promise their children to unknown mates, two young lovers forced to part by obtuse fathers, and a miracle of fate whereby the unknown mates turn out to be the young lovers themselves. First performed in Boston, like all of Eichberg's compositions, the *Doctor of Alcantara* was soon followed by a series of similar compositions, all built on mistaken identity, disguises, and star-crossed lovers, and colored by the exoticism currently in vogue on the Continent: *The Two Cadis, A Night in Rome, The Rose of Tyrol.*

During the period immediately after the Civil War, America was ripe for a series of importations.[3] Though *The Black Crook* had popularized musical entertainment in 1866, its strange combination of serious theater and girly show was not easy to imitate, nor did its naughty nature make it acceptable entertainment for all segments of society. The arrival of Jacques Offenbach's *Grand Duchess of Gerolstein* (in French in 1867, in English in 1868) capitalized on this wave of interest in musical theater, creating a short-lived but intense vogue for opéra bouffe. Set in a mythical tiny Central European kingdom—the kind which would dominate European and American operetta until World War II—*The Grand Duchess of Gerolstein* crystallizes a tendency to use the military as chorus (an approach already implemented by Bizet's *Carmen* and many other popular operas). A basic element of the fairy tale musical's semantic field, the regimental chorus permits not only picturesque use of national drinking songs, emphasis on national military costume, and the display of military architecture, but also the combination of martial music and military maneuvers as a substitute for the poorly justified but immensely popular ballet interlude. (Indeed, many of the most famous operetta composers began their careers providing music for marching bands: Arthur Sullivan, John Philip Sousa, Victor Herbert.)

By the early 1870s the public had soured on operetta-bouffe, thus ending the short-lived influence of French musical theater on American operetta. In spite of the spectacular successes of *The Black Crook* and *The Grand Duchess,* the average 1870s musical theater season in New York (now recognized as the mecca of musical theater) brought no more than a dozen or so new plays. The phenomenal success of Gilbert and Sullivan's *H.M.S. Pinafore* in 1878 overnight doubled that number. Perhaps more than any other single event, the success of *Pinafore* is responsible for the popularity of musical comedy in America. Ransacking the pastoral tradition, as had Offenbach and others before them, Gilbert and Sullivan hammered into place many of the building blocks of sophisticated operetta: mistaken identity, lovers of different classes, the use of a ship as a more modern equivalent of the self-contained Ruritanian kingdomlet. With these time-honored ploys, however, *Pinafore* offers two related novelties, the keys to its success and the foundation of Gilbert and Sullivan's strong but largely indirect influence on subsequent musical theater. Whereas French *opéra bouffe* most commonly makes fun of stock comic characters borrowed from a long literary tradition (e.g., General Boum of *Grand Duchess* fame is none other than the well known *miles gloriosus* of Roman comedy and all its vernacular imitators), *Pinafore* derives much of its laughter from a biting irony on current institutions. "Stick close to your desks and never go to see," the chorus opines, "And you all may be Rulers of the Queen's Navee!" Couple this ironic gaze on present-day British military practices with a light-hearted tone and music to match—what results is the first real alternative to the sumptuousness and sophistication of the Ruritanian operetta.

Ruritanian operetta derives its sophistication from the audience's delight in "naughty" situations: adulterous love, infidelity, risqué comments, double entendre. The aristocratic context not only provides the trappings of sophistication but the proper setting for humor that is "above" bourgeois morality. The sophistication of Gilbert and Sullivan comes from a radically different realm. No sex here, no innuendo, nothing but the good-old-fashioned star-crossed young lovers. The difference is that the lovers know that they are in a play. Constantly playing on the conventionality of their activity, on the unreality of the theatrical illusion, Gilbert and Sullivan's characters constantly challenge our "willing suspension of disbelief," transferring the source of our pleasure from mindless immersion in a dream world to self-conscious recognition of the fictitious, factitious nature of conventional theatrical fabrications. The Vienna audience gains pleasure from not being taken in by the conventions of bourgeois morality; Gilbert and Sullivan invite their audience to take pleasure—in an almost Brechtian way—from not being fooled by literary convention. Again and again, therefore, the spectator is reminded of the fabricated nature of the plot and dialogue. *Pinafore's* hero Ralph Rackstraw is accompanied in his first song by a chorus, to which he responds in this way:

I know the value of a kindly chorus
But choruses yield little consolation
When we have pain and sorrow too before
  us!
I love—and love, alas, above my station!

To which the chorus punningly responds: "He loves—and loves a lass above his station!" Puns, clever rhymes, verbal gymnastics—all are reminders of the text's fictitiousness and fabricated nature: a heritage passed on to Ira Gershwin, Cole Porter, and many another sophisticated lyricist.

If the 1878-79 season had firmly implanted Gilbert and Sullivan in American hearts, the mid-1880s would bring to New York's Casino Theatre the first American performances (in English) of no less than five operettas written between 1875 and 1885 by the first master of the Viennese School, Johann Strauss II. Here for the first time Americans thrilled at the sight of a world in which adultery is the rule, champagne flows freely, and a trip to prison is an amusing interlude rather than a moral blow. Viennese operetta thus becomes the upper class answer to *The Black Crook*. Responding perfectly to an aristocratic desire for intellectual eroticism (much as *The Black Crook* corresponded to the middle-class desire for physical, visual eroticism), Viennese operetta provides the American public, with its long history of puritanical mores, an opportunity to exercise, albeit phantasmatically, its desire for forbidden realms of experience. Besides this use of fundamentally titillating, amusing sex as a drawing card, the immensely popular Strauss operettas contributed numerous other elements to the operetta form as it would ultimately be borrowed by Hollywood. No longer dealing with the star-crossed young lovers of the pastoral tradition, but with mature individuals responsible for their own decisions, Strauss subtracts the parental figures so common

in the more naive tradition. Instead we have the servants, friends, and officials who haunt the fairy tale film tradition from *Love Parade*'s comic cabinet to the everpresent Eric Blore and Edward Everett Horton of Astaire/Rogers fame. Parental obstacles to young love can no longer, therefore, constitute the basic plot problem, as they do throughout the New Comedy tradition.

With Strauss a new kind of comic tradition enters into musical theater, later to be furthered by Lehar and Lubitsch, a tradition whereby consenting adults work out their sentimental life on stage (as opposed to the previous tradition in which adolescents come to the stage with their hearts already pledged). We thus find married couples engaged in courtship (usually of each other, and often in disguise), changes of affection during the course of the play (imagine lovers of the Romeo and Juliet school changing heart!), and love matches being blocked by the pride or conceit of one of the partners. Musically, Strauss broadens the repertoire to include increasingly more middle European music: Hungarian rhythms and harmonies, Gypsy music, and of course the famous waltz, which with Strauss—and especially after the success of Lehar's *Merry Widow* in 1907—becomes the hallmark of Viennese operetta. Emblematic of aristocratic society, associated from the first with sexuality (as opposed to earlier less physical or group dances), its whirling somehow vaguely identified with the dizziness caused by alcohol (from *Die Fledermaus* to *Gigi* waltzes and champagne somehow seem made for each other), the waltz encapsulates in music and in dance the forbidden and yet desirable, beautiful nature of the whirling, tempting, gay life of aristocratic Vienna. Commemorated on film by Duvivier's too little known masterpiece, *The Great Waltz*, the waltz is the first in a long series of dances/musical styles that permit the musical to carry a message of forbidden desire. From waltz to swing and from jazz to rock and roll, the musical has always been, at least in part, the vehicle of music's ability somehow to escape and protest against the culture of which it is seemingly so much a part.

Though Strauss may have been Vienna's waltz king, not until after the turn of the century did the operetta begin to turn resolutely around a waltz and the special demands which it makes on the cast. Just as *H.M.S. Pinafore* had once revived American interest in musical theater, so did the American success of Lehar's *The Merry Widow* (1907) serve to crystallize interest in—indeed, devotion to—Viennese operetta. Whereas Strauss used the waltz as finale, as celebration of the restoration of peace to the kingdom, Lehar makes the waltz the very agent of love. As it will be later for Fred Astaire and Ginger Rogers, the act of dancing—of dancing a waltz, that is—fans the spark of love as no dialogue, no other action could. With *The Merry Widow* is born the cliché whereby to dance is to love. It is hardly surprising, therefore, that Lehar's operetta should constitute *the* turning point in the history of male musical theater casting. Though no nineteenth-century actor could do without some voice and dance training, the mode in the latter part of the century decidedly favored the voice. Acting and

singing, singing and acting; these were the important talents, without which no major part was to be had or long held. Dancing could always be handled by the chorus, or by specialty actors—and thus was identified more with group movement, with ballet, or with picturesque tableaux than with couple dancing. Here then was the novelty of *The Merry Widow*: emphasis placed on an activity which requires men to hold women in their arms and carry them off to a land of whirling dizziness. A new standard was thus set for the male lead. Unlike male opera leads for decades, he could no longer be overweight, over-plain, or over-awkward; first and foremost he required grace of movement and magnetism of personality. A voice? What man needs a voice if he can . . . dance. The role of Danilo set a new high for male agility and attractiveness, and a new low for voice training. The Danilo of London's opening, Joe Coyne, actually spoke his songs, simply reciting the lyrics.

Coyne's heritage has heavily marked the history of the fairy tale musical. Following in his footsteps, the two most successful male stars of the fairy tale film musical, Maurice Chevalier and Fred Astaire, set the pattern for all the others. Both talk their songs, both make up in charm and rhythmical movement what they lack in voice. "Can't sing, can't act, can dance a little," goes the now familiar evaluation of Astaire's first screen test. If it hadn't been for the vogue started by *The Merry Widow*, nobody would ever have stayed long enough to hear the faint praise of the third clause. When the fairy tale film musical falls flat on its face it is almost without exception because the

In the London production of *The Merry Widow*, Joseph Coyne made the waltz an everyday word in the English-speaking world, and dance a necessary talent for fairy tale musical leading men.

Performing Arts Collection of the New York Public Library [NYPL]

male lead is held by a wooden professional singer, a Nelson Eddy, a Gordon Macrae, or a Howard Keel. Even in other subgenres preference for romantic roles regularly goes to dancers with little vocal training (Jack Buchanan, James Cagney, George Raft, George Murphy, Dan Dailey, Gene Kelly) or to straight actors chosen for their presence and charm rather than for their voice (John Boles, Peter Lawford, Van Johnson). Singing is not a learned art, this casting implies, but a natural expression of a character's emotions. Some of the film musical's most memorable moments are thus produced by the eccentric, raspy, talky delivery of non-singers like Mickey Rooney, Hoagy Carmichael, Walter Huston, Rex Harrison, and Walter Matthau. Pure singers rarely last long in Hollywood, but the film musical has always made a place for comedians (Eddie Cantor, Eddie Foy, Jr., Jimmy Durante, Bob Hope, Red Skelton, Phil Silvers, Danny Thomas) and dancers (Ray Bolger, Buddy Ebsen, Jack Haley, Bill Robinson, Jules Munshin, Bob Fosse, Donald O'Connor). Even those few men who owe their life in the film musical solely to their singing, as do Bing Crosby and Frank Sinatra, are the very model of effortless, seemingly untrained delivery, of song as speech with pitch. (Indeed, with Judy Garland, the crooners' female counterpart, a similar swerve sets in for female leads. What Jeanette MacDonald could get away with in the thirties Kathryn Grayson just can't quite carry off in the fifties.)

The phenomenal success of *The Merry Widow* meant more to operetta than unprecedented sheet music sales, innumerable *Merry Widow* fashions (right down to "Merry Widow Undergarments"), and an eternal reputation (it is said that Alan Jay Lerner, perhaps the most important postwar librettist of fairy-tale musicals, never lets a month go by without listening to a recording of *The Merry Widow*). In Europe, Lehar's operetta was imitated yearly, while in America the door was thrown wide open to the new generation of Viennese composers (Lehar himself, Oscar Straus, Leo Fall, Emmerich Kalman), as well as to a growing coterie of European-born Americans anxious to climb aboard the band wagon. In spite of the talent of these composers and their librettists, the first quarter of the twentieth century is a period of crystallization rather than invention. Seeds planted by Strauss come to fruition here. Gone are the star-crossed young lovers, replaced by worldly socialites whose emotions are buried deeper and thus harder to reach and reveal. Disguise, still a basic device, loses its comic function and takes on instead a necessary psychological role: the proud and the sophisticated can confess love only when protected by anonymity or false identity. With the courting process taking on more and more the look of a battle, neither partner will admit to having fallen without being tricked into an avowal (or at least having that excuse to fall back on). While the building blocks remain the same—class difference, mistaken paternity, disguise, unexpected reunions—*The Merry Widow* also sets a new standard for the way in which these motifs can be organized into a coherent plot. Whereas previous plays—with or without music—had bled the last comic drop out of such familiar devices, Lehar couples them logically with the Ruritanian motif of the small kingdom: the couple, for the brief period of their romance, *is* the kingdom. All eyes are upon them, all Marshovia counts on Danilo to win Sonia's heart and thus keep her fortune at home. Courting relationships are thus constantly tied to governmental concerns ("Have you ever had diplomatic relations with a woman?" asks Edward Everett Horton of Maurice Chevalier in MGM's 1934 film version). Within the tiny principality delineated by the film there can be no future until the principals of the love narrative discover their future; the bedlam in the kingdom *is* the confusion in the lovers' hearts. This equation of an aristocratic or even royal love affair with the affairs of government is one which will remain at the heart of the fairy tale musical as it is adopted by the film medium (though, as we shall see later, the age of kingdoms soon gives way to the more realistic kingdom-like closed societies constituted by a Grand Hotel, an ocean liner, a plush resort, or even simply a foreign city).

Plying its exotic wares on American stages from New York to San Francisco, the European operetta took the American spectator to Central Europe and to the Orient, to Venice and to the cinema's favorite fairy tale playland—Paris. In exotic song and exotic costume, but in familiar plots with familiar twists, the early twentieth-century European operetta soon had its American imitators. The first generation—and most successful of these imitators—were all European trained. Born in Dublin, Victor Herbert was educated in Germany; Rudolf Friml left Prague to study under Dvořak; Hungarian-born Sigmund Romberg received his musical training in Vienna. To all three, success came rapidly and continually, but perhaps only Friml leaves a recognizable mark on musical comedy, and that no doubt largely because of his librettist and lyricist. Just as *H.M.S. Pinafore* in 1878 and *The Merry Widow* in 1907 had revived a sleeping art, so did Friml's 1924 *Rose-Marie* take the country by storm. Whereas other American composers had simply imitated Vienna's middle-European exoticism (or like Wodehouse and Bolton with *Riviera Girl* boldly added two Jerome Kern songs to a previously existing operetta, Kalman's *The Gypsy Princess*), Friml turned to the Western hemisphere and its native color for his musical inspiration, as did his collaborators Herbert Stothart, Otto Harbach, and Oscar Hammerstein II for their story and lyrics. Now, the notion of an operetta set in America was hardly a novelty (indeed, the earliest American musical theater regularly dwells on native Americans and other local minorities), but to an extent theretofore unattempted—and with a level of success never before achieved—the authors of *Rose-Marie* managed to tie their production (plot, sound, and look) to the still mythical land of the Canadian Northwest. *Rose-Marie* is thus the first point in the history of the operetta where an ultimate split between the fairy tale tradition and the folk tradition is clearly visible. Laying the groundwork for the folk strain, with which Hammerstein would continue to be associated (*Show Boat, Rainbow, Sweet Adeline, Free For All, High, Wide and Handsome, Gentlemen Unafraid, Oklahoma!, Carousel, State Fair, Centennial Summer, Carmen Jones*), *Rose-Marie* nevertheless stands squarely in the line of its European forebearers. Along with the success of Kalman's *Countess Maritza* during the 1926-27 season it represents the last hurrah of stage operetta before the form's definitive appropriation by the cinema.

Even without the widespread development of sound cinema, the late twenties would have been a watershed period for staged operetta. European production was at an all-time low by 1930. Fall had died in 1925; Lehar, Straus, and Kalman had slowed their output. Competition from the cinema, economic difficulties, and a flagging of interest in traditional operetta all contributed to the decline (indeed, one of Germany's most successful stage operettas during the thirties was adapted from the film *Two Hearts in Three-Quarter Time*). In the United States the stock market crash had had a devastating effect on the theater business. By the early thirties nearly every major impresario went at least temporarily bankrupt: the Shuberts, Arthur Hammerstein, even Florenz Ziegfeld. Romberg and Hammerstein's *New Moon*, the operetta smash of the 1928-29 season, was the last book musical to run over five hundred performances until the forties.

The earliest history of the film musical hardly privileges the operetta. The quirk of fate which put sound cinema's first songs in the mouth of Al Jolson also set the fashion for Jolsonesque stories. Mammy-singing, actors in blackface, stagey situations, and non-stop mugging for the camera were the most immediate result of *The Jazz Singer's* success (1927). Jolson's next film, *The Singing Fool*, had an even greater—and more lasting—effect on the narrative situations of the early musical. Film after film from 1929 to 1932 borrowed the melodramatic tone, the tear-jerking songs, and especially the tender father-son relationship evidenced in "Sonny Boy." As strong as the Jolson influence may have been, however, the market for musical plots was so enormous that there was room for everyone and everything. By 1929 the success of a few key musicals had outlined major types for decades to come. King Vidor's *Hallelujah* gave the folk musical genre

both its first masterpiece and a major impetus. MGM's *Broadway Melody* established the backstage musical as king of the Hollywood backlot. The fairy tale musical recorded its first major successes with *The Desert Song, Rio Rita,* and *The Love Parade.*

Constantly deriving its appeal from a more or less overt display of sexual desire, the fairy tale musical demonstrates from its earliest presence on film the extent to which it is driven by the spectator's need for quasi-sexual satisfaction. Part of the charm of Viennese operetta had always been its willingness to deal openly with society's favorite topic—sex. Adultery, infidelity, innuendo, double-entendre—such was the menu that whetted the appetite of many an operetta spectator. Just as the disguises, mistaken identity, and comic misunderstandings which operetta borrows from the pastoral tradition permit the characters on stage to play out their hidden desires, so the naughtiness which the Viennese tradition borrows from nineteenth-century French boulevard comedy permits spectators to indulge in a few hours of deliciously forbidden pleasure. Whereas the Viennese stage did little more than reflect the mores of its audience, however, the American filmed operetta brought to the land of Prohibition and prohibitions a witty and sophisticated but nevertheless clear reference to that which was never before so openly revealed in American movie theaters: sex.

Not all fairy tale film musicals openly reveal their sexual thematics, however. If the Viennese tradition gives rise to a distinguished series of film musicals (largely identified with Paramount and its imported personnel, from 1929 to 1934) where the sexual energy driving the plot is clearly acknowledged as just that, an equally important group of films (including the RKO Astaire-Rogers classics) disguises the sexual energy that drives the plot behind a mask of courtship battles. A far longer-lived solution, but one which has received next to no critical attention, transfers the guilt and excitement associated with sexual energy to an outlaw figure, a foreign (usually male) adventurer who injects a sense of latent sexual pleasure into the exotic locations and travel motif so characteristic of the fairy tale musical. In tracing the history of the fairy tale musical, this chapter will thus follow these three approaches to sexuality separately:

—*Sex as sex*: the plot is driven by overt sexual desire (e.g., MGM's *The Great Waltz*, where Johann Strauss's musical inspiration is continually and specifically identified with an adulterous relationship);
—*Sex as battle*: sexual energy is projected onto bickering, fighting, or competition between potential partners (e.g., RKO's 1934 *Gay Divorcee*, where Astaire alternately charms and enrages Rogers by tearing her dress, romancing her, running into her with a car, dancing with her, insulting her, and so on);
—*Sex as adventure*: one partner's apparent fear of sexuality is compensated for by the other's lawless, uncontrolled drives (e.g., MGM's 1940 *New Moon*, where it takes the forced attention of rebel chieftain Nelson Eddy to break down the aris-

tocratic defenses of proper Jeanette MacDonald).

The material which inspires the fairy tale musical varies little. Only the approach and the level and type of sublimation differ.

Sex as Sex

Even before his first sound film (*The Love Parade*, 1929), Ernst Lubitsch, the dumpy little German with the cigar in his mouth, was known to one and all as Hollywood's master of sexual innuendo. Equally famous for his treatment of light sophisticated comedy (*Ich Möchte Kein Mann Sein, The Marriage Circle, Kiss Me Again, Lady Windermere's Fan*) and sumptuous, sexually alive costume drama (*Madame Dubarry, Sumurun, Anna Boleyn, Rosita, Forbidden Paradise*), Lubitsch had not let the absence of a sound track keep him from basing films on operettas. Long a devotee of the Viennese tradition (Jeanette MacDonald claimed that she never saw him when he didn't play a waltz on the piano), Lubitsch spent the better part of his career borrowing plots from the operetta repertory. Already in Germany he had pillaged Strauss for *The Merry Jail* (*Ein fideles Gefängnis*, 1918, based on a scene from *Die Fledermaus*, with Emil Jannings as the jailer Frosch), Bizet for *Carmen* (entitled *Gypsy Blood* for its 1918 American release, in order to suggest a link with the gypsy titles and music of the Viennese tradition), as well as the French operetta *La Poupée* for *Die Puppe* (1919), and, in the same year, the well known titles of operettas by Lehar (*Der lustige*

Ehemann—The Merry Husband, from Lehar's *Merry Widow*) and Fall (*Die Austernprinzessin—The Oyster Princess—* from Fall's *Dollar Princess*, both in 1919). After moving to Hollywood in the mid-twenties Lubitsch once again returned to *Die Fledermaus* (this time going directly to its French source) for *So This is Paris* (1926). The following year he directed a full-blown production of Romberg's well known *Student Prince*. *The Love Parade* was thus by no means Lubitsch's first go at operetta—it was just his first shot at *sound* operetta.

Adapted from a ten-year-old French play entitled *Le Prince consort*, *The Love Parade* tells the story of a certain Count Renard (Maurice Chevalier) and his Queen (Jeanette MacDonald), who has him recalled because of his amorous escapades as Sylvanian military attaché to Paris. What polite society might regard as reprehensible, however, entices the Queen (along with the entire audience). We thus meet here for the first time a major leitmotif of the fairy tale musical tradition: what makes a man desirable is his very indulgence in forbidden activities; the queen goes for her Renard in much the same way that the audience revels in the film's innuendo, bedroom scenes, and generally spicy atmosphere. Once married, the royal couple find themselves unexpectedly becalmed. Reduced to the role of Prince Consort, Chevalier is forced to shed his independence and thus his lively personality. Forbidden to initiate political activity, Chevalier refuses to follow MacDonald's orders, resulting in a separation which jeopardizes Sylvania's financial health. Finally, Chevalier agrees to save the country's finances, but vows to di-

vorce the Queen, who only now fully recognizes the independence of her personal desires from the needs of her national person. With a final chorus of "The Love Parade" they renew their marriage as equals, in affairs of state as in those of the heart.

The building blocks of *The Love Parade* are typical of the semantic elements which the fairy tale film musical inherits from its stage uncle. Set in aristocratic Europe, from the vaguely recognizable outline of Paris to the conventional big white set of Ruritanian royalty, the film draws its situations, sets, costumes, and props from a typically American storybook version of Old World Kings and Kingdoms. The main characters are mature individuals, not adolescents, and of different classes (compared to that of Queen, the title of Count is a lowly one indeed) and thus identified by two different modes of dress (his military regalia creating a striking contrast to her gowns and negligées). This contrast is carried into the sound track as the opposition of a highly trained operatic voice to the almost rasping, accented voice of a chansonnier who owes his training to street and café. Along with numerous duets and their individual reprises, Victor Schertzinger's music includes the *de rigueur* military march (authorizing regimental rhythmic movement in a film surprisingly light on dancing), a traditional Wedding March, and the requisite waltz ("Dream Lover"). The secondary characters are those we might expect to see in any aristocratic household (and which proliferate in the fairy tale musical): manservants, maid-servants, ladies-in-waiting, butlers, and the like. No children, no

A sumptuous palace and the uniformed palace guard constitute a typical early fairy tale musical background for Jeanette MacDonald in *The Love Parade*.
[BFI]

parents, no adolescents, no old people, no peasants, no manual laborers—nothing to remind us of the real world. All is distilled down to an imaginary kingdom which seems created for the mature, attractive, desirable and desiring—but unmarried—pair of individuals on whom all the others wait hand and foot.

The extent to which the fairy tale musical concentrates on adult couples calls for some explanation, since it contradicts common expectations about the operation of comedy. The comic plot most familiar to the Western world, called "New Comedy" by Northrop Frye and identified with major writers from Menander to Molière, reveals a pair of young lovers frustrated in their desires by an older figure, often the girl's father, whose allegiance to cultural values (birth, class, money, etc.) is ridiculed and eventually overcome by the young lovers' seemingly natural and just cause (often energetically defended by a tricky servant). The New Comedy system thus aligns youth, servants, and spectators in defense of love (and "nature") against the older blocking character and the conservative world which he represents ("culture"). The fairy tale musical, following an eighteenth-century French tradition most fully embodied in the plays of Marivaux, displaces the resistance to the lovers' union, radically modifying the familiar New Comedy system. Instead of pitting the lovers as a unit against an enemy who is ridiculous (from the Latin meaning "laughable"), the fairy tale musical typically places an obstacle within each lover, in the form of pride or vanity (which the French aptly call "amour-propre" or love of self). The role of rival is thus no longer played by an unattractive but rich character chosen by the New Comedy father, but by the self. As the play takes on a strongly neo-platonic look, with self-love competing in each of the two principals with love for the other, the New Comedy notion of a unified couple facing the world together disappears. More often, it appears that the two would-be lovers are pitted against each other, using the barbs of dialogue to avenge themselves of Cupid's arrows. The older generation thus loses its reason for being, ultimately disappearing altogether and leaving the way clear for lovers played as adults whose life has been sufficiently complex and long to justify a certain measure of pride and a healthy suspicion of love, suitors, marriage and all the other values which New Comedy takes for granted. With the major roles held by mature, self-possessed individuals, this new brand of comedy gains a capacity for sophistication and adult humor entirely lacking in New Comedy. Indeed, if "sophisticated" implies experienced, worldly, even artificial values (as opposed to naive, natural, untutored virtues), then New Comedy is the least sophisticated of comic forms and the romantic comedy represented by the fairy tale musical the most sophisticated. In New Comedy, the young couple are already in love when the curtain rises, they openly confess their love (always their first) and give themselves fully over to it. In *The Love Parade*, and throughout the fairy tale musical tradition, the eventual lovers have not even met when the film begins. In New Comedy, marriage is an utter guarantee of future happiness, whereas the fairy tale tradition often takes us past marriage and into the second courtship on which the success of a marriage may depend.

The debt of the fairy tale musical—and of the musical in general—to romantic comedy radically dislocates the meaning of the term "comedy" in the familiar but misleading label "musical *comedy*." Not only does romantic comedy express its meaning through structures absent from New Comedy, but the type and use of laughter in the two traditions is radically divergent. The fundamental New Comedy structure involves the opposition of the young (love, energy, justice, nature) to the old (money, conservation, power, culture). This opposition arises in the text through a competition of the two groups for the same desirable object (e.g. both father and son want to marry the same girl), through an alternation between scenes of confrontation between the two groups and scenes which present the planning for those confrontations, and through the defection of the servants from the camp of the masters (who pay them) to that of the lovers (who charm them with the innocence of their love and the justice of their demands). As spectators, we are thus constantly called upon to measure the difference between two groups: lovers and their numerous allies on one side, powerful blocking character and his diminishing support system on the other. Romantic comedy leaves little room for such diametrical opposition of lovers to those who block their love—especially since the lovers and those who block their love are one and the same. The entire New Comedy system is thus turned sideways, with one lover now opposed to the other. This opposition of lover to lover provides the very basis for the film musical's thematics and structure. As outlined in chapters two and three, the musical's dual focus on a pair of characters permits the introduction of diametrically opposed values or value systems which are "carried" by the would-be lovers. The resolution of the love plot thus assures not only the coupling and marriage of the lovers but the merging of cultural values once defined as mutually exclusive. Instead of being asked to compare the lovers as a unit to their enemies, the spectator must constantly compare the prospective lovers one to another, teasing out of this opposition an understanding of the thematic and cultural stakes underlying and, as it were, energizing the couple's rocky courtship. More than the other musical subgenres, the fairy tale musical plays this opposition between the would-be lovers to the hilt. In a typical New Comedy, say Molière's *Miser*, the opposition between love, freedom, and energy on the one side to money, careful accounting, and conservatism on the other eventually calls for the radical dismissal of all those values which are not identified with young love. Not unlike the epic in its structure, New Comedy often takes on the appearance of all-out war in which no prisoners are taken nor survivors condoned; the winning side is left alone triumphant to reorganize its new society.

Instead of attributing its opposed values to different generations, *The Love Parade* allots them to the main male and female characters. Sylvania's Queen MacDonald, in spite of an early moment of personal weakness, repeatedly defines herself in terms of public concerns—the budget, external politics, and other impersonal national needs—while Count Renard Chevalier continues to exude the energy, desire, hunger and other libertine attributes for which foxes are known. To her early move toward his libertinism corresponds his attempt, after marriage, to exhibit interest in the government's problems. When he is rebuffed, the couple—and the entire nation of Sylvania—reach a stalemate. The resolution can come only when the Queen recognizes the needs of her private self—and of the Prince's public self. Instead of damning one system and adopting the other, as New Comedy might have done, *The Love Parade* manages, through the success of the royal love affair, to save them both. The couple will reflect the values brought by Chevalier from Paris to Sylvania, while the country will continue to thrive on its traditional values, now renewed by exposure to the new approach represented by Chevalier. The ship of state, as well as the sovereigns who both symbolize and pilot it, will now lack neither energy nor direction.

Related to the redistribution of meaning-bearing structures in romantic comedy as compared to New Comedy is a new type of spectator identification and thus a radically reformulated role for laughter. In New Comedy the spectator identifies immediately and wholeheartedly with the young couple in their struggle against adversity. Anything and everything which retards or blocks the young lovers' union is judged negatively by the spectators, most often in open, audible fashion—through laughter. In New Comedy, laughter comes easily, for we are quick to judge the blocking character (Hobbes' theory of laughter), we laugh at his quasi-mechanical devotion to his projects (Bergson), we judge him to be more childlike than children (Freud). The fairy tale musical presents a vastly more complicated situation. Like the main characters, whose vanity precludes an early and open avowal of love, the fairy tale musical spectator is too sophisticated to succumb to the belly laughs of farce or the complicitous laughter of New Comedy. No, hilarity doesn't come easily to the fairy tale musical spectator; his/her medium is more the chuckle, the smile, the guffaw, that is the barely externalized sign of an internal judgment of superiority. From Vienna to Paris to New York, the staged operetta was always an occasion for the aristocracy and/or intelligentsia to celebrate their dominance over all other classes, groups, cities, and what-have-you. Reflecting big-city morals, big-city manners, big-city mating customs, the operetta has always offered the ideal opportunity to make fun—albeit obliquely—of all that is provincial.

From Offenbach's supposed *pièces à clef* to the repeated use of newspaper gossip columns and *Variety* headlines in the musical, the in-joke lies at the center of the fairy tale musical's rhetorical structure. (For the film musical, Hollywood in-jokes often take the place of New York or Vienna fare. Our first view of Sylvania near the beginning of *The Love Parade* reveals a group of tourists riding in an open-topped vehicle sporting a banner proclaiming "See Sylvania First." Only when the monetary value of the sights is mentioned do the sightseers pay attention to the announcer's patter. "And on the left Pickfair," the tour guide might have been saying, "worth today over a million dollars!") For the in-joke shares the rhetorical structure of the romantic comedy from which the operetta derives so much of its material. To appreciate an in-joke I must know something that others do not. In laughing I am not so much judging the person(s) at whom I am laughing as I am celebrating along with the author of the in-joke our special community of privileged knowledge. Lubitsch and I know that all of this is really a send-up of Hollywood and the American way. The characters certainly don't know and neither do you, in all probability. In fact, the characters are unaware of the extreme conventionality of their every scene. I who know the conventions am amused at their unwitting obedience to forces far stronger and far older than themselves. If they knew what I do, then perhaps things would go differently. Indeed, every now and then one of them covertly admits that he too is in on the joke; but Lubitsch and I are happy to let one of them join our little coterie when Chevalier winks into the camera as if to say "Aren't we putting one over on them, now!" Together, Chevalier, Lubitsch, and the spectator constitute by themselves a class apart, an aristocracy of intelligence ready to celebrate at a moment's notice the discursive power they share. In the same way, Marivaux regularly provides the audience with an on-stage reflector of their knowledge and pleasure. While the lovers-to-be of *Le Jeu de l'amour et du hasard* unsuccessfully resist the temptation to fall in love with their promised mate's servant, we spectators follow the all-knowing brother and father in deriving pleasure from the limitations of the lovers' knowledge. The lovers think they are wooing servants; we know that they are wooing each other.

Every mistaken identity, every disguise, every comic misunderstanding potentially celebrates this same spectator power through knowledge set in motion by in-jokes, winks into the camera, and the sophisticated New York lyrics and rhymes of an Ira Gershwin or a Cole Porter. Indeed, the same function is played by a long list of fairy tale musical devices which simultaneously distance the spectator from the text and identify the film as something specially made for the spectator by a complicitous "author." Any line whose full meaning is lost to the film characters fits this bill, from in-joke to double-entendre, passing through echoes of other texts, puns, and innuendo. So does parody, whether internal to the film (as when Chevalier's rendition of "Paris please stay the same," with regular intercutting from Chevalier to groups of society ladies regretting his departure to Sylvania, is followed by similar sequences with his butler and corresponding servant ladies, and then finally his dog—and the pining lady dogs!), or in reference to an entire tradition (as when MacDonald and Chevalier are pronounced "wife and man"). Even the over-sumptuous, over-stylized sets of the entire fairy tale tradition tend to recall to the spectator the artificiality of the fairy tale world. But only we sophisticated spectators recognize this directorial wink—others probably miss the point and thus the joke. Comic shadow couples work in the same fashion. The servants who mimic their master (Lupino Lane and Lillian Roth in *The Love Parade*) serve more as a send-up of their masters' hesitations than as an independent center of interest. Such is also the function of the even more common single comic servant, an important specialty role of the fairy tale musical from its earliest days (ZaSu Pitts, Stanley Holloway, Hugh Herbert, Charlie Ruggles, Eric Blore, Edward Everett Horton) to the MGM revival in the forties and fifties (Red Skelton, William Bendix, Jimmy Durante), but which tends to die out in the last quarter-century (except in the films of Elvis Presley and other relatively low-budget productions). Numerous manipulations of the camera can serve precisely the same function. From keyhole shots to complicitous views of closed doors, Lubitsch is a master of both the conventional distancing ploy and the less expected but nevertheless ironic move like the series of cuts, twice repeated during the first Chevalier-MacDonald kiss, from close-up to medium shot and from medium shot to long shot.

Whether literal—as here—or figurative—as in a host of other situations—the process of distancing in the fairy tale musical nearly always implies distancing from the characters and screen illusion, accompanied by simultaneous reduction of distance between the spectator and the complicitous composer, director, author and their confederates. We are too sophisticated to accept such a banal plot without dissociating ourselves from it; in order to permit belief, we must cover that belief with a coded mark of our non-acceptance of the text's discourse, a mask of unbelief in the form of irony, parody, and the numerous other winks which bind us to the authors. In New Comedy, to laugh is to triumph—liberty and justice over all. In the romantic comedy of the fairy tale musical, to laugh is not to identify, but to rehearse the vanity of being better, more knowledgeable, closer to the center of things than other spectators. We wouldn't identify with those lovers any more than their own vanity would permit them to fall in love.

And yet their vanity permits them to do just that. In spite of initial protests and insistent pride, each member of the couple eventually succumbs to the goddess of love, as do we to their charm. Though sophisticated, we are human, and all the world loves a lover. For all the distancing devices built into the fairy tale musical, we can nevertheless not maintain our distance indefinitely. Just as the on-screen lovers must be wooed to the point where they trade self-love for love of the other, so must we be wooed by the screen personalities into eventually shedding our vanity and admitting that pleasure is to be found in something more than simple power games. To this end the fairy tale musical's distancing devices are heavily front-loaded, with fewer and fewer occurring toward the end of the text. In *The Love Parade*, for example, we are treated within the first few minutes to Chevalier's

winks into the camera, the ironic sequence of his butler's and dog's departure, the "See Sylvania First" tour, MacDonald's surprising "other leg" joke, the couple's supercilious courting procedure, numerous keyhole shots, patterned servant appearances, camera distancing during the first kiss, repeated spoofing of the principals by their personal servants ("I am the farmer's daughter," says she to her shorter mate as she sits in a gauche, spread-leg position), the pronouncement of "wife and man," and a radio program "Brought to you by Sylvania hardware."

Shortly after the marriage, about midway through the film, the tone slowly changes. At first Chevalier's utter dependence on his wife is uproariously funny (she alone can command her people), but Chevalier's frustration soon becomes real, culminating in his almost pitiful rendition of "Nobody's using me now." Whereas earlier we identified with our all-powerful author crony, we now transfer our affections increasingly to a very real and very frustrated Prince Consort. From our elevated perch conducive to lording it over the characters, we ever so imperceptibly enter the fray on the side of love and proper government. We want the Queen to satisfy the Prince's urge to govern so that he can satisfy her need for love. In fairy tale musical after fairy tale musical, this pattern is repeated: early irony, parody, dramatic irony, innuendo, and other directorial winks at the audience, thus creating a bond of knowledge and emotion between author and spectator, followed by increasing illusionism, emotionalism, and character setbacks, thus eventually assuring the spectator's allegiance to a permanent coupling which that same spectator would have blushed to support during the early parts of the film. Rhetorical rule number one of the American film musical: play the audience like game fish; hook them on their own weaknesses, give them plenty of line, convince them they have plenty of distance; then slowly, imperceptibly, reel them back in, so that they end up at one with the film's main couple.

At the root of the fairy tale musical's syntax we find the love/government parallelism which *The Love Parade* borrows from the Viennese tradition. The Kingdom is in disarray—a fact made all the more salient by the kingdom's insularity and smallness. The rulers' love life is deficient—a situation lamented by the entire kingdom. Solution: simultaneous resolution of the two plots, the one dependent on the other. Government is simply a question of proper marriage, and, conversely, marriage is but a question of proper government. In order to develop this plot literally, nearly every operetta tradition has recourse to the creation of small, imaginary kingdoms run—as in former times and distant states—according to a personal type of reign. The importance of the government/love metaphor and plot connection explains the regularity with which every operetta tradition chooses its characters from the upper aristocracy or royalty (or their equivalent in uncharted regions: the military and outlaw chieftains). Gilbert and Sullivan give us Japan and the Mikado, Offenbach a series of closed principalities from Gerolstein to Hades, Lehar contributes Marshovia, Luxembourg, and the Orient, and every subsequent Viennese composer follows his lead. The film musi-

cal in the thirties often adopts the solution suggested by the fragmentation of nineteenth-century Germany and its many mini-courts (in fact as late as 1953 Liechtenstein was used for the same purpose in *Call Me Madam*, as would be Siam for the 1956 *The King and I*, and an Arabian sheikdom for the 1955 *Kismet*).

Quite early, however, film eschews Graustark in favor of more up-to-date fairy tale material. In 1929-31 alone we find a series of fairy tale musicals capitalizing on the current Parisian mode (*Paris, Hot for Paris, Battle of Paris, Playboy of Paris, Fifty Million Frenchmen*), another series gaining us cheap entry into the watering spots of European aristocracy (*Monte Carlo, Viennese Nights, One Heavenly Night, The Smiling Lieutenant*), while a third group of films is our ticket into local high society (*Vagabond Lover, Let's Go Places, The Big Pond, Madam Satan, The Hot Heiress, One Hour With You*). Borrowing their overt approach to sexuality from the libertinism of the Viennese tradition, these films also borrow, albeit in a displaced manner, the government/love connection of the Ruritanian plot. No longer do we find actual royalty sorting out the problems of a closed world clearly similar to a small kingdom. A mansion in disarray, uproar in a grand hotel, pandemonium at a swank resort, dissension at the country club, fancy footwork on an ocean liner, even night-club panic or the problems of a swanky business can provide a more modern version of palace upheaval. In all these cases the lack of order in the big white set is seen as parallel to the mistaken distribution of hearts among the residents. Like a neo-platonic Renaissance pastoral novel, the fairy tale musical sets about simultaneously matching hearts and restoring order—for the two are one and the same. Proper government, proper marriage—and vice versa.

Never possible independent of a certain sexual fascination, the fairy tale musical nevertheless presents its sexual energetics overtly over no more than a five-year period, from *The Love Parade* to the 1934 tightening of the Hays Code marked by the appointment of Joseph Breen as Hollywood's chief moral guardian. From these years not a single "naughty" musical has endured without the presence of at least one of *The Love Parade* trio of MacDonald, Chevalier, and Lubitsch. Together they made the infidelity-pocked 1932 *One Hour With You* (remake of Lubitsch's 1924 *Marriage Circle*) and the 1934 MGM *The Merry Widow* (which, as Lubitsch's last musical, Chevalier's next-to-last American musical for a quarter century, and MacDonald's last sexy role, marked the end of an era), while Lubitsch and MacDonald teamed up on *Monte Carlo* (1930, with Jack Buchanan) and Chevalier and Lubitsch together did the most salacious parts of *Paramount on Parade* (1930) and *The Smiling Lieutenant* (1931, with Claudette Colbert). The only film which Chevalier and MacDonald made together without Lubitsch, *Love Me Tonight*, remains one of the few films of the period still regularly screened and admired today.

Directed by Rouben Mamoulian, whose earlier stage credits included the basic opera repertory followed by the best known operettas (1923-25, at Rochester's Eastman Theatre) and a handful of New York's most artistically acclaimed

plays (*Porgy, Marco Millions, R.U.R., A Month in the Country, A Farewell to Arms* —1927-30), and whose film credits already included *Applause, City Streets,* and *Dr. Jekyll and Mr. Hyde, Love Me Tonight* appears at the very ebb of interest in the musical. After the successes of 1929, 1930 proved to be the musical's biggest year ever (with only 1943 and 1944 providing close competition), yet by early 1931 critics and the public alike had turned a cold shoulder to the genre: together, 1931 and 1932 produced little more than a quarter of the 1930 output. Clearly influenced by Lubitsch, *Love Me Tonight* is nevertheless remarkable for the overall coherence which it achieves, largely through the establishment of a new relationship between music and plot material. Now, in 1929, technological limitations required the recording of music simultaneously with the image. While this approach assured synchronization, however, it limited character and camera mobility and for all practical purposes restricted the use of synchronized music to single scenes conceived theatrically as a single audio-visual entity. This is the method used, for example, in the archetypal backstage musical, *The Broadway Melody*. Location photography of course created problems which simultaneous recording could not solve, given the primitive state of the microphone art. A film like Vidor's *Hallelujah* was thus shot silent, with music added in the studio. Only Lubitsch's *The Love Parade* makes a move toward more modern, i.e. freer and more music-oriented, practices. Convinced of the overriding importance of rhythm to the musical film, Lubitsch regularly photographed the most complex parts of the film (e.g. the massive wedding scene) to a beat, with all movement, right down to hand lifting and head nodding, regulated by the beat. The orchestra was later conducted according to the same beat, thus producing fully choreographed mass scenes not seen again until the extravaganzas which characterize MGM during the Freed years (especially the well known transportation numbers "Atchison, Topeka & Santa Fe" in *The Harvey Girls* and "The Trolley Song" in *Meet Me in St. Louis*, as well as the park scenes in *Summer Holiday*, the opening of the 1951 *Show Boat*, the finale of *An American in Paris*).

Another Lubitsch innovation successfully, though in a cumbersome and expensive manner, overcame simultaneous recording's seeming limitation to a scene-by-scene approach to the music. Unwilling to forego the freedom over space which characterizes the cinematic medium as compared to its theatrical cousin, Lubitsch insisted on joining cinematically (by inter-cutting), and not just theatrically (by temporal or spatial continuity), the stock scenes in which the comic servant couple parody the activities of the masters. Conceiving the scene as a double duet with crosscutting between the two couples throughout, Lubitsch simply had a single orchestra play the music on stage (the standard 1929 practice) while two crews simultaneously shot the two separate scenes, masters and servants. This two-camera technique provided complete freedom in the editing room to intercut the two scenes in any way desired. As innovative and effective as this technique may have been, however, it clearly had severe limitations. The invention of the "playback" system in late 1929 would seem to have removed many of these. Once recorded while cameras whirred, extras shuffled, and onlookers coughed, the orchestra and singers were now recorded prior to filming. This solution not only removed unwanted noise, it also permitted easier manipulation of tone quality (either through choice of room size and acoustics or eventually through mechanical tampering, i.e. adding reverb, recording voice and orchestra separately, even patching flubbed passages), as well as ideal recording circumstances (which, parenthetically, contributed markedly to the notorious American penchant for singers who sing effortlessly, i.e. those who look like movie singers, who, having left their physical efforts in the recording room, can act out the spiritual side of singing for the camera, and never let on that producing the sound cost them any effort). In spite of the enormous possibilities made available by the playback system (which every studio was using by early 1930), few directors treated it as any more than a convenience, a way to get the film in the can a little quicker, a little cheaper, with a little better sound quality. Each number continued to be treated separately, as if the onstage orchestra were still needed.

With *Love Me Tonight*, Mamoulian proves to be one of the first to take full advantage of the pre-recording process. Having recorded the entire score before finalizing plans for the visuals, this musically trained Armenian immigrant regularly succeeded in linking not just two but multiple scenes through the use of synchronized music apparently emanating from onscreen action. Thus contributing to the breakdown of the typical *spatio-temporally unified scene* to which cinema reverted when the coming of sound drove it back to the theatrical model, Mamoulian repeatedly builds *musically unified sequences* out of shots which have little spatial unity. The most famous of these sequences are to be found near the beginning of the film. The opening, borrowed from Mamoulian's staging of *Porgy*, and best known to most audiences by its incorporation in Mamoulian's staging of Gershwin's *Porgy and Bess*, orchestrates the noises of an awakening Paris (recalling audibly the visual "city symphony" genre of the twenties). Then, in a passage which prefigures the passed-along song which later became a stable element in the folk tradition, Chevalier's song is "carried" out of his tailor shop by a friend, who in turn passes it on to a taxi driver, whose fare, a songwriter, begins to take it down and then adds his own words; he, in turn, is heard by a platoon of marching soldiers, who transform it into a rousing march until the violin of a nearby gypsy picks up the tune and bends it toward the Viennese tradition, thus setting the stage for the final passing of the melody, this time through a cross-country pan to a nearby castle and a dissolve to the lovesick Jeanette MacDonald, Ruritanian princess *par excellence*, who lends operatic elegance to the tune. Here, in a single sequence (the term scene no longer applies) we have witnessed a lesson in musical style that prefigures the film's handling of plot problems. From the typically French Chevalier chansonnier style we follow the populace to the clever lyrics and offhand delivery of Tin Pan Alley, and from there to the only

form shared by popular and aristocratic modes, the march, which leads us further and further into the aristocratic style associated with Vienna, opera, castles, and the distant upper classes. Encapsulating all MacDonald and Chevalier's previous screen roles in this one film, Mamoulian builds *Love Me Tonight* around an opposition between the idle rich and the working poor—yet paradoxically this very first sequence assures us that contact is possible between Paris and provincial palaces, between penniless Maurice and loveless Jeanette, but only through the magical continuity provided by music and song (thanks to Mamoulian's new-found mastery of the sound-image relationship).

Bridging their disparate styles as well as their classes, "Isn't it Romantic" constitutes one of the most original solutions to the stock fairy tale musical opening. In order to establish a fundamental parallel between the fairy tale musical spectator—who is captivated by the screen world of luxury and lust—and the film's middle-class hero—seduced by the unaccustomed attractions of a distant, desirable world—the fairy tale musical often begins by propelling one member of the couple from a humdrum daily life into the fairy tale world. From city, the flight is to the country (*Love Me Tonight, Damsel in Distress, Holiday Inn, White Christmas*); or to a distant resort (*Gay Divorcee, Monte Carlo, Moon Over Miami*). From the recognizable workaday life of these United States the trip is to Europe (*Gold Diggers in Paris, Royal Wedding, Call Me Madam*) or to South America (*Flying Down to Rio, Blondie Goes Latin, Weekend in Havana, Ship Ahoy, Yolanda and the Thief, Holiday in Mexico, The Road*

Rough tweed jacket, turtle neck shirt, informal cap—Maurice Chevalier's costume contrasts with Jeanette MacDonald's aristocratic satin and lace, just as his raspy chansonnier voice and delivery contrast strikingly with her smooth operatic tones (*Love Me Tonight*).

[MOMA]

to Rio). Any place which crystallizes spectator dreams will do, even the city (*Hair, The Wiz*), eighteenth-century America (*New Moon, Naughty Marietta*), the distant past (*Maytime, A Connecticut Yankee in King Arthur's Court, On A Clear Day*), or a land whose imaginary origins match its image-based presentation (*The Wizard of Oz, Brigadoon, Alice in Wonderland*). However the flight is handled, it serves to cement the spectator to the local commoner and to identify the other partner with fantasy, with the far away, with

the imaginary—in short with the image itself. For in a most profound way, the love stories of the fairy tale musical are never the courtship of a man and a woman alone, they always imply the romance of spectator and image as well.

The most basic opposition operating through the fairy tale couple is thus the very one which sets in motion the plot of *Love Me Tonight*. Maurice Courtelin is a tailor. He has to work for a living, like you and me. That is, he has to get paid for his work, and there's the rub. The

Vicomte de Varèze, Princess Jeanette's brother, has skipped town without paying his tailor. With the support of the other businessmen whom the Vicomte never pays, Maurice decides to mount an attack on the château, as in revolutionary times. To travel to the castle is thus to go up the river of time to those pre-revolutionary days when men rode horses (rather than cars and trains) and measured a man's worth by his birth (rather than by money). *Love Me Tonight* is thus set up from the very beginning as the confrontation of two value systems, symbolized by Maurice and Jeanette and embodying the divergent reality of the spectator and the film image:

Maurice	*Jeanette*
present	past
city	country
lower class	aristocracy
work	recreation
money	birth
car	carriage
train	horse
popular singing	operatic training
reality	image
spectator	film

Love Me Tonight thus perpetuates the basic fairy tale structure whereby one side of the couple is identified with reality, the other with the imaginary, divine, or unreal (with the male commonly standing for the real—the body—while the woman figures the ethereal—the soul). Maurice and Jeanette are thus an image of our split selves, in that their opposition parallels the opposition of our daily needs and habits to the desires of our nights, our weekends, our imaginary life (cinema and otherwise). Cleverly, though, Mamoulian has used this formal parallelism as a front for a shameless scam. The film cheats by setting up its real vs. imaginary opposition on the imaginary end of the spectrum:

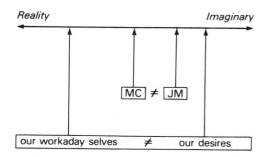

Maurice Chevalier as the image of the American working man! Ever the one to reverse stereotypes, Mamoulian has here taken the romantic idol of millions, the professional Frenchman par excellence, and turned him into the formal equivalent of the American man-in-the-street. As Paramount's pressbook for the film so aptly claims, Chevalier is "The Aristocrat of the People." The revolution is thus won before it starts—but not by the bill collectors.

Whereas at the beginning of the film Maurice goes to the country to collect his bills, once he has met the beauteous Princess Jeanette he turns his attention to proving that he is a nobleman himself, i.e., that he is not the sort of man who has to worry about money at all. By the end of the film questions of money will have entirely disappeared. By what leger-demain does Mamoulian displace attention so completely and effectively from the commodity originally given as the driving force of society? Indeed, the process does have something magical about it—in fact it is this very magical quality that justifies the labeling of this subgenre as the fairy tale musical. In the traditional fairy tale (Grimm, Perrault) evidence of personal value often justifies the coupling of an individual of lowly birth with a royal partner. Stress on the element of personal value—typically identified with beauty for women (e.g., Cinderella) and with feats of valor for men (e.g., climbing a glass hill)—supports the fairy tale's general function of wish fulfillment by convincing the listener that happiness depends not on birth but on acts, even in a world dominated by the aristocracy. Eighteenth-century romantic comedy naturalizes a similar solution. Eschewing the pastoral resolution whereby the common partner is found to be the long-lost child of noble parents, a playwright like Marivaux induces his noble characters to choose their partners on the basis of personal qualities rather than birth. This is often a long process, requiring the major characters to overcome a pride instilled by society's class-consciousness, but even when the supposedly plain partner turns out to be a disguised nobleman, the stress is laid on his personal qualities. Attention is thus drawn to the insufficiency of birth as a basis for societal organization, thus paving the way for the revolutionary use of romantic comedy in the works of a Beaumarchais—the most direct link between eighteenth-century romantic comedy and musical theater.

Now, the fairy tale musical is hardly so open regarding its social project, but its methods are a combination of those used by the fairy tale and by romantic comedy. As we enter the movie theater we carry with us a bevy of personal problems, with financial concerns no doubt figuring strongly among them (to be sure, these problems were even more pressing during the depression, but given the universality of such difficulties it would make little sense to expect depression films alone to reflect them). The fairy tale musical regularly recognizes these financial concerns right at the beginning of the film. Maurice wants his pay, Marshovia needs to keep its rich princess (*The Merry Widow*), Dorothy is threatened by a combination of the sheriff's power and Miss Gulch's money (*The Wizard of Oz*), Fred Astaire is after Lucille Bremer's money (*Yolanda and the Thief*), Gene Kelly is broke (*An American in Paris*), the mailroom is no career (*How to Succeed in Business*), and so forth. Faced with a commoner in an aristocratic world, a man without money in a world where only money talks, in short a man like us with little economic security or future, the fairy tale musical has but one choice: to redefine the text's economics in such a way that success can be offered both to the deficient character and to the film's audience. The plot must so organize things that initial concern for birth or fortune becomes secondary to a skill which the postulant character possesses. For Fred Astaire this skill is dancing ability, for Nelson Eddy it is an appealing voice, for Maurice Chevalier it is that well known Gallic charm (read s-e-x). Indeed, the last words of Mamoulian's film, uttered by the Macbeth-like witches who appear intermittently throughout the film weaving their tapestry, provide the clue to *Love Me Tonight*'s politics as well as a description of the now completed tapestry on which the film ends: "Once upon a time there was a Princess and a Prince Charming, who was not a Prince, but who was charming . . . and they lived happily ever after."

Used in a figurative sense throughout the fairy tale tradition, the term "Prince Charming" only here comes into sharp focus. During the age of the epic, from Homer to the late Renaissance, nouns have a special force because they, like the level of an individual's birth, permit us to predict with certainty the characteristics and actions of individuals. From the Bible's identification of the Philistines with ungodliness to the seventeenth century's linking of the *honnête homme* and noble birth, aristocratic and epic practices concur in subordinating all other parts of speech to the noun, all other activities or characteristics to birth, as source of national, religious, or class identity. With the eighteenth century this system begins to be undermined, not only in literature but in social life as well. Aristocrats become villains, commoners become heroes, verbs and adjectives begin to replace nouns as predictors of value, fortune, and eventually station. One is no longer "Master" by birth, but more and more by achievement. It is during this period, from the late seventeenth century to the mid-nineteenth, that our most popular fairy tales reach print, and with them the magical notion of "Prince Charming," the one who can solve all our problems, who alone is an adequate mate. The success of the term can no doubt be laid to

its delicious ambiguity. A prince who is charming? A charmer who is a prince? The old, epic, solution would have been to interpret the charm as derivative of the title. All princes are charming; this man is a prince; therefore this man is charming. The new solution, the one operative throughout the fairy tale musical tradition, reverses the syllogism quite exactly: All charmers are "princes"; this man is charming; therefore this man is a "prince." A Prince, in the same sense that we now say "a Prince among men." As the best at what he does (swatting home runs), Babe Ruth merits a title, and so it was that the Babe became the "Sultan of Swat." As the best in his class, Maurice merits one as well. He is Prince Charming, that is Prince of charm, that is Prince *because* of his charm. As such he is part of the new aristocracy created by the eighteenth century, according to which nouns and adjectives are now subservient to verbs and adverbs. Noble is who nobly does.

Now since charm is primarily a sexual attribute, associated with the magic of courtship (i.e., the ability to induce another to share one's own desires), the sliding from an emphasis on money or birth to an emphasis on charm is easily attached to the musical's primary interest in forming couples. A basic moment in the fairy tale musical is thus that moment when the financial or governmental plot dissolves into a love plot. Certainly the extraordinary success enjoyed by Lehar's *The Merry Widow* comes in part from its overt and immediate subordination of diplomacy to courtship. What's more, Lehar's play provides a model for the musical by defining charm in a musical fashion. Danilo is charming because of his ability to dance (just as Fred Astaire's charm is always lost on Ginger Rogers until they dance together, or Gene Kelly's wooing of Leslie Caron in *An American in Paris* is unsuccessful until they dance together by the Seine). Whatever the source of the commoner's charm—fancy footwork, a way with a tune, or simply sexual prowess—the refusal of the prospective partner to fall immediately prey remains a necessary plot device. Not only to whet the spectator's appetite, but especially to transfer interest from one problem (the monetary one) to another (the romantic one), resistance must be strong. In this way the plot's conclusion will no longer correspond to the plot's inception, yet the conclusion will be acceptable to the audience, because it will solve the only problem which the audience has taken to heart. Perhaps the French are right to call entertainment "diversion" (*divertissement*), given that popular entertainment, like the fairy tale musical, spends so much of its energy engaging the audience's attention on the basis of real world problems and then diverting that attention and energy to problems of its own choosing, problems which serve its own ideology.

"Charm is the greatest gift in the world. If you have it, you don't need to have anything else; if you don't have it, it doesn't matter what else you have." This conclusion (quoted by John Kobal from James Barrie, author of *Peter Pan*!)[4] is precisely the goal to which the musical must bend the spectator, thus erasing the importance of money (society's value, which the spectator can't have) and substituting that of charm (Hollywood's value, which the audience can enjoy for the price of admission, and no doubt even become convinced that they possess themselves). Queen for a day, King for a night—such is the musical's ideological program.

Indeed, the ending of *Love Me Tonight* not only corresponds to the early transfer of allegiance from monetary to amorous matters, but through the culminating treatment of pastoral imagery it also symbolizes that transfer of interest. From their very first meeting, tailor Maurice and Princess Jeanette have inhabited a world of conventional pastoral imagery opposing the animals of the country to the mechanized ways of the city. When Maurice first sights Jeanette he is trying to repair his motor car, while she is having trouble with the horse pulling her cart. Later, the horses of the hunt will be implicitly opposed to the methods of mechanical modernism through the explicit use of fast motion and then of slow motion photography. After Maurice has definitely won Jeanette's heart thanks to his charm, but seemingly lost her hand forever on account of a forced admission of his lowly profession (the passed-along song "The Son of a Gun is Nothing but a Tailor" echoing the passing along of "Isn't it Romantic" at the film's opening), Maurice decides to leave the palace and return to his lowly life as a tailor. Recognizing *in extremis* the force of her love, Princess Jeanette takes out after Maurice, to the strains of their "Love Me Tonight" duet. With Maurice on the iron horse and Jeanette urging her country horse on, we spectators recognize the extent to which this final race, simultaneously echoing Griffith's last minute rescues and

Lubitsch's "Beyond the Blue Horizon" number, represents a competition between city and country values. Successful in her race against progress, Princess Jeanette thus wins the right to keep her lover in her never-never land where money is no object. Implicitly accepting the credentials established by his charm, the Princess is thus proclaiming her right to choose a mate according to personal needs rather than society's conventions. Not only is Maurice-the-tailor's monetary claim forgotten, along with his common origins, but the victory of meat horse over iron horse (as L. Frank Baum would have said) clearly proclaims the film's proposition that pastoral solutions alone are worthwhile and effective.

That Princess Jeanette should stop Maurice's train on the frontier between the magical palace-land and a mundane urban destination reminds us of the importance of Ruritanian insularity in the fairy tale musical. Whether we go to Graustark, to a resort, or to a fancy hotel, we must be insulated from the outside world in order for the fairy tale musical to work its magic on the spectator. Only in the closed confines of a tiny German principality (like those popularized by Offenbach, Lehar, and the operetta tradition in general), an ocean liner, or the literary Paris of yesteryear, can the old European norm of birth, gentility, and unquestioned riches be successfully combined with the American ideal of liberty, individual prowess, and personal charm. The fairy tale world must be a utopia, but in order for that utopia to have substance it must be a limited realm, one seemingly cut off from the outer, evil world, accessible only through the magical action of

song, love, and belief. Romance has always postulated this special kingdom, from the forest of Brocéliande into which Arthur's knights once wandered, to the realms of Oz, Pan, and Seven dwarfs. What distinguishes this special romance kingdom is the impression it offers that here the action of a single powerful and benevolent individual—or the action of a single loving couple—can make a difference for the entire kingdom and for all time. Ruritania is in a sense the American dream of democratic autocracy, of benevolent despotism. It is that land, free from material concerns, where charm can indeed replace money as society's standard.

Sex as Battle

Though it had an enormous effect on the development of the fairy tale musical, the sophisticated approach whereby sexual attraction is recognized as sexual attraction is hardly the rule in the history of American filmmaking. Always identified with Europe (and especially with Lubitsch and Chevalier), the more or less overt treatment of sexual energy thrived only during the final years of Prohibition, as if the forbidding of one pleasure triggered the surfacing of another. Indeed, the history of American popular entertainment may be seen in part as a series of compensatory reactions. Outlaw sex as a subject for adolescent conversation? Turn to couple dancing as replacement. Outlaw couple dancing because of its connections with sexual activity (as in the Protestant South)? Invest religious vocabulary with strong sexual overtones (as in the hymns of that same Protestant South). The facts of life are such that certain processes, certain activities never disappear, but are only displaced to less conspicuous, less overt events (which, by virtue of the very fact that they are a displaced version of something else, retain a symbolic quality). This process is a never-ending one, active in all countries at all times, but particularly salient in the United States, where legislation of morality is the rule. With the doctrine of separation between Church and State requiring displacement of religious law and doctrine onto the more legislatable moral law, that overriding moral law in turn triggers the displacement of innumerable prohibited activities or subjects onto less offensive simulacra. The extent to which the development of the fairy tale musical recapitulates this process is striking. Until 1934 Hollywood enjoyed a nearly European freedom in its choice of subjects, treatments, dialogue, etc. Indeed, this freedom was so liberally exercised that conservative elements among the early thirties' public began to give voice to their concerns. Fearful as always that it might lose part of its audience, Hollywood responded by appointing Joseph Breen to the Hays Office of the Motion Picture Producers and Distributors Association. Supported by the newly formed Catholic Legion of Decency, Breen immediately set to work strengthening and enforcing Hollywood's self-applied code: crime doesn't pay, love is supreme while sex is absent, the sanctity of marriage is absolute and never violated, all married couples sleep in twin beds, even the term "sex" is outlawed. The power of the Breen office was extraordinary. Every script had to be submitted for review; "suggested" changes were in fact mandatory. The impact of the reinforced Code was all the more obvious given the freedom which European countries enjoyed. Even Hollywood films, when made for another market, were subject to far less control. Take the case of Chevalier's last American film in the thirties, *Folies-Bergère* (1935). In the French version of the film (*L'homme des Folies-bergère*) the topless style of the famous cabaret was revealed for all to admire. The American version, however, depicted an oddly sobered Folies-Bergère, where Ziegfeld-like costumes covered all. Titillation reached its height when New York audiences were promised a look at the French version of the film. The dialogue was in French, all right, but the stage scenes from an American copy had been substituted for the more risqué French version!

The common American habit of forbidding public exposure of human sexual functions or the sexually marked parts of the body has a number of direct repercussions pertinent to the development of the musical. First, the European country most directly associated with the libertinism banned in America—France—receives the lion's share of the interest not only in the fairy tale musical (either through location, casting, or language) but in American mythology as a whole. Second, the energy which society refuses to let us invest openly in sexuality is transferred to a related concern, courtship, which must thus simultaneously stand for, cover over, and lead to the sexual source of its energy. Finally, and most important for the fairy tale musical, society's unwillingness to recognize openly the importance of sexuality leads to a transfer of sexual attraction to other types of attraction. In particular, two other types of attraction stand out: fascination with violence, mystery, and banditry, and a tendency to represent the process of courtship through the energy, repartee, and adversary relationships associated with battle. Identification of sex with battle will be covered in the present section, while the final section of this chapter will treat the sublimation of sexual energy onto the excitement of adventure.

From the very beginning of the Lubitsch-Chevalier-MacDonald films at Paramount, there can be little doubt about the source of the audience's fascination. The plot's energy, and thus our attention, clearly derive from a desire which is overtly sexual. From the start of *The Love Parade*, for example, the setting, the language, *and* the morals are defined as French. As the consummate Frenchman of the early sound period, Maurice Chevalier easily seduces us into sharing his mores: pleasure first, remorse never. Faithful not even to his mistress, but only to (sexual) pleasure, Chevalier leaves little doubt about the nature of his activities. Not content with verbal implication of the nature of Chevalier's activities, Lubitsch shows Maurice fastening the dress of the woman whose husband has just accused her of infidelity. Now, we could take this activity to be scurrilous, reprehensible, morally indefensible; we could read Chevalier through the eyes of a D.W. Griffith. However, Lubitsch makes such a reading virtually impossible. In melodrama infidelity may be the highest sin, but in comedy the most unpardonable sin is being ludicrous. The girl's husband at the beginning of *The Love Parade* unconsciously makes us laugh *at* him, while Chevalier is all the time inducing us to laugh *with* him. The rhetorical strategy of the opening scene thus prohibits anything but an identification with the enjoyment of (sexual) pleasure. Even if we were to miss this point, however, MacDonald's interpretation of this first scene would bring it home. When she reads the minister's report on Chevalier's activities she reveals an intense and personal fascination which draws us in to a close-up revealing the surfacing of her repressed desire. Instead of punishing him, she rushes out to primp, thus initiating the thematic thrust of the film whereby each expected punishment is turned through sexual desire into a continuation of the forbidden pleasure (just as the audience, who know that this infidelity stuff is hardly to be recommended, are not punished but rewarded with more for their fascination with sex). Drawn in by the naughtiness of France, drawn on by the pleasure to be found in naughtiness, we are directly identified with the *id*, which pushes couples on to mating. More or less the same configuration is to be found in all those early films where sex is still an overt concern of the musical. The first time he sees MacDonald in *Love Me Tonight*, Chevalier shocks her with a rendition of "Mimi," ending with the extraordinarily direct "I'd love to have a little son of a Mimi by and by." The rest of the film remains under the sign of this confrontation—especially the long sequence in which Chevalier as tailor undresses, measures, and in general visually appreciates the semi-dressed MacDonald. Borrowed from *Monte Carlo*, where Jack Buchanan as MacDonald's hairdresser enjoys the special rights of the professional to manipulate parts of her body, the tailoring scenes go as far as it was possible to go (until recently) in audience titillation. Energized by the illicit, the sex-as-sex films which we owe mainly to Paramount labor very hard to deliver conclusions which correspond to the sexual nature of our and the characters' desires.

It is precisely in the domain of audience interest and energy that the Astaire/Rogers films differ most notably from their predecessors. Though their first film together acknowledges its precode status and thus its debt to the sex-as-sex approach (primarily through Ginger's number "Music makes me do the things I never should do," which serves as catalyst to the Dolores Del Rio-Gene Raymond love affair and thus to the film's entire narrative), and though they meet in their first starring film (*The Gay Divorcee*) when Ginger's dress is caught in a trunk, thus revealing her legs in typical MacDonald style, neither of these films focuses on the sexual potential of its opening scenes to propel the plot forward. Instead, from their earliest films on, the energy of the Astaire/Rogers RKO series is derived from an entirely different source. Typically, the initial contact between the two simultaneously gives Ginger a reason to fall in love with Fred *and* good cause to despise him. He is suave, talented, different from other men, but at the same time self-satisfied, flippant, conceited, bordering on disrespectful.

In *The Gay Divorcee*, Astaire comes to the rescue of an embarrassed Rogers who has caught her dress while closing a trunk. Now, the romantic solution to this plight would have Astaire neatly and in a gentlemanly manner free the Princess from the grasp of the monster. She would be eternally grateful, but so that the plot would not end there she would have an old-fashioned father who has vowed never to marry his daughter to anyone short of a Prince. Up to Astaire to prove his mettle or somehow to come up with noble birth. But ninety minutes is a long time to sustain such a banal plot, so a pair of bonehead comics would probably be thrown in for good measure. Such a recipe, always avoided in the Astaire/Rogers films, is scrupulously followed in *Damsel in Distress* (1937), Astaire's only infidelity to Rogers during the late thirties. If *Damsel in Distress* seems lifeless by comparison, it is precisely because Astaire's relationship with Joan Fontaine lacks a primary component of his interaction with Rogers. The way in which Astaire acquits himself of the rescue in *The Gay Divorcee* is indicative of his relationship to Rogers throughout the entire series: he botches the job, tears the dress, and has to lend her his raincoat to cover her shame. In short, while rescuing the maiden, while winning her heart, this Prince acts in a way which is alarming, not to say harming, and yet for all that disarming. Astaire's bumbling thus inaugurates the twin, coinciding plot lines: the process by which he falls in love initiates the process whereby Rogers falls in hate. Astaire's very attraction for Rogers is identified with Rogers's negative attraction for Astaire. No recalcitrant father here, therefore, since the obstacle to their union is built into their relationship. The initial equation is written in such a way that any increase in Astaire's attention only produces an increase in Rogers's rejection. Astaire and Rogers are always adults, old enough to make their own decisions; they are thus old enough, in typical romantic comedy style, to provide their own obstacles.

The energy toward union (identified with Astaire's overt desire to woo Rogers) is thus matched by an energy against union (Rogers's constant tendency to refuse, to quarrel, to challenge, to oppose), the two born together out of the same event. When in *The Gay Divorcee* Astaire finally finds his lost Princess he does it in characteristic fashion—he runs into her with his car. Reunion must always be synonymous with—and the cause of—separation, lest the plot itself die and with it the text. Again in *Top Hat* the initial meeting of the pair provides the opportunity for their initial quarrel; no wonder, since Astaire's dancing has awakened Rogers out of a deep sleep (other couples meet in their dreams; only Astaire and Rogers interrupt dreams for wide-awake quarrels). In *Roberta*, Astaire unmasks Rogers from their very first meeting, for he alone recognizes the aristocratic Scharwenka as Lizzie from back home—the girl next door. Symbolic of their relationship throughout the series, this combination of Rogers's masquerading and Astaire's ability to see through her mask explains the approach-avoidance relationship between the two. Posing as a Countess who is above common sensations like love, Rogers has a vested interest in keeping secret her true identity—and her hidden desires. Her animosity toward Astaire, and not just in this film, derives from his ability to bring out the very attributes and desires which she would conceal. In *Swing Time* Astaire nearly causes Rogers

to lose her job as a dancing teacher. In *Shall We Dance* it is Astaire's turn to masquerade (as a Russian) and Rogers' turn to unmask him mercilessly. *Carefree*'s plot is set in motion when Rogers chances to overhear Astaire's evaluation of her as just another dizzy female. Throughout the series this approach-avoidance relationship is the one irreplaceable aspect of the Astaire-Rogers relationship.

Not yet established as a principle in *Flying Down to Rio*, the sex-as-battle approach comes into its own in *The Gay Divorcee*, where the animosity created by the dress-tearing episode risks being overwhelmed by the romance of the "Night and Day" dance until, at the culmination of this dance, Astaire speaks the magic sentence which identifies him (Rogers mistakenly thinks) as the professional correspondent in her divorce. Just as she is about to be eternally bound to him by the chains of love, a new misunderstanding tears them asunder. That their battle is here somehow mysteriously to be identified with their love is elegantly implied by the ambiguous dialogue:

> Mimi (Rogers): You? You?
> Guy (Astaire): Me? Why, yes, of course it is.
> Mimi: So you're the man I've been waiting for.
> Guy: None other.
> Mimi: I'll be waiting for you in my room, 216. At midnight.

Astaire's nocturnal visit to Rogers's room is thus for him an assignation, a tryst, while for her it is a business proposition, a legal necessity for her divorce proceedings, and a good reason to cancel all the warm feelings developed for Astaire in the previous scenes.

For all the opposition between Astaire and Rogers in *The Gay Divorcee*, however, it is not until the next film, *Roberta*, that their quarreling becomes the source of one of their dance routines. Much has been written of the glorious Astaire/Rogers romantic dances—"Night and Day," "Cheek to Cheek," "Change Partners"[5]— yet for all their charm and plot functionality, these dances are relatively standard numbers in the dance musical. From *The Merry Widow* to *The Boy Friend* and beyond, dance has often been used as a culmination, as celebration of a love affair. Far rarer in the history of the musical is the generation of dance out of bickering. More than the romantic dance, it is the challenge dance that constitutes the Astaire/Rogers trademark—the dance that grows out of difference, out of quarreling, even out of mutual insults, and which during the course of dancing bends that opposition and its energy toward concerted effort and thus toward a preliminary model of union, later developed in the conclusive romantic dance. Already in *Roberta*'s "I'll Be Hard to Handle" we find Astaire and Rogers arguing into a dance, which overtly reflects in its steps and structure the argumentative nature of the couple's relationship.

Top Hat's "Isn't It a Lovely Day to Be Caught in the Rain" makes the pattern if anything still clearer. Finding Rogers taking shelter from the rain in a bandstand, Astaire breaks into song, after explaining that showers are nothing more than the courtship of the clouds. She begins to beat the rhythm with her cane. He hops up and walks lightly in time around the stage formed by the bandstand. As if mocking him, she falls into step behind him, imitating his every step, even as the walking turns to a shuffle and then to increasingly complicated tap breaks. Finally, they touch; he takes her into his able arms and they whirl around their isolated stage like a pair of courting clouds riding the same wind. Not a word has been spoken, yet the magic of dance has brought their love along as no dialogue ever could. With other couples such a development would imply the burying of the hatchet and the triumph of a purely romantic relationship. With Astaire and Rogers, however, quite a different meaning is to be gleaned: "Isn't It a Lovely Day to Be Caught in the Rain" establishes not the demise of quarreling, but rather the continuity of conflict and cooperation. At first Ginger is mocking; her moves are dictated by Fred's and thus her eyes must constantly be upon him (how important their eyes are for retaining narrative content in dances which are otherwise utterly devoid of such a lowly concern). As the interlude progresses, however, this challenge dance regains its equilibrium. Sequential similarity becomes simultaneous similarity, with each dancer seemingly anticipating the other's moves, or simply responding in similar fashion to the music. Now their gazes are symmetrical; first toward each other, then apart, now up, now down. Finally they merge into a single whirling form—the union which grows out of conflict.

Again and again this technique is repeated in the Astaire/Rogers canon. "Let Yourself Go" (*Follow the Fleet*) doesn't really take off until the dancers start to insult each other. In the same film, "I'm

Putting All My Eggs in One Basket" begins without character but soon picks up the pace—and the interest—as it turns into a dance floor battle built on missed steps. *Shall We Dance* also doubles our pleasure in the adversary dance line. First the two arch enemies (read future mates) are forced to dance together in front of a night-club audience. Neither can refuse and neither is about to be out-danced by this particular partner. Thus from ballet to rock and from ballroom to jazz, "They All Laughed" slides from one challenge to another. Never was a fight so rhythmical, so varied, and so beautiful to watch. And not surprisingly our pleasure seems to rub off on the dancers. Angry at first, intent on upstaging a rival, they slowly begin to take to what they're doing. Slipping from scowls to smiles, and from there to a broad grin, they seem more surprised than anyone that fighting could possibly be so much fun. Fred and Ginger are great dancers, make no mistake, but the reason why their dancing is so effective is that they don't forget to be actors as well. Later in the same film the challenge technique is translated into music and words. "You say eether and I say eyether," the lyrics begin, and until the final duet the song is a non-stop challenge song. (Since Astaire and Rogers the challenge dance has never again been used with the same effectiveness, but the challenge song returns regularly, and successfully, as in *Annie Get Your Gun*'s "I Can Do Anything Better than You" or *Pajama Game*'s "There Once Was a Man".) In *Carefree*, Rogers has to blackmail Astaire into doing the "Yam" with her. In plot and dance alike, Astaire and Rogers are magnets. As one advances, the other re-

treats by virtue of the very magnetic force invested in them. Each time one moves, the other responds, backing away until, suddenly, one partner whirls around, reverses polarity, and sticks with all that same magnetic force to the other.

The progression of the Astaire/Rogers films thus depends on the simultaneous growth of their quarreling and of their love, with that ambiguous growth expressed through the dance. So formulaic does the pattern become that by *Top Hat* a routine is established which is rarely varied throughout the remainder of the series. The accompanying table clearly reveals the growth of this pattern through *Flying Down to Rio*, *The Gay Divorcee*, and *Roberta*, to *Top Hat*, the last of the series to use a concluding new dance number simultaneously as a celebration of the couple's union and an invitation to the audience to join them in that union. After *Top Hat* we note a growing tendency to multiply the adversary numbers, to the point where *Swing Time* and *Shall We Dance* have three apiece, carefully balanced between straight challenge, insult, or comedy dances and ironic songs or satiric routines. Though not the source of a memorable dance, a duet like "A Fine Romance" clearly perpetuates the quarrelsome, ironic tone associated with the challenge dances. Its syncopation and constant accented drops contrast sharply with Kern's folk and romantic numbers (e.g., "An Old-Fashioned Wife," "The Song is You," "All the Things You Are," "I'm Old-Fashioned," "All through the Day"). With the lovers and their affair compared to such delights as two old fogies who need crutches and yesterday's mashed potatoes, it is hardly surprising

	Astaire or Rogers alone (song stressed)	FA & GR—challenge dance (or ironic song)	FA—specialty number (dance stressed)	FA & GR—romantic dance	FA & GR—new dance
Flying Down to Rio 1933	1. Music Makes Me-GR		3. Flying Down to Rio		2. Carioca
Gay Divorcee 1934	2. Needle in a Hay-stack		1. Don't Let It Bother You	3. Night and Day	4. Continental
Roberta 1935	1. Let's Begin	2. I'll Be Hard To Handle	3. I Won't Dance		
Top Hat 1935	1. No Strings	2. Isn't This A Lovely Day To Be Caught in the Rain	3. Top Hat, White Tie and Tails	4. Cheek to Cheek	5. Piccolino
Follow the Fleet 1936	1. We Saw the Sea 2. Let Yourself Go-GR	3. Let Yourself Go-dance contest 6. I'm Puttin' All My Eggs in One Basket	4. I'd Rather Lead a Band 5. (Let Yourself Go-GR bicarbonate reprise)	7. Let's Face the Music and Dance	
Swing Time 1936		1. Pick Yourself Up 2. The Way You Look Tonight 4. A Fine Romance	5. Bojangles of Harlem	3. Waltz in Swing Time 6. Never Gonna Dance	
Shall We Dance 1937	1. Beginner's Luck	3. Walking the Dog 4. They All Laughed 5. Let's Call the Whole Thing Off	2. Slap That Bass	6. They Can't Take That Away From Me (sung only)	
Carefree 1938		3. The Yam	1. Since They Turned 'Loch Lomond' in-to Swing (golf dance)	2. I Used to Be Color-Blind 4. Change Partners	

Even in his early years, in vaudeville routines with his sister
Adele, Fred Astaire was already characterized by the top hat,
an enduring mark of his ties to the fairy tale tradition,
exemplified in a 1934 *Top Hat* routine.

[a = UW, b = MOMA]

that a long list of activities is given as preferable to love—things like Jello, cactus plants, and playing bridge with old maiden aunts. The very existence of a song like this one is a testimony to the importance accorded by production personnel to the couple's skirmishing.

Whereas most musicals in the thirties either borrowed pre-existent music or produced new music for a yet-to-be-determined cast, the music for RKO's Astaire/Rogers efforts, from *Top Hat* to *Carefree*, was commissioned, developed, and tailored for the Astaire/Rogers team. Thus the Irving Berlin score and lyrics for *Top Hat, Follow the Fleet,* and *Carefree,* the Kern score (with lyrics by Dorothy Fields) for *Swing Time,* and the Gershwin numbers for *Shall We Dance* were all created in careful collaboration with the studio, each as a new episode in a by now clearly defined story. One effect of this close collaboration is a trim sense of integration, a reduction of distance between narrative and number (except in Astaire's specialty dances) to the point where the dance and song numbers *are* narrative. (It is interesting to note, by contrast, that in the last two Astaire/Rogers films—*The Story of Vernon and Irene Castle* and *The Barkleys of Broadway*—the notion of integration tends to disappear along with the challenge dance. The dances that occupy the challenge dance slot in these two films take for granted a married couple's togetherness instead of creating that union out of conflict. "Waiting for the Robert E. Lee," "Too Much Mustard," "Bouncin' the Blues," and "My One and Only Highland Fling" are thus disappointing in their inability to embody a quarrelsome relationship which is otherwise hardly absent from the couple's last films—especially *Barkleys.*) The other important effect of this continual collaboration is the increased emphasis on the quarrelsome relationship between the two principals: romantic songs fit anywhere, but a number like "A Fine Romance" could only be written for two screwballs like Astaire and Rogers.

Indeed, it is hard not to draw the parallel between the antics of the Astaire/Rogers team and their equally quarrelsome counterparts in the exactly contemporary screwball comedy. From Gable and Colbert (*It Happened One Night*) or Barrymore and Lombard (*Twentieth Century*) in 1934, to Grant and Hepburn (*Holiday,* 1938; *Bringing Up Baby,* 1938; *Philadelphia Story,* 1940), the screwball comedy as a genre regularly focuses on a couple who attract us not so much by their romantic attachment but rather by the masking of their attraction for each other behind an antagonistic front. Some films are successful to the extent that the lead couple are successful lovers; these films succeed when the principals are effective opponents. Indeed, as Andrew Sarris has suggested, screwball comedies, like the Astaire/Rogers films, derive their energy from a displacement of sexual attraction necessitated by the 1934 tightening of the Code. When you remove sex from a sex comedy, it has to go somewhere; in many films of the period it reappears as adventure, but here it resurfaces as battle. Growing up alongside the non-musical screwball comedy, the Astaire/Rogers series clearly borrowed from *and* influenced the films of Hawks, Capra, and Cukor, not so much through image design (for the non-musical screwball comedy often presents a real America as a backdrop, even though the plots may be heavily stylized) but rather through antagonistic dialogue and especially through the characteristic plot construction whereby sexual energy is transmuted into quarreling and the progression of romantic attachment is made, paradoxically, to parallel the intensification of the conflict between the two would-be lovers. The current tendency to treat Hollywood genres as watertight compartments has obscured the relationship between the non-musical screwball comedy and the Astaire/Rogers series; the connection needs to be restored and the generic boundaries broken down.

In order to understand the workings of the Astaire/Rogers-screwball comedy couples, and thus the history of American film in the late thirties, it is essential to recognize the operation of two separate but related types of historical displacement. As posited by literary theoretician Northrop Frye, the term displacement refers to the historical process whereby the materials of myth are transferred over time to stories with increasingly realistic presentation. The original, mythical intentions are not entirely lost; they are simply disguised as plot patterns, as metaphoric configurations, as overall structures imbedded within the more and more realistic texts. Behind the Astaire/Rogers conflict, indeed behind the screwball tendency as a whole there lies, I would submit, a mythical event, one which all films must repress because of its unconventional nature, but nevertheless an origin which we can postulate by moving upstream from the severely repressed post-1934 era to the, by comparison, libertine 1929-33 period, and from there to

a posited source itself implied by a little-known 1930 film.

Rarely seen today because of the disfavor into which the revue has fallen, *Paramount on Parade* nevertheless boasts three sequences directed by Ernst Lubitsch. One of these, "The Real Origin of the 'Apache' Dance," provides a vision, albeit incomplete, of a certain 1930 evaluation of French morals and sexual practices. Returning home late one night with his wife (Evelyn Brent), Maurice Chevalier finds her surprisingly distant. Soon this cold shoulder turns into a full-fledged argument as Chevalier is blamed for flirting with another woman. Increased dialogue volume and rapidity of movement mark the transition from argument to quarrel and eventually to outright battle, as each strips the other, in turn, of a garment. Visibly violent at first, the strip-battle then moves off-screen as the camera tracks down to the couple's naked legs and the growing pile of clothes, to which are soon added the conclusive undergarments. The traditional connection between violence and sexuality, recognized in Western culture at least since epic heroes took to wedding the daughters of conquered kings, is here condensed into a single extremely significant scene. Now, the "Apache" is a dance, a conflictual, violent affair reputed to be representative of the twin French traits of overt interest in sexuality and a tendency toward violent male domination. Dancing, as seen through the model of the "Apache," is thus thinly disguised sex, and that sex is defined as the product of conflict. Fighting is not opposed to sexual activity, according to this myth, it *is* sexual activity. Conflict produces rhythmic quarreling (expressed simultaneously as dance and as stripping), which fades imperceptibly into sexual activity.

Now the Chevalier-Lubitsch sequence from *Paramount on Parade* of course does not present this myth directly, but it alludes to it in such a nearly undisplaced fashion as to leave little doubt about the nature of the original of which this is a displacement. Indeed, through his connection to libertine scenes such as this, the very presence of Chevalier for five years served to suggest the sexual overtones of dance and song fairly clearly to American audiences. From *The Love Parade* to *The Merry Widow*, Chevalier's character makes no bones about what it is he is after. As we move through the thirties, however, the sexual implications of courtship recede further and further into the background, while at the same time they are increasingly projected onto quarrelsome behavior, itself less and less physical and increasingly verbal. From Chevalier we pass to the domineering but self-restrained Gable of *It Happened One Night* or *San Francisco*, and from there to Astaire and his tendency to channel all violent emotions into rhythm and art, whence we move to Cary Grant, the ultimate step in displacement from the physical to the verbal and from overt sexuality to symbolic spats with Hepburn and others. The farther we move from "The Real Origin of the 'Apache' Dance," the more we are in need of the notion of displacement to make sense of the identification of bickering with courtship. Though the linking of conflict to courtship may be presented in an increasingly "civilized" (i.e., repressed) fashion, it always harks back to the (mythical) identity of violence and sexuality. To say that the Production Code banishes the topic of sex is really only to say that after 1934 sex appears on a different level—disguised, displaced, dislocated, but certainly not to be discounted. As a model for historical investigation, the notion of displacement has received too little attention; without it, numerous aspects of American film history are destined to remain isolated from a larger context and thus only partially understood.

A second type of displacement is clearly operative in the Astaire/Rogers films. If we once again move upstream from the naturalized, quasi-realistic settings of most recent fairy tale musicals (*Hair, On a Clear Day, Sweet Charity*, etc.) back toward the aristocratic but American hangouts preferred during the forties and late thirties (resorts, country clubs, night clubs, and so forth) to the European palaces of the early sound years, and then project a source beyond them, we find ourselves speculating about the royal protagonists of operetta, eighteenth-century comedy, and the Renaissance pastoral, or even the gods identified with classical mythology. Indeed, so many classical myths begin with a quarrel between Jupiter (Zeus) and his mate Juno—a quarrel projected onto the created world as chaos, divisiveness, and disorder—that a preliminary connection between aristocratic disorder and divine contentiousness, while surprising, may not be entirely out of order. According to this interpretation, the fairy tale couple always retain something of the divine nature from which they descend. From kingdom to palace to liner to resort to business office there is created a direct line, each somehow calling forth memories of the previous more exalted realms. Held together by the theme of government, of restoring order to a chaotic situation, all these films seem implicitly to refer back to the divine order symbolized by the peaceful union of the divine couple. For disorder in the realm and disorder in the couple are implicitly equated throughout the tradition, with the solution to both branches of the plot traditionally arriving simultaneously and by the same sequence of actions.

The process of displacement moves us from the stage operetta's imaginary Ruritania or extremely stylized middle-European kingdom to the exotic but real cities and watering spots of Western Europe, and from there to the less romantic but no less aristocratic resorts of the Western Hemisphere, and finally to the infinitely more prosaic yet still formally similar business and professional world. The history of the fairy tale musical thus constitutes a fall by steps from a divine origin. If the history as a whole represents a fall, however, individual texts take on a compensatory redemptive function. Typically beginning close to home, fairy tale musicals regularly transport the spectator to a place which is at the same time farther from our reality and closer to the divine/royal origins of the fairy tale plot. Musicals which start in Paris end up in a mythical castle; those which start in New York typically travel to Paris; those which start in the hinterlands often conclude in New York. Faced by the Manifest Destiny of the fairy tale musical's democratization, each film reverses that displacement, adopting a nostalgia for a lost world of divine origins as its structural model. This interlocking of the structure of individual films and the destiny of entire genres is far from an isolated case. Unexploited as a model of historical understanding, the process of textual compensation for a genre's fall into history deserves increased attention by critics and historians alike.

A second method of compensating for the fall from divine to royal to aristocratic to rich to middle-class is borrowed directly from the eighteenth century, whence cometh the operetta form on which the fairy tale musical is based: as the notion of innate value acquired by birth recedes into the distance, it is replaced by the more mobile notion of value acquired through individual action. Now, as we have seen, this sliding from "noble" to "common" values is mediated throughout the fairy tale musical tradition by the ambiguous notion of charm. Though not a Prince by birth, the man who is charming finds the locked doors of social class opened for him. Seen in this light, the notion of charm serves as one half of a tandem which works to put away, to conceal the very real barriers of money and class. The basic fairy tale musical configuration opposes a commoner to a potential mate of far higher social class, thus establishing as a strong theme the problem of class and/or riches. The pastoral solution, inherited by the operetta and passed on to a certain class of films, simply reveals the commoner actually to be of noble birth, thus erasing the problem, and rendering the class-oriented thematics superfluous. The fairy tale musical solution is at the same time more radical and more perverse. On the one hand, charm is treated as the universal social solvent, dissolving away all class barriers. On the other hand, the very real differences between the two mates are expressed as antagonistic behavior, with the resolution of their conflict being taken for the resolution of their differences. The second solution conceals the fact that while quarrels may have been created by difference, the typical resolution of a quarrel rarely involves solution of those differences, but rather transmutation of the quarreling energy into courtship energy, as in the "Apache." The first solution neglects to recognize that "charm" is elevated by the new mass media into the basis for a new aristocracy, a cult of stardom nearly equivalent to a new divinity.

In fact, even in the notion of charm there is a progression parallel to class-oriented displacement. Chevalier's charm derives directly from his foreignness; we can admire it, but we can't quite have it. Likewise for the talent of the many highly trained opera stars borrowed by Hollywood during the early years of sound film. With Astaire a radically new relationship to the audience is born. Sure, we can't dance like Fred Astaire, but then most of the steps aren't that hard, if you take them one by one. Maybe if we only had the right teacher. And so were born a line of Fred Astaire Dance Studios, a business dedicated to the proposition that we can be equal to Fred—or at least good enough to impress our own private Ginger. And the voice, well, that's no problem. I mean, the man has no voice. He just sort of talks those songs with little more training and talent than I do. Why, every time I sing them or play them on my piano I can somehow see myself whirling around those gorgeous sets. I

can convince myself I'm Fred Astaire talking his songs or Bing Crosby or even Frank Sinatra because they don't *seem* to be doing anything more than I do when I sing. Whatever training they have, they have hidden it; however they may differ from me, they have labored to conceal that difference in a way that old Maurice just never could. As time goes by, the model of charm provided by the fairy tale musical comes closer and closer, until by the time of *Hair* (1979) I find movie-going strangely like looking in the mirror. Why, that guy from Oklahoma is no different from me. Sort of naive, but polite and concerned. If that's all that's needed then I've got what it takes. As displacement progresses, therefore, a process of compensation parallels it. The farther we fall from the divine, the regal, the more we are made to feel that we have access to a new kingdom, to the Hollywood world of stardom which is made to appear increasingly less distant.

Before we leave the Astaire/Rogers films it is important to take a close look at the way in which a single film as a unified whole handles the repression associated with the transfer of sexual energy onto quarreling. In many ways *Top Hat* is *the* quintessential Astaire/Rogers film. It is the only film to combine the finale introducing a new dance (characteristic of the first half of the series) with the challenge dance which would become the couple's hallmark. Typical in its unwillingness to reveal semi-clad bodies or stress sexual desire, *Top Hat* nevertheless engages the spectator in a journey into the forbidden, a detour around the obstacle of censorship. From the *fact* of infidelity present in earlier films, *Top Hat* seems dedicated to leading the spectator astray, inducing us to abandon society's conventional values in favor of the values which the genre proposes as a more pleasurable substitute.

From the very first, the relationship between Fred and Ginger is defined as an impossibility—as long as they both respect the conventional limitations for behavior within their society. When Fred awakens Ginger with his tapped rendition of "No Strings," she very properly complains not to the perpetrator of the evil deed but to the manager, the necessary intermediary provided by a society which prohibits individuals from conversing without prior introduction. Informed by phone that "a lady" desires to speak to him, Astaire's host and manager Edward Everett Horton heads downstairs to meet her because, as he tells Astaire in no uncertain terms, a lady simply does not come to a man's room alone at night. If society's strictures were respected, Horton would see the manager, who would, on behalf of an unidentified lady, request that he and his guests adhere to the hotel's policy of late evening quiet. Astaire and Rogers would never meet. *And that is the one thing that the spectator cannot accept.* Already in this first meeting, a basic principle of Hollywood is at work: oppose societal to entertainment conventions at a point when all spectators are bound (by the very desire to get their money's worth) to reject the societal conventions which under any other circumstances they would have espoused. In this way, through little sins, the spectator will eventually be won over to a life of crime, of utter rejection of society's principles in favor of entertainment's pleasures. So it

is, then, that we choose the unconventional but generically necessary solution of a nighttime bedroom meeting between unknowns. When Ginger gets so frustrated that she decides to take matters into her own hands she is not so much obeying her own inner impulse as she is adhering to the generic logic expressed in the audience's desire to arrange a nocturnal meeting of the two stars.

"Qui volerait un oeuf volerait un boeuf," as the French say. The road leads straight from petty theft to grand larceny. Though up to this point we have been unfaithful only in little things, our habits have been established. Romanced by Fred, finding him attractive enough to be worthy of quarreling with, Ginger soon learns—so she thinks—that Fred is none other than her best friend's husband. Now the comic misunderstanding, or *quid pro quo* (taking *quid* for *quo*, i.e., one thing for another), is one of the oldest devices of romantic comedy. At times permitting characters to play out forbidden desires, at other times blocking their desire, misunderstandings *always* serve to satisfy spectator desire—the desire, that is, for power. For the *quid pro quo* always leaves the characters in the dark while elevating the spectator to an all-knowing, all-powerful ironic position, thus giving the spectator the impression of sitting with the author and director in the manipulation of the characters. But this very illusion of power is part of Hollywood's gambit to subordinate us as spectators to its own narrative power. We think we gain power from our knowledge that Fred is not the man Ginger thinks; in fact this knowledge simply draws us in to a life of greater crime. While we know that Fred is not the husband of Ginger's best friend (married in fact to Edward Everett Horton), we delight increasingly in Ginger's willingness to be danced, romanced, and embraced by the forbidden Fred.

The effect of "Cheek to Cheek" depends to an unrecognized extent on our sense that Ginger and Fred are becoming lovers in spite of the taboo which Ginger feels. When we zoom in on a table next to the dance floor we find Ginger sitting with her best friend Madge (Helen Broderick). When Fred approaches, Madge suggests first that Ginger dance with him, and then that she hold her partner much closer. At first horrified that Madge would encourage her to get friendly with the man she believes to be Madge's husband, Ginger finally gets caught up by the music and dance and decides to let herself go. In so doing she once again responds not so much to her inner conscience as to the spectator's desires. While we have not yet reached the point of desiring the forbidden, we have begun to take immense pleasure in the quasi-illicit knowledge that Ginger believes her desires to be forbidden. What better and more innocent way to displace forbidden desire and thus get around the Code than to substitute for actual infidelity a character's belief that she is involved with an unfaithful husband (and at the wife's suggestion, at that). "Cheek to Cheek" derives its intensity from this sense that dance and song alike represent that miraculous moment when the search for pleasure has won out over the more conventional respect for morals.

For "Cheek to Cheek" is more than just a song, it is a hymn to pleasure.

Sung by Astaire against a religious hush (all diegetic noise is cut out), the song names its suit from the first two beats: "Heaven," Astaire sings, sliding from the attack of the first-beat A to the release of the second beat G as if he were sighing with pleasure, while the accompaniment marks a hymn-like progression from the sub-dominant to the tonic (IV-I). In this most complex of popular songs (the structure is a-a-b-c-a with lengths of 16-16-16-8-16 measures), the initial measure is repeated no less than nine times (measures 1-3-5 of each "a" section, with the lyric for measure 5 displaced to "heart beats"). Decidedly, the conventional religious notion of heaven is central to this song, yet the entire lyric delineates an alternative (non-religious) method for achieving heaven. Though each "a" section begins with "Heaven" and the accompanying IV-I cadence, the syncopation of this first measure paradoxically gives a preliminary feeling to a word expressing finality. Only at the end of the "a" section will melody and harmony alike settle on the tonic, and on an accented beat, this time with the more traditional popular music cadence (IV-V_7-I), with the lyric explaining the new source of the divine experience: "out together dancing, cheek to cheek." Whereas other songwriters would equate climbing a mountain and the experience of heaven (cf. Oscar Hammerstein II in *The Sound of Music*), Berlin makes reaching "the highest peak" nothing more than a rhyme and a foil for dancing "cheek to cheek." The tension and excitement are redoubled when Astaire, already alternating between piano and forte, suddenly belts out a second release rather than return to the

original sixteen-bar "a" section. "Dance with me, I want my arms about you. The charm about you will carry me through to"—and suddenly we are back to the now familiar, comfortable, and redefined "Heaven." Clearly reminiscent of one of George and Ira Gershwin's first and best known songs ("I'll build a Stairway to Paradise": "Let me tell you there are a lot of features/Of the dance that carry you through/The gates of Heaven"), this unexpected second bridge does indeed carry us through to that familiar heavenly song and dance material of the final section.

At the end of the song the orchestra swells and the entranced couple dance in long shot across a bridge and onto a patio where they are alone. As we cut in from extreme long shot to full shot, the sunburst floor pattern (rendered symmetrical in typical Astaire style by placement of the camera on the center line) seems at the same time to concentrate attention on the dancing couple at the center of the pattern and to turn them into another ornament in RKO's Van Nest Polglase set—more mobile than the others perhaps but still part of the set design, Fred's formal black and Ginger's feathery white picking up dominant patterns throughout. Now, as they dance alone, tap sounds are added, the music swells, then suddenly stops almost dead, inducing the dance into a sort of slow-motion ending. Their energy drained, they walk to the adjoining balcony and are about to kiss when Ginger is shocked to remember that this wonderful man, this partner of partners,

is married to her best friend. Amused at her ignorance and still warm with the afterglow of their glorious dance, we laugh at her moralistic reaction to his proposal, little dreaming of the shocking turnaround that Ginger has in store for us.

Within minutes Ginger's marriage to Beddini (Erik Rhodes) is announced. The shoe is now on the other foot. We have all along derived easy, innocent pleasure from our knowledge and Ginger's ignorance. We have been successful in keeping "clean" of any unauthorized desires by projecting them onto Ginger. Our generic desires have been fulfilled without challenging society's conventions, and yet because of Ginger's ignorance we have also tasted the tangier fruit of forbidden desire. She has crossed the line of illicit desire, we have not (and yet through our identification with her we have nevertheless had the thrill of that forbidden desire). Now all that has changed. True to the genre, we cannot avoid wanting Fred and Ginger back together, yet this time to want them back together is to desire, quite literally, the forbidden. While the concluding scenes are constantly played for comedy, even such light treatment cannot conceal the fact that we have as spectators entirely abandoned our allegiance to conventional morals. We have been led so far from the limits which we accept in our daily lives that when Fred and Ginger escape from pursuit on the lagoon, we are more than happy to watch them spend the evening together. The "Piccolino" number, clearly a climax, thus occurs at a point when both Astaire and Rogers believe that the other is married, and when we as audience still believe Rogers to be. This climactic dance

Magic moments in a magic dance—*Top Hat*'s "Cheek to Cheek."

[MOMA]

thus operates fully, according to a time-honored generic convention, as the consummation of a perfect romance. Yet that romance is at this point a strictly forbidden one. At first we reveled in the unconventional nature of the couple's initial encounters. Soon, we found ourselves delighting in Ginger's willingness to be courted by a man whom she believes to be married; we didn't desire the forbidden, but we desired Ginger's desiring the forbidden. Now we find ourselves not only encouraging adulterous activity, but actually openly celebrating the emotional consummation of an adulterous love affair.

From beginning to end, the conventions of society have been in conflict with those of the genre. From the moment when the graphic of a top hat behind the credits (already the Astaire trademark, and thus that of entertainment) turns into a real top hat on a terribly proper British Lord, the opposition is defined. When we enter the Thackeray Club seconds afterward the opposition gains substance. "Silence" the sign reads. And silence there is within the hallowed parlors of this ancient British institution. But musicals and silence cannot cohabit and so we soon find ourselves desiring if not a song at least a word, a sign of life. What we get is a volley of taps from Astaire, who thus reiterates his identification with a certain kind of life, a certain set of values. In a nearly self-conscious fashion the film constantly foregrounds the opposition developed in this opening scene, to the point where the entire film seems defined by an insistent set of paired dualities, with new pairings added regularly, but always without disturbing the overriding con-

trast between the conventions of society (as they are unfairly and self-servingly encapsulated in *Top Hat*) and those of the musical genre:

British	American
aristocrat	commoner
closed society	open society
silence	noise
formality	informality
repression	freedom
business	pleasure
legality	love

Nearly every move within the film serves to reinforce this set of oppositions. For example, the British aristocrats in the Thackeray Club are framed in such a way as to cut off their feet, as if the lower parts of the body, like noise, were somehow an evil which it is society's responsibility to destroy or at the very least conceal. When the camera reaches Astaire he is framed in this same footless fashion, but not for long; a slight pan reframes Astaire, this time including the feet which will later become synonymous first with noise and then with entertainment and love. Indeed, the film's strategy seems to be much like that of a salvation preacher: to use every possible device to move all right-thinking people, all those who still stand a chance of being saved, toward support of entertainment, love, and those faithful to them. At first Ginger is identified with the British aristocracy. Silence is what she wants, more than any other thing—until, that is, she takes a shine to tap-happy Fred. Even the spectator who hangs back, like Ginger unconvinced, eventually finds it impossible not to choose the conventions of a pleasurable genre over those of a repressive society, made to seem more so in order to lionize the products of Hollywood, those irreplaceable promoters of a pleasure which alone can induce us to forget our moral training in favor of a dance.

Sex as Adventure

Whatever the difference between the early thirties' recognition of sex as sex and the later thirties' representation of sex as battle, the musicals spawned by these two approaches nevertheless have much in common. Clearly conceived with a sophisticated audience in mind, these films abound in distantiation devices designed to remind and reassure the audience of their sophistication. From injokes, innuendo, and impertinent rhymes to intertextuality, implicit irony, and impish into-the-camera winks, the self-conscious fairy tale musical of the thirties uses every conceivable device to distinguish itself from a competing strain of more naive but equally successful fairy tale musicals. Aimed primarily at a female audience, this third approach, which developed alongside the sex-as-sex and sex-as-battle strategies throughout the decade, had its roots less in the stage musical than in the strong tendency in American films of the twenties to substitute violence, mystery, and banditry for sexuality.

The first two decades of the century saw a concerted effort to transfer to the screen the overt message of melodrama: live a clean life, neither smoke nor drink, frequent only those who look and believe like you, stand up for the truth, lend succor to children, the aged, and damsels in distress, and in the end you will be rewarded (with a mate who resembles you in every particular save sex). Villain after villain is undone, as their evil countenance, ungentlemanly manners, and foreign origins suggest they must be. Such a clearcut and unchanging system could hardly be expected to last forever. Built into dualistic systems like that of melodrama is the necessary similarity of all heroic figures. At first their righteousness is sufficient to attract and fix our attention, but after continued exposure to the same basic plot, with its stereotyped hero, our attention begins to wander to the character who changes from play to play, from film to film. In spite of his evident lack of morality, the villain soon becomes the focus of the plot, the more interesting role, and the more captivating figure. For it is easy to become bored by virtue when that virtue is stripped of the sexuality which we long to sense in a courting young couple. To be sure, the teens attempted to compensate for the colorless hero inherited from Griffith by forging a hero who would be increasingly required to substitute physical for moral superiority, but even that move—typified by the western—would prove insufficient. Bitten by a fascination with the villain, the American public increasingly sought films which acknowledged the romantic attraction of the forbidden, of the violent, foreign, sexually active, amoral hero. Ever revealing a love of violence as the visible symptom growing out of repression of sexuality, America has never since World War I been able to shake an identification of (sexual) attraction with danger.

The form which the new romance took during the twenties is bound up in the screen careers of three men: Douglas Fairbanks, Sr., Rudolph Valentino, and Ramon Novarro. Beginning with Fairbanks' *Mark of Zorro* (1920), where the leading lady swoons over the dashing outlaw hero, while rejecting his proper but lifeless alter ego, the twenties' adventure film exactly reverses the rhetoric of the melodrama. The hero must be violent, not peaceful; foreign, not local; outside the law, not its most faithful servant; in short he must, like Zorro, at one and the same time play the two roles of melodrama. As outlaw, it is the hero himself who endangers the heroine, but as inoffensive good boy the hero must fight himself and his own animal appetites in order to ensure the safety of the heroine. The typical plot, therefore, is that of the film which catapulted Rudolph Valentino to international fame: *The Sheik*. " 'When an Arab sees a woman he wants he takes her'— Ancient Proverb of Arabia," says Paramount's publicity.

> That was the meaning of love in the desert until The Sheik met the English girl. That is the heart of the plot of *The Sheik*, which in book form is the year's sensation on both sides of the Atlantic and which as a Paramount Picture finds and thrills a multi-million audience. Don't miss the thrill of seeing the proud mad-cap English girl snatched from the sand by the hard-riding Sheik of a hundred tribes. You will be amazed at her life within the tented luxury of the Sahara. You will see love making by the handsome Rudolph Valentino as The Sheik which is the full torrent of Oriental tradition. How shall the lovely and aristocratic Agnes Ayres, as the English girl, escape with life and honor? *That* is the plot of it, the shiver of it—the odds are so great—that is the

> drama you see against a background of infinite desert,—of a thousand wild Bedouin horsemen with long rifles and flowing robes,—of the bride-market at Biskra where the slave-brides are sold,—and of desert fighting between Sheik and Bandit, and between their troops, of a ferocity only equalled by tigers. Does love emerge supreme and glorious at the climax? Is a pure spot found in the heart of the bronzed Sheik? The answer to that will make you draw the deepest breath of all,— and recognize that once more Paramount has given you the best show in town or state.[6]

The Sheik's struggle is thus between love and sex, with love conquering all in the end, but deriving its very reason for being, its excitement, its energy, from the sexual potency of Valentino. Until his early death, Valentino's roles (especially *Blood and Sand*, 1922, and *Son of the Sheik*, 1926) brought to the female moviegoer a sensuality whose intensity was assured by the danger and forbidden nature of Valentino's activities, and whose security was guaranteed by its celluloid nature. This same approach was immediately and successfully imitated by Ramon Novarro. As *The Arab* (1924) he forces his attention on a Christian missionary (Alice Terry); in *The Red Lily* (1924) he enters the underworld; *The Road to Romance* (1927) makes him a Spanish adventurer; his first sound film, *The Pagan* (1929), strips him to the waist and has him abducting the daughter of a white trader (not to mention singing the song which might well serve as theme for all twenties' adventure movies—"The Pagan Love Song"). During this time Fairbanks was turning out a major adventure

Rudolf Valentino as the Sheik—the original dream lover.
[MOMA]

film per year, ever identifying his sexual attractiveness with physical prowess and an outlaw role (especially in *Three Musketeers*, 1921, *Robin Hood*, 1921, *The Thief of Baghdad*, 1923, and *The Black Pirate*, 1926). With this trio of leading men dominating American production during the twenties, it was inevitable that the early musical should look to their combination/identification of love and adventure for one of its basic models.

During 1925-26 the revolt of the Riffs against the French protectorate in Morocco was headline news all across America, reinforcing interest in North Af-

rica enough to inspire Sigmund Romberg's 1926 *Desert Song* (with book and lyrics by Otto Harbach, Oscar Hammerstein II, and Frank Mandel). One of the last great successes of Broadway operetta (471 performances), *The Desert Song* was, according to *Photoplay*, "the first all-singing and talking operetta to reach the screen." Produced in 1928-29, *The Desert Song* was Warner's attempt to turn John Boles into a competitor with MGM's Ramon Novarro for the right to wear the mantle of the dead master Valentino. Clearly influenced by *The Sheik*, as well as by Fairbanks' *Mark of Zorro*,

The Desert Song is the first musical to fashion out of the clichés of exoticism a coherent thematics, a syntactic bond between the spectator's overt fascination with unknown lands and that same spectator's unavowed but intense interest in the uncharted seas of sexuality. While the film spectator is treated to a series of romantic scenes—the Riff encampment, exotic dances, Ali Ben Ali's desert palace, the ladies at the bath, the "Room of the Silken Divans"—young Margot Bonvalet, freshly arrived from France, is expected to disregard the excitement around her and stick close to home. Soon, however, her fascination matches ours; when she meets a man who embodies the excitement and danger of her desert world she loses all composure and self-restraint. Now, we know that that man, the Riff chieftain known as the Red Shadow, is none other than the dashing, Zorro-like alter ego of the Governor's foppish son Pierre (both played by Boles). Though Margot's affection for Pierre is great, he lacks the element of danger, of novelty, of excitement represented by the Red Shadow. Of Pierre she says: "Sometimes I wish he were more of an outlaw and a ruffian. I wish he would make the decision for me." Only with an outlaw can she find the quality of feeling which she seeks. That is, the desire to break her own law (which defines strictly and clearly under what conditions and with whom she may satisfy her sexual desires) is neatly projected onto the man of her dreams. Law-breaking in one arena—civil law—is thus made to stand for transgression in another—moral law. The sin of illicit desire is thus erased from the woman's slate and attributed to the

man—as it is throughout the Beauty and the Beast tradition. Far from having sexual yearnings herself, she is apparently carried off by a bandit who forces his attention on her. *He* is the one to blame, not she. That his outlaw status is actually dear to her becomes increasingly clear as she sings the "Sabre Song," nearly immobile in frontal medium shot, while fondling the Red Shadow's sabre. As the sign of his manhood as well as his adventuresome nature, the sabre is an ambiguous item indeed, simultaneously representing to Margot the promise and the danger embodied by her man.

As if the sabre song scene were actual and not symbolic love-making, it precipitates the romantic climax of the film. Dressed now as the foppish Governor's son, Boles is told by Margot that she loves the Red Shadow, that she desires his advances. Forgetting that he is dressed as Pierre, Boles responds with a kiss, leading directly into "The Desert Song" duet ("Blue Heaven and You and I") and eventually to a clinch. Short minutes later the now impetuous Pierre reports that he has killed the Red Shadow, thus reducing the safe but sexless brother figure and the attractive but dangerous outlaw to a single acceptable partner. Margot now happily consents to a life with Pierre, for she knows that behind his proper facade lies the desire and excitement of an outlaw. Like *The Sheik*, which reveals the "bronzed Sheik" to be a quite safe and civilized British lord, *The Desert Song* creates, through the outlaw approach to exoticism, the dream of every woman: a terror of a man, dangerous, adventuresome, sword-wielding, mysterious, romantic—yet as sweet, safe, and brotherly

John Boles in *The Desert Song*—as ineffectual, effete, brotherly Pierre; as the dangerous, masked, sword-wielding Red Shadow

[UW]

as good old Pierre. For those not sophisticated enough to swing with Chevalier's innuendo, *The Desert Song* provides an alternate model, just as effective but less compromising. The film thus becomes a medium of satisfaction and the film theater a place of pleasure, a way of introducing danger and sex into daily life without the risk of a battle with one's conscience, father, or husband. Just as the outlaw Red Shadow satisfies Margot Bonvalet's desires without engaging her responsibility, so the fairy tale musical serves as the spectator's outlaw, a (Red) Shadow world which permits us to live out our fantasies with impunity.

The fantastic success of *The Desert Song*, coupled with the nearly immediate and equally spectacular success of *Rio Rita* (again with Boles, but this time for Radio Pictures), firmly fixed the relationship between the subgenre's travelogue exoticism and the dynamics of the main couple. No matter where a film might be set, at least one of the members of the main couple would be identified as a legal transgressor, thus covering and, as it were, justifying the other member's desire for moral transgression. In modern sets alone, the leading man's transgressions range from imposter (*Vagabond Lover*—1929), to river gambler (*Cameo Kirby*—1930), to rum-runner (*Roadhouse Nights*—1930), to gun-runner (*Women Everywhere*—1930). Indeed, all sex-as-adventure musicals might well have borrowed the title from an unlikely Jeanette MacDonald vehicle while she was on loan from Paramount to Fox. Surprised one night by a burglar, the lucky lady takes him in, teaches him how to . . . sing, and falls in love with him. The title: *Oh,*

For a Man! (1930). Following in the vein of *The Desert Song*, numerous early fairy tale musicals adopted a military backdrop (e.g., *Bride of the Regiment, The Toast of the Legion, Golden Dawn*—all 1930), while others followed the lead of *Rio Rita* and headed south of the border (e.g., *The Singer from Seville, One Mad Kiss*—both 1930—and *The Cuban Love Song*, 1931). More common still was the historical approach, often concentrating on a revolutionary period or personality (*Devil May Care, The Vagabond King, The Rogue Song, Song of the Flame, Captain of the Guard, Sweet Kitty Bellairs,* and *New Moon* in 1930 alone). Like *Love Me Tonight*, which induces us to trade monetary values for the currency of charm, all these sex-as-adventure fairy tale musicals lead us to substitute the romance of banditry for more traditional values. The most successful of these films manage to establish and hold a tension between danger and security. Excitement is generated by such rousing numbers as Romberg's "Riff Song," which opens *The Desert Song*. Solos and duets release the energy pent up by sexual repression. The principals appear to succeed in remaining within the bounds of moral decency only by virtue of a strong—and visible—repression of their desires. Sexual desire must not be allowed to becloud the dialogue, nor may it reach the level of visibility that it attains in the many longing looks at the female body which the sex-as-sex approach permits, but if desire is to be hidden, the visible repression of that desire must not be. The audience must not see or hear the desire, but must nevertheless sense its presence for the heirs of *The Desert Song* to succeed.

Perhaps this is why MGM's most successful series of the decade seems to have lost so much of its luster today. Reviving the sex-as-adventure syntax during the latter half of the thirties, the films which teamed Nelson Eddy with Jeanette MacDonald, now under contract with MGM, enjoyed an extraordinary level of success. MGM's most popular couple would no doubt never have been created had it not been for the 1934 success of Grace Moore's operatic voice in *One Night of Love*. Now, Hollywood had already suffered through one opera era. In 1930 anyone with a voice was fair game, but of all those brought to the screen at that time (including Everett Marshall, John McCormack, Dennis King, Nino Martini, Alexander Gray, and Bernice Claire) only Lawrence Tibbett managed anything resembling continued success (in *Rogue Song* and *New Moon*, 1930; *The Prodigal*, 1931; *The Cuban Love Song*, 1932). After Moore's restoration of box-office dignity to opera stars in 1934, not only did Tibbett make a comeback (*Metropolitan*, 1936; *Under Your Spell*, 1937) but opera theaters from San Francisco to Denmark suddenly found their casts plundered by Hollywood. In a first wave came George Houston, James Melton, Carl Brisson, Jan Kiepura, Marion Talley, Mary Ellis, Gladys Swarthout, Lily Pons, Gita Alpar, Evelyn Laye. They were followed in the late thirties and early forties by a second wave—Rise Stevens, Miliza Korjus, Martha Eggerth, Jarmilla Novotna, Ilona Massey—and then in the late forties and early fifties by Joe Pasternak's one-man-ministry-of-culture attempt to bring classical musicians into American lives: opera stars Lauritz Melchior and Mario Lanza, conductor José Iturbi, plus guest performances by countless others.

The 1935 match-up of star MacDonald with newcomer Eddy was thus a natural—and well rewarded—attempt to capitalize on the public's momentary romance with a particular style of singing. How fitting, then, that Eddy, chosen for his voice (and in spite of his lack of acting experience or talent), should find himself in a film version of Victor Herbert's *Naughty Marietta*, in which he gets the girl solely by virtue of his ability to complete the song ("Ah, Sweet Mystery of Life") whose ending she has forgotten. On the surface, *Naughty Marietta* seems to possess every element requisite for a sex-as-adventure success. Rebelling at an arranged marriage, Princess Marie (MacDonald) proves her independence by sailing to America disguised as her maid Marietta, where she is first captured by a pirate, then rescued by handsome young Captain Warrington (Eddy). In order to escape marriage, she feigns immorality ("Naughty" Marietta) and takes a job in a marionette show. At the very moment that she is winning Warrington's heart she is recognized as Princess Marie and taken into the Governor's custody until the night when Warrington completes her enigmatic song and the two flee together into the wilderness. In a way, this plot perfectly matched Eddy's lack of presence on the screen; possessing a more than adequate voice, but rarely able to project a sense of power or danger, Eddy was never fit for the sexually alive outlaw role which the sex-as-adventure approach requires. MacDonald, on the other hand, had six years of nearly unbroken success as the queen of lingerie, double-entendre, and spicy plots. No wonder then, that she is cast as the naughty one, while Eddy spends his time protecting her rather than stealing her heart. With a John Boles or a Ramon Novarro in the Eddy role the level of sexual tension would remain consistently high (compare any Eddy-MacDonald film with the Gable-MacDonald *San Francisco*—1936—in which Gable's piercing eyes and surly, animal-like behavior infuse the film with an unmistakable sensation of desire), but however adequate Eddy's voice he suffered from an inability to mix aesthetic pleasure with the suggestion of sexual pleasure—a talent in general sadly lacking in the period's opera-trained leading men and certainly one of the reasons for the near disappearance of the sex-as-adventure approach to the fairy tale musical. What's more, Hollywood's growing self-consciousness about its moral responsibilities deprived MacDonald as well of her considerable talent for sophisticated repartee. With Chevalier she had carried half the innuendo; with Eddy she was rarely allowed to be so much as sexy (a talent which nevertheless seemed to come naturally to her). As if sensitive to a lack of flashiness in the Eddy/MacDonald films, MGM regularly assigned Slavko Vorkapich, their prize-winning montage effects specialist, to enliven the show, to provide technically what they felt might be lacking humanly. Ten years later they would simply have added Jimmy Durante or Red Skelton to the cast, but in the late thirties no comedian was ever allowed to steal the thunder of MGM's much loved pair.

Only in their 1940 match-up in a remake of *New Moon* does MacDonald regain some of her sauciness and Eddy finally merit the acclaim which the team had received at every outing over the past five years. With a score rivaling *The Desert Song* as Romberg's best (again with lyrics by Oscar Hammerstein II), *New Moon* exactly reverses the configuration of *Naughty Marietta*. This time Eddy is the revolutionary, being deported as a bondsman (though he is actually an aristocratic political enemy of the king). After charming MacDonald as her servant, Eddy organizes the moonlight escape of his fellow slaves and revolutionaries. Their tub-thumping march ("Stouthearted Men")—one of Romberg's most durable songs and certainly Eddy's single best number—is effectively shot in high angle dollying back just ahead of the accelerating marchers, Eddy in the lead. (One wonders if Director Robert Z. Leonard was aware that he was thus borrowing the shooting arrangement of Berkeley's just completed "Babes in Arms" number in the movie of the same name.) When MacDonald decides to leave New Orleans with a group of mail-order brides her ship is rapidly captured by none other than the rebellious Eddy, now turned pirate. When all are deposited on a small island by a sudden storm, MacDonald and Eddy must begin their relationship anew. But this time the element of desire is hardly lacking. While the plot has Eddy marrying MacDonald in order to protect her from the other men, with MacDonald reminding him on their wedding night that she married him only for protection, the images tell another story: if she is attracted to Eddy it is because he represents danger. Slave, revolutionary, pirate, he is exactly what her body and eyes tell us she wants. The release which we feel when they finally kiss is marked by a cannon shot and the news that all France is now liberated. In rapid succession we then reprise nearly all the film's excellent songs ("Lover Come Back to Me", "Stouthearted Men", and "Wanting You", with the "Marseillaise" thrown in for good measure), producing an emotional climax entirely fitting in this extremely well handled effort.

The relative disrepute into which the MacDonald-Eddy films have fallen merits explanation, for it is only a special case of the general disdain for the musical as a genre, the fairy tale musical in particular, and more especially the sex-as-adventure syntax. Overall, the musical is marked by a process according to which the spectator's reality is opposed to the ideal image which the film represents (the musical being the quintessential product of Hollywood's "dream factory"). The fairy tale musical reinforces this opposition by setting its characters in a class, a plot, and a locale which are as far as possible from those familiar to the audience (and known to the audience only through the prettifying lens of travel publicity or society column chatter). The sex-as-adventure film relies particularly heavily on the real/ideal opposition, because it is out of this opposition that the tension between man and woman must grow. She is frustrated by the pedestrian nature of her reality; he seems identified with the exoticism and danger of the very land around him. For the film to work, the surroundings must appear as exotic to the spectator as they do to the character; the film must appear to be a sort of ideal newsreel, giving us a privileged view of life in the many worlds which arouse our curiosity by the very fact that they are imperfectly known to us. What happens, however, when the mass media and the jet age combine to destroy our ignorance? What once may have appeared ideal or mysterious now clearly seems to result from misrepresentation. For here lie the pitfalls of exoticism: just as the real can easily be unflatteringly opposed to the ideal, so can it be advantageously opposed to the unreal. Many of Hollywood's most successful musicals began their careers by convincing audiences of the ideality of their vision, only to find decades later that that same vision is seen simply as unreal:

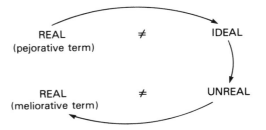

Again and again in the history of the musical this evaluative circle has operated. Only those films which recognize their unreality and use it to attract the spectator into a conspiracy of irony, thus building the evaluative circle into their structure, are able to ensure security from the ravages of time and taste. (It is thus Chevalier's wink that guarantees him—and his directors Lubitsch and Mamoulian—immortality). It is somehow saddening to think that MGM, with the complicity of the contemporary public, should have so rapidly wrenched Jeanette MacDonald from a series of sophisticated films which will live forever and thrust her into a series whose survival ability was doomed from the start.

Among the least self-conscious films of the period—and the least likely to retain any charm for posterity—are the Latin films which supplanted MacDonald and Eddy (as well as Astaire and Rogers) in the public eye. After the 1929 success of *Rio Rita* and the 1930 flowering of the South-of-the-Border craze, Latin settings settled down to an average of one a year throughout the remainder of the decade (1931—*The Cuban Love Song*; 1932—*The Kid From Spain*; 1933—*Flying Down to Rio*; 1935—*Under the Pampas Moon*; 1936—*Rose of the Rancho, Hi Gaucho!, The Dancing Pirate*, and *The Gay Desperado*; 1938—*Tropic Holiday*). Then in the forties, the bottom dropped out. Thanks in large part to the popularity of Latin music, embodied in the U.S. in the person of Xavier Cugat, and to the immense box-office success of Lupe Velez and especially Carmen Miranda, all America seemed ready to lay out a bill or two to go *Down Argentine Way* (Miranda's first film in 1940). The over two dozen South-of-the-Border musicals produced during the forties (along with scores of isolated Latin numbers) are a reminder that in some ways the evolution of the fairy tale musical is no more than a record of the general evolution of American utopian thought. An analysis more firmly rooted in sociology than my own would no doubt stress the extent to which the twenties' romance with Araby was quickly replaced by an understandable depression interest in high society, upper class mores, or any other situation where money is simply no problem. The fascination with opera corresponds to a general

explosion of the arts under Roosevelt, while wartime interest in South America might easily be explained as natural attraction to the only continent in reach not torn asunder by war. Just as the waltz had once signified romance to Vienna, so the series of Latin dances popular throughout the late thirties and forties identified our southern neighbors with rhythm, life, and a certain looseness of morals. If *Mardi Gras* represents the New Orleans tradition of feasting before the fast, then the characteristic Latin fiesta appeared to North Americans as a perpetual feast, a symbol of life in what seemed like an unhurried utopia.

Perhaps the most striking aspect of Hollywood's forties' Latin romance is the absence of MGM from the fiesta until mid-decade. By the time *Yolanda and the Thief* appeared in 1945 no fewer than six other studios had beaten MGM to the punch an uncharacteristic fourteen times. The wait turned out to be worth it, for *Yolanda* is one of the true lost gems of the musical world. Vincente Minnelli's first chance to let his surrealist color sense run wild, *Yolanda* inaugurates the only distinguished series of fairy tale musicals by a single director in the post-war era (*Yolanda, The Pirate, An American in Paris, Brigadoon, Kismet, Gigi, Bells are Ringing, On a Clear Day You Can See Forever*). In many ways *Yolanda* is a fitting heir to the sex-as-adventure operetta tradition. As in *The Merry Widow*, a parallel is established between the future of the kingdom of Patria and the marital plans of Yolanda Acquaviva, its richest and most important citizen. Even the National Anthem draws its lyrics from the parallel realm of romance ("This is a day

Fred Astaire as Lucille Bremer's angel in *Yolanda and the Thief*. The camera placement in the film differs from this production still—the camera is placed farther to the right, shooting directly through the harp at Bremer. As Astaire plays, he thus appears to be playing Bremer as well as the harp. Woman as instrument, man as instrumentalist: a configuration developed visually and thematically throughout the film musical tradition.

[MOMA]

for love, this is a day for song"). The celebration of Yolanda's twenty-first birthday prefigures a characteristic fairy tale musical sliding from monetary to amorous concerns; at first the question of majority is linked to control over the Acquaviva fortune, but soon we realize that Yolanda is far more enthralled with the freedom which her sentimental majority brings. The plot seems to grow straight out of the Zorro-Sheik-*Desert Song* line. Falling in love with the criminal Johnny Riggs (Astaire), whom she believes to be an angel, Yolanda eventually recognizes that it is not the angelic in him that she desires, but the masculine traits of mastery and adventure. Eventually she frees herself from the constraints imposed by her convent upbringing, while he resigns himself to the bonds of marriage, thus rejecting his wandering, lawless past.

The plot and characters may be familiar, but *Yolanda and the Thief* is hardly just another remake of *Rio Rita*. Minnelli's film is perhaps the first simultaneously to place a heavy emphasis on the visual delights of a foreign land and to distance itself from that emphasis. Much of this distancing grows out of Minnelli's developing passion for saturated, garish colors which seem to draw attention to themselves and say "Feast your eyes on me (here and now, because you'll never see anything like me in real life)." In addition, a series of staged scenes, recognized as such, contributes to the film's self-conscious stand. The opening scenes at the convent reveal a short passage from a religious play. Says Yolanda: "I was so frightened." Responds her interlocutor: "I wasn't worried for a minute. I saw the rehearsal." So might we say as well, after seeing so many similar films. Shortly afterward Yolanda rides to meet her angel at his hotel (in my humble opinion this scene, played in the confinement of a carriage to an orchestral rendition of "Angel, I've an Angel", represents an intensity of repressed sexuality which will never be equaled on film). As the naive, indeed gullible mark of Astaire's scam (he is posing as an angel in order to bilk Yolanda out of her fortune), Yolanda is treated by Astaire and his henchman Frank Morgan as an audience of one. In preparation for her arrival they create in the hotel lobby a stage set, arranging props, even aiming spot lights. To "set up" a mark, this sequence implies, is to treat her as a spectator, to draw her into the illusion of a performance. It is thus hardly surprising that Astaire's reversal, his falling in love, is also treated as an involuntary surrender to a world of illusion.

Choreographed by Eugene Loring, the esteemed dancer-choreographer of the new American school (*Yankee Clipper*, *Billy the Kid, City-Portrait, The Great American Goof, Prairie, The Invisible Wife*), Yolanda's dream ballet simultaneously suggests the internal conflicts of the main character and moves toward their resolution—a practice derived from the recent stage successes of *Lady in the Dark* and *Oklahoma!*, both of which make extensive use of the device. In *Yolanda*, however, the surrealistic sets and Minnelli colors combine with dream-like continuity (the movement from sequence to sequence clearly reflects the connections perceived by Astaire's unconscious as he reviews the daily residue in his sleep) to produce a piece of such originality that it has rarely if ever been equaled. The plot of the dream sequence is hardly original, however: will the male lead follow the evil designs which come naturally to him, or will he let himself be tamed by a woman? By any yardstick a striking movie, *Yolanda and the Thief* is one of a very few movies that actually tried to *do* something with the South-of-the-Border craze. In spite of the zaniness of the plot (it turns out at the end that Leon Ames, assumed all along to be no more than another fortune-seeker, is in fact a real guardian angel!), *Yolanda* merits more attention than it has received.

The only other film to make truly creative use of Latin motifs is Minnelli's next full-length musical effort, *The Pirate*. Once again proclaiming through Minnelli's hi-fi colors the artificiality, the imaginary nature of its supposed Caribbean setting (the director refused to use location photography *in order to* assure an artificial look), *The Pirate* is perhaps the only American film to merit compar-

Always on the lookout for talent, in whatever field, MGM hired noted choreographer Eugene Loring to choreograph the dream ballet in *Yolanda and the Thief*. Literally ensnared by a bevy of colorful washer women at the start, Fred Astaire is then taken in by the very money he set out to steal (and the attractive Lucille Bremer who offers it to him).

[BFI]

ison with Renoir's *Golden Coach*, a tribute to the theater by another lover of theatrical artifice. Immediately identifying the desires of young Manuela (Judy Garland) with a literary model—the picture-book story of the pirate Macoco on which the movie opens—Minnelli never lets us lose from sight the basic syntax whereby character and spectator are identified. Manuela's desire is to have the hero of her reading hours leap off the page and appear in front of her; our only wish is the one which the film grants: to travel magically to the exotic lands which fill our dreams. Indeed, the film reinforces this parallel by having Manuela fall not for the real Macoco (Walter Slezak, the man she is to marry), but for the actor Serafin (Gene Kelly), the one most fully able to imitate the pirate of Manuela's imagination. She, like the spectator, is thus captured by the show's illusion, a process symbolized in *The Pirate* by the process of hypnotism. Having talked her governess into one short trip before her arranged marriage, Manuela for the first time travels to the sea, the turbulent realm ruled over by the beloved pirate of her dreams (thus tying together the metonymic chain of sex-romance-travel-sea-pirate). As she stands enraptured watching the pounding surf, she is accosted by the unprincipled Serafin, a man known to us only by his acrobatic song "Niña," which simultaneously reveals his wandering eye and his danger-defying acrobatic abilities (to my mind these Fairbanks-like physical qualities make "Niña" Kelly's best routine ever). That night, on the public square, the courtship of Manuela and Serafin is carried

out not only during but *as* the publicity for the actor's show. By getting Manuela to gaze into a revolving mirror and repeat three times the phrase "Beneath this prim exterior there are deep emotions, romantic longings," Serafin hypnotizes her. Once she is hypnotized it is precisely those romantic longings that appear in Manuela's behavior. What is important here, however, is not solely the familiar freeing of repressed emotions through hypnotism (or dream, or danger, or simply solitude), but the way in which those emotions surface. On the moralistic, conscious side all was speech, but once Manuela has slipped out of the moral mold and across the barrier of consciousness she *sings* her desires (and not only does she sing them, she belts them out with an energy level rarely seen even in Garland's energetic repertoire). Singing is thus doubly suspect. In keeping with a recurrent musical motif whereby dance is seen as an illicit activity (from the waltz as adultery in *The Great Waltz* to dance as hallucination in *Hair*), not only is music here identified with performers, but it is used to reveal that which a proper young lady had best keep hidden.

Minnelli's use of hypnotism as the hinge on which Manuela's personality turns provides a veritable lesson in fairy tale musical syntax. Now the device of "make-believe" is as old as theater itself. Whereas earlier comedy invariably uses disguise, mistaken identity, and comic misunderstanding as devices to further the plot and provoke laughter, romantic comedy regularly uses disguise as a psychological crutch, an invitation to "dress up" mentally, to try on other, normally

Acrobatic Gene Kelly struts his stuff in the "Niña" routine near the beginning of *The Pirate*.

[MOMA]

forbidden roles. Disguised as her own maid, a proper young lady may with impunity (not only from her guardians, but from her own vanity as well) use familiar forms of language, speak more frankly than usual, even admit sentimental attachment. That is, she may, without hurting her own pride or awakening her societal censor, express a hidden but desirable side of her personality. Used in this way, the motif of disguise has more in common with dream work, free association, or psychoanalysis than it does with farce. Though the fairy tale musical, like

the romantic comedy often occurs in a *land* of make-believe, it takes place more importantly in a *state* of make-believe, a situation where even the most sophisticated dare to speak the language of love. By transforming the familiar motif of disguise into hypnotism, *The Pirate* foregrounds the always implicit connection of the make-believe motif to literary, theatrical, or filmic illusion, thus explicitly identifying the spectatorial activities of the audience with the desires of the film's characters. Instead of concentrating solely on the bond linking sexual desire to forbidden activity (as in a long line of sex-as-adventure fairy tale musicals from *The Desert Song* to *The Wiz*), Minnelli's film, by casting Kelly as a performer, establishes a further link between the exoticism/forbidden activity complex and the artistic illusion itself. What's more, by identifying singing as the immoral revelation of one's other self, and by portraying the performers as itinerant, that is as vagabonds, as travelers, the film completes the fairy tale musical's triangle of desire. What the proper, repressed homebody wants is just what she has never been able to have: the exotic (travel), adventure (the forbidden), and the artistic illusion (including the right to sing).

Looking back over the fairy tale tradition with this triangle of desire in mind, we recognize the extent to which the illusion of art is to be identified with banditry and the exotic. In *The Desert Song* Margot is looking not for a man of flesh and blood, but for the Sheik himself. Her desire is clearly mediated by the Valentino tradition (or rather, to put it more accurately, the spectator projects onto Margot's desire the mediating factor for her/his own). Jeanette MacDonald is forever awaiting that consummate literary figure, Prince Charming. To find him is to enter into the artistic illusion, to leave behind this limited world. The desire to share the stage with one's heroes in large part justifies the constant identification of song as either a marker of desirability or as an expression of desire. The opening male song is typically a rousing, hearty march, beer song, or other expression of man's adventuresome nature (e.g. "The Riff Song" in *The Desert Song*, "Ride" in *Balalaika*, "Niña" in *The Pirate*, "Fate"

in *Kismet*, or "Paris Loves Lovers" in *Silk Stockings*), while the woman typically does not sing until her desire surfaces to the point where she cannot do otherwise. By singing she is simultaneously passing across the border of life to art, of repression to expression of desire, of immobility to the exotic (her man representing the latter). This identification of artistic illusion with banditry and adventure helps us to see just how parallel the fairy tale musical is to the show musical. While the garden variety backstage musical makes no bones about its division into two levels, the stage and the city, with the couple's courtship bridging the two, the fairy tale musical normally masks its bilevel structure, refusing to reveal to the audience the extent to which their own story is projected onto the screen before them. As always, Hollywood champions Hollywood values: in desiring desire, adventure, and the exotic, the fairy tale musical heroine is only expressing her desire for Hollywood, purveyor of desire to her excellence the American spectator.

The Pirate thus reveals yet again the importance of the entertainment/business split as a fundamental Hollywood musical theme. Not only are the rivals for Manuela's hand identified as entertainer and rich businessman (whose fortune derives from a life of pirating, thus suggesting an identity of business with theft—every mayor and businessman is but a pirate in disguise), but the fairy tale musical's typical motif of the restoration of order is accomplished not by the corrupt local official (the disguised pirate, whence disguise as lying, as harmful) but by the entertainer (the one who poses as pirate, whence disguise as artful, as expressing a deeper truth). Even the governor seems to recognize the importance and nature of this opposition, for it is he who keeps the disguised Macoco from interrupting the entertainer's attempts to unmask him, saying "Hold your tongue, Don Pedro. I will not have the performance ruined by your bourgeois possessiveness." Though it may be treated with Hollywood's characteristic superciliousness, to which is added a strong dose of Minnelli illusionism, *The Pirate* is clearly a morality tale in the medieval style. Never was the desire to extol entertainment and denigrate everything else so clear as in *The Pirate*. Little wonder then, that the film ends on an anthem to entertainment, one of many within the Hollywood tradition. "Be a Clown" reveals Kelly-Serafin doing what he has been doing all along—donning a mask and providing entertainment. For Garland, however, this is a new experience. Her desire for adventure, while clearly deriving its energy from sexuality, lacked specificity. With the "Be a Clown" number her desires finally achieve definition. Just as "Niña" reveals Kelly-Serafin indulging in sexual overtures as a function of his role as entertainer, "Be a Clown" affords Garland-Manuela the opportunity finally to express her longings through entertainment. Entertainment afforded Kelly an opportunity for sexual overtures and Garland a chance to release her repressed desires. Now Hollywood self-servingly reverses the formula, with sexual energy now feeding a desire for entertainment. In *The Pirate*, as throughout this tradition, sexual desire is expressed through adventure; it is just that the adventure proposed by *The Pi-*

rate is none other than the Hollywood adventure itself, the process of producing entertainment.

After *Nancy Goes to Rio* (1950), the Latin craze disappears from Hollywood for good, only to give way to nearly a decade of passion for Paris. If South America had provided an obvious alternative to the war-torn North Atlantic, post-war Paris seemed to satisfy peacetime pressures for a new utopia. The City of Light thus becomes the backdrop for some of the decade's best musicals (*An American in Paris, Funny Face, Silk Stockings, Les Girls, Gigi)*, as well as many of the least inventive fairy tale offerings (*Rich, Young and Pretty, Lovely to Look At, April in Paris, Gentlemen Marry Brunettes*, and *Paris Follies of 1956*). Since the musical's fifties romance with Paris, a new trend has emerged, privileging no single geographical location, but seeking to discover the flights of fancy possible within everyday situations. The basic fairy tale notion of disorder in the kingdom remains, but it is displaced to a series of self-contained worlds which are a far cry from the Ruritanian palace (and yet clearly in a direct line with the resorts, ocean liners, and hotels of the golden days of the fairy tale musical). *Bells Are Ringing* (1960) features the switchboard operator of a large apartment building; *How to Succeed in Business without Really Trying* (1967) takes place in the offices of a large New York firm; *On a Clear Day You Can See Forever* (1970) invades the university campus.

While the increasing naturalization of the fairy tale musical brought the subgenre within range of fifties conventions of realism, such a taming necessarily made it harder and harder to retain a sense of sex-as-adventure. Outside of sundry remakes (*Pagan Love Song*, 1950; *The Desert Song*, 1953; *The Vagabond King*, 1956) and a few gangster-oriented or exotic films with strong male leads (*Kismet*, 1955; *The King and I*, 1956; *Party Girl*, 1958), nearly all the fairy tale musicals of the last three decades cast children, flower-children, or man-children in lead roles (Rex Harrison, Christopher Plummer, Zero Mostel, Tommy Steele, and *Hair*'s John Savage, not to mention various versions of Jesus, sundry child stars, and a handful of cartoon characters). Indeed it can be argued that the demise of the fairy tale musical grows out of the increasing displacement of its sexual origin and mythology to the point where, from the fifties on, the spark of sexual attraction is almost entirely absent from the genre. Even through their exoticism, their superciliousness, their I've-seen-it-all irony, earlier fairy tale musicals had a sort of elemental power about them, an attraction which we may no longer feel in an era of sexual liberation, but which clearly attacked millions of viewers like an infectious disease whenever Nelson Eddy and Jeanette MacDonald appeared on screen. Always aimed at that part of the film-going public whose ambiguous attitudes toward sexuality dictated preference for an oblique approach to sexual attraction, the sex-as-adventure fairy tale musical rose and fell on its ability to satisfy a repressed need. Sexuality must not be too prominent, but remove it entirely and the form curls up and dies.

For this reason the films of Elvis Presley stand out like a beacon within the pro-duction of the late fifties and sixties. Poorly made in every way, overloaded with stereotyped characters (often played, however, by quality actresses like Angela Lansbury and Barbara Stanwyck), slowed down by dimwitted comics (whose lines seem to have been scripted by more of the same), burdened with plots which seemed to be suggested (indeed, sometimes were suggested) by poor song lyrics, many of Elvis' films nevertheless exude a sense of life present in few other musicals of the period. Approximately split between allegiance to the show motif (get the girl, get the singing job) and fairy tale exoticism in a resort setting (Miami, Acapulco, Las Vegas, Hawaii), the films lay increasing emphasis on the role of Elvis (and his new musical style) as misfit. Exiled from conventional society, Elvis paradoxically finds himself attracting increasing female attention because of his very unconventionality. What's more, not just one girl is attracted to Elvis, but nearly every young woman in the movie—and thus by extension, in the audience. *Blue Hawaii* (1961) is exemplary in that it pairs Elvis with not one but five girls. As the maverick son of an influential island pineapple family, Elvis has rejected the easy life which his high birth facilitates. Taking a job as vacation tour operator, Elvis thus becomes identified with Hawaii for the four women he escorts. For these love-starved lasses, to travel is not to learn, but to find love. "You know I've taken a vacation every summer, looking for romance," the school-teacher tells him. Playing on the latent identification of travel and romance which underlies not only the fairy tale

Elvis Presley bringing life to the landscape, from the folk atmosphere of the carnival in *Roustabout* to the travelogue backdrop of Diamond Head in *Blue Hawaii*.

[MOMA]

musical tradition but the travel business as well, *Blue Hawaii* is only fulfilling an archetypal plot by making Elvis into the tour operator, the one who can simultaneously provide tourism and romance.

Yet it is not his identification with the romance of the islands that provides Elvis' greatest attraction. Most of the time, Elvis is a nice guy, a straight arrow, a sweet Mama's boy who says "No, Ma'am" and "Yes, Sir." Little marks him as the firebrand, the instigator of sexual desire which he becomes when he sings. Now *Blue Hawaii* is no *Jailhouse Rock*. It is a quiet sort of a movie, where the sexuality comes from warmth of delivery (and added reverb) rather than from the pelvis. *Blue Hawaii's* sexuality is not the overt sensuality of "Don't Be Cruel" but the quiet pleading of "I Can't Help Falling In Love with You." Yet there is no question about the nature or intensity of the experience. In fact so intense is the experience that the tourists, like the film audience, soon discover that Elvis' singing is what they have come to see and hear. Like the films of Valentino, which were conceived as throwaway packaging of a few supreme moments, the films of Elvis all build up to that instant when we discover that a song is the supreme adventure and the supreme locus of sensuality. With no help from his directors, and even less from his supporting cast, indeed with little acting talent of his own, Elvis nevertheless dominated a decade of musical filmmaking because of his understanding of the sexuality of song. Often lumped together with the totally vacuous American International beach party films featuring Frankie Avalon, Annette Funicello, and

usually directed by William Asher, Elvis' films clearly outstrip these unworthy rivals by his ability to seduce his female audience—the basic ingredient for the successful sex-as-adventure fairy tale musical.

While Hollywood was going Parisian and turning increasingly toward rock stars, Broadway was enjoying its most successful days since the twenties. During the thirties, when book musicals rarely outlasted a single Broadway season, Hollywood had regularly bought up the rights to musical plays, only to discard the scanty plot and half the music for the movie version (which thus resembles the original only in title). Now, in the wake of *Oklahoma!, Carousel, Annie Get Your Gun, My Fair Lady,* and other long-running Broadway successes, Hollywood returned to the late-twenties practice of bringing book musicals to the screen relatively untouched. Whereas a film like the 1929 version of *The Desert Song* takes the operetta out of doors, thus capitalizing on the freedom afforded by the change of medium, the adaptations of the fifties and sixties stick painfully close to the Broadway version. The freedom from scenic construction achieved by Lubitsch and Mamoulian a quarter-century earlier is here abandoned in favor of a staginess that testifies more to a poverty of taste than to any limitation of means. In the thirties even the otherwise filmically uninteresting MacDonald and Eddy films had the montage sequences of a Slavko Vorkapich, Berkeley treated his sound stages like oversized editing tables, and even the most undistinguished studio productions created a sense of visual and aural space that far surpassed the simple unity of the proscenium stage. Compare to these modest but honestly acquired riches the unexpected poverty of the "I Believe in You" number from *How to Succeed in Business*. With the possible exception of Harold Arlen, no Hollywood composer since Gershwin can match Frank Loesser for his mastery over syncopation, over unexpected voice leading, over eccentric harmonies. Even his ballads zigzag their way to an emotional and musical climax. Nothing straightforward, nothing still, nothing obvious. Yet the David Swift film somehow manages to shoot "I Believe in You" without a single camera movement, and without the least cut. Just turn the camera on and let it run. Worse than a return to the common early thirties camera-in-the-fifth-row-of-the-orchestra technique, this arrangement puts the camera in a head brace. Throughout the fifties and sixties such lack of independence from the stage production was the rule (e.g., *Call Me Madam, The King and I, My Fair Lady, The Sound of Music, Camelot, A Funny Thing Happened on the Way to the Forum*). Even when directors went out of their way to exploit the versatility of the film medium, they often did so in the servile and uninventive manner of a Joshua Logan, whose ever-present filters in *South Pacific* strive to create an atmosphere of mystery otherwise desperately lacking. Even Vincente Minnelli seemed doomed to his least exciting and original films when he turned to Broadway adaptation. While *Brigadoon, Bells Are Ringing*, and *On a Clear Day* certainly don't fall to the level of *Kismet*, they are still far below the level of Minnelli's original musicals, or for that matter of his melodramas.

Neither the loss of the sex-as-adventure formula, nor Hollywood's renewed dependence on Broadway can alone explain the fairy tale musical's post-war loss of vitality, however. A third contributing factor is to be found in the post-war growth of the folk musical subgenre. In the early years of the Hollywood musical, typically American locations are used more for their picturesque qualities than for the real problems and concerns which they might evoke. Fairy tale exoticism and not folk drama is the rule in portraying the old South, for example. Throughout the thirties, therefore, the folk and fairy tale subgenres remain largely undifferentiated. There is little difference between the treatment of Hungarian gypsies and colored slaves, or between Ruritanian princes and Southern aristocrats. When the folk approach begins to receive a new impetus in the late thirties (and especially after the 1943 opening of *Oklahoma!*), it is thus first seen as little more than a variant of the fairy tale approach, a final step in the evident displacement of the genre from aristocratic foreigners toward middle-class Americans. When the folk musical took flight unexpectedly after *Meet Me in St. Louis*, however, it began to diverge rapidly from its fairy tale precedents, concentrating on a quasi-serious, quasi-mythological approach to the American homeland rather than the typically supercilious look which the fairy tale musical takes at distant disorder.

The success of the folk musical (particularly at MGM and Fox, two of the largest producers of fairy tale musicals in previous years) effectively sapped the fairy tale musical's remaining strength. In fact it is interesting to note the extent to which the fairy tale musical accommodates itself to folk conventions in order to perpetuate its very life. Gone are the operatic scores which characterized the subgenre in the pre-war years (to be sure, Joe Pasternak, now moved from Universal to MGM, continued to include a high-art number or two in nearly all his productions, but the film as a whole rarely was built around these arias or symphonies). More and more accessible to the untrained voices of the average audience, these new songs often owed their existence to composers and lyricists well versed in the folk tradition (e.g. Rodgers and Hammerstein, who move from the folk musicals *Oklahoma!* and *Carousel* to the fairy tale atmosphere of *South Pacific* and *The Sound of Music).* In the thirties, fairy tale musicals were virtually devoid of children; now they become a major factor of spectacle and plot (*An American in Paris, South Pacific, The Sound of Music, Oliver, Mary Poppins*—not to mention the growing number of fairy-tale inspired cartoon musicals). Folk motifs like clambakes and amusement parks abound (*Clambake, The Wiz, Damn Yankees, Mary Poppins, Half a Sixpence*). Once New York City was restricted to theaters and publishers (the show musical) or night clubs and sumptuous apartments (the fairy tale tradition); now, in the wake of *On the Town,* we find ourselves wandering the streets *(On a Clear Day, Hair, The Wiz).* Even the films which take us farthest from home and dwell most on the power of imagination create a folk thematics and a more

complete and classless society than their Ruritanian predecessors (*Brigadoon, An American in Paris, The Sound of Music, Blue Hawaii).*

Dissipating its energy into cartoon fantasies, innumerable straight transfers from Broadway, a never ending flow of beach movies and Elvis shows, and a desperate output of remakes of previous successes, the fairy tale musical's drop in energy level must nevertheless be seen in terms of the overall context of musical production. Previous study has concentrated so heavily on MGM, the Freed Unit, and thus the period stretching approximately from 1944-55, that the genre's basic statistics have been too often forgotten. The drop off in production after 1948 is striking. The average annual production of the musical's first two decades (defined in Hirschhorn's fairly strict sense) was 48 films. The next decade halves those figures (1949-58 = 23 per year), while the subsequent decades have reduced even that low figure by two-thirds (1959-80 = 7+ per year). Such a spectacular drop in production is hard to imagine from our vantage point, for we remember (and, alas, usually write our film histories on the basis of) only a small fraction of the total production. The vitality of the genre, however, can clearly not be measured by the few masterworks alone. Just as the Freed Unit's continued existence permitted the production of numerous artistically innovative films, so the existence at every major studio of a large stable of composers, lyricists, writers, artists, choreographers, musicians, arrangers, dancers, singers, and so forth made it possible for the musical to develop—even in its most average productions—beyond the level of musical films produced elsewhere in the world.

To understand the magnitude of the drop-off in production it is perhaps helpful to consider that the production of the war years alone matches the entire production of the last three decades. Or to put it another way, it took just twelve years to produce the first third of the total musical production from 1927 to the present (1927-38 = 457 films). The second third took even less time to produce; by 1947, i.e. in 9 years, two-thirds of the total output was history (1939-47 = 462 films). By contrast it has taken the last thirty-seven years to produce the final third of the total production (1948-84 = 466 films). More than any theory or analysis, these figures eloquently explain the debt which the musical owes to Hollywood's assembly-line genre film production system. Once production falls below the critical minimum of some two dozen films a year in the mid-fifties, it no longer remains possible to turn out a full-fledged musical with permanent studio personnel alone. Too little produc-tion means too few permanent personnel, which in turn spells too little production. Just as Hollywood's investment in the artistic and technical crews necessary for the production of musicals once forced the studios into constant production, with or without ideas, simply to amortize their investment, now the lack of investment in permanent personnel made it all the harder to undertake projects as mammoth as the creation of an all-new large-scale musical film (a further reason for dependence on Broadway's prepackaged spectacles, which has the added benefit of also providing prepackaged personnel—personnel who could be, as it were, "leased" rather than bought or put on long-term contract). More perhaps than any genre, the musical reveals the mechanisms which kept Hollywood together, and those which tore it apart. In Hollywood's glory days, the musical was Hollywood, its proudest possession and production. When the musical began to decline, Hollywood as a whole could not be far behind.

The Show Musical

OF ALL THE TRADITIONALLY RECOGNIZED TYPES OF MUSICAL, the backstage variety is certainly the best known and the most often commented upon. Responsible for the genre's revival in 1933, the backstage musical has usually been considered a category by itself, having little in common with films which do not take place in and around the Broadway theater. This emphasis on semantics has not served the musical well; by identifying the subgenre with its setting rather than with a particular syntax (replicable in other circumstances), critics have privileged both a narrow range of films and a limited approach to them. For the purposes of this chapter, therefore, a wider and more syntactic approach will be taken to the subgenre which includes the backstage films. In general, the films dealt with in this chapter all construct their plot around the creation of a show (Broadway play, fashion magazine, high school revue, Hollywood film), with the making of a romantic couple both symbolically and causally related to the success of the show. The show musical subgenre thus includes films like *Babes in Arms* and *Lady in the Dark* as well as *Footlight Parade*; it covers *Anchors Aweigh, Singin' in the Rain,* and *Lili* as well as *The Band Wagon*; it even includes the many films which concentrate on the makers of musicals themselves, from the biopics of the forties to the compilation films of the seventies. The standard is not whether the film takes place backstage, but whether it is primarily concerned with putting on a show.

The Sources of Show Musical Semantics

In the preceding chapter I described the process whereby a half-century of European operetta and a generation of American imitations provided convenient models for the sound cinema. Commonly advertised as

"The $7.70 Show That Thrilled Broadway for Two Seasons Now Bigger, Grander, Funnier on the Vitaphone Screen" (*Fifty Million Frenchmen*, 1931), these adaptations first introduced Viennese violins and Parisian morals to the American hinterland. Already in the earliest years of the talkies, however, a different strain of film arose, recognizable by its recourse to indigenous rather than European forms of music and entertainment. Where the fairy tale musical borrowed its material from a long and prestigious—and rather cultured—tradition, this other type of musical scoured the American scene for its musical idiom. Even before the show musical developed the syntax to which it owes its name, therefore, it was a distinct form, recognizable by its debt to nearly a century of characteristically American forms of entertainment.

Perhaps the single most continuous source of show musical semantics is American vaudeville.[1] When vaudeville first developed out of the mid-nineteenth-century music hall tradition, it was decidedly a male pastime. Which provided the greatest attraction for the mainly male patrons we shall never know: the stage acts, the female waitresses, or the liquor they served. We do know, however, that during the sixties and seventies a campaign to clean up matinee performances for women culminated in the 1881 institution of Tony Pastor's 14th Street Theatre in New York as a source of respectable family entertainment. In 1885 the opening of the Keith/Albee theater in Boston reinforced this tendency, which grew along with the Keith/Albee and Proctor circuits to nationwide propor-

tions. With the disappearance of liquor and the definitive replacement of the "Beer Garden" arrangement (tables plus stage) by the now familiar proscenium theater, both the Keith and Proctor groups adopted a continuous performance format, with one act succeeding another from late morning to midnight. Soon the well known "two-a-day" pattern crystallized: performers would do a turn in the matinee program, then return for another in the evening. As vaudeville moved away from its single-sex beerhall origins, its influence expanded considerably, especially with the turn-of-the-century development of a so-called "small-time" vaudeville, increasing both the overall size of the vaudeville audience and the intense competition for quality acts: opera singers, scenes from the legitimate stage, and foreign stars now took their places alongside the more familiar solo or duet comedy routines. The growth of the Loew circuit during this period and the opening of the famous figurehead New York Palace Theatre in 1913 contributed to making the teens and twenties the veritable heyday of vaudeville.

From vaudeville the show musical borrows three major aspects: performers, format, and thematics. Restricted to the operetta tradition, the film musical never would have developed its characteristic combination of music and comedy. Borrowing from vaudeville, however, Hollywood found itself overrun with performers used to alternating between comedy routines and songs. From Moran and Mack to Jimmy Durante, former vaudevillians could be counted on for light touches and comic interludes. Conceived as a disconnected series of ten to twenty minute "turns," however, vaudeville provided no model whatsoever for the narrative function of short comic numbers. In its tendency toward brief comic scenes inserted randomly into an episodic plot, and thus in its early preference for the revue format, the musical reveals its debt to vaudeville's tradition of short, unconnected turns. Indeed, it is interesting to note how many narrative musicals seem organized solely to justify a long, usually final, multiple-number revue: *Footlight Parade*, *The Gang's All Here*, *Thousands Cheer*, *The Band Wagon*, *The Glenn Miller Story*, *Woodstock*, many more. With the shortness of turns forcing vaudeville to abandon the large group numbers characteristic of the minstrel show and the stage spectacular, life on a vaudeville circuit settled into an uneasy relationship between each act and all the others making up the show. Built into the vaudeville experience, therefore, is an intensified version of the familiar actor/ troupe theatrical dichotomy. On the legitimate stage, competition must be limited to the period of casting, for as soon as the cast is set each person's job depends in part on the performances of the others. If the show folds, everyone is out of a job. In vaudeville, on the other hand, contracts are handed out to each individual act. Individualism and personal ambition perpetually threaten a general ambience of concern and cooperation. In those films which owe the most to the vaudeville tradition (e.g., *For Me and My Gal*), we thus find the opposition of individual desire to the good of the group elevated into a major thematic role.

Growing up alongside vaudeville were the minstrel show and its step-child bur-lesque. Inaugurated in the 1830s and 40s by such innovators as Thomas D. Rice and Edwin Christy, the minstrel show typically employed forty singers arranged in a semi-circle on a necessarily large stage.[2] The "first part," as it came to be called, was made up of comic dialogue between the three named characters (The Interlocutor, Mr. Bones, and Mr. Tambo) interrupted by group songs and ending with a showy "walk-around." Then came the "olio," a specialty number—often a stump speech—while the stage is reset for the "second part," characterized by individual specialties followed by the all-important "afterpiece," which often reproduced a complete play. Performed entirely in blackface (blacks entered the business only in the 1870s, and even then they too had to make up in black face), the minstrel show gave us the banjo and the formulaic straight man/funny man comedy team (the farcical Bones and Tambo always getting the better of the serious Interlocutor), as well as the transfer of laughter from an external audience (as in legitimate theater, where a joke on stage is met with laughter in the balcony) to an audience located within the spectacle (on stage in the minstrel show, on the laugh track in TV situation comedies). Whenever a Bones or Tambo would get the best of the Interlocutor all others on stage would howl with laughter, thus leading the theater audience and showing them when to laugh. While the actual borrowings of the show musical from the minstrel show are limited to a few fairly idiosyncratic films (e.g., *Babes on Broadway*), the entire organization of the show musical depends on this important identification of one audience with another—

the one within the proscenium, the other without. There is perhaps no shot in the show musical tradition more characteristic than the shot of the audience, either over the spectators' backs or from the point of view of the performers. As in the popular arts in general, the show musical limits the freedom of the external audience by forcing it to identify with an internal audience which can be controlled by administrative decision rather than artistic principles. A stand-up comic writes his jokes, then rises or falls on the audience's evaluation of his material and delivery; Mr. Bones appears to be following the same principle, but in fact he is only part of a larger text wherein the funny joke is by definition the one that the boss tells everyone to laugh at. Audience manipulation through the careful use of an internal audience enters the American scene through the minstrel show.

Until the Civil War, burlesque had little connection with minstrelsy, and certainly nothing of the bawdiness associated with it in this century.[3] Derived from the English burlesque tradition best represented by Gay's *Beggar's Opera*, burlesque in America meant humorous stage shows based on the parody of a well known classic (e.g., *Hamlet* in 1828). In the 1860s, however, the decline of legitimate burlesque and the arrival of numerous less-than-decorous European female troupes concurred to change forever the course of burlesque. From Britain came Lydia Thompson and her British blondes; from France came the Great Parisienne Ballet Troup, with their scandalously revealing tights. When chance gave the Parisian ladies an opportunity to show off

their wares as a dancing chorus in an otherwise undistinguished play, *The Black Crook* (1866) set off an explosion of condemnation—and of curiosity. Taking advantage of this atmosphere, Michael Leavitt in 1869 had the bright idea of replacing the men of the minstrel show semi-circle with lovely ladies clad in tights (with Tambo and Bones dressed as men!). This new arrangement provided ample opportunity to display the talents—and the bodies—of forty lovely ladies at a time. The afterpiece for the first year was a travesty of *The Mikado*; every year thereafter the Rentz-Santley shows added a new burlesque to their program, along with such risqué imported dances as the can-can. Nevertheless, there was not yet any attempt to turn this new form of burlesque into strictly male entertainment. No double-entendre jokes, no salaciousness, no nudity. By the turn of the century, however, things had changed somewhat. Little Egypt had introduced the hootchy-kootchy dance at the 1893 Chicago World's Fair, thus providing burlesque with a staple individual dance whose sexual implications could hardly remain hidden; sales of pornography before and during the show increased; emphasis on large, buxom, fleshy girls grew (to the point where Billy "Beef Trust" Watson insisted on girls weighing at least 200 lbs.). During the early part of this century the Columbia burlesque circuit was formed on the vaudeville model. Soon nudity was introduced, first in human tableaux imitating well known classical art works, then as a matter of course. Not until the era of sound film, however, did the familiar striptease come of age.

Though burlesque, like the minstrel show, provides the subject matter for relatively few musicals (e.g., *Applause, Dance Girl Dance, Gypsy*), it contributed in a major way to the identification of the show musical spectator with a male internal audience. In this, burlesque is strongly supported by its high-class sister, the chorus girl spectacular. Borrowed in part from the French music-hall (i.e., Folies-Bergère) tradition, the high-class spectacular was first popularized in this country by Florenz Ziegfeld, who in a series of yearly Follies stretching from 1907 to 1931 did not so much flaunt nudity as suggest it by a variety of tricks and lavish costumes. Imitated by Earl Carroll in his Vanities and George White in his Scandals, Ziegfeld made it *de bon ton* to go to the theater to watch scantily clad women performing simple but visually effective routines. More than any other showman, Ziegfeld is responsible for the show musical's tendency to deemphasize individual talent and to concentrate interest on the visual patterning of costumes and bodies. This now-familiar approach deprives woman of her status as an equal partner in a shared act; instead she becomes a pretty "hoofer." Not just in the films of Busby Berkeley, but throughout the entire show musical tradition, this vision of woman inherited from burlesque and Ziegfeld will be reiterated.

By the time sound invaded Hollywood, Americans were thus thoroughly conditioned to a definition of "entertainment" that was largely passive in nature. Whereas earlier generations thought of singing, dancing, and baseball as something entertaining *to do*, early twentieth-century Americans were already quite likely to think of those activities as spectator sports. More and more, it was necessary *to be entertained* in order to have a good time. This concentration of pleasure in the senses of sight and hearing is nowhere more obvious than in the development of the fashionable night club as a place where entertainment is served up with the same style and on the same drop-in basis as the food. Launched in 1911 by Lasky and Harris's enormously successful rooftop club, the Folies-Bergère, the night-club has served ever since as a special showcase for worldly wise crooners, while creating an easy parallel between the love songs warbled on stage and the pairs of lovebirds sitting at the surrounding tables. In Hollywood, Al Jolson and Frank Sinatra have especially benefitted from the opportunities afforded by the night club model.

When the talkies were born in the late twenties it was no doubt natural, as many commentators have pointed out, for Hollywood to turn to indigenous forms of entertainment for its music, performers, plots, and settings. The stage already had a tradition, and so Hollywood simply borrowed that tradition. We must remember, however, that the percentage of actual on-stage time in the backstage musical is in truth quite small. Far from simply borrowing the material which the stage had to offer—as the fairy tale musical often did in the early years—the show musical regularly displaces interest from the stage show itself to two related phenomena. In the theater everything takes place on stage; in a backstage musical the stage is instead the intersection of the audience's gaze and the actors' backstage efforts. The theater audience sees only the show; stage activity thus remains primary. In the backstage musical, however, the film audience not only watches the theater audience watch the show, but it also observes the theater actors rehearsing the show. The show itself thus loses its primacy, making way for the new primary concerns of observing the show and making the show. Now, just as the show itself has a history (the one I have just sketched in terms of indigenous American entertainment forms), so the concerns of observing and making the show have a history. Though we could well trace the motif of actor as character to the baroque play-within-a-play tradition stretching from Shakespeare and Corneille to Pirandello and Anouilh, it is perhaps more pertinent to recognize the extraordinary predilection revealed in the years prior to the rise of sound film for plays dealing with theatrical personnel.

Quite apart from the more intellectual Pirandellian strain of *mise-en-abyme*, the Broadway stage from 1919 to 1928 waged a love affair with the backstage lives of all manner of entertainers. No doubt influenced by Hollywood's growing tendency to implement a star system stressing the off-screen lives of actors and actresses alike, Broadway's fascination with backstage affairs began with Avery Hopwood's 1919 The Gold Diggers, produced by the famous David Belasco. While Hopwood's play is set entirely in the girls' apartment, it lays sufficient stress on the connection between stage life and real life to give the impression that it takes place entirely backstage. Af-

ter the then unheard of number of ninety consecutive weeks on Broadway, the company went on tour for another 528 performances, until 1923, when a silent film version took over, only to be replaced in 1929 by the 100 percent Natural Color Vitaphone version, *Gold Diggers of Broadway*. In the wake of this success, the twenties brought to Broadway an unending series of plays concentrating on the entertainment profession, its problems and joys. Among the most successful plays of the 1926-27 season, for example, was George Abbott and Philip Dunning's *Broadway*, soon to be made into a Paul Fejos film (Universal, 1929) which inspired many other musicals mixing music and the underworld in shady night-club back rooms (e.g., *Broadway Babies, Go Into Your Dance, Wonder Bar, Ziegfeld Girl, Party Girl, The Joker Is Wild, The Blues Brothers*). Here the backstage area unveils the evil underside of the stage rather than its supporting cast. The same season revealed the carnival world in Kenyon Nicholson's *The Barker*, the multiple realms of Samson Raphaelson's *Jazz Singer*, soon to be given over to the immortal Al Jolson, and Hammerstein's stage version of Edna Ferber's *Show Boat*, with its concentration on yet another area of American entertainment. The following year brought 322 Barbara Stanwyck performances in George Manker Watters' and Arthur Hopkins' *Burlesque*, a savvy alternation of off- and on-stage scenes soon to be transferred to celluloid as *The Dance of Life* (Paramount, 1929). Still other early films derived directly from currently popular novels, e.g., *Show Girl* (First National, 1928) and *Applause* (Paramount, 1929). The early growth of the backstage musical is thus not so much a mark of Hollywood's reflexivity vis-à-vis Broadway, as others have claimed; it is rather a sign of Hollywood's attentiveness to Broadway themes, and of Hollywood's perpetual willingness to borrow those themes and turn them to its own purposes.

Hollywood's tendency to split its attention between audience and performers, stage and backstage, performance and box office, has the effect of fragmenting the show musical's semantics. There is not one set of semantic elements in this subgenre, but three or four. Traditional criticism of the backstage musical commonly splits the form into "narrative" and "number," treating the two categories as equivalent of "real" and "ideal" and as very nearly mutually exclusive. As I have already suggested in chapter four, however, such diametrical oppositions in the musical tend to be resolved by the use of one or more mediating factors. It is thus more fruitful to identify a series of four "sites" within the backstage musical which, taken together, constitute two complementary series of three, each with a pair of terms seen as diametrically opposed and a third which serves as a mediating factor. For the characters in the film, the entire world is divided into the city and the theater. On the one side the New York City black-and-white world which characterizes the genre from its very beginnings: a simple unisex apartment or two, bus or taxi, elevator or stairs, a store or a street. On the other side the glitter of opening night, the marquee, the lights, the color, the orchestra,

and dancers stepping in time to the music. In between the two stands that world which is neither city nor stage: the practice halls, rehearsal spots, backstage areas, and dressing rooms which lead from the drabness of the city to the glamour of the stage. Here it is that ragged movements are refined, stilted speech made silky, make-up applied, costumes adjusted, identities transformed. For the backstage area, like Janus, turns both ways. Two doors—one opening onto the street, the other onto the stage. Only here do the problems of life and those of the stage cross. The backstage area is that crucible in which actors are turned into characters, actions into gestures, and real life into art, as well as, in the other direction, the place where ham actors are turned back into real people and vessels of dramatic fiction into solid citizens of the real world. Because it is continuous visually with the real world as well as thematically with the stage world, the backstage middle-world serves to establish an unexpected continuity between the diametrically opposed realms of reality and art.

For the audience, however, the values are precisely reversed. The end of the actor's quest is the performance; in it the actor finds momentary utopia and escape from the world of time. The audience, however, is looking for something quite different. Why should backstage activity so captivate audiences throughout the history of the musical? What is it about the wings of the theater that makes them seem even more fascinating than the stage? On the answer to this question hangs much of our understanding of the show musical as a functioning system. In

Even in a stylized production number, the set and backdrop of the show musical typically represent a familiar urban setting realistically portrayed, as in this Berkeley extravaganza from *Forty-Second Street*.

[UW]

a general way we might say that the semantic elements of the show musical's narrative component derive entirely from a single source: stars doing what they do when they are not on stage. The show musical gives us the illusion of seeing something which theatergoers cannot perceive: the theater audience's gaze is stopped by the stage backdrop, but the film audience can see right through that backdrop and into the wings. To put it schematically:

theater : film ::
stage : backstage ::
public : private.

In other words, the show musical camera becomes an agent of voyeurism. When we go to a backstage musical we lift a veil; by pulling aside the backdrop or peeking into the wings we are able to satisfy our natural desire to look beyond, behind, and beneath.

A keen sense of this privileged vision is provided by the opening scenes of *Thousands Cheer*. In the first scene José Iturbi conducts an orchestra accompanying Kathryn Grayson's rendition of *La Traviata*, then announces that she is leaving music in order to follow her father to his new Army post. Into this scene shots of the audience are constantly intercut, as if to remind us that this is a public performance, available to all. Immediately after a second song we cut to a dressing room where the conductor and the singer say their goodbyes: he calls her Kathryn and she calls him José. Now there is no audience, nobody present but the two stars, so only now does director George Sidney reveal the fact that their fictional first names in this movie correspond to their real first names. The effect is to convince the viewer that he is witnessing, thanks to some technical wizardry, a scene between the stars themselves rather than between two fictional characters. This device clearly presents the stage production as public and illusionist (Kathryn Grayson plays a woman whose father is about to be transferred), while the backstage scene is private and real (José and Kathryn are called by their real names). Only the cinema—the screen that serves as a window on hidden realities—can produce this sensation of looking through the stage at the private lives and production secrets beyond. In short, whereas backstage space serves as an intermediary for the actor striving toward the stage, for the audience it is the stage that mediates between our limited workaday world and that imaginary ever-so-glamorous life lived by the stars. Stage and backstage space thus serve as a reversible intermediary between two real worlds, that of the audience and that of the actors:

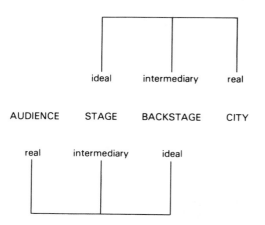

Invariably, then, constitution of the show musical's semantics must begin with the establishment of a firm sense of the "real," against which the show's "ideal" will be pitted. Indeed, with few exceptions, the show musical offers a particularly partial view of reality, and thus a peculiarly limited set of semantic possibilities. Providing a strikingly middle-class view of the process of producing and marketing a commodity (the show), the show musical takes for granted most of the activities normally performed by a working class. The backstage musical rarely shows the work of production (sets are not built, they appear; lighting is not planned, it is as natural as the stars; curtains aren't cranked open, but rise on their own); the fashion magazine needs no printer; when a group of adolescents get together to put on a show they can always count on free instruments, costumes, props, music, even a stage—never is anyone shown actually procuring or making these essential elements. In other words, the show musical is a white-collar genre, consistently showing only upper-echelon production personnel and performers, while masking the blue-collar work of production. This preference for a middle-class view of production has an enormous effect on the semantics of the show musical's narrative sections. In general these sections are characterized by a realistic look, but it is a middle-class version of the real, which gains audience acceptance thanks to the same sleight of hand prevalent in *Love Me Tonight*. In the previous chapter we saw how Mamoulian made Maurice Chevalier—the dashing Parisian—into a symbol of everyday reality simply by opposing him to a manifestly unreal fairy princess. Even reality in *Love Me Tonight* is colored by fairy tales, for only in a fairy tale musical could Maurice Chevalier represent reality. In the same way, the opposition of the seemingly realistic narrative of the show musical to a patently unreal stage show makes it possible for us to accept as realistic a version of production which so obviously hides all the work. The semantics of the show musical plot are thus based not so much on the production of a show (magazine, film, etc.) as on a particular middle-class view of what it is to produce a show. As such, the show musical perpetuates a romantic mythology whereby creativity is vested in the hands of the few—the same mythology that

gave rise to *auteur* criticism.

If the fairy tale heroine sleeps in a castle, and the folk musical's leading lady in the maternal manse, the show musical's protagonist typically lives alone in a modest but tastefully decorated apartment. When the protagonists are children or adolescents, the middle-class domicile usually houses the entire family (*100 Men and a Girl, Babes in Arms, Strike Up the Band, Ziegfeld Girl, Bye Bye Birdie*), but as a rule one essential set places one sex or the other in a bachelor apartment, often shared by more than one character (*Broadway Melody, Gold Diggers of 1933, Broadway Melody of 1940, Two Sisters from Boston, Les Girls*). Even when the film heavily emphasizes the theater or film world, this middle-class bachelor apartment set remains a staple (as in *For Me and My Gal, Anchors Aweigh, Easter Parade, Singin' in the Rain*, and even *The Band Wagon*, where Fred Astaire's temporary lodgings are personalized by the introduction of his private record and art collection). In the relatively few show musicals where the protagonists are married, the bachelor flat approach is perpetuated by the use of separate but parallel dressing rooms (*Sweethearts, Barkleys of Broadway, The Country Girl, A Star Is Born* [1976]). Though clearly reflecting the type of show produced, show musical semantics never fail to deploy the sets, costumes, ambitions, and mannerisms that serve to play up the fundamental differences between the sexes, thereby serving the underlying thematics of the genre as a whole.

Backstage: The Syntax of Illusion

With the coming of sound, the film industry looked in every possible direction for plots which would take full advantage of the new technology. The backstage plot was a natural, for it permitted a maximum of singing with a minimum of justification. Part-talkie films could restrict sound (and often color as well) to the staged numbers, while the increasingly popular all-talking, all-singing films found in the backstage plot an ideal way of showing off sound's full potential. This process of cannibalization of an established medium (the stage) by a new technology (sound film) is a familiar one. During the late Middle Ages the oral story-telling tradition provides the subject matter for the newly popularized manuscript technology (Boccaccio, Chaucer, Marguerite de Navarre). With the rise of printing a new form was born—the novel—which relied for centuries on a compilation of so-called manuscript forms (particularly the memoir, the letter, and the chronicle). When cinema was invented, it turned immediately to the novel for its material, with a special predilection for theatrical adaptations of Tolstoy and Zola. In these cases and many others like them, the new technology tends to borrow the old form along with its thematics, only slowly working out syntactic relationships specific to the new combination. Boccaccio's *Decameron* makes relatively meager use of the interplay between frame story and included stories, while two centuries later a lesser author, Marguerite de Navarre, will fully exploit that relationship in her *Heptameron*; seventeenth-century epistolary authors use the letter primarily for verisimilitude, while a late eighteenth-century writer like Laclos builds the entire structure of his *Les Liaisons dangereuses* around the properties peculiar to the letter form. In the same way, the early musical treats the backstage plot as a convenience, a simple ploy to justify showing off the full range of sound technology; only later will that technology and its borrowed subjects be fully integrated in a syntax particular to them.

Perhaps the most insistent plot of all the early semantic musicals was the one introduced by Al Jolson in *The Singing Fool* (1928). Jolson, the singing waiter, marries Molly, the club's beautiful performer. As long as things are sunny, Molly sticks with him, but soon, with Jolson's singing career on the rocks, Molly two-times him, leaving him to console their three-year-old child, "Sonny Boy." As the October, 1928, *Photoplay* review puts it: "If you have tears to shed, prepare to shed them now." *The Singing Fool* uses the sound track to reinforce its melodramatic plot, jerking tears at every turn. While this attempt to establish a tragic syntax for the musical (music = separation) did not survive far into the thirties, it nevertheless had many imitators in 1929 and 1930. Numerous films simply repeated the Jolson plot, emphasizing the plight of the child caught between quarreling parents or abandoned by a dissolute mother (*The Rainbow Man, Honky Tonk, Not Quite Decent, Is Everybody Happy*). Others followed the *Broadway Melody* example of having two friends fall in love with the same man. Sooner or later, someone has to make a sacrifice (e.g., in 1930 alone, *The Grand Parade,*

Chasing Rainbows, Be Yourself). Still other films developed new approaches to the backstage paradigm: the egotistical ventriloquist unable to express himself without the aid of his dummy (*The Great Gabbo*, 1929), the broken-hearted nightclub hostess (*She Couldn't Say No*, 1930), the over-the-hill burlesque queen trying desperately to protect her daughter (*Applause*, 1929). So popular in 1929, the backstage plot dwindled considerably—along with the musical in general—throughout 1931-32. It is tempting to conjecture that it declined not because the public wanted more variety (after all, the Warners/Berkeley backstage formula lasted for years), but because the public tired of the equation of music with sadness.

Whatever the cause of the musical's temporary decline, the genre's reemergence in 1933 provided the opportunity for a radical reorientation. If the pre-1933 musical was, as often as not, a weepie, the post-1933 backstage musical almost never seeks to provoke tears. No longer a sign of emotional stress or the product of a broken heart, song is from 1933 on freed to become both the symbol and expression of happiness, community, and success. In other words, the backstage musical of 1933 brought a new syntax not only to the backstage subgenre; it also for the first time established the illusionist and happy-go-lucky syntax of the genre as a whole. We often call a film a musical when it contains at least a certain minimum of diegetic music; we are sure the film is a musical if it turns on a love plot. Not until the music is fitted to the love plot in a certain way, however, is the genre's characteristic syntax established.

In short, the semantic musical *adds* music to the love plot, while the syntactic musical *equates* music with a successful love plot. Because this equation was first fully developed in the Warners backstage musicals of 1933, there has been a common tendency ever since to take the backstage subgenre as a model for the genre as a whole.

The development of musical syntax out of the plot necessities of the backstage musical is easily traced. Logically, three steps may be recognized (with historical progression approximating, but not exactly replicating, the logical progression).

1) From the earliest days of sound, staple Hollywood plots were mated with new devices to highlight the sound track. The simplest of these, as we have already seen, combined Hollywood's favorite formula—the romantic triangle—with the production of a stage show or equivalent. The common presence of these two elements within the same film soon led to the establishment of a causal sequence: either *show* ⟶ *love* (hero and heroine are thrown together by their common profession; their make-believe love on stage leads to a real romance off-stage), or *love* ⟶ *show* (only by the joint efforts of a romantic couple can the show be brought to a successful conclusion). While both of these solutions establish close causal ties between the couple and the show, neither provides a fully coherent thematic relationship between the two elements.

2) Such a thematic tie becomes established as soon as the success of the show is sensed as a displaced display of success in love. Any show could be produced by lovers, from *King Lear* to *Who's Afraid*

of *Virginia Woolf?*, but only a joyous show properly reflects a successful romantic union. When the show matches the lovers' mood, it becomes a celebration of their mating, a ritual reenactment or prefiguration of their coming together. The energy invested in the show no longer appears unexplained or misplaced, but rather *dis*placed; i.e., it is the sexual drive itself that energizes the show. If the backstage musical of the mid-thirties consistently places the major numbers at the end, it is not without reason; indeed, the typical Berkeley finale has the camera aiming at the center of concentric patterns or tracking between the legs of semi-nude chorines. Not only does love inspire the show (or vice-versa), but love *is* the show—the climax of the one must serve for the other as well.

3) Steps one and two apply to the entire musical as a genre as well as to the show musical subgenre in particular. Love is song; the energy driving the one derives from the other. Step one establishes a causal relationship between art and love; step two adds a symbolic tie; the third step finally establishes a full equation between art and love. Perhaps the clearest explanation of this equation occurs in a rather lifeless Jeanette MacDonald vehicle sandwiched between pictures with Nelson Eddy. In *Broadway Serenade*, MacDonald is married to a hot-tempered songwriter (Lew Ayres) who, jealous of her success, packs to leave. At this point MacDonald enters the apartment and delivers a touching speech to her frustrated husband. She tells him that being in love is like Peter Pan: just as the spectator must believe in Peter Pan to make him live, so a couple depends on each partner's believing in the other. Jealousy, in love, thus corresponds to an unwillingness to suspend disbelief in art. Equating herself with the show and her husband with the spectator, MacDonald provides an elegant justification of the backstage musical's fundamental love = art syntax. Not only does the romantic couple make music as a team, but the female partner is typically represented as deriving her beauty and talent from the attention lavished on her by the male. She is a vision, a song, a melody; he is a viewer, a singer, a composer. If she is music, he is a music-maker. If she is the show, he is the appreciative audience. Borrowing its formula from the well known metaphor, show musical syntax depends on couples who "make beautiful music together."

Before we turn to a consideration of specific strategies and individual films, however, we need to set the syntax of the backstage musical into the Romantic context to which it belongs. According to the lucid analysis of Denis de Rougemont, the notion of love as an all-consuming passion is a product of the early Middle Ages.[4] The troubadour poets were the first to elaborate a theory of love as a desire for the unattainable: passion resides not in the possession of the object of desire but in the tension between that object's unattainability and the lover's desire for possession. Destroy the gap between lover and loved, and the passion itself is destroyed. Courtly love, as this rather bizarre arrangement was termed, generally takes for granted the active role of the man (the lover) and the corresponding passive role of woman (the loved one). She is married, unattainable, identified with figures of purity (especially the Virgin Mary), while he is unattached and by avocation a poet. Inspired by his loved one to sexual desire, but unable (by definition) to satisfy his passion, the lover sublimates that desire into poetry, thus appearing to be poetically inspired by the woman. This configuration quite naturally leads to a correspondence between the actors of the "love plot" and those of the "show plot," a correspondence not only operating thematically but also justifying the very existence of troubadour poetry:

male role	relationship	female role
subject of desire	love	object of desire
poet	poetry	muse

To love is to write poetry; to be loved is to inspire poetry. Love *is* poetry.

This simple homology lies at the very heart of the interplay between sexual and artistic relations in the modern world. Largely replaced by more classical models between the Renaissance and the Enlightenment, the love = poetry equation resurfaces with Romanticism, never to be submerged again. For the Romantic poet, the woman—Nature—is an often contemplated but never possessed Muse; she is the raw material of his desire and his poem alike. Solitary, heartbroken, the Romantic poet basks in the bittersweet limelight of genius and passion, states equally dependent on the poet's inability to attain his goal. It is thus hardly surprising that the Romantic theater should have depended so heavily on a sense of spectacle and star worship, making every male spectator into a poet rapturously desiring his favorite female star. Indeed, the theater provides a special opportunity for the reinterpretation of the troubadour/Romantic paradigm. Already in the troubadour model the visual component was heavily stressed: the woman is set on a pedestal, she is a perfect vision, a work of art; the man is primarily a pair of eyes, a voyeur intent on consuming the woman visually. In Petrarch this motif is still more prominent, with love always being born *per gli occhi*—through the eyes. The poet is thus vision, and Laura his visible Muse. Only during the course of the nineteenth century is this configuration transferred fully to the popular theater, and that only by the progressive baring of the female body, with a resultant identification of the audience with man's prying eyes and the stage with the revelation of female beauty. Not all theater plays directly on this relationship of course, but the theater of the late nineteenth century does so increasingly. Not only does it turn a few talented actresses into veritable symbols (e.g., Sarah Bernhardt), but with the rise of burlesque and the revue, a theater is created which specifically acknowledges the sexual identity of its components: the spectators are men, the performers are women (no doubt the source of the lingering cliché whereby all male ballet dancers are suspected of homosexuality). This division is an actual one only in the lowest forms of burlesque, but even in those forms which attracted a large female clientele (e.g. the Follies), the structure of the entertainment depends on this model. The audience is the passionate male eye, the show is the unattainable female vision, unattainable precisely be-

MGM's *Broadway Serenade* places Jeanette MacDonald on an enormous pedestal, thus actualizing the familiar metaphor.

[BFI]

cause it is a show, a theatrical illusion, a fiction. Even the raunchiest burlesque presents a fiction, a sense that the woman on stage is willing to lend her body to all who ask, when in fact she is available only to the male eye—for just as poetry is displaced passion, so is the eye a figure for, a fiction for the phallus. The performer only pretends to offer up her body to the male phallus; the spectator only pretends to prefer sexual consummation. In fact, the condition of his passion is that consummation not take place, that the tension between his desire and her unattainability be maintained—and this can

be achieved only through the agency of a fiction. She is on stage, distant from him, because the sensation which he desires depends on her being kept at a distance: the distance of fiction, which the proscenium stage replicates physically. She must remain like a dream vision—higher, bigger, brighter, and sexier than life, yet utterly unreal and unattainable.

This production still from Warner's 1934 *Dames* graphically exhibits the characteristic show musical configuration: men in the dark with their cameras, watching and filming the brightly lit women on the stage before them.

[MOMA]

For every one of their early show musical efforts, Warner Brothers shot a series of publicity stills of scantily clad chorines, destined to lure male viewers, like this one from *Forty-Second Street*.

[UW]

The American musical theater was born, it is said, from the 1866 chance mating of a melodrama entitled *The Black Crook* and a French ballet company whose concert hall had burned down. With this spectacle a new kind of male spectator position was forged as well. The years after the Civil War were a libertine era in America, witnessing the visit of numerous risqué foreign troupes as well as the birth of domestic burlesque. *The Black Crook* is no exception: boast-ing scantily clad French girls clad in pink tights and "thin gauze-like material allowing the form of the figure to be discernible," this new show included one song which serves as a fit admonition to the audiences of its film descendants. "You Naughty, Naughty Men" is said to have been sung provocatively by Milly Cavendish not to the characters on stage but to the men in the audience, their eyes straining for a better look at the demoiselles on stage. The accompanying se-

The "Pettin' in the Park" number from *Gold Diggers of 1933*—a typically irreverent Berkeley "crotch shot."

[UW]

quence from *Applause* (Mamoulian, 1929) demonstrates the extent to which certain films are self-conscious of the identification of the spectator with the male point of view. The men are a mass of black below while the single point of light is provided by the woman who hovers over them like some vision in the night. The Dubin and Warren song lyric identifies a show's power quite specifically with woman's lure: "What do you go for, go see a show for. Tell the truth you go to see those beautiful dames" (*Dames*, 1934). Indeed, Busby Berkeley follows this formula to its most graphic conclusion; his camera is constantly aimed at the mid-section of his lovely chorus girls. The famous track along their faces, so that each one can be seen in close-up, thus personalizing a seemingly impersonal line-up, is matched by an equally important track, this one undoing the individualization of the face-level track: I speak of the track between the legs, the voyeuristic movement which equates the eyes/camera with the phallus and which reduces each individual girl to the area between the abdomen and the

Rarely has a director been as sensitive to the potential inherent in a new form as Rouben Mamoulian. His first film, Paramount's 1929 *Applause*, tells the story of an over-the-hill burlesque queen (Helen Morgan), who is desperately trying to make a better life for her daughter (Joan Peers). The following sequence, in which the daughter first discovers her mother's occupation, constitutes a veritable glossary of the show musical's eventual clichés. In shot 4, Mamoulian capitalizes on burlesque's traditional opposition of the male orchestra to the female dancers, the phallic trombone penetrating the shimmying woman. In shot 6 (as later in shots 7 and 17) we receive graphic proof that spectacles such as this are not meant for women's eyes; while the men leer at the dancers, the daughter hides her eyes, refusing to gaze at her mother's nakedness. Shot 9 cuts from a neutral, above-the-crowd shot to an over-the-shoulder shot identifying us with the internal audience. This shot, limiting our vision to the women from the waist down, contrasts the intense darkness of the audience to the bright legs up front. From horizontal shot, we then move to a high angle, and finally to a vertical top shot (11), turning the women into pure pattern. In shot 14 we move from one side of the audience to the other, with the camera actually hidden behind the loge curtains, thus compounding the sense of dark privacy soon to be associated with show musical spectatorship. Shot 20 provides an interesting pendant to shot 9. Both drop down to a lower angle, but whereas shot 9 identified us with male vision, shot 20 dips to the level of the women's knees, revealing all too clearly the object of the men's gaze. With the close-up of legs in shot 23, we begin an increasingly rapid alternation between the female body and the male gaze. With shot 31, the general ecstacy reaches the orchestra leader, and then in shot 37 the string bass player, who, by dancing with his instrument, clearly identifies his music-making as a sexual activity. The trombonist then contributes his suggestive back-and-forth motion, again quickening the cutting pace and increasing the shot scale. As if she has witnessed an illicit sexual encounter—and she has—the daughter finally stands up and leaves. All of this in two and a half minutes (the last 22 shots in a breathtaking 30 seconds)—an extraordinary lesson in show musical editing.

[pers]

1

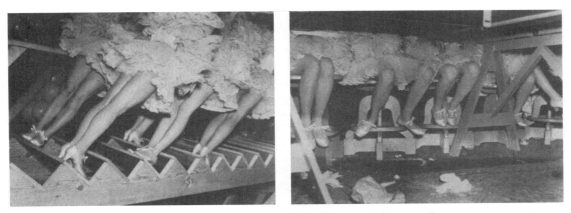

Studio photographers apparently carried the show musical's overall patterns into their private picture-taking, as we all too easily see from these two extracurricular shots taken backstage on the set of MGM's *The Great Ziegfeld*.

[MOMA]

knees. Those "crotch shots" are by no means restricted to Berkeley, for that matter; they show up in scores of show musicals, from *Footlight Parade* to *Singin' in the Rain*, and from *Words and Music* to *Cabaret*. If, as Hedy Lamarr's violinist husband in *Ziegfeld Girl* puts it, dancing is "showing yourself to other men," then the crotch shot is the semantic unit *par excellence* of the show musical, while the identification of the camera/audience as male and the show as female constitutes the very foundation of the show musical's syntax.

The voyeurism of overt sexuality thus joins the mental voyeurism associated with the viewer's ability to see backstage, to see through curtains and behind sets into the private lives of the stars. Indeed, so much show musical energy is concentrated on the pleasures of voyeurism, that the cost of the spectator's indulgence is too often forgotten. For voyeurism is here bought only at the price of a corresponding blindness. Because we are permitted

"backstage" within the film, we fail to recognize that there is no such thing as backstage in the film world, only "on-stage." We never go behind the set but only behind the stage part of the set. In short, the more we see back*stage*, the less we realize that we cannot see behind the *set*.

Fundamental to the backstage musical tradition, the stock casting of woman as visible and man as viewer has far wider ramifications for the society in which the musical flourished. We can best come at the omnipresence of this model by considering the ambiguous role played by make-up in twentieth-century American life. For this purpose a simple example from *The Broadway Melody* (1929) proves most instructive. Bessie Love and Anita Page have brought their sister act to New York in hopes of making the big time. Desperately in love with Charles King, Bessie sees that he loves her sister and decides to play the martyr in order to free him to declare his love. Immediately

The first major show musical success, MGM's *Broadway Melody* attracted crowds—and imitators—for years to come.

[MOMA]

after this scene a long take reveals Bessie Love crying over the pictures of Anita Page and Charles King, then removing her make-up with cold cream, and finally accepting her uncle's offer for a job teamed with a different girl. Embedded in this sequence lies a basic assumption of show musical syntax: to break up a romance is to break up an act. Instead of setting these two homologous activities side-by-side, however, director Beaumont inserts the seemingly gratuitous cold cream scene. This placement suggests the ambiguous, intermediary status which we as a society accord to make-up. Women wear make-up, but so do actors; make-up is used to attract a man, but make-up is

also used to deceive an audience. By removing her make-up, Bessie Love simultaneously symbolizes the end of the love relationship (she no longer wants to "make herself beautiful" for her man), as well as the end of the sister act.

It is no accident that the performer removing her make-up should be a woman, for in our society woman is constantly on view (particularly during the heyday of the Hollywood musical); she has an image, she is a work of art, she wears costumes not clothes, she is pretty as a picture, she goes to a beauty salon not a barbershop, in short she is made-up, created. In the theater, make-up is used to facilitate identification of an actor or ac-

On the sound stage of *The Broadway Melody*. Songwriters Arthur Freed and Herb Nacio Brown are at the piano.

[MOMA]

tress with the character he/she plays; that is, it serves the theatrical illusion without which the (traditional) show cannot go on. For woman it is no different. Make-up leads to a "cover girl" complexion. But what is a cover girl? She is a woman photographed, cropped, and framed in such a way as to transform her into a work of art, an otherworldly vision impossible in this world of flesh and blood. To achieve a cover girl complexion is to abandon humanity for art, to climb back up on that pedestal of perfection and unattainability where the troubadours first set woman. To be made up is thus not to heighten one's natural beauty, but to don a mask, a theatrical prop which changes the identity of the wearer. Just as

society has made woman into a show, so that same society has forged man as an eye, as a spectator of woman's show whose most important function is to validate the power of the illusion.[5] A show must be shown to someone in order to be a show. In the show musical, man is that someone.

The applicability of these remarks to the backstage musical extends even further than might at first be expected. As a group of French theoreticians has recently shown, the technology of cinema creates a necessary identification between the spectator and the cinematic apparatus.[6] What the spectator consumes at the moment of projection is precisely that which the camera earlier recorded; the marks of

Perpetuating the twenties' immensely popular night-club setting, *Broadway* also helps to inaugurate the show musical's characteristic parallel between the show and the couple. Says Billie Moore (Merna Kennedy) to Roy Lane (Glenn Tryon), "Don't say the act is off, Roy. I'm willing to do my share."

[UW]

perspective inscribed in the film image thus place the spectator at the precise spot of the camera. He is both the creator of and the consumer of the film. This correspondence is of more than passing importance, for it provides the very basis for the syntax of the show musical. Earlier we saw how the Western lyric tradition from the troubadours to Romanticism identifies the desired woman with the Muse, the lover with the poet, and ultimately love with poetry. The doubling of the male role (poet *and* lover) makes the man alternately the creator and consumer of the woman. In the apparatus of the cinema a similar configuration is implicit

(camera = spectator, creator = consumer), but only in the show musical is this correspondence between Romantic mythology and cinematic technology fully explored. Man is the director, producer, songwriter, or teacher; he is Pygmalion and Svengali. But he is also the admiring eye, the loving, desiring gaze unable to possess its object. Woman is alternately the source of man's creative desire, and the product of that same creativity. The identity of camera and spectator, when combined with the Romantic identity of poet and lover, justifies both the backstage musical's equation of making art and gazing at women, and the allotment of two different but complementary roles to man: producer and consumer.

The merit of fully elaborating this syntax must go to a series of Warner Brothers musicals created by the same stock company in 1933-34. With choreography by Busby Berkeley and songs by Harry Warren and Al Dubin, these films all featured a dancing Ruby Keeler and a crooning Dick Powell as the young couple whose romance and show is ineffectually opposed by the grumpy, anti-entertainment, moralistic *senex*, Guy Kibbee (often seconded by Hugh Herbert). With a chorus line filled out by Joan Blondell and/or Ginger Rogers, these four films constitute an extraordinarily influential nucleus of the backstage mode: *Forty-Second Street, Gold Diggers of 1933, Footlight Parade*, and *Dames*. Throughout this series the problem of putting on a Broadway show and constituting a romantic couple are so effectively intertwined that the two separate activities come to be equated, with the long final number celebrating the successful conclusion of show and romance alike.

From the very start of *Forty-Second Street*, the show ("*Pretty Girl*") is identified as a collaboration between male artistic direction (Warner Baxter, the director, and a pair of "famous" songwriters, played by Dubin and Warren themselves) and female bodies (chosen during an early sequence on the basis of good-looking legs, lovingly caressed by the camera throughout the scene). When the star (Bebe Daniels) breaks her ankle and has to be replaced by the inexperienced Ruby Keeler, the relationship between artistic and sexual relationships is firmly reinforced. Young Ruby is an ingenue who has not only never danced the lead; she has never been kissed either. When Warner Baxter asks her to take the star's place, however, he kisses her to provoke sufficient emotion to assure a good performance. The transfer is complete when Dick Powell declares his love and returns sexual significance to kissing. By intertwining stage success with sexual initiation, this sequence sets the stage for the show to follow. At the opening, as the girls come down the stairs they are shot from underneath; the camera peers between their legs, thus mixing its creative and sexual functions. It is hardly surprising that the next number should be "Shuffle Off to Buffalo," portraying Keeler and Powell as a just-married couple on their breathless way to a Niagara Falls honeymoon. If this number overtly models the show on sexual relationships, the next redefines the show/sex tie in audiovisual terms. We first hear Dick Powell singing "I'm Young and Healthy," thus identifying the sound track with the male voice; next we see a single woman who soon multiplies into dozens, creating a link between the image track and the female silhouette. As the number progresses, men enter the image and surround the women, leading ultimately to a track between the women's legs, reducing to a graphic pattern the sexual thematics obvious in the previous number.

The Berkeley pattern is a simple one: develop the young couple's love simultaneously with the show (preferably by making the success of one depend on the success of the other), project the thematics of the couple into the thematics of the show by having the lovers outside the show play the lovers inside the show, then drop the thematic concerns in favor of graphic equivalents to the show = sex equation. With little variation, this is the progression followed throughout Berkeley's career. In another realm, however, *Forty-Second Street* does represent something of a throwback within the show musical genre: at the end the director is given no credit for the show's success; while Ruby Keeler is applauded, Warner Baxter wanders, alone and dejected, outside the theater. Recalling *On With the Show*, the 1929 film on which the plot of *Forty-Second Street* is based, and prefiguring the lonely figure of Jean Gabin in Renoir's *French Can-Can*, Warner Baxter represents a fundamental Romantic myth which the show musical leaves behind in constituting a syntax. In a general way we may recognize two basic performance myths in Western theater:

1) *the sad clown*: there is only so much happiness available in the world, so the performer must sacrifice his own happiness in order to assure that of the audience, all the while covering over his own misery with the clown's mask. This is the Romantic myth *par excellence* (its *locus classicus* is the pelican metaphor in Musset's "Nuit de mai," whereby the poet/pelican eats his heart out in order to feed his readers/children); the poet, performer, or director is a martyr who can reach the higher plane of artistic contribution only through self-sacrifice. As the fading actress says to the new girl on the way up in *Show Girl in Hollywood* (1930): "There's a tear for every smile in Hollywood."

2) *the happy clown*: happiness is like the loaves and the fishes; we have only to share it in order to multiply it. The more the clown clowns, the more the audience laughs; the more the audience laughs, the happier the clown is; the happier the clown is, the more he clowns. And so on, forever and ever. According to this sunnier myth, it is enough to "put on a happy face" in order to chase the clouds away and make the sun come out. Consecrated in two famous songs ("Be A Clown" from *The Pirate*, and "Make 'Em Laugh" from *Singin' in the Rain*), this approach is an essential one throughout the heyday of the show musical. Whenever the "happy clown" syntax begins to falter, however, it is precisely because the correlation between performer pleasure and audience pleasure begins to break down, thus suggesting a return to the "sad clown" paradigm (e.g., *Dance Girl Dance*—1940, *Ziegfeld Girl*—1941, *The Red Shoes*—1948). Indeed, when in the mid-fifties show musical syntax comes under frontal attack, it is the disparity between audience and performer perceptions and pleasure that leads the way (e.g., *A Star Is Born*—1954, *The Country Girl*—1954, *The Joker Is Wild*—1957).

Forty-Second Street is the last of the early thirties musicals to lay such a heavy stress on the sad clown motif. Revealing its debts to the melodrama influence of earlier years, but foreshadowing the direction which the musical would take for the next two decades, *Forty-Second Street* is truly a transitional masterpiece.

The syntactic solution discovered in Berkeley's first film of 1933 is repeated nearly intact by the second, *Gold Diggers of 1933.* Once again Ruby Keeler is the chorine who dances to Dick Powell's songs, which this time he writes as well. Indeed, we learn from the couple's first love scene, where Powell leaves a frustrated Keeler in order to return to his songwriting, that music results from repression of the sexual urge, that inspiration derives from desire unfulfilled. As in *Forty-Second Street,* the first number specifically adopts the thematics of the narrative itself, revealing Keeler and Powell "Pettin' in the Park," while the second ("The Shadow Waltz") redefines that thematic material graphically, leaving the third and final production number free for a specialty routine ("Remember My Forgotten Man"). Of the three it is the second that most interestingly develops the elements of backstage syntax, finally justifying the previous film's identification of singing as a male art and dancing as its female counterpart. At the start Dick Powell warbles "In the shadows let me come and sing to you" to Ruby Keeler clad in a platinum wig. As he sings he plays a violin, thus establishing him as the source of the song in three different ways: as songwriter, singer, and instrumentalist. As the dance develops, a chorus of violin-playing girls in double-hooped white skirts make their way along serpentine paths to a darkened stage where their luminescent instruments lend an eerie glow to their concentric patterns. At the climax of this kaleidoscopic progression, the girls together form a single enormous violin, their separate violins illuminating the pattern while a gigantic bow moves across the bridge, "playing" the outsized human instrument. (How different—and yet how similar, *mutatis mutandis,*—from one of the more risqué lines of the recent *Fame:* "It's a violin bow, hold it like your dick.") All of the thematic motifs of the previous number are here redefined. Instead of giving us a series of duet shots, with men and women together (as in "Shuffle Off to Buffalo," "Pettin' in the Park," or the corresponding number of *Footlight Parade,* "Honeymoon Hotel"), Berkeley gives us only a single shot of a man, then spends the rest of the number on visions of beautiful women. For the sexual opposition has here been transferred to a contrast between the image track and the sound track (woman = image, man = sound). At the beginning of the number Dick Powell sings and plays the violin; the number itself successively redefines woman as the inspiration of his song, the accompaniment of his singing, and finally as the very instrument which he must play in order to produce music. Just as the composition of the music was inspired by repressed sexual desire, so the playing of the music is equated with the fulfillment of that desire. As the phallic bow is drawn across the human violin, we recognize Berkeley's ability to make pattern serve a symbolic purpose. For Berkeley, choreography provides more than a simple opportunity for men and women to sing and dance together. A Berkeley film does not just introduce men to women and both to the stage; Berkeley's choreography constitutes a disquisition on dance, an essay on the secret chain which makes a show grow out of courtship, which turns romance into a dance. In and of themselves, Berkeley's dances constitute a theory of art, a neo-

Romantic explanation of the origins of dance and song.

A double paradigm thus emerges from Berkeley's production numbers. On the one hand, woman is the dance and the image which constitutes it, while man is the prying eye of the titillated audience—a configuration which Berkeley shares with the rest of the show musical and with the culture in general. Berkeley's originality surfaces more clearly still in his treatment of the production number sound track, which he attributes almost exclusively to male performers, while the role of listener is reserved almost entirely for the female. "In the shadows let me come and sing to you," sings Powell to Keeler in the "Shadow Waltz" violin number. Song after song identifies woman as a listener, with the *locus classicus* of this phenomenon appearing in Warners' 1934 offering, *Twenty Million Sweethearts,* where Dick Powell plays a radio crooner with an entirely female audience. Throughout the backstage years, when Berkeley's influence was at its height, there reigned a careful complementary distribution of sexual subject positions. Strikingly, this complementary distribution governed script development and casting throughout the thirties, for no major backstage musical performer of this period was a woman singer or a male dancer. Male singers are plentiful (Jolson, Crosby, Dick Powell), as are female dancers (Crawford, Keeler, Eleanor Powell). Only Fred Astaire and Jeanette MacDonald seem at first to be exceptions, but in fact both are far more at home in the fairy tale subgenre.

Associated with the female image/male voice and male spectator/female auditor roles is a familiar circular myth: woman appears as an image; man sees her and is moved to praise her beauty in song; woman hears him and is moved to reveal her beauty in dance. And so on, *ad infinitum*. This myth clearly identifies man as creator, inspired by woman his Muse. How fitting it is that the sound track should be identified with creation in the one genre of films which actually does derive the image from the sound rather than vice-versa. In most films, it has been argued, the sound track is simply a tacked-on guarantee of the authenticity of the image; only in the musical does the sound actually generate the movement within the image. In standard musical practice, sound is recorded first, with the image synchronized later to the sound—dancers dance to the music, and not the reverse. By identifying woman with dancing and man with song, woman with the image track and man with the sound track, the backstage musical of the thirties thus puts the particularities of its technological heritage to work thematically, embodying in its very thematics and graphics the genre's peculiar sound-image hierarchy. (See chapter four for further comment on the musical's treatment of sound/image relationships.)

In *Footlight Parade,* Berkeley's third major film of 1933, the show plot/love plot parallel takes a new direction. Instead of spreading the three major numbers throughout the film they are all grouped at the end, once again in the familiar order of 1) song about the love relationship, transferring the lovers from the narrative to the stage ("Honeymoon Hotel"); 2) song inspired by the love relationship but which redefines the overt thematics of the first song in graphic terms ("By A Waterfall"); 3) specialty number not performed by or directly related to the romantic couple ("Shang'hai Lil"). Little new is added to the Keeler-Powell plot here, but there is an important new wrinkle in the treatment of the director, Jimmy Cagney. Like Warner Baxter in *Forty-Second Street,* Cagney is a slave-driver, pushing his girls as hard as he pushes himself. Unlike Baxter, however, Cagney is not a Romantic martyr; rather than sacrificing his life's blood for the sake of the show, Cagney is equated with the show itself. By taking his drunk star's place in the film's final number, Cagney breaks down the separation between production personnel and performers to which Warner Baxter fell prey. In so doing, Cagney reveals the general strategy typifying the closing moments of the backstage musical. As we have seen above, the backstage musical depends on an opposition of narrative to numbers, creation to performance, and man to woman; these oppositions are not final, however, they are set up only to be reduced, in accordance with the general practice of musical style which dissolves every level or category into the next. As a rule we might say that the backstage musical is generated by a situation like that which de Rougemont identifies with passion: a tension is created between two categories which seem wholly separate, each permanently separated from the other. Thus the narrative is separated from the numbers, the creation from the performance, the voyeuristic man from the exhibitionistic woman. Such a situation does not last, however, for once the film has established basic dichotomies, it

goes on to find various ways of resolving them.

The method used by *Footlight Parade* is an extremely common one: at the last minute a non-performer must be pressed into service to replace an injured, recalcitrant, or absent performer. By crossing the performance line, the non-performer thus reduces the distance between the world which he represents and the stage illusion into which he moves. In MGM's *Broadway Melody of 1940,* for example, Fred Astaire at the last moment replaces his friend George Murphy as Eleanor Powell's partner. This sleight of hand, brought on by Murphy's feigned drunkenness, not only brings Astaire together with the girl of his dreams, but symbolically merges the stage world (with which Powell has constantly been identified) and reality (thus far identified with Astaire). A similar effect is gained from the many films which end on the included show, implying a permanent merging in the spectator's mind of the couple as seen in the narrative and the same couple as actors in the show (e.g., *Broadway Melody of 1940, Stormy Weather, The Gang's All Here*). Working in the other direction, a bridge is established between narrative and number whenever a song is sung within the narrative portions or a stage direction given during a rehearsal.

In fact, seen from this point of view the rehearsal number in general performs the same intermediary function as the backstage portions of the film as a whole. During a rehearsal the actor represents both his character within the narrative (when he is receiving directions from the director or making eyes at one of the girls) and his character within the show (whenever he is saying his lines). The rehearsal thus functions as archetype of all the many devices commonly used to bridge the gap between the world and the show, the narrative and the numbers, the creative male and the created female. As the singing and dancing director of *Footlight Parade,* Jimmy Cagney inaugurates a function that will remain basic to the show musical throughout its long history. Without tension between plot and show, male and female, there can be no passion and thus no story, but without a collapsing of those oppositions there can be no marriage and thus no climax.

The fourth film in the Berkeley series, *Dames* (1934), is in many ways the most sophisticated and complex. Relationships only roughly sensed in the earlier films are here carefully worked out. By now Berkeley could count on an audience familiar with the Warner plot formula and the Berkeley choreographic touch—so much so, in fact, that he for the first time abandons the consecrated three-number formula guaranteed to establish thematic, visual, and structural links between the numbers and the narrative. The specialty number, "The Girl at the Ironing Board," comes first in order, while both the other major numbers (all Dubin and Warren songs) move directly to sophisticated play on the male = camera/eye, woman = image equation, without bothering to establish it by inserting the couple from the narrative into the number (that function having been fulfilled by the previous films of the series). Under the influence of Dick Powell's love, "I Only Have Eyes for You" turns a subway ad into a vision of Ruby Keeler, which soon multiplies into dozens of small Ruby Keelers, one enormous jigsaw composite of Ruby Keeler, and finally a montage of Ruby Keelers of various sizes and shapes. A strikingly clear summary of the visual structures informing Berkeley's previous backstage films, this song clearly identifies the feminine show as the product of a loving male eye. As such, it prepares the spectator for a generalization and reinterpretation of the optical/amorous metaphor in the final number, "Dames."

In analyzing the earlier Warner musicals, I have passed over the role of Guy Kibbee and other representatives of corrupt business, moralistic paternity, or self-serving censorship. In *Dames,* however, it is not possible to ignore the figures of Kibbee (the backer) and Hugh Herbert (Ezra Ounce, rich founder of the Ounce Foundation for the Elevation of American Morals), for the film makes an overt attempt to assimilate them to the already existent sex/show link. A closer look at their function is in order, for they typify the show musical's tendency to follow—more closely than the folk or fairy tale subgenres—the basic configuration of New Comedy (where the older generation father surrogates symbolizing money, power, business, and the established order stand temporarily in the way of youth, love, liberty, and an array of counter-cultural values). In many depression era musicals, performing is a job, a source of money in a jobless economy. The Gold Diggers series dramatizes this fact by portraying women intent on soaking men for all they are worth. Only in *Dames,* however, is gold digging fit into a larger structure. At first Kibbee and Powell argue about the approach which the show must take, a parallel montage highlighting the differences between the artistic approach (Powell as *auteur* of the show) and the business angle (Kibbee as investor in the show). The problem is not solved by direct confrontation, so it must be considered by the entire board of backers. A deadlock between the values of business and art is avoided only when the mediating notion of entertainment is evoked: people go to a show to see beautiful dames, who are good business as well as good art. This solution soon calls forth a long and elaborate number which realizes the visions running through the heads of the rich board members: girls are seen in bath tubs, at their mirrors, and arriving at the theater, with only their most private moments hidden from the camera lens.[7] This configuration repeats the pattern of "I Only Have Eyes for You," but with businessmen substituting for a lover, thus establishing a link between the love relationship and the business relationship. The question is, what will the backers put up money for? Comes the answer, anything that the public will pay for. The way to do good business is to be a good audience, and the audience wants dames (given that the audience is assumed to be, like the backers, all male).

> What do we go for, go see a show for?
> Tell the truth we go to see you beautiful dames.
> We spend our dough for bouquets that grow for
> All those cute and cunning young and beautiful dames.
> Oh, dames are necessary to show business—
> Dames, without you there would be no business.
> Your knees in action—that's the attraction.
> And what good's a show without you beautiful dames.

Throughout 1933, Berkeley developed a thorough analogy between sex, art, and vision; now that paradigm is expanded to include business. Man has all the money and he will spend it only when he gets something worthwhile in return; feminine beauty is that something. The monetary motif is driven home by Ruby Keeler's change of status in *Dames*. In *Forty-Second Street* Keeler's sexual ingenuity corresponded to her status as a theatrical neophyte; in *Dames* her falling in love is equated with her passage from amateur to professional performer. Constantly loaning her body to the audience, she feels that she should receive some sort of reimbursement for her services. Once again we return, but by a most circuitous route, to the model elucidated in an earlier chapter apropos of *Gigi*: man pays money in order to buy beauty; woman pays beauty in order to buy money. Here, however, the model has taken on its full theatrical meaning: we may have little in common with *Gigi*'s rich turn-of-the-century French industrialist, but we can certainly identify with spectators who pay good money for a ticket to observe feminine beauty, for the condition of our seeing *Dames* is precisely that we have already bought such a ticket. In other words, *Dames* is about us, the audience watching *Dames*. By extending the sex/show/vision metaphor to business, *Dames* completes the construction of show musical syntax around the position of the show musical spectator. The kind of entertainment represented by *Dames* is the meeting place of business and art, of morality and perversion, of repression and liberation. Rarely has a film so coherently summed up a cultural system as *Dames* embodies the underlying myths of Depression entertainment.

The influence of the 1933-34 Warner/Berkeley films is consecrated, as it were, by the influence which they had on the MGM musical throughout the following decade. From 1933 to 1943 hardly a year went by without a major Metro offering in the backstage genre. Whether the feature performers were Crawford and Gable, Astaire and Powell, MacDonald and Eddy, or Turner and Stewart, the backstage arrangement and Broadway locale remained stable. Not only did MGM regularly treat these films as top-line productions, investing in them both money and name stars, but the public continued to make the films in this series top-grossers:

> 1933-*The Dancing Lady*
> 1935-*Broadway Melody of 1936*
> 1936-*Born to Dance*
>   *The Great Ziegfeld* (Academy
>   Award for Best Picture)
> 1937-*Broadway Melody of 1938*
> 1938-*Sweethearts*
> 1939-*Broadway Serenade*
> 1940-*Broadway Melody of 1940*
> 1941-*Ziegfeld Girl*
>   *Lady Be Good*
> 1943-*Broadway Rhythm*
>   *The Gang's All Here*

Together, these two series—the Berkeley films for Warners and the highly successful MGM productions (many of which were choreographed by Berkeley after his

1939 move to Metro)—constitute the very heart of show musical syntax as it developed during the backstage years (1933-41).

Warner's syntactic solutions to the challenge of show musical semantics served as a model for decades to come. To choose just one interesting example from a highly overrated film, the major production number from MGM's Academy Award winning *The Great Ziegfeld* adopts nearly every detail not just of Berkeley's semantics but of his syntax as well. After a single male singer begins "A Pretty Girl is like a Melody," the curtain opens on an enormous rotating stage, revealing hundreds of sumptuously dressed, extraordinarily beautiful women. Woman as image, man as voice; woman as melody, man as the activator of that artistic quality. More is present here than the lush Ziegfeld set and Ziegfeld's legendary beauties. Director Robert Z. Leonard adopts in this extravagant film not only the visual semantics of Ziegfeld, but Berkeley's well developed syntax as well. Until a house style gets adopted next door it remains no more than a house style. In Hollywood, the ultimate form of consecration is to have your studio's style imitated by MGM. *The Great Ziegfeld* is thus the first important step on the way to generalizing the syntax developed by Berkeley at Warners. It remains to be seen what happens when semantic developments undermine the show musical's dependence on the backstage paradigm. Is the telling factor the semantics of Broadway stage doors? or will the syntax of the larger category—the show musical—outlast the loss of its favorite vocabulary?

Taking It Out of the Theater

By the end of the thirties, the backstage device was clearly losing ground to other, less stereotyped methods of motivating song and dance. In fact, the demise of the backstage paradigm is a classic example of how too much success can lead to failure. Such was the domination of the backstage model that in the late thirties no self-respecting musical could do without a staged spectacle. The fairy tale musical typically introduced a night-club act or a scene from an opera. The folk musical developed a long line of indigenous entertainment forms, each of which could be treated as a staged finale reminiscent of Berkeley's final numbers—parade (*Flirtation Walk)*, football game (*Pigskin Parade*), rodeo (*Girl Crazy*), and so forth—as well as a series of more traditional shows suited for insertion at any point within the narrative—operas, minstrel shows, native dances, saloon shows, and many others. In the backstage musical, the presence of a proscenium stage was a given; the shows inserted into other musicals, however, had to be motivated. Out of this concern for motivation grew a new kind of show musical, one in which putting on a show would no longer be mainly a professional responsibility, but an expression of shared exuberance. In the backstage musical the show exists, by and large, independently of any individual performer; "the show must go on" is the original theatrical cliché from which so many others emanate. About the time Hitler overran Europe, however, new forms began to appear, where the show usually doesn't even exist until the characters create a need for it. Perhaps the earliest musicals to motivate the show (rather than accept it as a given) were the Judy Garland/Mickey Rooney films which Arthur Freed produced for MGM (*Babes in Arms, Strike Up the Band, Babes on Broadway, Girl Crazy*). In each of these films the staging of a show grows out of the practical problems of a community of young people. Other non-backstage show musicals culminate in orchestra concerts, radio or television shows, benefit performances, or even puppet shows.

During the same period, the craze for the musical biography (or biopic) grew to epidemic proportions. Following the successful lead of *The Great Ziegfeld,* studio after studio portrayed producers, composers, and performers as inspired individuals who "just had" to create music. Now, of all the non-backstage types of show musicals, the one least likely to approximate the syntax of the backstage musical, it would seem, is the biopic. A man writes music, a man gets his music played and published, a man's music makes him famous, Hollywood films his biography: what could be more distant from the love = art syntax of Warner's backstage musicals? Such logic seems flawless, but what use is logic in the case of a form which against all odds for twenty years survived the abuse of critics, a form which never produced anything approaching a masterpiece, and whose high point may well have been its very first example, *The Great Ziegfeld* (1936)? Composers of every variety inspired screen biographies, from Viennese classical to Lower East Side popular. Band leaders and singers, dancers and lyricists, even drummers and disc jockeys are immortalized by biopics. Of the better than two films a year throughout the forties and fifties some of the best are: *The Great Waltz* (Johann Strauss II, 1938), *The Story of Vernon and Irene Castle* (1939), *Yankee Doodle Dandy* (George M. Cohan, 1942), *Rhapsody in Blue* (George Gershwin, 1945), *Night and Day* (Cole Porter, 1945), *Words and Music* (Rodgers and Hart, 1948), *Jolson Sings Again* (1949), *Look for the Silver Lining* (Marilyn Miller, 1949), *Three Little Words* (Bert Kalmar and Harry Ruby, 1950), *The Glenn Miller Story* (1954), *The Joker Is Wild* (Joe E. Lewis, 1957), *Beau James* (Jimmy Walker, 1957), *The Gene Krupa Story* (1960), and *Funny Girl* (Fanny Brice, 1968).

The greater the star, we might expect, the less it is possible for Hollywood to fit his or her biopic into the familiar syntactic mold of the backstage musical, for the public would certainly be aware of at least the basic outline of the star's career. Such, however, is far from being the case. A star is not a person but a public institution, a bright light both defining and defined by the galaxy which we call American popular mythology. MGM's *The Great Caruso* provides a perfect example. In post-war America, where opera was not one of the popular arts, the name of only one opera singer was a household term, nearly synonymous with opera itself (like Toscanini for the orchestra). In real life, Enrico Caruso was hardly a romantic figure; by the time he married into money he was already middle-aged and had a grown family by his first wife. As played by Mario Lanza, however, Caruso

falls in love with a wealthy socialite (Dorothy Benjamin) when he is still a young man; only after overcoming paternal disapproval can he marry her and settle down to a career in the opera. According to this new plot, Caruso's profession is dependent upon and a celebration of his romantic ties. Music is no longer just a job or a talent, it is an artistic consecration of the marriage vows.

This notion of music as dependent on a fusion of opposites is developed in the most varied ways throughout the history of the biopic. When Larry Hart (Mickey Rooney) first meets Richard Rodgers (Tom Drake) in *Words and Music,* he pays little attention to the latter's song; nor, for that matter, does the soundtrack, for "Manhattan" is realistically presented in a rather lackluster piano rendition. When lyricist again meets composer, this time with a full set of lyrics, the sound track celebrates the marriage of words and music by adding an orchestra to the piano rendition. No longer let it be said that the everpresent orchestra in the musical arises out of nowhere, unwarranted and unmotivated; the seemingly unmotivated orchestra represents the energy generated by the successful fusion of complementary forces. In *Words and Music* the title names the opposing forces. In *The Glenn Miller Story* the innovative band leader and his ever new arrangements are paired with the trusty play-what-you-give-them instrumentalists (a pairing doubled by the opposition of the visionary James Stewart as husband to June Allyson's super-practical wife). *Till the Clouds Roll By* provides a similarly doubled structure: Jerome Kern's melodies take on orchestra-inspiring stature

When the war came along, even the biopic turned to flag-waving: James Cagney and Joan Leslie in *Yankee Doodle Dandy*.

[UW]

THE "BACK-UP-THE-BOYS"
$5,000,000 World Premiere
YANKEE DOODLE DANDY
A Warner Bros. Production
Based on the Story of George M. Cohan
and Starring
JAMES CAGNEY
On Behalf of the N. Y. War Savings Staff of the U. S. Treasury Department

$25,000
LOGE
A 111

HOLLYWOOD THEATRE
Broadway at 51st Street
New York City
The 29th of May, 1942
at 8:30 promptly

Even the audience had an opportunity to participate in the war effort through the biopic—by way of wartime benefits like the one to which this ticket gave admission.

[UW]

only when they are married to an arrangement, while his personal life is illuminated only by a supposedly lifelong friendship with the arranger's daughter. Time after time, biographical events are ignored in order to make the semantic givens of the biopic conform to the syntax of the show musical. Music must never be seen as something one does solely to make a living. To make music is to make love; to make love is to inspire art.

With America's entry into the war, two new types of performance are added to the show musical's semantic field. Entertaining the men at home is the task of the servicemen's club, ably represented in *Stage Door Canteen* (1943), *Two Girls and a Sailor*, and *Hollywood Canteen* (1944). Even more popular was the troop show for the boys abroad. In 1943 alone, three films revolved around this most patriotic of entertainment formats (*Thousands Cheer, This Is the Army, Thank Your Lucky Stars*), while 1944 contributed still more (*Hey Rookie, Four Jills in a Jeep, Follow the Boys, Here Come the Waves*). Like the biopic, the military entertainment film labors hard to establish the basic couple/show relationship characteristic of the show musical. Nevertheless, it is interesting to observe how the nationalistic overtones of the war effort necessarily add to the troop show a twist more characteristic of the folk paradigm.

For the troop show was the very archetype of wartime volunteer effort, the one activity which turned hardened professionals back into amateurs for the duration of their tour, presenting the stage as a much sought-after place to demonstrate one's love of country (often actually op-posing the volunteer troop show to normal continuation of the performer's career). Two of MGM's wartime films provide particularly clear examples of the Janus-like nature of the troop show. In terms of spectacle and participants, the troop show clearly belongs to the same category as vaudeville, burlesque, opera, or Broadway; in terms of function, however, the troop show serves to hold together a community on the verge of dissolution. From this second point of view the troop show is not so much a spectacle as an exercise in solidarity. *For Me and My Gal* (1942) combines these two concerns in a simple but clever manner. Gene Kelly is the egotistical but talented vaudeville performer who, having recognized Judy Garland's charm and talent, has not only made her a performing partner but desires to marry her as well. They agree to marry only after playing the Palace, vaudeville's equivalent of Mecca. When they finally receive the coveted invitation, however, it is unfortunately timed to coincide with Kelly's draft notice. Ever unconcerned with the nation's plight, Kelly asks his agent to arrange a postponement. In responding to this selfish request, the agent sets up the relationship on which the rest of the film will depend. "I got you into the Palace but I ain't booking the war," he says, thus recalling the traditional metaphor whereby the war is divided into various *theaters*. Once Kelly has purposely injured his hand, thus avoiding the draft (but alienating the patriotic Garland), the only way to recover his stature is to star in the only theater which outranks the Palace: the theater of war. During Kelly's long road from shame to heroism Gar-

Stage Door Canteen bends the show musical about as far as possible toward the folk paradigm. Well-known performers (here, Ned Sparks) are reduced to waiters, while audience identification with the Canteen's patrons is heightened by the choice of military non-actors, ordinary guys like you and me.

[UW]

land is all the while singing for the troops, using her talents for the war effort rather than perceiving the war as a hindrance to a theatrical career, as Kelly does. The two are finally united on the Palace theater stage only after the Allied victory has made the world safe for vaudeville once again.

A schematic view of the syntactic relationships created by *For Me and My Gal* should illustrate quite clearly the extent to which this film uses the troop show not only to extend the show musical paradigm but also to harmonize it with the folk model. Throughout the first half of the film a rather traditional backstage pattern develops:

success in love ⟷ success in art.

The plot rebounds when another concern enters in, namely the performer's status as part of a national community. For Judy Garland, success in art is at this point superseded by success as a citizen, while for Kelly artistic success remains primary. From here on the reuniting of the couple depends on the ability to reconcile artistic and community success, the Palace with the war, the syntax of the show musical with that of its folk counterpart. Precisely this function is played by Garland's volunteer participation in troop shows. Instead of going from one extreme to another as Kelly does (nursing a self-inflicted wound in order to avoid the draft, playing the hero's role as a soldier), Garland finds the perfect union of opposites in the troop show. *For Me and My Gal* is a particularly clear example of the way in which semantic developments (the war and all it implies) can be simultaneously assimilated to one syntactic structure (war = theater) and yet force a reevaluation of that structure (the troop show may be theater, but it is also the paradigm of non-egotistical action).

In *Thousands Cheer* a similar reconciliation links the show musical's syntax of illusion to the folk musical's syntax of community. Gene Kelly's very first contact with Kathryn Grayson takes the form of role play: standing on a railroad station platform, Kelly watches all the other soldiers kissing their sweethearts goodbye; feeling left out, he suddenly grabs Kathryn Grayson, whom he has never met, and sweeps her away with an energetic kiss. Throughout the film this same structure is time and again reiterated; eventual realities (such as Kelly's love for Grayson) always begin as staged events in which the participants are only pretending. The question remains, however: at what point and how do the make-believe scenes turn into realities? Here a folk element is added to the familiar backstage illusionism. The troop show, and particularly the difficult trapeze routine done by Kelly and his circus family, serves as a

model for the production of a successful show. As an act in which the danger is real rather than illusory, the high wire specialty provides the perfect link between entertainment and the war effort, both of which depend for their success on trust and teamwork. The troop show which occupies most of the film's latter half thus celebrates not only the couple's success but the community's togetherness as well.

It is hardly surprising that Gene Kelly should in both these cases be the agent responsible for the merger of show and folk syntax, for like Judy Garland, Kelly tends to carry certain folk musical concerns along with him wherever he goes. As we saw in chapter three, Kelly is constantly seen in the company of children because his perennial problem is precisely his childishness, a positive trait in that it provides him with a boundless supply of energy, but a dangerous characteristic within the musical because it necessarily implies the very egotistical outlook which the musical as a genre takes upon itself to correct. It is this very connection, the transmutation of egotism into teamwork, of individuality into community, that typifies the Kelly film. As compared to Astaire's class and sophistication, which nearly always bend his show musicals toward the fairy tale subgenre, Kelly's down-home, all-American qualities push his show musicals toward the folk paradigm.

One of the most salient features of post-war show musical semantics was the attempt by producer Joe Pasternak and his many imitators to introduce classical music into the Hollywood musical. Now, the musical's openness to diverse musical

The show musical goes to war—and Private Kelly doesn't want to be left out of the important things that soldiers do.

[MOMA]

traditions is legendary. The fairy tale sub-genre draws from operetta, opera, and foreign song and march traditions throughout its history. The folk musical makes heavy use of ethnic rhythms and harmonies. The show musical itself has a long history of attention to jazz, from Jolson and Whiteman (*The Jazz Singer*, 1927, and *The King of Jazz*, 1930) to Ellington, Armstrong, and Basie (together featured in some two dozen films), as well as to big band swing, with early band leaders Ted Lewis and Fred Waring passing the baton to Glenn Miller, Harry James, Benny Goodman, Artie Shaw, and the Dorsey brothers, and even—especially during the forties—the Latin rhythms of Xavier Cugat and Carmen Miranda. No one before Pasternak, however, had dared to integrate classical music into the show musical. During his years at Universal, Pasternak had already succeeded in sugar-coating many an operatic pill with the sweetness of young Deanna Durbin (*Three Smart Girls, One Hundred Men and a Girl, Mad About Music, That Certain Age, First Love, It's a Date, Spring Parade,* and *Nice Girl?*). After his move to MGM at the start of the war he teamed singer Kathryn Grayson and orchestra conductor José Iturbi in a series of films mixing popular classics for voice

Imitating a forties show musical in the seventies, *New York, New York* could hardly do without a band leader—like this Tommy Dorsey look-alike.

[UW]

and orchestra alike, with emphasis on Iturbi's flamboyant piano style (*Seven Sweethearts, Thousands Cheer, Two Girls and a Sailor, Music for Millions, Anchors Aweigh,* and *Three Daring Daughters*). Surprisingly successful at the box office in his attempts to bring culture to the masses, Pasternak forged on with a series of films starring tenor Lauritz Melchior (*Thrill of a Romance, Two Sisters from Boston, This Time for Keeps, Luxury Liner*) or Mario Lanza (*The Great Caruso, Because You're Mine, The Student Prince*), as well as numerous

other films starring classical performers from home and abroad (e.g., Cyd Charisse in two films highlighting her considerable classical ballet training: *The Unfinished Dance* and *Meet Me in Las Vegas*). In the wake of Pasternak's success, the biopic as well took immediately and tenaciously to composers' biographies: *A Song to Remember* (1945, Chopin), *Song of Scheherezade* (1947, Rimsky-Korsakoff), *Song of Love* (1947, Robert Schumann), *Song of My Heart* (1950, Tchaikovsky), *Tonight We Sing* (1953, impresario Sol Hurok), *So This is*

Love (1953, soprano Grace Moore), and *Deep In My Heart* (1954, Sigmund Romberg).

If the troop show tends to draw the syntax of the show musical in the direction of its folk counterpart, the many musicals which depend on fashion photography have a natural tendency—like the films of Pasternak and his imitators—toward the fairy tale model. Already in the thirties *Roberta* (1934) uses the fashion show to explore the interaction between the artistocratic syntax of the fairy tale musical and the illusionistic paradigm of the show musical. Paramount's 1943 *Lady in the Dark* equates success in love with two separate results, the production of a "show" (*Fashion Playbill*) and the setting straight of a chaotic kingdom (the building in which the magazine is produced). If *Cover Girl* (Columbia, 1944) turns toward folk rather than fairy tale syntax, it can hardly be surprising to discover that this Columbia film stars Gene Kelly. America of days gone by, Brooklyn as a small town, photographs of generations past, tap dancing with the milk man, barbershop harmony, Gene Kelly dancing with his own reflection (but eventually closing his show to entertain the troops)—such are the clichés of which folk musicals are made. But *Cover Girl* is not by any stretch of the imagination a folk musical, because all these elements are redefined through the constantly present artistic metaphor of the "cover girl." This motif reaches its height in a stage production (borrowed by MGM for *Easter Parade* four years later) which captures extremely effectively the familiar equation between feminine beauty and artistic illusion. Repeated many times during the number, this sequence reveals a full shot of a woman on the left, soon accompanied by a soft-focus close-up of the same woman on the right; the right-hand shot is then transposed into the cover of one fashion magazine after another, the cinematic artifice which permits this transformation thus taking the credit for woman's ultimate consecration as an art object. The last woman to enjoy such an apotheosis is Rita Hayworth, who descends from her lofty position just long enough to dance with a group of (male) photographers, then disappears once again up her ramp into the clouds. Self-consciously borrowing the Ziegfeld apparatus on which depends the basic backstage syntax (man = eyes = camera = desire; woman = body = art = object of desire), *Cover Girl* recognizes the role of the camera as the new Ziegfeld, society's major method of "glorifying the American girl."

A dozen years later, Paramount's *Funny Face* takes up this definition of photography precisely where *Cover Girl* left off, only this time—as the titles suggest—the raw material needs far more work. In *Cover Girl* Rita Hayworth was a photogenic performer to begin with; *Funny Face* makes Audrey Hepburn into a bookworm. As fashion photographer, Fred Astaire must transform into an image a woman who is all words. For the umpteenth time in a long career, Astaire is asked to bring to life a girl much younger than he, to transmute raw material into art. The most poignant moments in the entire film come near the beginning, when Astaire does a photography test on Hepburn (a transparent figure for Hollywood's own screen tests). Rather

If the backstage musical brings us dancers, actors, and directors, other show musical forms concentrate on a broader range of fiction makers, like photographer Fred Astaire, who in *Funny Face* is charged with the task of transforming Audrey Hepburn's plain features into a cover-girl image.

[MOMA]

than submit to what she perceives to be demeaning photographic inspection, Hepburn simply runs off, hiding in the dark room. As Astaire develops and prints his pictures, this hiding motif takes on a new meaning. Hepburn is not unattractive, she is simply hiding from herself; what Astaire develops is only her hidden dimension. At the conclusion of his song, "Funny Face," he thus shines the light not on her now fully developed photograph, but directly on her face, suggesting that the song and their dance together have given her a real beauty not limited to the photographic image (though, of course, even this "real" Hepburn is an image within the film). A later sequence reiterates this material. Astaire takes pictures of Hepburn all over Paris, constantly using his personal romantic relationship with her to elicit the proper emotions. After each photo a stop-action sequence moves us from the original pose through the negative to the final developed picture. Soon, Astaire no longer needs to attract her into the artistic illusion by means of personal emotion, for she has begun to set up her own routines. From a plain Greenwich Village clerk, Astaire has turned her into an object of beauty, not by changing her nature but by bringing out the repressed self which only male attention, symbolized by the camera's attentive eye, can liberate.

In *Funny Face*, the older Astaire draws the youthful Hepburn carefully out of her shell and into womanhood. Indeed, for two full decades he continued to play this function for his leading ladies and the women in his audience alike. Earlier I suggested that the Kelly persona carries with it a specific folk syntax (the egotistical child vs. the adult community). The time has now come to consider the Astaire persona and the show syntax which it suggests during the post-backstage era. Primarily remembered for his RKO fairy tale musicals with Ginger Rogers, Astaire had a second career, stretching from the early forties to the late fifties, which in many ways contributed even more to the crystallization of his film persona. Throughout the earlier period Astaire was matched with a woman of his own generation and temperament, capable of bitingly clever repartee which only covered up a tender core. When the leading lady proved incapable of handling this screwball comedy-type role, the film was doomed from the start (e.g., *Damsel in Distress*, with Joan Fontaine). Even during this period, however, Astaire's relationship to Rogers always changed once they reached the dance floor. Again and again, an equal relationship during the strictly narrative portions turns into a teacher/student or at least leader/led relationship during the dance numbers. Dramatizing the accepted male role in ballroom dancing, Astaire always seemed to be showing Rogers how to dance, where to move, and when to embrace, thus turning numbers like "Night and Day" (*Gay Divorcee*), "Isn't This a Lovely Day?" (*Top Hat*), and "They All Laughed" (*Shall We Dance*), into dancing (= loving) lessons. Astaire moves, Rogers follows—this basic choreographic principle effectively turns the competition of the screwball comedy dialogue into danced harmony. Left to itself, the dialogue alone could never resolve the Astaire-Rogers conflict; when dance takes over, however, a competitive spirit (often visible within the steps themselves) slowly transfers its energy to a love relationship under the sure guidance of Astaire. Practically speaking, the on-screen relationship of Astaire and Rogers mirrored their off-screen situation perfectly, for their dances were always carefully choreographed by Astaire (usually with the assistance of Hermes Pan) who taught them to Rogers only after he had thoroughly mastered them himself.

With the forties, Astaire and Rogers went their separate ways. For years Astaire groped for a new partner, at first turning to women of Rogers' age, a marriageable eleven or twelve years his junior (Powell, Goddard). In *You'll Never Get Rich* (1941), however, Astaire was for the first time paired with a girl who looked as if she could have been his daughter (Rita Hayworth). From this point on, Astaire was never again paired with a woman of his own generation. Between 1941 and his first retirement in 1946, the average age difference is twenty-two years (Rita Hayworth, Marjorie Reynolds, Joan Leslie, Lucille Bremer, Joan Caulfield). After his short retirement until his last roman-

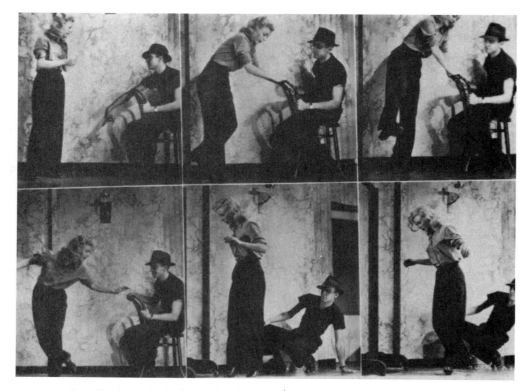

Once Fred Astaire had completed work on his RKO couple dances, Hermes Pan inherited the task of teaching them to Ginger Rogers, as in this rehearsal for *Swing Time*.

[MOMA]

tic lead (discounting the one return engagement with Rogers, in *The Barkleys of Broadway*), that figure swells to twenty-six years (Judy Garland, Vera-Ellen, Betty Hutton, Jane Powell, Cyd Charisse, Leslie Caron, Audrey Hepburn). While this age difference is constantly played down by means of make-up and Astaire's legendary energy, no viewer of this later period can miss the fact that Astaire's romantic relationships double as family ties: his age and wisdom always turn him into a father figure as well as a romantic partner for the leading lady (an arrangement which continues in Astaire's first non-mu-

sical part—*The Pleasure of His Company*, 1961—where he actually woos his daughter Debbie Reynolds for the ineffectual Tab Hunter).

It is this doubling that provides the Astaire persona with its fullest expression. To the dance partner = lover identification, on which the genre as a whole relies, Astaire now adds the more problematic (and potentially incestuous) equation of partner/lover/equal = older generation teacher/father/master. In three crucial films of Astaire's second period, all of these characteristics come out into the open and are joined in a representative syntax which does much more than relate one part of the film to another—it ties the Astaire persona to the show musical as a whole. In *Easter Parade, The Barkleys of Broadway,* and *Funny Face,* Astaire is not only the professional artist responsible for creating or reviving his sweetheart's career, he is also the one who takes a silly and inexperienced young girl and turns her into a woman (even Ginger Rogers, age thirty-nine when she plays Astaire's wife in *Barkleys,* is made to appear immature and naive, in order to let Astaire bring her to life). Astaire is thus the male initiator, simultaneously drawing his charges into life, love, and the dance. In many fairy tale musicals, Astaire is either a fine teacher (e.g., the RKO series), or an older initiator (e.g., *Yolanda and the Thief, The Belle of New York, Daddy Long Legs, Silk Stockings*), but it is only when these motifs are allowed to develop within the context of the show musical that the Astaire persona generates its full meaning. Just as Gene Kelly seems to carry folk motifs along with him, bending any fairy tale or show musical toward the folk paradigm, so Astaire exudes a sense of show musical syntax, even when the plot and set seem to call for something else (and even though, as I pointed out earlier, semantic considerations of class and costume tend to drive even Astaire's show musical efforts in the direction of the more exotic, aristocratic fairy tale tradition). Two final examples will demonstrate the extent to which Astaire's "second" career provided an outlet for this persona.

When Astaire returned to Hollywood to replace the injured Gene Kelly in *Easter Parade,* the script suddenly took on a new meaning, for here was Fred Astaire, owner of a chain of dance studios, claiming that he can take any girl out of a chorus line and turn her into a first-class dancer. Looked at from this point of view, *Easter Parade* is just as much about the Astaire persona as is the later *Band Wagon. Easter Parade* begins with the Astaire myth (called publicity when it is used to advertise his dance studios) and proceeds to subject it to careful scrutiny. At first Astaire tries to turn the girl he has chosen as his new partner (Judy Garland) into a replica of the high-stepper who has just abandoned him (Ann Miller). As rehearsal after rehearsal produces little results, however, it becomes increasingly clear that the solution to teaching Judy Garland to dance is not to be found in the area of technical expertise, but in that of human sensitivity: as soon as Astaire begins to fall in love with Garland he becomes the world's greatest teacher, not because his technique has changed, but because his affection loosens up Garland, permitting her to substitute spontaneous action for the rote repetition that characterized the earlier rehearsals. As long as teaching is seen as a skill, and learning a matter of practice, little progress is made; when the teaching/ learning process is recast in terms of male affection/female responsiveness, however, the team's success is instantaneous. (Whereas earlier the conception and performance of a number were separated by lengthy rehearsals, now the very first rendition of a song—"I Love a Piano"—dissolves directly to the number on stage.) The syntax common to Astaire and the show musical is thus maintained, but with a difference. Man is the teacher, director, and leader who turns woman into a work of art, but the manipulative aspects of the relationship have entirely disappeared. As long as Astaire insisted on turning Garland into another Miller, he failed miserably (in spite of the etymology, art is not artificial, it involves bringing out the most real aspects of the material), only when he helps his partner to discover her spontaneous self will he succeed in bringing out the dancer in her.

The second half of the film takes this distinction one step farther, by opposing the folk aspects of Garland's numbers (equality with Astaire, emphasis on emotion rather than spectacle, on spontaneity rather than practice) to the stagy exhibitionist quality of Ann Miller's final numbers. In particular, Miller's "Shaking the Blues Away"—as hot a number as ever hit Hollywood celluloid—identifies her as a whore rather than as a marriageable woman and thus recreates the voyeuristic/exhibitionist relationship proper to the backstage musical, but without any chance at the compensating love relationship which can bridge the gap between audience and performer. The same separation between male and female, audience and performer, is reinforced by the magazine cover number, which turns one woman after another into a magazine cover, fixing each one on film in precisely the way that Judy Garland has refused to be fixed. By exercising her own emotions, rather than simply submitting to her teacher's impersonal instructions, Garland has retained a sense of her own identity sufficient to permit her to parody the *male = artist, woman = art object* syntax of the backstage paradigm. By singing "In Your Easter Bonnet" to Astaire (rather than vice-versa, as we might expect), she reveals the extent to which she has reestablished the place of female initiative, spontaneity, and emotion within show musical syntax. She is willing to be the object of admiration in the film's closing Easter parade, but only on her terms, as an equal.

Astaire's next film, *The Barkleys of Broadway*, is even more aware of the Astaire persona; in typical Comden and Green style it provides the ultimate definition of Astaire's personal syntax, spoofing it all the while. Only a quirk of fate, like that which matched Astaire with the ready-made *Easter Parade*, provided him with a made-to-order partner for *Barkleys*. Garland was to have done the picture, in fact actually began it, but her emotional and physical instability eventually caused MGM to give Ginger Rogers the part—a perfect match, since she had, like the script's Dinah Barkley, spent a considerable period away from the musical genre. In an early scene Astaire provides what is perhaps the show musical's ultimate metaphor. Claiming to be responsible for all Rogers's dancing expertise (a claim which, as we have seen, is not so far from the truth), Astaire insists: "I molded you like Svengali did Trilby." As if this statement of authorship were not sufficiently insulting, the two performers spend part of the following day at an art exhibition given in their honor, where they witness the unveiling of a sculpture in which Ginger is represented as a pancake, Fred as a frying pan. Surprise turns to consternation as the sculptor explains (in a heavy Mediterranean

Fred Astaire as the creative frying pan, Ginger Rogers as the created pancake, in *The Barkleys of Broadway*.

[BFI]

accent) his would-be masterpiece: "As I see you, you are creative union. You [FA] creative frying pan in which the shapeless raw batter—you [GR]—are transformed by creative miracle into irresistible pancake. It is Pygmalion breathing life on Galatea." The substance of this analysis reveals the script-writing team's amazing sensitivity to the New York stage as it is portrayed in the Hollywood musical. Pygmalion/Galatea, Svengali/Trilby, even frying pan/batter—these are perfect metaphors to describe the male/female relationship as defined by the show musical. To foreground that truth, however, is tantamount to destroying stage illusion through the use of Brechtian alienation effects. In order to operate properly, a society's myths—and the syntax of the show musical is nothing if not a myth—must pass unnoticed. To call them myths, to draw attention to them, can only destroy the structures which they perpetuate. The rest of *Barkleys* is thus spent in restoring the element of secrecy to the Pygmalion/Galatea relationship. Having once revealed the show musical syntax on which films like *Barkleys* draw, the script then labors long and hard to hide that syntax once again, much as the backstage musical began by separating narrative and numbers, plot and show, only in order to collapse the opposition in the film's final moments.

Throughout the second half of the film Rogers tries to forge a new career on the "legitimate" stage. Her acting is terrible, but, as we are made to understand, that failing stems from a lack of direction, not of talent. When a telephone admirer begins to direct her she gains rapidly in composure, authority, and sheer energy. The telephone voice is of course Astaire, learning again the lesson which *Easter Parade* had forced on him: the meaning of the teacher/pupil, Pygmalion/Galatea myth is not that man is a demi-god, but that a man in love may have the power to release woman's stored-up capacities. As soon as the woman senses that she is being treated as an object, as material to be molded by a haughty and self-confident man, the flow of energy across the couple's bonds immediately ceases.

The backstage musical of the thirties gave the audience a fleeting view into the wings, thus destroying the illusion that art is real before restoring that illusion by creating a web of correspondences between the narrative and the numbers. *Barkleys* does precisely the same thing, but at a slightly different level: it provides a privileged glimpse into the syntax of the show musical (like the wings of the theater, the syntax is that hidden activity which makes art possible but which destroys art's illusion when seen too directly), thus affording a rapid view of the show musical's conditions of being before once again reducing the distance between the illusion and the means of its existence. Semantically, *Barkleys* has little in common with Berkeley, yet the syntactic similarities demonstrate the extent to which show musical syntax remains constant in form even as it changes radically in the details of its content (the content of *Barkleys* corresponding to the form of Berkeley).

Saving the Dying Myth: Reflexivity as Reinforcement

Throughout this study of the American film musical, I have insisted on the power of the musical to embody an American popular mythology. By doubling romantic relationships with the energy and beauty of song and dance, the musical endows the coupling process with the magical qualities that it must have if American society is to continue to be built on the foundation of marriage for love. A variety of secondary characteristics may thus be identified: man as a source of money paired with woman as a source of sexuality; man as the poet-teacher-artist, woman as his muse-pupil-art work; man as a wandering source of energy, woman as the stable factor who ties him down. These and many other relationships are implicit within the Hollywood musical. Now this does not mean that the musical simply *reflects*, at a more or less hidden level, the structures of contemporary society; nor does it mean that this or any other genre *creates* the societal structures. What it does mean is that society and the musical film (along with other popular genres, from Hollywood and elsewhere) stand in a symbiotic relationship to each other: each grows *out of* and *into* the other according to a simple scheme of mutual reinforcement. Spectators demand of reality what they have seen on the screen just as they demand for the screen what they have experienced in the real world—to the point where the screen world and reality no longer can be defined separately or even delimited successfully. The pleasure of spectatorship thus derives from the film's ability to induce viewers simultaneously to recognize and to rehearse the ritual of their own world. In order to operate successfully, of course, both recognition and rehearsal must occur beneath the threshhold of consciousness; those who take the greatest pleasure in the magical qualities associated with the musical marriage may be the very people who hold the least belief in the efficacy of marriage as an institution. It is thus essential that these people be allowed to take their cinema pleasure in their off-guard hours, in those very moments when they are not prone to question the value of an all-talking, all-singing, all-dancing romance.

The rub comes when a filmic structure becomes so obvious, or a film-going community so sensitive that the film's ritual patterns can no longer pass unnoticed. From this point on, the societal structures and the film's syntax can no longer remain in a hidden symbiotic relationship. Instead of acquiescing to the genre's mythology simply by following and accepting the film's plot, spectators find themselves rejecting the very assumptions that underlie the film. "She never would have done that," one may say, or "Who does he think he is," or perhaps "I don't see what that marriage solves, I wouldn't want to be married to that dope." As soon as audiences begin

to react in this manner, the genre's ability to serve a ritual function is seriously impaired. At this point in the history of a genre various solutions are possible:

1) Abandon the genre (a radical solution rarely adopted *in toto* by Hollywood, yet certainly a statistical factor in the decline of the musical during the last quarter-century).

2) Transfer the genre to a new and more naive public (e.g. the western's move to television since the fifties or, within the musical, the move from an adult to an adolescent audience since the fifties: Elvis Presley films, William Asher's *Beach Party* series and its many imitators, rock musicals of various sorts).

3) Subordinate the genre to a more prestigious art form, in the hope that some of the prestige will rub off, thus revalorizing the genre in spite of its shortcomings (e.g. Hollywood's wholesale transcription of Broadway musicals from the fifties on).

4) Begin each film by recognizing the outdated, reductive, unreal nature of the genre's syntax, thus lulling the spectator's critical faculties to sleep; then use the rest of the film to demonstrate the extent to which that seemingly outmoded syntax is not so devoid of sense after all (we have already seen this technique operating in *Easter Parade* and *The Barkleys of Broadway*, where the Svengali/Trilby syntax is first ridiculed, then recuperated).

These four basic reactions cover almost the entire film musical field since World War II. Alternatives two and three produce films not significantly different from their predecessors. The fourth approach, however, represents a new strategy characteristic of the later musical, a strategy important enough to be the major subject of this section.

As we saw in the preceding chapter, the fairy tale musical clothes its extreme artificiality in a persistent irony inviting spectators to feel throughout that they are far above this silly Ruritanian folderol (yet all the while they are in fact becoming more and more engaged in that very folderol). In a sense, then, the fairy tale musical always contains its own critique, but contains it in such a way as to permit the spectator to ignore it. Many backstage musicals take the same approach (particulary for a public already familiar with the clichés of the stage world, New York society, and trade papers like *Variety*), identifying their plot material, characters, and resolutions as banal and stereotyped—but only in order eventually to restore meaning to the very atmosphere that seems devoid of it. In short, the musical in general depends for its most basic rhetoric on the creation of a sham distancing device which exists only as a decoy: by reducing suspicion it actually aids in ultimately reducing the distance separating spectator and screen. Nevertheless, the approach adopted by many musicals of the late forties and after cannot simply be assimilated to this general framework. The musical of the thirties creates distance only through a general tone, not through a critique of the genre's syntax, whereas the reflexive musical of the later period foregrounds a specific problem within the genre's syntax.

As early as 1941, the conventional but simplistic syntax of the show musical was specifically contested through foregrounding. MGM's *The Ziegfeld Girl* begins with a regular litany of backstage commonplaces—not naturalized or concealed, but constantly emphasized, as if they were the film's true subject. Legs are "valuables"; dancing on a chorus line is "showing yourself to other men"; when Hedy Lamarr can't get her lipstick on straight, one of the other girls cracks: "Don't worry honey, they won't be looking at your mouth." As one backstage wag puts it, "The Follies is life." Indeed, the rest of the film demonstrates the interpenetration of the Follies and life in three widely divergent cases: desire for the grandeur of the show within her own life ultimately drives Lana Turner to loose morals, heavy drinking, and an early death; Hedy Lamarr eludes a similar fate only by leaving the Follies altogether; only Judy Garland, by reaffirming the typically Garlandesque folk values of family and friends, manages to withstand the pressures and turn the Follies into a personal triumph. Rather than radically contesting the familiar show musical equation of success in love and success on the stage, *Ziegfeld Girl* simply treats Turner and Lamarr as constitutionally unfit for the successful combination of personal and professional life that Garland's modesty and likable personality seemingly assure her. An initial threat to show musical syntax through ironic foregrounding is thus dissipated and the ritual effect of the genre reconstituted.

During the late forties, numerous major films followed this reflexive route, foregrounding and undercutting the conventions of show musical syntax only in order to reaffirm them all the more convincingly (if in a slightly more limited and better defined fashion). Besides the Astaire films treated above (*Easter Parade*

Jimmy Stewart wonders just where girlfriend Lana Turner gets her baubles, in *The Ziegfeld Girl*.

[BFI]

and *Barkleys*), these include such little-known gems as *Jolson Sings Again* (Columbia, 1949), which seeks to guarantee the authenticity of screen biographies of stage stars through the strikingly paradoxical technique of foregrounding the very technology that supposedly distances the filmed stage star. For *Jolson Sings Again* is not the story of just one more show in the long career of the country's best known entertainer, it is a record of the making of Columbia's earlier film, *The Jolson Story* (1946). Instead of hiding the fact that Jolson didn't play himself in the earlier film, *Jolson Sings Again* actually shows Jolson recording his songs while the actor who is to play him on screen mouths the words. While this scene thoroughly lays bare the biopic's devices, it also lays the groundwork for a complete reinstatement of the genre. When "Jolson" watches his stand-in mimic him, he is thoroughly touched by the fidelity of the actor's performance to the style of his early years. In other words, *Jolson Sings Again* reveals the technology behind the biopics—Hollywood's backstage arena—only in order to

Douglas Sirk observes as Don Ameche and Dorothy Lamour complete a scene in *Slightly French*.

[MOMA]

"prove" that even the great Jolson is impressed with the accuracy of Hollywood's portrait. In fact, of course, "the great Jolson" is played by the same Larry Parks who mouths songs as the young Jolson. The film foregrounds technology only in order to hide it more fully.

With the fifties this approach becomes dominant within the subgenre. Two MGM films in particular are often remembered for their role in this reflexive revival of the musical genre. From its very first moments, *Singin' in the Rain* foregrounds the sound track/image track relationship so characteristically important in

the musical. As Gene Kelly narrates his autobiography to the audience in front of Grauman's Chinese Theater, his tales of hard study and high art are translated onto the image track as monster movies, vaudeville, beer halls, piano accompaniment for silent films, stunt acts, and so forth. Now, the image track clearly tells Kelly's real story, while the sound track is nothing but an ego-boosting fabrication. Is this how it is with the musical as a genre? *Singin' in the Rain* seems to ask. Is the music nothing but window-dressing, nothing but crowd-pleasing rhetoric designed to cover up the inadequacies of the

In *Jolson Sings Again* Larry Parks practices playing Al Jolson in front of a mirror, then puts his practice to work on the sound stage.

[BFI]

The famous opening of *Singin' in the Rain* (Gene Kelly, Debbie Reynolds, Donald O'Connor), and its *Hollywood Revue of 1929* model (George K. Arthur, Marion Davies, Buster Keaton).

[a = MOMA. b = pers]

Gene Kelly—and a team of special effects men—recreate the Freed and
Brown standard, "Broadway Melody," in *Singin' in the Rain.*

[MOMA]

image? Is the sound film—of which the musical is the prime symbol—a sham? By admitting this possibility, the film seems to guarantee its objectivity. Later sequences contrasting the romantic acting of Gene Kelly and Jean Hagen with their ironic dialogue further reinforce this sense of objectivity. Throughout the first half of the film we are increasingly persuaded that the characters and audiences within the film know a bad film when they see one. Conversely, we begin to have faith in their ability to recognize a good film. The key scenes of the second half thus all concern the addition of a new sound track to the "bad" film ("The Dueling Cavalier") in order to turn it into a "good" one ("The Dancing Cavalier"). In order to effect this change, Debbie Reynolds must "loop" Jean Hagen's songs, i.e. add her voice to the actress's image. In terms of the earlier opposition between image and sound track, this activity should appear suspect, just as a separation between the two tracks exposed Kelly's lie in the opening scene. By this point in the film, however, careful rhetoric has maneuvered us into changing our standards of legitimacy: before, untruthfulness constituted the greatest sin (separation of sound and image), but now it is lack of beauty which seems most reprehensible. Jean Hagen's voice is her own voice, but it produces nothing but ugly sounds; Debbie Reynolds's voice does not emanate from the mouth portrayed by the image, but it is such a beautiful voice (at least within the context of this film!) that the impropriety of "lying" to the audience seems negligible. In order further to conceal the rhetorical shift which characterizes *Singin' in the Rain*, Reynolds's recording sessions are further legitimized by the addition of a specific audience at whom the lyrics are aimed: Gene Kelly. Instead of delivering lines as one might in a diction lesson, Reynolds gives the lyrics meaning; by "singing from the heart" she earns the right to the sound track. The illegitimacy of a "lying" sound track has now been reversed, for the film's rhetoric has put away one moral structure (truth/falsehood) and substituted another (beauty/ugliness, performance as expression/performance as business), thus reaffirming the backstage musical values which the film at first seemed to undercut.

In a more subtle way, another MGM film scripted by Comden and Green succeeds in recuperating from oblivion a seemingly lost genre. The world of *The Band Wagon* (1953, Vincente Minnelli), as we learn from the very first scene, is a world where Fred Astaire's famous top hat and cane have lost all symbolic value—and thus all monetary value—to their once faithful audience, a world where Astaire (as we learn in the next scene) is not even recognized by the very people who once constituted his fan clubs. If *Easter Parade* and *The Barkleys of Broadway, Jolson Sings Again* and *Singin' in the Rain* all confront the notion that the syntax of the show musical never had any value, that it never had any connection to the real world, *The Band Wagon* meets another problem head on. It suggests from the outset that the Astaire world was a real world once, but that such a naive world is long gone from modern life. The theater has changed a lot, Astaire is informed by the friends who greet him in New York (Nanette Fabray and Oscar Levant)—so much so that Astaire gets a shoeshine under the marquee of a theater which has been turned into a penny arcade. The musical was all right for the depressed thirties, the opening scenes seem to proclaim, but not for the modern world and all the new meaning that it brings.

The Band Wagon thus depends from the start on an opposition of the old to the new: musical comedy is old and cannot hope to keep up with a changing world. This initial situation prepares the spectator for the work which the text must ultimately do on him/her. By stacking the deck, marking the cards, and keeping an ace up its sleeve, *The Band Wagon* redefines its value systems in such a way as to reverse the initial configuration. Instead of ironizing progress, the film reformulates the passage of time as a degradation of established values, thus calling for a return to reinforcement of those values which are sensed to be *ab origine*—original and permanent. This reversal will appear most clearly through a simplified chronology outlining the slippage in the oppositions which inform the film.

1) The old (Astaire's hat and cane) is read as valueless; indeed, when it is compared to the new (a most youthful and appealing Ava Gardner, the new star), it appears as singularly sexless.

2) The old is associated with spontaneity (Astaire in the "improvised" shoeshine routine) while the new, at the very moment when it is praised by the Fabray-Levant writing team, is revealed as ossified (Jack Buchanan eats the same sandwich, prepared in the same way, after every performance). Throughout the film this essential dichotomy returns, always prejudicing the audience in favor of old-fashioned entertainment—and entertainers. At the first performance of "The Band Wagon," for example, we witness a group of stagehands playing cards on a scaffold high above the stage. Performance time has nearly arrived and yet not one of them moves, because, as one remarks, the director always makes a speech on opening night. And so Buchanan does, making the whole speech sound entirely canned: "Up to now, I've been giving you orders as director, but soon I shall be just as one of you—an eager ham anxious to do a good performance." (Casting the Englishman Buchanan as the multi-talented Cordova was a brilliant coup aimed at engaging—and debunking—the myth of the British character actor's innate superiority over American "entertainers.") When the performance is over, and a deadly dull show it is, Astaire becomes the center of a spontaneous festival that finally provides the film spectator with some enjoyable entertainment. It is no accident that Astaire at this point is associated with all the young people in the cast, while Buchanan—supposedly representative of the new style—is absent along with the elderly backers of the show. Already at this point the reversal has been effected: the "new" is associated with old age and the old with (eternal) youth.

3) The director of a "modern" show could have been portrayed in almost any fashion, but *The Band Wagon*'s rhetoric requires that Buchanan be seen as a master treating his cast (including Astaire) as slaves, in order to demonstrate how the direction will be reoriented toward a communitarian spirit under Astaire. Seen in this light, the new art appears to be achieved only at the expense of human concerns, whereas the old art grew spontaneously out of a coherent group's mutual respect and excitement. This motif is reinforced by its application to romantic relationships as well: James Mitchell treats Cyd Charisse just as Buchanan treats his cast, whereas she and Astaire together create a relationship of mutual respect and shared love.

4) As if these devices did not sufficiently stack the deck, *The Band Wagon* uses familiar Dietz and Schwartz music as its ace in the hole. You can tell us anything about Busby Berkeley's shallowness, you can say that Ginger Rogers can't dance, that Jeanette MacDonald is overweight, or that Nelson Eddy couldn't sing anyhow; you can demonstrate that the movies of our youth were shallow, fanciful, escapist, unartistic. You can tell us just about anything, but don't insult

our favorite songs. Young or old, movie-goers of the early fifties were brought up on the standards of the twenties and thirties. If they missed them the first time around, they heard them later in a new swing arrangement; if they missed them on the stage they heard them on the radio; if they missed them in person they heard them on record. Who, in 1953, had not danced, dreamed, and romanced to "Dancing in the Dark," "You and the Night and the Music," or "Something to Remember You By"? By consistently identifying Astaire and his cohorts with the surefire rhetoric of these universally recognized tunes, *The Band Wagon* builds a watertight case for the values of yesteryear.

Sliding and slipping, redefining and re-aligning, *The Band Wagon* ultimately reverses it polarities. Defined by the opening scenes as a film in which the shallowness of the traditional backstage musical would be revealed, *The Band Wagon* eventually moves the audience from sympathy with the new to a reaffirmed belief in the old way of conceiving musical comedy, the world, and life itself. Given this strategy, the film could hardly help but close on a reprise of "That's Entertainment." The first time this song was sung it was a rhetorical ploy to get Astaire to join the forces of the new; in this rendition entertainment included such items as *Oedipus Rex*, *Hamlet*, and by extension the musical version of *Faust* which Buchanan, Fabray, and Levant were trying to force on Astaire. The finale constitutes a corrective to this first, falsely old-fashioned version. This time the entire cast sings the song to celebrate not Astaire's conversion but their own. Like the

film spectators whom they are addressing, the members of the cast have all abandoned the pretension of high art and climbed aboard the band wagon.

Before we abandon the show musical, there remains one more major type of reflexive text which must be treated. The reflexive texts which we have seen thus far all develop the genre's natural reflexivity in a specific direction, foregrounding a questionable area of generic syntax in order to reaffirm it all the more conclusively. There is one class of text which we have not yet touched upon, however, in spite of the fact that its initial strategy is exactly that of the reflexive text just dealt with. I am thinking of the many musicals that foreground the conventions of closure associated with the syntax of the show musical. How does a show musical end? Logically it could end at any of a dozen points: at the end of the show, at the cast party, when the reviews come out, with the couple's marriage, when star status is achieved, after the show breaks even and begins to turn a profit, with an Academy Award, the success of a child star, or the establishment of a family act. To paraphrase a famous star, however, logic had nothin' to do with it. The show musical follows its own laws and thus typically draws to a close at the point where the genre's most basic syntactic relationship is at its most clear: the end of the show, where there is no longer any dividing line between narrative and number, characters and actors, reality and illusion. Because the film ends where the show ends (and where the love affair climaxes), the spectator leaves the theater still under the influence of the film's most powerful moment, that instant where all the film's vectors suddenly coincide. The spectator thus fails to recognize that the street outside the theater is radically different from the streets in the film, that the real world is neither described, defined, nor transfigured by that of the film. The show, the love affair, and the film all climax together in order to mask the fact that only the film permits the perfect success of the show and the romance. What happens to the show and the couple after the film ends? Do they live happily ever after, as the fairy tale states and the musical suggests?

To ask this question is to foreground an element of musical syntax in the very way that a number of musicals from the late forties on do quite openly. By continuing beyond the climax where success in love and art coincide, i.e. by portraying the couple's marriage as well as their courtship, the musicals in question here not only afford a look into that never-never land called "ever after," they also by extension permit spectators to glimpse before leaving the theater the fall back into reality which they must eventually experience after departure. (If in the old syntax the end of the show and the success of the romance spelled the end of the spectator's film, then the period which follows that ending in these new films may reasonably be taken to represent the spectator's fall into reality after leaving the theater.) Throughout the history of the musical, there have from time to time been couples who marry during the course of the film. This is especially true of biopics, from *The Great Ziegfeld* on. (Though one should not conclude too hastily that the biopic by its very nature requires a strictly biographical structure;

Night and Day, for example, is wholly structured around the boy-gets-girl, composer-gets-song motif, ending when Cary Grant/Cole Porter finally gets his Linda.) Here and there a non-biographical film has fastened on the life-after-marriage motif, only to show that as long as marriage is treated as courtship it can still obey the musical model (e.g. one each for the musical's two most famous couples: MacDonald and Eddy as husband and wife in the significantly titled *Sweethearts*, and Astaire and Rogers in *The Barkleys of Broadway*). By and large, however, the use of the married couple to question closure is a concern of the fifties, in a series of films that systematically avoid rebuilding a traditional musical syntax in the manner of the reflexive films treated in the earlier part of this chapter. Marriage is the cornerstone on which the genre's syntax is built, but the musical is concerned primarily to justify, indeed to necessitate marriage, not to provide a recipe for successful marriage. Given the key position that marriage holds within musical syntax in general, and within the show musical in particular, it is not surprising that assumptions of guaranteed matrimonial bliss should be the last aspect of the genre's basic syntax to come under fire, but the first actually to pull it apart. At this point, a word is in order about the relationship between courtship and marriage during the half-century of the musical's hegemony over American romance.

Marriage represents a very special phenomenon in American life. More than the dynastic, economic, and social event that marriage constitutes in Europe, American marriage is a mystic occasion. It is that moment when the good fairy visits a young couple, turning the man from beast to prince charming and the woman from cinder girl to radiant princess. Previously confined to the dim world of unfulfilled sexual drives, the couple is now transfigured, drawing to itself the force and radiance of the sun. Love it is that accomplishes this miracle—self-sacrificing, transfiguring love, the kind that releases a man from a witch's spell. Marriage in America, then, is not an institution but a celebration, a ceremony that cares little about sanctifying a legal union, but serves rather to project a momentary triumph of romantic love into eternity. In other words, the act and ceremony of marriage in American life serve not so much as a beginning, an initiation into the adult world of families—as is the case with marriage in most other countries—but as an ending, as the necessary capstone of a glorious romance, the symbol of a successful courtship. Like the fairy tale, like New Comedy, the musical ends with marriage (or its symbolic representation) in order to disguise the fact that *American mythology has no model for intersexual relationships other than that of courtship.* American popular narrative must conclude with marriage—the ending of courtship—for it has no way of dealing with married life (unless, as in screwball comedy, situation comedy, "women's" romances, or the "Total Woman" movement, it is simply by prolonging the courtship paradigm into marriage). By cutting off the narrative at the moment of marriage, by projecting the film's final image into eternity, American mythology attempts to disguise its failure to provide models for the interpersonal relationships of married life.

This situation was not conceived in twentieth-century America, it is simply heightened there. In general, it can be seen to have grown out of a Romantic paradox: love is a mystic experience, enabling ordinary mortals to escape momentarily from the tyranny of time and into the transcendent sphere of life perfect and eternal; yet love takes place within the world, where it is bound by the constraints of the body physical, time durational, and promises unkeepable. As the French Romantic novelist Benjamin Constant puts the dilemma in his *Adolphe,* "Love is but a point in time, but it seems to take on a duration of its own." That duration which love only seems to take on is, as it were, guaranteed by romantic marriage—as if any institution or myth could guarantee what time denies. Romantic marriage is not so much a solution of this dilemma as it is an attempt to disguise it, to hide from young lovers the fact that their romantic longing must necessarily be killed, not heightened, by satisfaction. De Rougemont claims that the logical consequence of romantic love—love as longing rather than possession—is death, the only state that assures continued "longing." The myth of romantic marriage is specifically designed to disguise that scandal: the end of the film represents the ending of romantic love (i.e. unfulfilled longing), yet it seems to present the beginning of an eternity of romantic love. Marriage is presented as the continuation, the celebration of courtship, precisely to hide the fact that it is the end of courtship. No more eloquent testimony to this fact exists than Flaubert's brilliant deconstruction of Romantic mythology in *Madame Bovary*. Emma Bovary, like generations of young women (and men) after her, expects marriage to transfigure her life, to eternalize her longings by fulfilling them. Marriage as a fact reveals the internal contradictions of marriage as a myth, however, and Emma finds herself constantly constructing new pleasures to long for, never learning from the fact that each pleasure is destroyed by its attainment.

Courtship is longing, marriage is possession. Between the two, Western mythology (and its American variety *a fortiori*) will always choose the former, for romantic love thrives on the longing and dies with the possession. Marriage thus loses its status as a *fact* and as a *state*, sacrificing all durational characteristics to its new role as an act, a moment, an all-encompassing point in time, a last sacred minute of courtship before the stultifying mode of possession takes over. Far from representing the state of possession, marriage in American mythology is that last second of foreplay, that instant when deferral has reached its height, when expectation will last increase the pleasure. The American Bride is not a cook or a housewife, not a mother nor even an executive—at least during the period of the musical's greatest success—she is a fruit ready to be plucked, a virgin wearing a white dress for the last time (yet clearly meant to appear super-attractive). She is for the first and last time both the sum of naïveté and the height of sexuality, inviting and yet virginal. American marriage, during the heyday of the musi-

cal, is never a lifetime shared but a dream concentrated into a single moment.

And yet, like Emma Bovary, those who dream continue to exist after the ceremony. "They lived happily ever after" is a convenient clotural device for fairy tale and Hollywood musical alike, but it hardly squares with our experience. Of all the subgenres of the musical, the show musical is the one that logically confronts this problem first. The permanence of the marriage union is sealed by its association with the creation of a work of art, by definition that which is outside the flow of time. Yet the performers live on; we see them in other films, read about them in the papers, follow their divorces and suicides in the news. It is thus natural that the biopic, along with other semi-biographical plots, should have contributed most heavily to the foregrounding and contestation of the musical's closure conventions. *A Star Is Born* clearly reflects the tragic events of Judy Garland's personal life; *The Joker Is Wild* and *Funny Girl* depict the broken marriages of Joe E. Lewis and Fanny Brice. When Liza Minnelli is cast in a musical where a marriage dissolves *(New York, New York)*, it is difficult not to see in her her famous mother, Judy Garland. The tragic biography is only a catalyst, however, not the main point. In all these films the plot reaches a high point, conflating success in love and art, only to reach beyond it—beyond the world of romantic mythology, as it were—in order to reveal the effect of that very mythology on a world where life and mythology are inevitably and eternally separate. As one of the least known but most finely crafted of these reflexive dra-

Is this a musical? Grace Kelly, Bing Crosby, and William Holden at a low
point of *The Country Girl*.

[MOMA]

mas puts it, "Just about anybody can face a crisis, it's that everyday living that's tough" (*The Country Girl*, Paramount, directed by George Seaton, 1954).

Before the clotural convention came under fire in the American musical, however, it was frontally attacked—not surprisingly—in one of the most successful and influential of European musicals, *The Red Shoes* (Michael Powell and Emeric Pressburger, British, 1948). Throughout the first half of this brilliant ballet film Vicky Page (Moira Shearer) as the rising ballerina and Julian Craster (Robert Helpmann) as the young composer are given parallel scenes concerning their similar careers, opportunities, success, and love for each other. Both are given their big chance by Boris Lermontov (Anton Walbrook), and respond by together creating the ballet, "The Red Shoes," which is shown at length by the film. In the syntax of the Hollywood show musical, this is the end of the film: the couple are in love, they have created art together, they have fulfilled their own purposes in life and entertained the audience in the meantime. The film has nothing left to do but end.

Yet this is precisely what *The Red Shoes* refuses to do. Instead of ending the film, the traditional finale number ends only the first part. Throughout the first half, a dark presence has inhabited the film: the inscrutable Lermontov, seemingly in love with Page, always makes her a new job offer at the very moment we expect him to declare his love, thus creating a conflict in the spectator's mind between love and art. It is precisely this opposition that projects the film into its second half. Lermontov, like the directors of the film, refuses to allow Page and Craster to remain with his troupe if they wish to marry. Instead of the traditional reinforcement of success in love by success in art, the couple must choose between the two. Eventually Page returns to the ballet stage, but by this time such a return has been defined as infidelity to her husband; she kills herself rather than return to a world where she cannot have love and dance simultaneously. Though this ending is fully as romantic as the mythology which *The Red Shoes* deconstructs, this influential film does succeed remarkably well in forcing a genre entirely devoted to exultation to consider the problems of duration and permanency. Not only does the couple fail to withstand the pressure of time, but the director as well is denied his traditional status. Ever since Jimmy Cagney jumped on the stage to replace an inebriated actor in the final number of *Footlight Parade*, the director has been a participant in his own show, a man married to the stage. Lermontov, like Danglard (Jean Gabin), the director in Renoir's *French Can-Can*, has no such relationship to the stage. Because he is the stage's slave he must be the dancers'

master. Like many later films, *The Red Shoes* presents the stage world as a nightmare. In *The Joker Is Wild* the audience are thugs; Bing Crosby in *The Country Girl* sees every spectator as his accuser; *Cabaret* reveals man's obsessions and nightmares rather than his dreams; *The Turning Point* undercuts—but gently—every sugar-coated cliché inherited from the backstage musical. The granddaddy of them all, however, the one film which most effectively contests the genre's clotural conventions while demythologizing stardom, the one film which most poignantly accuses the musical of lying, that film is Warner's 1954 musical remake of *A Star Is Born* (the original 1937 film was based, according to some, on a most ironic couple—Ruby Keeler and Al Jolson, Mr. and Mrs. Musical Entertainment of the thirties!).

From the very first shots of *A Star Is Born*, the spectator is aware of a radical dichotomy that never quite disappears from the film. Behind the credits, searchlights light up the sky of a distant city, announcing a show and its stars in a fashion at the same time traditional and picturesque, distanced and appealing. As soon as the credits—the stars—have faded from sight, however, we cut to the same scene viewed from close up, with the spotlights now seen from the uncomfortable perspective of a gala benefit traffic jam, overbright, with people yelling, screaming, pushing, shoving, trying to see the picture-perfect stars in their black limousines. Two views, two sensations, two overtones to the phenomenon of stardom; either distant and beautiful against the summer sky, or overheated, uncomfortable, and artificial to the close observer. The entire first half of *A Star Is Born* labors to erase this distantiating dichotomy. Every cliché of the show musical is trotted out in order to establish a situation in which opposing views of stardom—and of stage illusion in general—can melt into one. Like Fred Astaire in *Easter Parade,* James Mason finds Judy Garland in a glitterless night club and promises to turn her into a star. She has that "little something extra," says he, that turns an ordinary singer into a star. That night we reach back well beyond the backstage musical in order to draw upon the oldest cliché of Western dual-focus narrative: parallel sleepless nights, punctuated by a call to each employer, warn us of the love affair to come. The next day the Pygmalion/Galatea myth is trotted out in spades—Hollywood style. She is made up to the hilt by the studio's make-up department; from this block of Maybelline marble he removes just enough to restore her special nature. Shortly, in a scene borrowed from the thirties but which can no longer be done straight, Mason lures the boss into visiting his office then tricks him into giving Garland a chance. The only number that could possibly cap this sequence of backstage clichés is "Born in a Trunk," an utterly captivating amalgam of every commonplace not yet introduced. Within minutes, Mason and Garland are on their way to the Justice of the Peace, where even the use of their real names and the absence of an audience derive directly from cinematic tradition. The motel scene which ensues effectively resolves every opposition present up to this point. On the radio they hear her number one hit song, "It's a New World," its lyrics

clearly applicable to the happy couple's new world. He turns the radio off and insists on having her do the singing live; she does, thus at the same time reducing the distance between mechanical reproduction and live entertainment, and firmly establishing an equation between singing and love-making, the marriage of audience and performer paralleling that of husband and wife.

As in *The Red Shoes*, the final production number, where all the pieces fit harmoniously together, comes too soon. In the entire film, this is the only point—the point between the marriage ceremony and the wedding night—when this harmony will reign. For, as we soon realize, Garland's "little something extra" propels her to the top at the expense of her husband. Throughout the first half of the film, the conventional celebratory patterns of dual-focus narrative hold sway. His efforts to make her into a star are always matched by her malleability and talents. The second half, however, abandons the carefully paired patterns of the first. Instead of matched sleepless nights, which somehow seem to reflect each other according to some divine (generic) pattern, we witness instead Mason's fall into jealousy and self-degradation. From what seemed like a spatially conceived pattern of carefully matched scenes, shots, and situations paired two by two, we slide into a new world where time suddenly exists, where frustration is no longer subtracted out daily by the god of entertainment, but where each action instead induces another more desperate. Instead of the circle's wholeness and eternal return, an accelerating spiral of frustration. He began as her father (at first he

Is this a musical? James Mason and an over-the-hill actor's best friend in *A Star Is Born* (1954).

[UW]

makes decisions for her), at the center they are equalized (marriage), she ends as his mother (taking him into custody and making his decisions). Just as their triumph represented a breakthrough into a new world of harmony and realizable ideals, so the passage of time, the film seems to suggest, ever carries even the perfect moment forward to a new and different situation. Thus Garland's reprise of "It's a New World" serves as an ironic reminder that anything new can grow old: immediately after this reprise Mason wades out into the ocean, returning to the elements, whence he came.

Over this cynical treatment of stardom lost and nothingness regained, *A Star Is Born* attempts to throw a costume rather than a shroud. At the final benefit show, echoing the one that opened the film, Garland refuses to repudiate the drunkard husband who so often has publicly humiliated her. Rejecting her stage name as well as her real maiden name, Garland identifies herself as "Mrs. Norman Maine," a magnanimous gesture that temporarily hides the horror of their married life, but that cannot erase the extreme emotion required to bind the performer to the married woman. The gap between life and art, between real and ideal, so successfully bridged at mid-film, has now become an abyss never to be spanned again. As Garland's first film after a retirement forced by an overdose of stardom, *A Star Is Born* rings the death knell over the little girl who could play Pop Winninger's adolescent daughter or co-star with a cowardly lion. Along with numerous other mid-fifties offerings, it forever banishes the show musical's earlier automatic equation between success in romance and success on the stage.

During the watershed 1954-55 season, no fewer than five major musicals dared to confront the marriage realm so long shunned by the genre (*A Star Is Born, The Country Girl,* and *The Glenn Miller Story* among show musicals, with *Seven Brides for Seven Brothers* and *It's Always Fair Weather* in the folk subgenre). Indeed, from the mid-fifties on, plots that follow a couple from courtship into marriage and beyond dominate the adult offerings in the genre (as opposed to the increasingly common cartoon or rock musicals clearly aimed at the pre-teen and teenage crowd). From the fairy tale tradition come *High Society* and *Camelot,* while the folk subgenre contributes post-marriage films as varied as *Carousel, Beau James, Porgy and Bess, Paint Your Wagon, The Jazz Singer,* and *Pennies From Heaven.* Most abundant of all are treatments of married couples involved in show business: *The Joker Is Wild, I Could Go On Singing, Funny Girl, Funny Lady, A Star Is Born, New York, New*

York, and *All That Jazz.* The example of the 1954 *A Star Is Born* and the career of Judy Garland clearly weigh heavily in the post-marriage orientation of the show musical over the last three decades, for nearly all of the films mentioned owe an overt debt to the Garland persona, in and out of her films. Another group of films shares the bittersweet tone of the post-1954 marriage musicals, but permits the courting partners to discover their difficulties before the marriage vows are pronounced. Following the 1968 lead of Bob Fosse in *Sweet Charity,* numerous major productions have experimented with unhappy love as a potential source of artistic inspiration (*Cabaret, Nashville, The Perfect Couple, The Rose,* and even *Jesus Christ Superstar*).

This return to the sad clown motif reminiscent of the show subgenre's nightclub beginning seals the death warrant of the show syntax that reigned supreme over the genre for a quarter-century. No longer are music and spectacle generated by the energy of a successful courtship; no longer is a successful courtship guaranteed by the communitarian joy of an energetic musical spectacle. Where once singing and courting derived their value from common participation in a single wellspring of mystic power, now they have lost their status as uniquely valuable activities. Sexual attraction has been reduced to a bodily function like hunger or perspiration, while putting on a show has been stripped of its amateur overtones in favor of a more business-oriented approach. For decades, some might say, the American public has been hoodwinked by the musical into thinking that shows just happen, that they are made to appear

In the show musical, Bob Fosse-style, even Roy Scheider's open heart operation can provide the occasion for a production number.

[MOMA]

magically like a rabbit out of a hat; with the musical's new honesty with regard to show business and romance alike, no such misconception is possible. Perhaps ignoring the hidden values which myths may have for a society, these critics disregard the extraordinary energy which the myth of amateur theater has spawned in this country. From the Little Theater movement of prewar years to the school plays of the fifties, this country has been extraordinarily blessed with an impetus toward song and dance freely offered and graciously received. Even the breakdancing movement of recent years has continued this tradition. People perform best, this line goes, when natural talent is coupled with inner desire—desire that can be moved only by the emotions and not by money. That this myth conceals for a moment the fact that Hollywood actors work for money is incontrovertible, but one can't help wondering whether there is not a more useful truth to be found in the utopianism of *Flashdance*, where Jennifer Beals qualifies for conservatory training by adopting the techniques and the energy of youthful Pittsburgh breakdancers, than in the cynicism of Bob Fosse's painstakingly brilliant work.

However one considers the demise of amateurism and the vulgarization of sex in the new musical, one thing is clear: the illusion that nourished the musical and its audience for decades is now gone forever, from all but the very young and the nostalgically old. The production of music no longer possesses its own special narratives guaranteeing music's special, romantic, quasi-religious status. Instead, with music videos, a new multimedia poetry has appeared, recognizing the disc (and thus economic) origins of the music track, for which the stylization of the images appears as something like a compensation. The scandal of making music for money has thus not disappeared, it must simply be dealt with in a new manner. Once, it was the work of romance to disguise the financial side of music production; now that music's status as business venture has been unveiled, no traditional image can contain the malaise associated with such a sobering revelation. The illusion is gone, and with it—for some of us—much of the joy music produced in the vanished era of musical amateurism.

Looked at from a distance, the history of the show musical traced out in this chapter seems to follow the familiar pattern according to which preliminary accretion of key semantic units leads to development of a stable syntax, itself ultimately undermined through an increasingly reflexive approach that involves taking the previously established syntax as object of analysis. Such a neat, textbook description of the show musical's historical development misses the specificity of this particular subgenre's progression, however. A comparison with the fairy tale musical is instructive in particularizing the history of each type. Working with semantic material deriving from a half-century of European theatrical tradition, the fairy tale musical varies little over its history from traditionally accepted materials. What does change during the quarter-century when the fairy tale musical flourished is the syntax built out of a familiar semantic field. To be sure, there is a slight semantic displacement from the Ruritania of Chevalier to Astaire's contemporary European high society to the antebellum mansions of MacDonald and Eddy. Nonetheless, the operative changes that periodically give new life to the subgenre involve the confection of new syntactic bonds: sex as sex, sex as battle, sex as adventure. Indeed, one might well consider the folk musical as nothing more than a further link in this chain—sex as settlement—if it were not for the radical semantic innovations which the folk subgenre brings to its fairy tale godmother.

The show musical, on the other hand, depends heavily on shifting semantic traditions. While the first two important moments in the subgenre's history must clearly be defined syntactically—the early development of a melodramatic show syntax and its replacement in 1933 by the sunnier romance/show ties that would reign for the next two decades—nearly all subsequent innovations must be seen in terms of semantic developments deriving from multiple sources. While the biopic and the children's film clearly constitute conveniences for Hollywood, the changing styles in music and their related cultures obviously stem from the musical's heavy dependence on the nation's musical tastes. Further evidence of outside influence on the musical comes from the troop show and the genre's periodic tendency to turn toward new technologies in its search for semantic variety (radio, television, even film itself). While the reflexivity characteristic of recent decades certainly represents an important syntactic development, it must be recognized that the show musical, throughout its history, has remained more susceptible to semantic variation by virtue of its dependence on currently viable forms of musical entertainment. More closely tied to the recording industry than either of the other two subgenres, the show musical traces out a half-century path that closely parallels the history of musical taste in America outside the musical. Using top performers when they are at the top of their form—and box-office potential—the show musical, for all its amateurism, reveals a history inseparable from economic considerations.

The Folk Musical

AS A GENRE, THE FILM MUSICAL SATISFIES THE SPECTATOR'S desire to escape from a humdrum day-to-day existence, each musical subgenre meeting this need for a fuller life in a different way. The show musical involves the spectator in the creation of a work of art; the fairy tale musical creates a utopian world like that of the spectator's dreams; the folk musical projects the audience into a mythicized version of the cultural past. In each case a different device mediates between the spectator's reality and the unreal world for which he/she yearns. In the show musical it is the show itself that serves this mediatory function, by virtue of its dual status as real (the show actually exists, including actors, sets, and props) and unreal (all the elements of the show represent something that they are not). In the fairy tale musical, this mediatory role is assigned to the Big White Set, which thus plays the part occupied by Hollywood within American society as a whole: at one and the same time it authenticates our dream visions (proving that fairy tale kingdoms and careers actually do exist, even if only in Hollywood), yet makes them seem impossibly distant from the lowly status of our daily life. The mythical vision of the folk musical is in many ways more complex, because it must grapple more seriously with a lived reality. The art and dream worlds of the other subgenres create an atmosphere of make-believe which by definition combines the real with the unreal. The folk musical, on the other hand, colors every corner of the world with the transforming power of memory. Now as a mediatory factor (between real and unreal, between present and past), memory is far less stable than either art or dreams. Memory can tame a sailor's language, clean up a barnyard in nothing flat, turn bankruptcy into a picnic, and a picnic into a banquet. Nothing so dulls hardship or magnifies pleasure as memory. And it is in the folk musical that the genre film's general tendency to glorify the past reaches its highest point. Yet memory can also reproduce the past faithfully, recall hardship, filth, and defeat, or bring back experiences best forgotten. Suspended between observation and dream vision, memory is the perfect—if unstable—mediatory factor for a subgenre simultaneously grounded in the American heritage and the American myth. The folk musical thus neither depends entirely on American history, nor ignores it completely; it takes place within that intermediary space which we designate by such terms as tradition, folklore, and Americana.

Observation and dream vision, the two components of memory, define quite clearly the limits of the folk musical subgenre. On one side lies a large group of films, almost all produced during the early history of the subgenre, which stress the picturesque almost to the exclusion of observed reality. These semantic folk musicals—films like *Hallelujah I'm a Bum*, *The Little Colonel*, *Mississippi*, *Shipmates Forever*, *Rose Marie*, *Girl of the Golden West*, and *In Old Chicago*—place so much emphasis on the romance of Central Park, the Old South, or the Mounties that they recall the unreality of the fairy tale musical. When being a tramp is a cause for rejoicing, when shipmates are forever, when the West is Golden and Chicago Old, when a Southern mansion is treated as the privileged meeting place of Southern gentlemen, then we might as well be in Ruritania. These quasi-utopian musicals of the thirties are matched by another group, this time from the sixties and seventies, that so stress the realistic aspect of American life that they threaten to abandon the musical's stylized nature all together. When Elvis Presley and Mary Tyler Moore play a blasé doctor in a New York slum and a Catholic nun committed both to social work and her vows of chastity, then the conventions of the musical are clearly being stretched to the breaking point (*Change of Habit*). In *Nashville* they are snapped cleanly in two: too much realism threatens a film's identity as a musical, even a film with twenty-seven separate musical numbers which takes place in the capital of American folk music. From total dependence on the picturesque, anecdotal elements of Americana, with little respect for realistic portrayal, the folk musical progresses through a period of structured tension between real and unreal (observation and dream vision, threats and pleasures), moving finally to a careful undercutting of the picturesque by emphasis on the observed.

Elements of the Folk Musical

Of all the characteristic concerns of the folk musical, none so clearly separates it from the show and fairy tale traditions as its emphasis on family groupings and the home. In the fairy tale musical, parents are second-rank characters at best, often serving as a mild but nevertheless functional barrier to the couple's marriage. Family ties as such are reduced to the conventional role that they play within the aristocracy. For some characters, parental relationships seem downright impossible: in what movies, for example, do Maurice Chevalier, Jeanette MacDonald, or Fred Astaire have parents (or children, for that matter) who play an important role in the plot? The mere presence of multi-generational relationships—and particularly the presence of children—tends to bend the fairy tale musical in the direction of its folk counterpart (e.g. in *Stowaway, The Wizard of Oz, The Sound of Music,* and *Oliver!*), though more often than not the fairy tale musical manages to reduce the distance between the generations through a successful intergenerational romance (*Yolanda and the Thief, Daddy Long Legs, Gigi, My Fair Lady, The Sound of Music*). The status of the family in the show musical differs little. The older generation may represent the recalcitrant parents of the New Comedy tradition, a potential bankroll for a show, a doting mother, or a force opposing entertainment, but we rarely find a close-knit family unit in which the unity of the generations is as important as the unity of the couple. Indeed, the few times when family relationships are emphasized, the show musical takes on certain characteristics of the folk musical (e.g., *Babes in Arms, Strike Up the Band, Bye Bye Birdie*). Typically, the hero and heroine of the show and fairy tale musicals are free agents, tied to no responsibilities except those which attach them to the creation of a work of art or the government of an imaginary kingdom. The folk musical, on the other hand, cannot survive without a sense of community, and in the America portrayed by the folk musical, no group so clearly embodies the joys and difficulties of community as the nuclear family.

During the thirties and early forties, the family grouping is often represented by a substitute family, such as the students and faculty of a college (*Flirtation Walk, Shipmates Forever, Pigskin Parade, Girl Crazy*). With *Meet Me in St. Louis*, however, the multi-generational family (previously emphasized in *Hallelujah, The Little Colonel, High, Wide and Hand-*

some, and *Little Nelly Kelly*) becomes permanently fixed as a standard element of the folk musical: four separate generations are necessary for a proper portrayal of the Smith family (grandfather, parents, marriageable daughters, and young children, not to mention the family maid). Hardly a single folk musical after 1944 lacks a strong family relationship; among those that do, most tend either toward the fairy tale world (*On the Town, Two Weeks with Love, Guys and Dolls, Girls! Girls! Girls!*) or the show musical (*Varsity Show, Take Me Out to the Ball Game, It's Always Fair Weather*). The presence of more than one generation facilitates the doubling of the youthful romantic couple(s) with an already married couple whose relationship is rejuvenated during the course of the film, thus increasing family closeness and establishing a link between the marriage bond and the family bond. The interchangeability of romantic and family ties is often underscored by making the members of the young couple also members of the same household (*Hallelujah*) or close neighbors (*Meet Me in St. Louis, Summer Holiday, One Sunday Afternoon*), or by giving the young couple an older relative or friend whose parental advice serves the couple's love (especially in Rodgers and Hammerstein films, e.g., *Oklahoma!, Carousel,* and *Flower Drum Song,* but also in *High, Wide and Handsome, Living in a Big Way, This Time for Keeps, West Side Story, The Music Man, Roustabout,* and *Finian's Rainbow*). Whether or not the older generation shares youth's romantic interests, it always serves in the folk musical to reassure the audience of the ability of young people to remain sensitive to ro-

Starting in the late thirties, Fox produced one folk musical after another, reproducing familiar situations like this lunchroom scene from *Margie*.

[MOMA]

mance years after the glow of courtship has faded. The family residence, whether farmhouse, mansion, or humble flat, thus takes on a symbolic value, for it serves not only as the stable and constant backdrop of the folk musical's action, but also as a permanent reminder of the strength and stability of the American family and home.

The presence of an extended family in the folk musical almost by definition implies a vision of America as a galaxy of small towns, with the impersonality of the big city permanently banned. Indeed, the small town or agricultural setting is one of the most tenacious of folk musical semantic traits. In many cases the action of the film is entirely limited to the type of town where everyone is a neighbor, where each season's rituals bring the entire population together. Other folk musicals portray large cities, but at a time when they were still made up of coherent neighborhoods in which everyone knows the local iceman, policeman, or shopkeeper (e.g., *San Francisco, In Old Chicago, Little Nelly Kelly, Meet Me in St. Louis, Centennial Summer, In the Good Old Summertime, Flower Drum Song*). In the familiar context created by the folk musical, even the world's largest city can be tamed and made to appear no more

Never short for a stage or an audience, the folk musical excels at turning places as banal as this farm kitchen from *Summer Stock* into a dance floor for Gene Kelly.

[MOMA]

than a slightly bigger version of one's hometown (*Hallelujah I'm a Bum, It Happened in Brooklyn, On the Town, The Belle of New York, It's Always Fair Weather, West Side Story, Change of Habit,* and *Saturday Night Fever*). As long as Gene Kelly and Vera-Ellen try to impress each other with their sophistication in *On the Town* they do little more than get on each other's nerves, but when they finally admit that they both grew up in the same small town (and thus had the same school teachers), their love is assured. It is fitting that their first love duet—"Main Street, U.S.A."—should be as much an ode to the American hinterlands, to "small town people, the backbone of American civilization" (as one says to the other), as it is a declaration of love. Love is only possible, the folk musical seems to affirm, when we are in familiar territory, with familiar people, and speaking a familiar language. Just as the recognition of familiar places is reassuring for the film spectator, so the support of the characters' own past is necessary to help them envision the future with clarity.

In keeping with the principle that all folk musical elements are borrowed from the American past and colored by a euphoric memory, the typical folk musical set represents aspects of the American scene as transformed by the popular arts. Two major directions can be identified here: 1) the construction of sets based on the conventions of American painting, printmaking, and photography, and 2) the use of location photography, with the location carefully chosen to recall a cinematic or other pictorial precedent. In the section of his autobiography on *Meet Me in St. Louis*, Vincente Minnelli recalls

how he "felt the whole picture should have the look of Thomas Eakins's paintings, though not to the point of imitation." [1] The sets for this film thus never aspire to the status of reality, but rather to that of remembered reality. Kensington Avenue is not like the street we grew up on, but like an old engraving of that street, as the film's seasonal vignettes reveal. By borrowing the Eakins style, Minnelli assimilates his set not to an actual memory, but to our memory as filtered through the transforming palette of an artist. In *Summer Holiday* Rouben Mamoulian performs a similar operation with the help of other American artists. Like Godard, reputed to give his cameraman directions by simple reference to shots in earlier films, Mamoulian designates his desired color scheme in terms of a certain style of painting. Instead of the standard contrasting colors, Mamoulian wanted "just tints within a very narrow chromatic range—various degrees of yellow, beige and green . . . the colors of 'Americana'—like Thomas Benton, John Curry and Grant Wood."[2] "From them," he says, "I learned what marvelous things you can do just by using different shades of the same color" (Fordin, 191). Mamoulian does not just ask for a typical American landscape but a typical American landscape done in "Grant Wood or American primitive style" (Fordin, 195), not just a period feeling but "a period feeling like Currier and Ives prints" (Fordin, 197). Furthermore, in Mamoulian's New England town every piece is in place—the soda shop, the park, the old Victorian mansion, the Fourth of July picnic—so much so that we feel we are viewing a carefully staged version of the past. The camera records only those moments worthy of a painting, shying away from subjects which are less than fully representative or perfectly constituted. The scene in the soda shop focuses on Mickey Rooney and Gloria de Haven sharing a malted with two straws; at the graduation exercises the camera picks up a statue of Abe Lincoln (artistically shot through ferns), notices a statuesque group of women in front of a painting of Washington crossing the Delaware (thus reconstituting Grant Wood's "Daughters of Revolution"), and freezes on a living tableau version of Grant Wood's "American Gothic"; at the picnic the food is depicted as beautiful and untouched (rather than strewn all over, as it would be at any time other than the moment when a picture was about to be taken), while the dance is captured from above, as it could be seen only by the mind's eye. In *The Belle of New York* Charles Walters self-consciously imitates the compositions of Currier and Ives. Whether or not a specific model is employed, however, the effect is always the same: folk musical sets are characterized by a conventionalized realism in which the conventions are borrowed from the vocabulary of American regional art. Instead of recalling the visions of the spectator's personal past, the folk musical brings back instead those works of popular art through which previous generations have taught us how to see the American past: postcards, engravings, calendars, magazines, photographs, paintings, and films.[3]

The problem of location photography is a stickier one. On this subject nearly every general history of the film musical takes three propositions for granted:

1) *On the Town* (1949) was the first musical to make extensive use of location photography;

2) the primary function of location photography in the musical is an increase in realism;

3) the use of location photography frees the musical from artistic precedents by removing the last vestiges of staginess. I believe that all three of these propositions are fundamentally wrong, that they stem not only from an inadequate knowledge of the history of the musical, but also from a mistaken apprehension of the status and function of realism in the musical.

1) As early as 1929, King Vidor used extensive location photography in *Hallelujah*. From cotton fields and shanty towns to the final chase through the swamp, *Hallelujah* succeeds in recording the poor man's South. Using scenes shot on location in Chino, California, Mamoulian's *High, Wide and Handsome* (1937) is able to create a sense of openness and closeness to the land which would have been impossible indoors. Many other films before *On the Town* use location photography.

2) The use of location photography in *On the Town* has been cited to document the growing realism of the post-war musical. To be sure, there is an added realism here, an unretouched view of real buildings in a real city, but they are rarely seen as a typical New Yorker would see them. Just as Minnelli, Mamoulian, and Walters compensate for the realism of their sets with the painter's palette, so *On the*

Continuity of inspiration in the folk musical—from a shared milkshake in *Summer Holiday* to a hardly changed soda shop in *Grease* thirty years later.
[a = MOMA, b = BFI]

As early as 1930, the folk musical called on the western to provide the look of Americana, as here in *The Song of the West*, one of the first of many contributions which Oscar Hammerstein II made to the folk musical.

[MOMA]

Town counters the realism of location photography by freeing the camera from its spectator's eye view of the city. Throughout *On the Town* the camera dances, making New York obey its rhythm rather than vice-versa. The camera does not *record* New York, it *animates* it. Never straying from the folk musical's combination of perceived reality and compensatory memory vision, *On the Town* transforms its perceived reality cinematically, just as MGM's trio of directors had done in a painterly fashion. This transformation of a photographed location is even more obvious in the many films of the fifties and sixties which use extensive location shooting in the wide open spaces of the West. Films like *Oklahoma!*, *The Unsinkable Molly Brown,* and *Paint Your Wagon* all use the conventions of the filmic medium in much the same way that Mamoulian uses that of painting; they refer to the American countryside indirectly, through the intermediary of a popular genre. Our vision of the American West is colored by the western, just as our vision of small-town America is colored by regional painters. Whether Thomas Eakins or John Ford provides this vision, whether

Throughout the thirties, the folk musical periodically turned to location photography to achieve a realistic picture of the American landscape of our imagination: a southern river in *Hallelujah*, the cold Northwest in *Rough Romance*, wagon trains west in *The Song of the West*, the cliffs of Chino, California in *High, Wide and Handsome*.

[a-c = MOMA, d = BFI]

the raw material is a studio set or a western landscape, the function remains the same: to keep simultaneously before the viewer's eyes the true stuff of America *plus* the mythifying vision which turns it into Americana.

3) We can thus see how misguided it is to take location photography as an escape from artistic precedents. Quite to the contrary, location shooting simply represents a change in the precedent chosen. Instead of the stage (as in the backstage musical), instead of historical romances and other versions of aristocratic life written for lower- and middle-class consumption (the fairy tale musical), instead of painting and the related arts (the Minnelli-Mamoulian-Walters strain), the location-oriented folk musical simply turns to other film genres for its artistic precedents (in particular the western and the travel documentary).

With traditional characters living in a small town and seen through the eyes of

Lacking an effective form of couple dancing, the early folk musical turned instead to formation marching, as in Warner's tribute to the U.S. Naval Academy in *Shipmates Forever*.

[UW]

the popular arts, it seems that the folk musical would have a ready-made dance medium: the folk dance. Indeed, it is the square dance, the line dance, and other group dances that support the folk musical well into the forties. As a group, however, these dances have a drawback which eventually required their replacement by a more versatile style: all these dances are done only at a set time, in a set place, by a set number of dancers. Whereas Fred Astaire can turn a walk into a solo dance with only a slight variation of normal walking rhythms, or an argument into a

dance by simply provoking properly timed responses from Ginger Rogers, the square dance is tied not only to a specific social milieu but also to certain ritual moments in the life of the community. These moments can of course be used to great musical advantage, as the films of John Ford clearly demonstrate. But the folk musical in general aspires to a connection between life, music, and the dance far too close to permit restriction of the dance to a particular situation. For this reason it is fortunate that contemporary with the growth of the folk musical as an independent subgenre a new dance style was growing up within the staid world of American ballet.

As early as 1934, Leonide Massine transformed a moment of cultural history, the building of the first transcontinental railroad, into a modern ballet. Employing stylized period costumes by Irene Sharaff (later head costume designer for MGM's Freed Unit), *Union Pacific* launched a new look in American dance. The new style was further developed in Martha Graham's *Frontier* (1935), which combines familiar gestures and stylized traditional dances with a quasi-historical set drawn from the American past. Within a few years this new approach, again used by Graham in 1938 (*American Document*) and 1944 (*Appalachian Spring*), was tried by a number of other choreographers. Lew Christensen set *Pocahontas* (1936) and *Filling Station* (1938) to the work of American composers Elliott Carter and Virgil Thomson. Catherine Littlefield combined nineteenth-century folk tunes with a farm motif and came up with *Barn Dance* (1937); the setting was changed, but not the technique, for *Terminal* (1937) and *Café Society* (1938). Ruth Page borrowed her motifs from folk mythology, especially in *An American Pattern* (1938) and *Frankie and Johnny* (1938), and her costumes from current popular culture (the chorus was dressed in Salvation Army costumes, a happy solution which was to be copied many times in the film musical). Sophie Maslow turned to the folk strains of Woody Guthrie for her *Dust Bowl Ballads* (1941), which was followed in 1942 by *Folksay*. Eugene Loring was even more prolific, turning out six major folk ballets in as many years before his departure for Hollywood: *Yankee Clipper* (1937), *Billy the Kid* (1938—the first of Aaron Copland's many folk ballets), *City Portrait* (1939), *The Great American Goof* (1940), *Prairie* (1942), and *The Invisible Wife* (1942).

Not until Agnes de Mille's repeated triumphs, however, did the new dance style achieve popular acclaim. In her autobiography, de Mille explains quite clearly the essence of the new style which she had used in *Rodeo* (1942), the stage productions of *Oklahoma!* (1943) and *Carousel* (1945), and the ballet *Fall River Legend* (1948):

> Ballet gesture up to now had always been based on the classic technique and whatever deviated from this occurred only in comedy caricatures. The style throughout, the body stance, the walk, the run, the dynamic attack, the tensions and controls, were balletic even when national folk dances were incorporated into the choreography.
>
> We were trying to diversify the root impulse and just as Gershwin impressed on the main line of musical development characteristics natural to his own unclassical environment, we were adding gestures and rhythms we had grown up with, using them seriously and without condescension for the first time. This is not a triviality; it is the seed and base of the whole choreographic organization. If dance gesture means anything, it means the life behind the movement.
>
> The younger choreographers believed that every gesture must be proper to a particular character under particular circumstances . . . The new choreographer does not arrange old steps into new patterns; the emotion evolves steps, gestures and rhythms.

With the forties, the dream ballet became an almost required interlude within the folk musical tradition, thanks largely to the success of Agnes de Mille's choreography for the 1943 stage production of *Oklahoma!*, reproduced nearly intact for the 1955 film version illustrated here.

[MOMA]

And for this reason, the line between dancing and acting is no longer clearly marked.[4]

This last sentence can hardly be overemphasized for an understanding of the folk musical as a whole. Whereas classical ballet is often narrative but rarely ritual, whereas folk dance is always ritual but never truly narrative, the new style was both ritual and narrative, able to tell a story but particulary well-suited to telling a familiar story *again*. The titles of the new dances read like the chapter headings of a book on American popular mythology; each dance recreates a myth, but a myth close enough for the spectator to feel a sense of participation. The new style had, as Martha Graham put it, an "aura of race memory." When integrated into the musical, the narrative flow of the new style permits a constant interweaving of dialogue and dance, such that dancing and acting are even less separate than in the new ballet itself. Borrowing the new style, Hollywood also borrowed its makers: choreographers (Loring, de Mille, Jerome Robbins), designers (Oliver Smith,

Lemuel Ayers), costumers (Irene Sharaff), even dancers (especially Michael Kidd). Supported by such talented and sympathetic personnel, the narrative folk dance element in the musical was in a position to maintain its quality well into the fifties.

The situation of music in the folk subgenre was in many ways much like that of dance. With no shortage of folk music to draw from, the early folk musicals simply did as Catherine Littlefield did for *Barn Dance* or Sophie Maslow for *Dust Bowl Ballads*: they used American folk songs as is, thus providing a corpus of popular, rhythmical, and familiar tunes to which any spectator could tap his feet and hum along. In King Vidor's *Hallelujah*, for example, all the songs are traditional, with the exception of two numbers written by Irving Berlin. Spirituals never disappear from the musical, as we can see from such diverse films as *The Little Colonel, Mississippi, Cabin in the Sky*, and many others. The problem with spirituals—and other folk tunes—is that like folk dancing they are hard to fit into the narrative flow of a film without special preparation. What was needed was a type of music which would share the popular rhythms, downhome subjects, and ritual qualities o. the folk song, but which would be composed by contemporary composers aware of certain Broadway and Hollywood conventions of harmony, phrasing, and instrumentation. In fact, by the time sound hit Hollywood, such a style was already well on the way. As far back as 1919, Jerome Kern had begun his association with the Princess Theater, which was at that time experimenting with a new style of musical theater in direct reaction against the aristocratic and unreal aspects of European operetta, then the rage of New York. Rather than writing songs of an extravagant nature, meant to match an operetta star's costumes and stature more than the plot, Kern aimed for something of a more intimate nature. To logical stories acted out by recognizable characters in a modern setting, he added songs which were well integrated into the action and which borrowed their rhythm and their style from daily American life. *Mutatis mutandis*, the communal experiments of the Princess Theater represented for the musical stage what the realistic innovations of Antoine's Théâtre Libre had meant to the dramatic stage more than a generation before.

Nevertheless, the Princess Theater period was only a beginning and not a source of masterpieces (from this period only *Very Good Eddie* is regularly revived). When in 1925 Kern teamed up with the young scriptwriter and lyricist, Oscar Hammerstein II, such influential masterworks were not far off. Under the influence of Kern, Hammerstein began to concentrate on material derived from the American national heritage. With the colossal success of *Show Boat* in 1927 a new style was born. In earlier musicals, every song constituted a "number," a radical break in the story line accompanied by lavish production techniques, including unmotivated chorus lines. For *Show Boat*, however, Kern and Hammerstein conceived the music and the script together. Every song was to grow directly out of and further the plot. When a chorus was needed, it was to be provided by characters whose presence on stage was justified by more than just the need for a chorus. Songs were to appear natural; by far the majority were conceived as expressions of heartfelt personal emotion rather than as public performances. For this reason a new musical paradigm was needed, one which reflected the problems and concerns of people along the Mississippi. Where the style of Viennese operetta no longer seemed appropriate, the syncopated rhythms of ragtime, the plaintive tones of the spiritual, and the happy-go-lucky melodies of the minstrel show provided just the right note. Unlike the music of most contemporary musicals, *Show Boat*'s songs clearly belong together in the same show; they benefit from a unity of style and inspiration which characterizes the folk musical throughout its history.

Drawing on the models provided by Kern, many of this country's greatest popular composers would soon be providing shows with songs based on the traditional music of regional and ethnic America: Irving Berlin, George Gershwin, Richard Rodgers, Harold Arlen. Before long, plot necessities broadened the range of folk-type songs available for use in the folk musical: onomatopoeic tunes imitating the rhythm and sounds of modes of transportation ("In My Merry Oldsmobile," "The Trolley Song," "The Surrey With the Fringe on Top," "The Wells Fargo Wagon," "Coach Comin' In," "When the Midnight Choo-choo Leaves for Alabam," "Let's Choo-choo-choo to Idaho," "Get on Board Little Chillun," and Harry Warren's three standards, "Chattanooga Choo-choo," "On the Atchison, Topeka, and the Santa Fe," and "Stanley Steamer"), songs built around community rituals ("Our State Fair," "This Was a Real Nice Clambake," "County Fair," "Goin' to the County Fair," many others), songs celebrating a particular place ("All I Owe I-o-way," "Dixie Melody," "Pennsylvania Polka," "It's the Little Things in Texas," "Allegheny Al," "San Antonio Rose," "Sioux City Sue," and myriad others from "The Brooklyn Bridge" to "San Francisco" by way of "Poughkeepsie," "Kalamazoo," "Paducah," "Gary, Indiana," "The Black Hills of Dakota," "Kansas City," "Tallahassee," "New Orleans," "Oklahoma!," and "Nevada," not to mention all the traditional place songs reused by the folk musical such as "Manhattan," "The Sidewalks of New York," "Chinatown, My Chinatown," "Carolina in the Morning," "Chicago," "Meet Me in St. Louis," and "California Here I Come"), as well as songs of the seasons, songs stressing particular ethnic groups (often stressing that group's characteristic rhythms and harmonies), songs recalling the style of an earlier period (particularly barbershop harmony), and many other categories all of which emphasize on the one hand the situations of Americana, and on the other hand the rhythms, harmonies, and melodies which have come to be conventionally associated with the American tradition.

Perhaps the single most important attribute of the "native American style" is a certain ease of delivery, stemming from a belief—like that which Agnes de Mille expressed in relation to dance—that song is not art but the expression of emotion. It is thus less important to know that much of the musical idiom of the folk musical is influenced by jazz and ragtime (particularly through the influence of Gershwin) than it is to know that song is a natural attribute of folk musical characters, rather than a learned one. Professional musicians rarely appear as folk musical characters (unlike the show and fairy tale subgenres) because music is a natural means of expression, not the privileged possession of an aristocratic, artistic culture. Few folk musical stars are blessed with the vocal versatility and training of a Jeanette MacDonald or a Kathryn Grayson; those who do display outstanding voices are most often "natural" singers, people like Judy Garland, Gene Kelly, and Frank Sinatra, who seem to sing effortlessly, without training, in a manner which evokes not the opera or concert stage but the expression of personal emotion. They don't perform, they just sing. In other musicals poor singers either avoid singing or sing for comic effect (does Eric Blore ever sing? does Edward Everett Horton? does Frank Morgan?). In the folk musical everyone sings, from the littlest tyke to the oldest grandparent (not to mention barnyard animals, pots and pans, morning sounds, and many other non-human sources of music). Expression, and not esthetic quality, is the goal.

Music is not something to be saved for unusual moments; it is as much a part of the life cycle as eating and sleeping. Indeed, nearly all the major moments of the folk musical form part of a cycle: the cycle of the day (mealtime, work, bedtime), the cycle of the year (seasonal rituals), the cycle of life (graduation, leaving for school, getting a job, marriage, having a family, moving). Rarely does the folk musical dwell on an activity which takes place only once—an event whose very appeal is that it certainly could never hap-

pen again—such as we regularly see in the show and fairy tale subgenres. Making catsup, going to the fair, arguing at dinner, putting out the lights—these cyclic rituals are the events of which most folk musicals are made. To be sure, every film has one or two events which are entirely out of the ordinary, but by and large the film is made up of events meant to be repeated. It is this cyclical quality of the folk musical's semantics that permits such a strong connection between spectator and film, for we spectators still take part in the cycles represented by the film. We still go to Fourth of July picnics, linger at the dinner table, and argue with fellow family members; recognizing our own family on the screen, we easily project ourselves into the space represented by the film's world. Even when the film represents an era forever gone by, it is by convention an aspect of the American spectator's mythical past, a world to which we feel connected by virtue of our family and the land on which we tread.

Such a golden version of the spectator's past can be achieved only at a price, however, for in nearly every folk musical there is one character or event which the spectator's exuberance cannot control, one point which escapes memory's transforming action, seemingly gathering unto itself all our doubts that the past ever was—or that the future could ever be—all we want. Other subgenres take great care not to place too much emphasis on those who oppose the couple's success. The show musical typically depends on weak rivals (a friend, like George Murphy in *Broadway Melody of 1940*; a kook, like the phony Parisian intellectual in *Funny Face*; an easily converted sophisticate,

At the center of the folk musical world lies the family piano. Gathered around it, family and friends sing their solidarity, making up in good will and mutual concern what they lack in professional training. In *Centennial Summer* even Walter Brennan gets a singing part.

[MOMA]

like "Baby Essex" in *Babes in Arms*; a self-satisfied playboy like Franchot Tone in *Dancing Lady*), or a general lack of funds, often symbolized by a financier, producer, or conductor who can resist young love and good entertainment only so long (Guy Kibbee in *Dames, Footlight Parade*, and *Gold Diggers of 1933*, Edna Mae Oliver in *Little Miss Broadway*, the school officials in *Varsity Show*, Leopold Stokowski in *One Hundred Men and a Girl*, José Iturbi in *Anchors Aweigh*). In the fairy tale musical, the marriage is typically blocked by recalcitrant but easily convinced parent figures (*Love Me Tonight, Call Me Madam, Daddy Long Legs, Damsel in Distress, Gigi, The Pirate*), or even more often by a misunderstanding between the members of the couple (the very basis of the Astaire-Rogers films, as well as *An American in Paris, The French Line, Gentlemen Prefer Blondes, The Love Parade, The Merry Widow, New Moon, On an Island with You*, and *Yolanda and the Thief*). All these situations manage to provide just enough opposition to the couple's formation or marriage to generate a plot, but

Life in the folk musical is made up of a cycle of seasonal, ritual events, like the jam judging from *State Fair* (1945).

[BFI]

never enough to arouse the audience's anger or fear. Furthermore, the couple's problems are easily solved without the need to exclude anyone from the film's final community. These films are properly termed musical "comedy" because at every point we retain both the tone and the plot associated with the comic genre.

In the folk musical, on the other hand, emphasis is commonly placed directly on the blocking character, so much so that the film periodically loses its self-assured, joyous, comic nature. Nearly every folk musical contains a single figure, or closely related group of figures, who seem genu-inely evil, who actually threaten the continued well-being of the romantic couple and their world. The joyous nature of the folk world is compromised by characters as diverse as a loose woman and her gambling partner (*Hallelujah*), a tough Eastern syndicate (*High, Wide and Handsome*), the devil himself (*Cabin in the Sky*), the "mean man" down the street (Mr. Braukoff in *Meet Me in St. Louis*), a vengeful hired hand (Jud Fry in *Oklahoma!*), a "bad influence" friend (Jigger in *Carousel*), gang warfare (*West Side Story, Grease*), or even a never seen but constantly threatening Immigration Department (*Flower Drum Song*). Other films suggest the element of danger by evoking natural or man-made catastrophes: the San Francisco earthquake (*San Francisco*), the Chicago fire (*In Old Chicago*), a hurricane (*Porgy and Bess*), sickness induced by exposure (*Riding High*), or even death (from natural causes in *Little Nelly Kelly*, at man's hand in many others). It is as if this single terrifying memory were the price paid for so much dependence on rose-colored glasses, as if a solitary ominous element were left remaining in order that it might be overcome. It is as if the folk musical represented the final step in the long process of domesticating our memories, of systematically erasing every threatening recollection. The genius of the folk musical is that it manages both to mythify the American past and yet, by making the process of mythification visible, to retain before our eyes the very dangers which necessitated that process to begin with. The folk musical thus guarantees the veracity of our happy memories, but it does so only by recalling the one memory which threatened that happiness. The evil figure in the folk musical invariably provides a touch of melodrama, but what is melodrama if not the ritual reassurance that the serpent in man can be laid to rest, that man's loftier side can triumph?

Building A Folk Syntax

From its very beginnings in the *Jazz Singer* (1927), the musical has been associated with black faces. Indeed, the early popularity of the all-black musical determined the fate of the folk musical for an entire decade. In the late twenties black performers might as well have played in black face, for the roles they were given always corresponded not to their daily life but to the white man's vision of "colored boys and girls," of "darkies," of the "dusky race," as they were patronizingly called on film posters. Blacks were in no sense a part of the American "we"; instead they represented a picturesque and mysterious "they" living among us, a source of romance hardly differentiated from the operetta version of aristocratic Europe. Just as the show musical represented an impossible trip to Broadway and its theatrical center, just as the fairy tale musical realized the Grand Tour of our dreams, so the all-black folk musical served as a romanticized substitute for direct experience of the Old South. As a full-page *Photoplay* ad for one of 1929's biggest musicals puts it:

> *Hearts in Dixie* is the first authentic screen record of the Old South ever produced. It is a singing, dancing comedy with music—all the actors speaking their parts in a 100 percent Dialog Dramatization of Dixieland and its people. 200 native entertainers, including the famous Billbrew Chorus of 60 voices, relive the vivid romance of Anti-Bellum Days below the Mason and Dixon Line. All the happy-go-lucky joy of living, laughter and all-embracing gusto of plantation life has been re-created with thrilling realism. Forty negro spirituals are sung by a magnificent chorus—a plantation orchestra struts its stuff—folk songs are hummed by roustabouts and stevedores as the "Nellie Bly" pulls into the wharf. Cake-walks, folk dances—breathlessly

The presence of blacks in the musical began as an excuse for introducing picturesque southern scenes, as in this steamboat loading episode from the 1929 *Hearts in Dixie*.

[MOMA]

beautiful, crowd the action of this greatest of all Fox Movietone productions.[5]

The contradictions contained in this hype are characteristic of the early folk musical: the film claims to provide an "authentic screen record," yet also advertises a "vivid romance." The key to this paradox lies in another passage from the same poster: "HEAR THOSE HEARTS BEAT THE CADENCES OF THEIR RACE . . . along the levees and in the cotton fields . . . strummin' banjos . . . chanting spirituals . . . where life is infused with an ageless melody—throbbing with emotion—epic in its simplicity." The Negro race is taken as a primitive people more in tune with the source of life; their very life is a throbbing song, full of suffering but for that very reason somehow closer to the land and to God. In its attention to Americana and its interest in the daily routine of an American minority, the all-black musical clearly initiates the folk subgenre; yet in its desire to romanticize a "primitive" people and its dependence on the religious "spiritual," the all-black film provides a model which eventually will be left behind by films attempting to develop a more generalizable version of the American scene.

Among the early all-black folk musicals, one stands out by the quality of its music, the consistency of its performances, and particularly the coherent vision imposed on it by its director, King Vidor. The story of *Hallelujah,* filmed on location in 1929, is a banal one. Zeke, the oldest son of a poor family, gambles away the family earnings and, to make things worse, shoots his brother rather than the sharp who cheated him. Repentant, he becomes an evangelist, preaching to the faithful and baptizing the sinners in town after town. Still haunted by Chick, the girl who caused his earliest troubles, however, he backslides and runs away to a life of hard work in the mill. He soon discovers her affair with Hotshot, the original card-sharp, and eventually kills him after an eerie chase through the bayou. Finally, having served his time in prison, he returns home to his former fiancée Rose. The family is thus united once again.

The beauty of Vidor's conception lies in his ability to enrich the meaning of religious experience in black life by a series of metaphors. The fundamental metaphor, on which the entire film depends, concerns the relationship between religious fervor and sexuality. From the very first scene a causal chain links religious music to sexual drive. When Rose plays the Wedding March on a wheezy organ Zeke cannot restrain himself from forcing a kiss on her. The devil was in him, he says. This striking combination of the divine and the diabolical becomes a leitmotif of the entire film. When Zeke preaches to the multitude, his words become rhythmical, his steps carefully cadenced, to the point where he is dancing an imitation of the "Gospel Train," the apocalyptic special taking us straight to Hell—unless we get off at the way-station of vir-

tue. Intercut with his gospel dance are closer and closer shots of the woman who caused his original problems, the Eve who tempted him down the path of sin. His sermon soon becomes a love scene. "Won't you come?" he woos her. She struggles, clearly in the grip of a powerful force. Suddenly she cries out that she wants to be saved. Shortly, Zeke baptizes her in the river, but it is sexual desire that consumes them and not the Holy Ghost. He carries her to his tent, possessed by her charms at the very moment when she is supposedly full of the Lord. Torn away from Chick by his Mammie, Zeke can resist temptation no longer than the next revival service. Imitating a fist-fight with the devil, Zeke chants his sermon to a frenzied crowd. At the high point of that religious fit, Zeke's fervor suddenly turns to sexual desire; he picks up Chick and carries her off into the night.

Vidor keeps us constantly aware of the risk involved in religious zeal; when it can be tempered by the family (Rose, the good woman, the permanent couple, the old homestead, planting cotton on your own land) it leads to the tempered rhythms of the spiritual, sung in unison by the gathered community; but when it is associated with a temptress (Chick, the bad woman, the vagabond life, shanty towns, paid indoor labor at the saw mill) it leads only to the syncopated rhythms of jazz and the chaotic sexual drive which they invoke. Both music and dance are thus ambiguous forms, for the fervor they reveal duplicates the ambiguity of religious feeling itself. This uneasy relationship can only be solved by a metaphysical match, an apocalyptic duel between the

In subject matter and style, the depression era American Scene movement produced paintings strikingly similar to numerous film musical scenes. John Steuart Curry's 1929 "Gospel Train" shares the high contrast lighting, hands in the air exaltation, and collective hysteria of the Gospel Train sermon and revival meeting of King Vidor's *Hallelujah*, made in the same year. The shared hands-in-the-air posture surfaces throughout the film musical tradition as a reminder of the community religious fervor that lies at the root of much American popular music. (Vidor, it is worth noting, was a major purchaser of works by American Scene artists.)

[a = MOMA, b = Syracuse University Art Museum (Syra), c = BFI] warring impulses in man. This *psycho-machia*, or war in the soul, is represented by the magnificent chase through the bayou, beginning with Chick's death as she falls from a runaway cart (recalling the medieval *topos* where lust—*luxuria*—is finally undone by her runaway emotions/horses), and ending with Hotshot's murder at the hands of Zeke. Treated with the same apocalyptic high contrast lighting previously used for the dance hall and revival service scenes, the bayou chase is clearly a Harrowing of Hell, an opportunity for Zeke finally to catch up with the devil in himself and to conquer him.

The ambiguity built into the religious experience in *Hallelujah* is matched by another metaphor, this one explaining religion rather than contesting it, and set up by the various circumstances in which Irving Berlin's "At the End of the Road" is sung. When Zeke and his brother take the cotton crop to the gin, they hear a group of men playing jugs and singing this carefully crafted imitation of the folk tradition. The song itself plays on the familiar apocalyptic motif so common in spirituals; Vidor, however, uses the song quite differently. At the end of this road is the cotton gin, the pay-off for a season's effort. For the poor farmer there is little difference between two ultimate rewards: payday for the crop and the Judgment Day for life's harvest. It is thus natural that the family should have *prayed* for a good price, since economics and religion are one and the same. For the same reason, Zeke's religious sin (killing his brother) is linked to his economic sin (squandering the pay for the crop). The

most graphic representation of the tie between economics and religion, however, is the montage sequence which accompanies Zeke's rendition of "At the End of the Road." We normally think of Lewis Milestone as the early talkies' most ardent student of Eisenstein, but the cotton gin sequence in *Hallelujah* is far more effective than any of Milestone's Eisensteinian experiments. As the cotton goes through the gin, shots of the mechanism are intercut with medium shots of Zeke and long shots of the entire group singing. Like the cream separator sequence in *The Old and the New (The General Line),* Vidor's montage elevates the mechanical to the level of the holy; ginning and baling the cotton is tantamount to transubstantiation, "At the End of the Road" providing an appropriate anthem. A sacred relationship is thus established between the fruits of the earth and community singing. This community is specifically redefined as the family when Zeke finally reaches the end of *his* road. To the strains of Dvořak's New World Symphony, Zeke is seen on a cotton boat, on top of a freight train, and walking through the countryside as he returns home. Now, at last, "At the End of the Road" achieves its fully apocalyptic status, for Zeke has conquered the devil and earned his reward: the adopted sister whom he is to marry and the family which provides him with his definition of Heaven. Finally, all the pieces fit together. At the end of the road lie family harmony and a bountiful harvest, both symbolized and expressed through song and dance. Just as song and dance embody the diametrical opposition between sin and vir-

The high-contrast lighting of the black musical: its sources and its symbolism. Top: Gustave Doré's Bible illustration of the exile of Adam and Eve from Eden. Eden was pure light; heavy shadows are a mark of exile from that light. Middle: Rouben Mamoulian's 1927 stage production of *Porgy*. Again, it is an absent side light source that divides the world into blinding bright and fearsome dark. Bottom: a shot from the apocalyptic bayou chase in *Hallelujah*. The moral universe matches the lighting; good and evil coexist in the universe, but they are as recognizably different as the extremes of light and dark used throughout Vidor's film.

[a = pers, b = NYPL, c = BFI]

Chick's dress figures the ambiguity characteristic of both sex and religion in *Hallelujah*: the dice display a winning combination, but no man can count on continually rolling a seven with this woman.

[MOMA]

tue, so they create a symbolic tie between the fruits of this world and those of the next.

Had *Hallelujah* gained the critical and popular attention which it richly deserves, then the folk musical subgenre might have been fully constituted, syntactically as well as semantically, by the early thirties. Unfortunately, it was the show and not the sensitivity of Vidor's film that was remembered, the picturesque semantics and not the apocalyptic, agricultural syntax. Instead of following the carefully controlled structure and

studied ambiguities of *Hallelujah*, the regional musical of the early period imitated the varied and grandiose scenes of the 1927 stage success, *Show Boat*. Before long the all-black musical would give way to an aristocratic, almost operatic regional musical, set on a romantic ranch (*Montana Moon*), in New Orleans (*Dixiana*), lumberjack country (*Rough Romance*), an old-time wagon circus (*Swing High*) the world of Amos 'n' Andy (*Check and Double Check*), the Canadian Northwest (*Under Suspicion*), old Kentucky (*A Song of Kentucky*), or even

Hallelujah's cotton gin, where Zeke sings "The End of the Road"—but where his road begins. Stretched out in a long line, waiting their turn for the cotton gin, the wagons evoke the generalizing quality to which the folk musical aspires: stories are told not because they vary from the ordinary, but because they are representative of the regional American experience of yesteryear.

[MOMA]

Mexico (*Rio Rita*). Instead of providing materials for an American mythology, folk elements remained an excuse for new costumes and sets. For this reason, the folk musical never really got off the ground during the thirties; it remained largely undifferentiated from other musical subgenres. Wherever folk elements were present they were used for their picturesque qualities rather than for their ability to engender a myth of the American past. Thus a 1934 film about West Point begins with a Hawaiian love feast, centers on the Academy's legendary "Flir-tation Walk" and "Kissing Rock," and ends with the class show and graduation parade (*Flirtation Walk*). Only the constant presence of American history and the use of marching as the film's primary rhythmical movement permit us to identify this Borzage film with the folk subgenre. Myriad other films, such as a trio of Jeanette MacDonald vehicles (*Rose Marie, San Francisco, Girl of the Golden West*), take a few basic folk elements and use them as a backdrop or a catalyst for a romantic story hardly distinguishable from those developed in MacDonald's

In *Cabin in the Sky*, the medieval notion of *psychomachia* is actualized—angels and devils compete for the soul of Little Joe (Eddie Anderson), perpetually tempted by the local siren (Lena Horne).

[BFI]

fairy tale roles. Vidor's *Hallelujah* had no influence whatsoever. Blacks remained confined throughout the thirties to subordinate and/or comic roles, usually as the valet or maid of a sympathetic aristocrat.

This situation might never have changed had it not been for a single individual whose influence on the American arts has never been sufficiently proclaimed. If the folk musical is the joint product of Hollywood and Broadway (whereas the show musical tended to be a Hollywood monopoly and the fairy tale musical a European import), if the folk musical takes advantage of the best available in *all* the forms of American art, if the folk musical has a syntax at all, it is largely due to one man: Rouben Mamoulian. Yet nothing in Mamoulian's background would suggest such an affinity for American folk forms. Born in Armenia, initiated into his craft at the Moscow Art Theater, Mamoulian soon turned from Stanislavskian naturalism to the opera and operetta repertory as director of George Eastman's American Opera Company in Rochester, New York. With the coming of sound, Mamoulian was immediately pressed into service in the film industry. His very first effort was a backstage musical already stamped with the Mamoulian trademark: close observation of the American scene combined with a keen sense of rhythm (*Applause,* 1929). Throughout the thirties, Mamoulian continued to experiment with the film medium, applying his stage experience to new problems and constantly coming up with new, more filmic, answers.

Two of Mamoulian's experiments during the mid-thirties stand out for their contribution to the establishment of folk musical syntax: the stage production of *Porgy and Bess* (1935) and Paramount's *High, Wide and Handsome* (1937). Already in his production of *Porgy* (1927), Mamoulian had sensed the importance of affirming the fundamental musicality of the blacks on Catfish Row. Rather than simply follow the cliché whereby blacks sing out of misery and religious sentiment, however, Mamoulian developed a musical and rhythmical model which was to lie at the heart of folk musical syntax. As the curtain rises on Catfish Row all is silent. "Then you hear the Boum! of a street gang repairing the road. That is the first beat; then beat 2 is silent; beat 3 is a snore—zzz!—from a Negro who's asleep; beat 4 silent again. Then a woman starts sweeping the steps—whish!—and she takes up beats 2 and 4, so you have: Boum!—Whish!—zzz!—Whish! and so on. A knife sharpener, a shoemaker, a woman beating rugs and so on, all join in. Then the rhythm changes: 4:4 to 2:4; then to 6:8; and syncopated and Charleston rhythms. It all had to be conducted like an orchestra."[6] Instead of linking music to the other-worldly, to transcendental sufferings or apocalyptic religion, Mamoulian simply makes it grow out of daily life, out of the noises of a folk community, with the people's unity symbolized by their ability to stay in time with each other. When Mamoulian developed this approach for the screen in *Love Me Tonight* (1932), it retained its charm, but lost its symbolic quality as an expression of the bond which unites man to man, and each man to the land through his occupation. When this "symphony of sounds" was returned to the stage for Gershwin's version of *Porgy and Bess* it took on an even fuller meaning, however. When music is added to a dramatic play, the music often seems out of place or tacked on; Mamoulian's device served to justify the presence of Gershwin's music by making it seem to grow directly out of the life of the folk. As such, "the symphony of sounds" represents an apology for the folk musical in general, an explanation of the relationship between dramatic and musical materials.

Mamoulian's return to folk material in *Porgy and Bess* initiated a period of profound reflection on the American scene. The success of the second film version of *Show Boat* (directed by James Whale, 1936), seems to have convinced him that the time was right to apply to the cinema the insights gained in the theater. In *Show Boat*—one of a very few previous plays or films to sustain a regional musical style throughout—he also found the song and script-writing team that corresponded to his folk interests. Jerome Kern and Oscar Hammerstein II had a sense of American rhythms and speech, to which Mamoulian added an extraordinary feel for the daily realities of provincial life. *High, Wide and Handsome* thus became the first musical—with the possible exception of *Hallelujah*—in which a folk syntax is openly and actively at work. *High, Wide and Handsome* tells the story of the discovery of oil in Titusville, Pennsylvania, in 1859. Peter Cortlandt (Randolph Scott) befriends a wandering snake-oil salesman (Doc Watterson, played by Raymond Walburn), eventually marrying his daughter Sally (Irene Dunne) in spite of competition from a local tough (Red Scanlon, played by Charles Bickford). On their wedding day, Cortlandt's faith in the land is rewarded as his well spews forth oil, covering the entire wedding party with black gold. Soon, however, Eastern tycoons get wind of the fortunes to be made in western Pennsylvania; Walter Brennan (played by Alan Hale) tries to force the farmers to sell their valuable land by refusing to transport the oil to market on his railroad. Undaunted by the big city tyrants, Cortlandt and his neighbors decide to build a pipeline to bring their crude oil to the refinery, but in order to acquire all the land they need, Cortlandt is forced to give up the hill on which he and his wife have planned to build their dream-house. Unable to distract him from his all-consuming attempt to get the oil through, she leaves him and returns to the stage and eventually to a big job with the circus. In the climactic moments of the film, the farmers realize that they are beaten unless they can pipe their oil up and over a massive cliff. As they struggle to raise the pipe up the face of the cliff in time to beat a deadline, they are attacked by Brennan's mob, led by Red Scanlon. Just as the farmers' doom seems certain, Sally arrives with her circus friends, elephants and all; the battle which follows has rarely been matched for sheer scale and overall effect. Top shots from the summit of the cliff alternate with close-ups and horizontal medium and full shots to create a circus-like atmosphere in the realest of locations (Chino, California). Eventually, the farmers and their allies carry the day, thus assuring the delivery of their oil just prior to the deadline. Brennan is defeated, the farmers triumph, and the Cortlandt couple is reunited—not on the hill they dreamed of, but on a far more meaningful one.

This summary cannot begin to evoke the care with which Mamoulian recreates the small town atmosphere of nineteenth-century America. As in the thirties films of John Ford, Mamoulian masks the strong dramatic development of his film behind a series of ritual events. The film opens on a traveling salesman's pitch, obviously a big event in this little town, since the entire community is present, their attention riveted on Doc Watterson and his pretty daughter. Nearly every other scene of importance takes place in a traditional context: the Saturday night square dance (culminating in a fistfight between Cortlandt and Scanlon), the wedding (at which the oil strike is finally made), the local bar (at which Sally declares her independence and Cortlandt sells off "their" hill), and so forth. Recreating a small working farm, the rolling countryside of western Pennsylvania, and the rather colorless—but all the more real—streets of a provincial village, Mamoulian provides every touch necessary to differentiate this film from its many predecessors which employ the American scene solely as a source of the picturesque.

Furthermore, by creating a series of metaphors, coincidences, and comparisons, Mamoulian succeeds in integrating the regional semantic components into a coherent folk syntax. The most important of these metaphors establishes a relationship between the making of the couple and the exploitation of the land. When Cortlandt strays from his usual calm disposition to fight Red Scanlon, in the opening scene as well as at the square dance, he seems simply to be obeying a Hollywood law: the good guy protects ladies from unwanted attention. In Mamoulian's hands, however, this cliché becomes a metaphor: when Cortlandt sees Sally, he *erupts;* his sublimated sexual drive is suddenly forced to the surface and gushes forth. The implicit tie between Cortlandt's sexuality and the discovery of oil is made explicit by the timing of the oil well's initial eruption; by placing that eruption on Cortlandt's wedding day, Mamoulian equates human sexuality and fertility to that of the land. This parallel is further developed by the pipeline. Cortlandt gets his idea for a pipeline from a water pipe in a rainstorm, thus assimilating the oil pipeline to an irrigation system; like water irrigating the desert, the pipeline in *High, Wide and Handsome* will bolster the economy of western Pennsylvania, giving new life to farmers unable to make an adequate living off the land. When the pipeline is finally completed, we see the precious black liquid spurt out of a small, stiff pipe into the waiting vats. Just as the initial eruption could not occur until Sally came to the Cortlandt farm, so the ultimate consummation of this romance with the land (and with location photography) cannot occur until she has returned; now that she is back, with her entire circus in tow, the oil can spurt forth once again. The ultimate union of man and woman thus takes place not on the hill of the couple's dreams (always shot in the studio, with an obviously fake backdrop) but on a real hill, with real earth, real trees, and real oil. Mamoulian openly rejects the stagy romance solution of the fairy tale musical, preferring to emphasize the interdependence of marriage success and territorial development.

The sexual symbolism of the pipe, the liquid, and the vat must not, however, be read on a psychological plane, but on a mythical one. The marriage between Peter Cort*land*t and Sally *Watter*son is not just a civil ceremony, but a hierogamy as well, a mystic union of the elements themselves. Sally is a free spirit, repeatedly equated to a bird and seen with the circus animals; she is a wanderer, a performer, a girl without a mother and without a home. Peter is the farm, the community, the land itself, with all the stability that those terms imply. When Sally comes to the Cortlandt home she serves as a catalyst for new activity; the excitement of an outsider—a showgirl of doubtful morals—incites Peter to violence, the land to eruption, and the whole community to a new energy level. Only by harnessing that energy can the farmers derive full profit from their land. The rousing finale thus represents more than a simple triumph of local interests over intrusive railroad barons; it also provides a

Rouben Mamoulian's brilliant wedding sequence from *High, Wide and Handsome* begins with Irene Dunne singing her dreams ("The Folks Who Live on the Hill") to husband Randolph Scott on their own private hill. As their emotions swell, the earth erupts, leading to a renewed and oh-so-awkward embrace between the pristine Dunne and the oil-drenched Scott. From this point until the very end of the film, the oil will come between them.

[pers]

Echoing the wedding scene, the end of *High, Wide and Handsome* begins with penetration, proceeds to the spurting forth of the precious fluid, and concludes with an embrace. Now that the marriage between Scott's farmers and Dunne's circus performers has been consummated, the couple can happily trade in the idyllic but unreal hill of their earlier dreams on a new hill, the center of a new and shared life.

[pers]

resolution of all the dualities carried by the Sally/Peter couple:

female	male
wandering	stable
entertainment	business
wild animals	work animals

The merging of the farmers and the circus people (with their elephants) clearly breaks down the oppositions developed throughout the film. The union of Sally and Peter thus heralds and symbolizes a larger union, that of energy and order, of the sky and the land.

In every area of the film, this union of opposites operates. When Sally first visits the Cortlandt farm, Peter's mother (Elizabeth Patterson) corrects her picture-book image of farm life. A farm is hard work, Grandma Cortlandt maintains, yet when Sally goes out to feed the animals—dressed in a stage costume and singing an operatic air—the animals love the music and actually sing the chorus! This montage sequence, reminiscent of Mamoulian's earlier "symphony of sounds," manages to rhythmify the farm, to turn it into music, without overly romanticizing it. Instead of sacrificing reality for the sake of romance, Mamoulian achieves a sense of the romantic by highlighting the reality itself. The key is Sally's ability (identified with the filmmaker's montage) to lend rhythm to natural sounds. The farm is not just hard work, nor is it a picture book; it is the one transubstantiated into the other.

The same mediatory effect occurs with the problem of morality and mob rule. Normally Titusville is a peaceful community which generates little energy. A dance hall in an upstanding town, however, is quite enough to turn law-abiding citizens into a mob bent on chasing the harlots out of town. This situation sets up two parallel oppositions, each implying a different set of values:

PRUDES	vs.	ENTERTAINERS
Morality		Immorality
Inertia		Energy
SOLITARY	vs.	MOB
PROTEST		RULE
Order		Chaos
Inertia		Energy

Each sex is forced into one of two diametrically opposed categories: for the women the alternative is energyless morality or energetic immorality; for the men the choice is between energyless order and chaotic energy. The goal of *High, Wide and Handsome* is clearly to create a strategy to mediate these oppositions, thereby combining energy, morality, and order. The prude/entertainer opposition is resolved by the presence of moral female entertainers: the dance hall singer (Dorothy Lamour), who eventually warns the farmers of the financiers' plot, and Sally, who saves the day only by virtue of her job with the circus. In the new community formed during the film, morality and entertainment will never again be sensed as mutually exclusive categories. Morality will be more exciting because of its marriage with entertainment, while entertainers will by marrying avoid the pitfalls of the wandering life. Likewise, the lifeless/chaotic, individualistic/mob oppositions are mediated by the farmers and their union. They tear down their own fences in order to build the pipeline; they collaborate as they have never done before, deriving energy from their very union. For the first time they form a group capable of generating the mob's energy but at the same time restrained enough to direct that energy toward the common good. The productive farmers' cooperative thus stands in direct opposition to and replaces the threat of mob rule.

Paradoxically, this new community could never have been formed, this new energy would never have been generated were it not for the reprehensible actions of the eastern tycoons. Fully integrating the villain figure into folk syntax for the first time, Mamoulian treats the evil outsider in much the way he is treated by nineteenth-century nationalist movements in Europe: the outside threat crystallizes support for the internal community. The choice of financiers as the external threat serves more than just a plot function, however, for the economic aspect of *High, Wide and Handsome* is far more than just an afterthought. At stake throughout the film is the claim of the farmer to own, enjoy, and operate his own land, and to make *local* decisions regarding its disposition. The folk musical would not be the folk musical were this connection to the land, often expressed economically, not present. The folk musical carries along with it an impression of pioneer days, when the land was free for the asking—but only to those who would work it. The only deed which counted was the work of one's hands and the sweat of one's brow; the only applicable theory of value was the labor theory. Even when this notion is reduced to the simple problem of parking a car (as in *On the Town*), the belief remains that the

world belongs to those who make the fullest use of it.

The fundamental syntax of the folk musical is clearly present in *High, Wide and Handsome*, even if only in a preliminary form. Not until Mamoulian adds a dancing chorus in his next stage production, however, can we think of the folk musical as a fully constituted genre. More than any other single production, on the stage or on the screen, the Broadway production of *Oklahoma!* (1943) is responsible for crystallizing the separate elements of the folk musical into a coherent whole. With Oscar Hammerstein's script (from Lynn Riggs' novel *Green Grow the Lilacs*), songs by Rodgers and Hammerstein, sets by Lemuel Ayers, choreography by Agnes de Mille, and the direction of Rouben Mamoulian, *Oklahoma!* brought together for the first time a full complement of artists versed in the folk tradition. Reproduced almost intact for the 1955 Todd-A-O screen version, directed by Fred Zinnemann, *Oklahoma!* does not simply group various semantic elements in a picturesque whole, but organizes them into a stable syntax. The plot itself is inconsequential: the farm girl Laurie is courted by the rancher Curly, but out of spite agrees to go to the box social with her surly hired hand Jud Fry instead. At the box social Jud and Curly bid against each other for the picnic basket prepared by Laurie; Curly wins, but he has to sell his horse, saddle, and gun to win the right to Laurie's wares. That evening he proposes, she accepts, and their marriage is planned. On the marriage night, however, Jud attempts to exact revenge, but is instead accidentally killed himself. Curly is acquitted on the spot and permitted to retire with his bride to the sounds of the title song, celebrating the territory's impending statehood. Parallel plots arrange the marriage of two supporting couples: 1) Will Parker (just back from Kansas City) with Ado Annie Carnes (who can't say no), and 2) Ali Hakim the peddler (Will's rival for Ado Annie) with Gertie Cummings (Laurie's rival for Curly).

As the examples of *Hallelujah* and *High, Wide and Handsome* have already suggested, the semantic folk musical begins to build a syntax when American regional or historical traits are no longer employed simply for their picturesque value, but are tied thematically to the land out of which they grow. Where the semantic genre proposes a series of elements borrowed from a familiar but idealized American past, the syntactic genre creates a system in which every element is linked to the earth, to its appearance, to its history, to its fruits. The rest of this chapter will be devoted to a description of the "rules" of folk syntax, each one exemplified primarily by reference to *Oklahoma!*

1) *The sounds of nature inspire man to make music and serve as a model for the music itself.*

As *Oklahoma!* opens, Curly translates the beauty of the landscape into a song; "All the sounds of the earth are like music," he says, thus openly proclaiming a traditional link between seasonal change and ritual song. Indeed, it sometimes seems that every folk musical song describes either a place, a season, or some other aspect of nature. Song is no longer perceived as a cultural response mediated by society's institutions (e.g., religion in *Hallelujah* or stage training as in *High, Wide and Handsome*) but as an entirely natural response to one's own position in life. When we sing we feel *key*ed into, at*tune*d to, in *harmony* with a predetermined order. As an intransitive verb, "to sing" means "to be in harmony with," to participate in the natural order, to belong (whatever the community might be). Harmony is not something manufactured by a composer but the unrehearsed concordance of a community of voices, each responding in its own way to the same natural impulses. As an expression of community togetherness, music may absorb the individual into the group ("Oklahoma!" serves as the couple's final love song), pass a local or natural song from one member of the community to another (the opening songs in *Meet Me in St. Louis, Summer Holiday, Centennial Summer,* and *State Fair*), or reinforce an individual's lament with a supporting chorus of the same sex (e.g., "Many a New Day" in *Oklahoma!*, "It's a Great, Big World" in *The Harvey Girls*, "Wedding in June" in *Seven Brides for Seven Brothers*). Likewise, the feelings of any given individual are said to stem from seasonal or other natural causes, thus generalizing them and enlarging the space of the song to include the audience (who also experience the daily and yearly cycles). Never the province of professionals alone, always inspired by impulses which the entire community (and audience) can share, music in the folk musical regains the sacred status which it had lost in the show and fairy tale subgenres. Only in the folk musical can we say with Johan Huizinga that "All true ritual is sung, danced and played. We moderns have lost the sense for ritual and sacred play. Our civilization is worn with age and too sophisticated. But nothing helps us to regain that sense so much as musical sensibility. In feeling music we feel ritual. In the enjoyment of music, whether it is meant to express religious ideas or not, the perception of the beautiful and the sensation of holiness merge, and the distinction between play and seriousness is whelmed in that fusion."[7]

2) *The rhythm of life already constitutes a dance.*

Just as nature itself provides a model for song, so it induces people to move rhythmically and thus walk into a dance. From the opening frames of *Oklahoma!* this principle holds: as Curly ambles across the prairie and through the corn, his horse walks in time to the song. Attention to such simple details has the power to turn a pretty picture into a thematically rich system. When the men help the women off their wagons they do it rhythmically; when they fight they move with the music; when Will Parker starts telling his story about Kansas City all those around him naturally slide from normal activity to rhythmified normal activity to dancing. There is never a point where we can say: "Here is where normal life stops and here is where dance begins." Life properly lived *is* a dance. One could of course say the same of Fred Astaire or Gene Kelly, but with an immensely important difference. Astaire and Kelly are personally graceful, they impress us with their ability to move imperceptibly from a walk to a dance step, but what they do is their own, they do it because they are performers, because they are special people, because they are Astaire and Kelly. Try as we might, we are not. But the folk musical starts from the premise that the daily activities of the country's ordinary people have a certain nobility, a certain beauty, a certain natural rhythm. Picking cotton is a lyric activity (*Hallelujah*); barking for a carnival sets the entire world into rhythmic motion (*Carousel, Roustabout*); running a farm, building a house, grooming a horse, swinging an axe—all contain the seeds of the dance (*State Fair* and *Summer Stock, Living in a Big Way, Riding High, Seven Brides for Seven Brothers*). Mamoulian's "symphony of sounds" is not an isolated example; it is the very model on which folk music and dance depend. Just as the folk music appeal to the community and to the seasons engages the spectator, increasing chances of identification, so the treatment of daily activities as intrinsically beautiful appeals to spectators who know they will never be an Astaire or Kelly.

3) *One of the lovers represents the stability of the earth, the other energy and movement.*

We have already seen how *High, Wide and Handsome* identifies Sally with the birds and the sky, the wind and the flowing streams, while Peter is assimilated to the land. *Oklahoma!* reverses that pattern, setting the model for years to come. Curly is a rancher; his world, as the film demonstrates graphically, is a wide-open realm in which herds of cattle wander aimlessly. Laurie is a farmer; her fenced world is characterized by orderly arrangement, with everything in neat rows. Ado Annie and Will Parker provide a comic inversion of the main couple's relationship. Annie is the flighty one; she sings "I

Though *Summer Stock*'s poster emphasizes the film's show musical side, the images consistently recall the folk musical tradition, where breakfast has to be cooked, where eggs must be collected, where milk comes from a cow and not a bottle.

[MOMA]

Cain't Say No" at the beginning, to which the faithful Will responds at the end: "I'm a one-woman man" ("All 'Er Nothin"). In *Meet Me in St. Louis* the women all want to stay in St. Louis, while the men either go to school in the East or want to move there for business purposes. The male lead in *Centennial Summer* is a Frenchman, paired with a local girl. The title character in *The Music Man* is a traveling salesman, while his counterpart's stability is guaranteed by her title

as "Marian the Librarian." Throughout the folk tradition, three separate levels are combined in this energy/order opposition, corresponding to three different meanings of the term stability: physical, financial, and emotional. The literal sense of the term is typically satisfied by allotting the woman a function which is so identified with a single location that it can be done in no other (housewife, librarian, farmer, teacher), while the man—consistent with social practice in the first half of this century—is the only one able to travel. This wanderlust is not solely geographical, however, it is also emotional. The man often appears to be unfaithful (though most often he is not), thus jeopardizing the stability of the couple's romantic relationship. The woman, on the other hand, is a staunch defender of fidelity, monogamy, and the American way of marriage. The opposition also holds on an economic level. Most often the man seeks to widen his horizons financially as well as literally: to build an empire, to establish a new clientele, or just to increase his family's standard of living. The woman, quite to the contrary, only wants to guarantee stability.

4) *The creation of a couple is parallel and simultaneous to the formation of a community.*

The dancing chorus introduced by de Mille and Mamoulian in *Oklahoma!* serves a double function. On the one hand it serves to underline the importance of sexual parameters, as it does throughout the show musical's chorus line tradition (e.g. the balletic style, feminine costumes, and indoor setting of "Many a New Day" contrast with the rope tricks, ragtime, and acrobatics in the outdoor rendition of "Kansas City"). The main couple cannot be conceived in terms of the (primary) sexual distinction alone, however, for in the folk musical an extraordinary amount of emphasis is always given to the (secondary) thematic oppositions which the couple embodies. In *Gigi* Louis Jourdan represents one generation, while Leslie Caron stands for another; the bond which relates either character to his/her generation remains largely symbolic, however, for neither is closely inte-

grated into a *community* of the same generation. In the folk musical such a community is rarely absent. Laurie and Curly not only embody the values of farmer and rancher, they are also seen in the company of their respective groups. When the two lovers come together, they are thus accompanied by their friends, setting the stage for parallel resolution of 1) the romantic plot, and 2) the split between ranchers and farmers. Not only is the secondary split (farmers/ranchers) symbolically healed by the marriage of the primary pair (Laurie/Curly), but the use of the community dancing chorus permits us to witness the merger graphically. At the box social square dance, a choreographed fight is followed by a musical peace treaty:

Oh, the farmer and the cowman should
    be friends.
One man likes to push a plow,
The other likes to chase a cow,
But that's no reason why they cain't be
    friends!

Territory folks should stick together,
Territory folks should all be pals.
Cowboys, dance with the farmers'
    daughters!
Farmers, dance with the ranchers' gals!

Here the dancing chorus changes function. Instead of simply setting up an opposition, the pairing off of cowboys with farmers' daughters and farmers with ranchers' gals overcomes an important split, turning two separate but opposed groups into a single unified community. Whether the community thus created is a state (*Oklahoma!*), the family (*Meet Me in St. Louis, State Fair, Summer Holiday,*

Centennial Summer), the town (*Harvey Girls, Living in a Big Way, It Happened in Brooklyn, The Unsinkable Molly Brown*), or some other unit, the primary coupling is never a solitary venture. Fred and Ginger can solve their own problems and the audience rejoices, but in the folk musical, a resolution resolves nothing unless it creates or renews a sense of community.

5) *The permanence of this community, consecrated by marriages whose celebration recapitulates the cosmic act of creation, authorizes the colonization of the wilderness and thus the mythic transformation of chaos into cosmos, of untamed land into civilization.*

The mechanics by which this symbolic process takes place in *Oklahoma!* are fascinating to observe. In order to claim the right to Laurie's affections, Curly must outbid Jud Fry for her picnic basket. The courtship ritual is here reduced to an auction characteristic of American marriage in general: in order to get Laurie to cook his meals, Curly must assure her financial security. It is the slight twist that *Oklahoma!* gives to this traditional symbiotic relationship that marks its true originality, however. She *donates* her services to the community; he *pays* his fee not to Laurie but to the community. The money thus collected is used to build a roof over the schoolhouse, on whose unprotected floor the violence-marred dance has just taken place. In other words, the community schoolhouse is the by-product of the box social; civilization is a by-product of the marriage auction/ritual. To marry is to create, not only a family, but a community as well. It is thus more than appropriate that the song "Oklahoma!"

should simultaneously celebrate the marriage of Laurie and Curly (their initiation into the adult world, the world of families) and the impending statehood of Oklahoma (the territory's initiation into a mature community of states). *Oklahoma!* catches a country at exactly that point in its history when a period of expansion gives way to a period of consolidation. Such is precisely the case of *The Harvey Girls, Annie Get Your Gun, Seven Brides for Seven Brothers,* and *Paint Your Wagon* as well.

6) *A similar transformation takes place in the couple; the wandering male, tamed by the civilized female and thus sublimating his wanderlust, endows the civilized community with his energy and knowledge.*

In order to understand this process as encapsulated in *Oklahoma!* it is necessary to consider the two basic steps in the civilizing process (presented here in reference to the taming of the prairie, but the basic relationship is the same whether the arena is the West, New York City, or River City, Iowa):

a) Pioneering exploratory efforts, typically carried out by rough and ready men, result in the informal use of the virgin forest or open range for purposes of hunting, trapping, grazing, or other random activities for which ownership of the land is not a concern.

b) Permanent settlement of the land for purposes of farming requires fencing of the range, clearing of the forests, and reduction of unplanned land use, whence the importance of land ownership.

That is, an initial step of expansion, characterized by a rather chaotic energy, is followed by a process of consolidation requiring order and restraint. This two-part process is clearly replicated in the folk musical:

a) Nearly every folk musical begins with the discovery or arrival of a new source of unrestrained energy, usually provided by the male romantic lead, e.g. the discovery of oil in *High, Wide and Handsome*, arrival of the man-about-town Mickey Rooney in *Girl Crazy*, the new boy next door and the offer of a New York job in *Meet Me in St. Louis*, the Frenchman come to plan the Exhibition in *Centennial Summer*, the sailors on leave in *On the Town*, Fred Astaire bringing dance to the Salvation Army in *The Belle of New York*, the traveling salesman in *The Music Man*.

b) As the film progresses, the man must progressively abandon his wandering ways and put his energy to work for the community, e.g., Mickey Rooney must give up his playboy habits to help the school (*Girl Crazy*), John Hodiak must give up his saloon in favor of Judy Garland's quiet little valley (*The Harvey Girls*), Leon Ames abandons a chance for advancement in his profession so his sentimental women can stay put (*Meet Me in St. Louis*), the reporter in *State Fair* (both versions) gives up a life on the road for the farmgirl he loves, Elvis Presley leaves the Easy Rider life and takes a job in order to prove a point (*Roustabout*).

Excess (sexual or pioneering) energy is needed to set the wheels in motion, but order and constraint are essential to guide them. The very energy involved in music or dance testifies to this necessity: without the initial impulse of energy neither can exist, nor can they exist without the ordering factor of rhythm.

A strong relationship ties the folk musical's characteristic pattern to the development of these United States. As the Turner thesis would have it, the country's history is marked by the constant availability of free land to the West. Our past is thus marked by a natural desire to move West, just as each sex possesses a natural desire for the other. In order to colonize each new settlement, however, it was necessary to import women and to overcome the male desire to continue further West. A high proportion of (syntactic) folk musicals are thus localized between the Mississippi and the Rockies (*Girl Crazy, Meet Me in St. Louis, The Harvey Girls, State Fair, Annie Get Your Gun, Calamity Jane, Seven Brides for Seven Brothers, Oklahoma!, The Unsinkable Molly Brown, Paint Your Wagon*).

Without the energy of the rancher (or hunter, or trapper), the West goes untapped; without the civilizing influence of the farmer, the West goes untamed. This pattern is clearly paralleled by the love-making activities of the couple: one member makes an advance, without which the exploitation of the sexual parameter cannot take place; the other member refuses the advance, but in such a way as to demonstrate that it is the incivility of the offer that causes it to be rejected, not the offer itself. If the sexually aggressive partner will only restrain himself, guarantee fidelity, and "fence himself in" then the passive partner will gladly have him. In *Oklahoma!* this process is symbolically represented by the fee which Curly pays for Laurie's picnic basket. By abandoning the tools of his rancher's trade, Curly is giving up his wandering ways, bringing his energy and strength to the working of Laurie's farm, and thus gaining the right to Laurie as well. Only through the simultaneous presence of sexually aggressive male and restraining female (simulating the sequential presence of pioneering impulse and settler caution) can the couple be formed and thus family stability be assured (symbolizing the spread of a permanent civilization). This is the story of the world and of the folk musical alike. Without a source of energy there is no power to drive the wheels of civilization; without a technique for harnessing that energy the power cannot be directed, ordered, and properly used.

7) *The ambiguity associated with sexual drive, nature, or memory, is expressed by a competition between the hero and a villainous rival.*

There is a certain class of texts, constituting the very lifeblood of western narrative, which derives its energy from the ambiguity associated with sexual power. Stretching from the Greek romance to the Beauty and the Beast tale, from the Tristan material to the melodrama, from Renaissance pastoral to the folk musical, these texts are generated by the risk associated with (usually male) sexuality: necessary to human creation, the sexual drive nevertheless threatens to break free at any moment and become destructive. In many traditions (folk tale, Gothic novel, horror movie), this risk is expressed by the presence of complementary characters embodying the benign and malignant aspects of sexuality: Prince Charming and the Beast. In the show and fairy tale musical, no real risk is attached to the process of courting; love is banter even when (especially when) it is serious.

In the folk tradition the contrary is true; courting is always a deadly serious affair, precisely because of the risk involved. To remind us that something may go wrong in the courting process is the constant function of the dark rival: Chick in *Hallelujah*, Red Scanlon in *High, Wide and Handsome*, Georgia Brown (Lena Horne) in *Cabin in the Sky*, the saloon singer (Angela Lansbury) in *The Harvey Girls*, and many others from Crown in *Porgy and Bess* to the rival gang leader in *Grease*.

Oklahoma!'s Jud Fry provides a particularly clear example. The first time we see Jud he enters the frame from behind the camera, instantly blacking out half the frame with his enormous shoulder. This configuration, repeated many times within the course of the film, encapsulates Jud's role as a dark shadow. (Fairy tale musicals have comic shadow couples; the folk musical has dark shadow rivals.) Like Curly, Jud is in love with Laurie and would like to marry her and take over the care of her farm (of her person). Unlike Curly, however, Jud is characterized by illicit sex. Curly proposes a romantic ride in a "Surrey with the Fringe on Top;" Jud's advances lead to a wild ride in a buckboard pulled by runaway horses. Curly shows no interest in loose women; Jud has pictures of scantily-clad women posted all around his dingy room. For Curly, women are to be identified with the beauties of nature; for Jud, women are the objects of a Peeping Tom's illicit desire. The potentially destructive aspect of Jud's sexuality is best represented through a metaphor cleverly developed by a newfangled device brought from

Characterization by horse and buggy: Jud Fry takes Laurie to the box social in an old buckboard drawn by a pair of high-strung dark-colored horses which soon break out of control endangering Laurie's life. This symbolic presentation of the threat which Jud's runaway emotions pose to Laurie is matched by Curly's "surrey with the fringe on top," with its ultra-civilized paint job and high-stepping white team.

[MOMA]

Kansas City by Will Parker, sold to the traveling salesman in exchange for Ado Annie, and then bought by Jud in order to murder Curly. When the men look through the peep hole in this "Little Wonder" they see pictures to delight the eye, visions of naked women to fire the imagination. The device also includes a "pig sticker," however, a spring-loaded knife aimed at the head of the peeper. Improper thoughts, this little device implies, can be deadly. Indeed, they almost are, for when Jud shows the device to Curly he intends to release the "pig sticker," thus sealing Curly's doom. Only the timely arrival of Aunt Eller saves Curly. The "Little Wonder" clearly identifies Jud with the destructive aspects of sexuality, with the animal lust which must be tempered in order for civilization to maintain permanence.

The sexual pairing of Curly and Jud as productive and destructive sexuality is matched by another opposition, this one relating not to the ambiguity of sexual energy (—→ fertility of women) but to that of nature (—→ fertility of the land). From the very opening shots Curly is identified with the sky, the sun, the open range, while Jud is characterized by darkness, shadow, and in particular by an underground abode. Curly puts it quite clearly: "In this country there's just two things you can do if you're a man. You can live out of doors or you can live in this filthy hole." Each represents a radically different aspect of nature: Curly is the warm sun, without which the crops cannot grow; Jud burns like the fires of Hell, consuming everything in his passion and anger. (In 1943 Jud would surely have recalled for many the recent Dust Bowl days when the sun's fire had turned the land to dust; Curly would have evoked the promise of a better and more fertile life to come.)

Curly will thus eventually cultivate the farm whereas Jud will try to burn it down. Living as he does beneath the earth, Jud seems to represent the evil spirits within the earth which man must overcome before he can domesticate the land and turn it to his own purposes. In many other films nature's potential threat is directly represented: the earthquake in *San Francisco*, the twister in *The Wizard of Oz*, the storm in *Riding High*, the snowslide in *Seven Brides for Seven Brothers*, the hurricane in *Porgy and Bess*. Even more often, however, it is symbolically depicted as a crackling fire or apocalyptic glow (the high contrast lighting of *Hallelujah*, the Wizard Oil fire at the start of *High, Wide and Handsome*, the great fire of *In Old Chicago*, the Halloween pyre in *Meet Me in St. Louis*, the burning of the restaurant in *The Harvey Girls*, the haystack fire at the end of *Oklahoma!*, the church fire in the closing scenes of *Finian's Rainbow*).

The many folk musicals which depend heavily on historical reconstruction of times gone by develop a third type of ambiguity, that of memory. As a general rule, the folk musical presents the past as tamed by memory, yet given memory's uneasy position between dream vision and reality, there is always a chance that memory will recall to us the upsetting aspects of the past rather than the reassuring ones. The subgenre is thus peppered with moments that we recognize perfectly well as elements of our past, but which are terrifying rather than nostalgic. In *Meet Me in St. Louis*, when Tootie Smith (Margaret O'Brien) goes nearly berserk, smashing her snow family in order to leave behind no living

being when the real family moves to New York, we recognize that more is involved than a little girl's whims. By creating a residue of uneasiness which cannot be assimilated to the glowing version of the past presented by the film as a whole, Tootie's violent action serves to remind us that our past, like our childhood, was not all roses (as do many other macabre events: the Halloween trick-or-treating, Tootie's "doll cemetery," the girls' attempt to run a trolley off its tracks, and so forth). It is precisely this willingness to come at least partially to terms with the real past that gives the syntactic folk musical its characteristic melodramatic tone. When the past is so prettified that its threatening side is hidden, there is a corresponding loss of seriousness and depth. Consider, for example, the moment in *Show Boat* when Julie is about to be arrested; as a mulatto she has no right to marry a white. At this point in the 1936 Universal version directed by James Whale, Steve (Donald Cook) flashes a switch blade and slowly, deliberately, ever-so-painfully slashes the back of Julie's delicate hand (Helen Morgan); he then sucks her blood openly and quite visibly, in order to be able to claim that he has black blood in him, thus saving Julie from arrest. This intensely emotional scene, reminding us graphically of the importance of birth, blood, and race in the otherwise picturesque world of the Old Mississippi, is all but removed in MGM's 1951 version. Director George Sidney shows us no knife, no violence, no blood, thus creating no fear in the spectator.[8] Memory remains an unproblematic device to erase the threat of the past, rather than the complex, ambiguous faculty which it had been in the 1936 version, and which it remains in the most complex and interesting examples of the subgenre.

We are now in a position to make some final comments about the nature and type of folk musical syntax. In general we may say that the folk musical is never solely about a young couple in love, for the couple is always taken as representative of an entire community. The sexual risk taken by the couple is matched on other levels by other risks: religious fervor may become passion (*Hallelujah*), the community may turn into a mob (*High, Wide and Handsome*), the family may be split (*Meet Me in St. Louis*), the horse may lose or die (*Riding High*), the gangsters may triumph (*It's Always Fair Weather*), the foreigner may be expelled (*Flower Drum Song*), and so forth. The successful making of the couple thus always heralds the overcoming of other risks, particularly in the realm of civilizing the land, of transforming nature's potential into civilized actuality. The folk musical thus follows the scenario of a cosmogony, of the creation of a new world: chaotic energy is subdued by the forces of order, of stability, and of civilization. To tie down the wandering male, to stabilize him, is to make the soil fertile by coupling the wind to the earth, the masculine divinity to his female counterpart. In a fundamental sense the cosmogonic act represented by the American folk musical is achieved through a hierogamy, a cosmic marriage. Serving as a guarantee of the harvest, itself a sign of the civilizing of nature, the folk couple stands as the mythic microminiaturization of the civilizing process itself.

We can now see the function of the folk musical's serious tone, evil characters, and emotional scenes. Throughout the history of popular narrative, two basic plots repeatedly appear, which we might call hierogamy and apocalypse. In the hierogamy plot a divided world is brought to new unity by the creative linking of two opposed principles. Often, the two principles are associated with nature, the one representing the stable land, the other a mobile element required to fertilize the land (rain, clouds, wind, or even man). The notion of hierogamy is thus closely associated with the earth and its fertility, as well as with the fertility that comes from sexual union. The apocalyptic plot inverts this pattern, destroying rather than creating, separating rather than uniting, ending rather than beginning. Whereas hierogamy invokes the simple joy of creation through union, apocalypse always implies preliminary suffering, a dark hour for all mankind, a period of fear and trembling, and ultimately a moment of moral judgment, where questions of good and evil cannot be avoided. When employed in literary texts, the hierogamy and apocalypse forms create a strong sense of the sacred; they are not mythical as such, but they are so close to myth that they retain much of myth's seriousness of purpose and sense of the holy. When reduced to the level of pastoral and melodrama, these basic plots still reveal mythic origins. Moving yet another step away from the mythical level, we reach the comic genre, which deploys certain mythic patterns but deprives them of their seriousness. A young couple (the hierogamy component) clashes with a judgmental father (the apocalyptic element), but in a context which precludes a sense of the sacred: instead of worshiping the young couple we laugh with them; instead of sacrificing to the Father we laugh at him. We thus arrive at the following configuration:

Creation myth   Destruction myth
    Hierogamy   Apocalypse
      Pastoral   Melodrama
          Comedy

The greater the distance between corresponding genres, the greater their seriousness and mythic import. As a genre, comedy thus appears as a strategy to domesticate myth, to reduce it to the level of a social laughter-producing device. To be sure, laughter recalls (stands for) worship or sacrifice, but it only *recalls* such ritual activities. So it is that the fairy tale and show musical—musical *comedy*—are light and entertaining, requiring little investment of energy or thought on the part of the spectator. The folk musical, however, is perhaps better termed *pastoral melodrama*—after two genres known for their musical origins—for it brings a mythic problematics, submerged in comedy, back to the surface. In order to achieve the high seriousness associated with hierogamy, a sense of risk must be felt. It is this sense of danger, of impending doom, of the possible wrong use of (sexual, economic, or pioneering) energy, that is provided by the apocalyptic influence. The syntax of the American folk musical ultimately depends on a fundamental tension between hierogamy and apocalypse, between mythic creation and mythic destruction. The main couple takes on added importance, because it is their union, interpreted cosmically, that permits the victory of the creative forces, the settling of the land, and the founding of a new society.

A Folk Art in the Age of Mass Media

Born of the depression, the show musical celebrates man's never-ceasing ability to overcome despair by retreating into the world of make-believe. The folk musical grew to maturity only during the war and thus works with radically different parameters. To protect the land, to glorify the country, to oppose our Folk to their *Volk*—such is the implicit function of the folk musical. The folk musical's mode of creation is thus radically different from that which defines the show musical. In the show musical a creative encounter between the raw material (woman as clay) and the artist who molds it (man as sculptor) produces an aesthetic work, an entity radically greater than a simple sum of the parties involved. In the folk musical a similar process applies to the land: woman is the earth and man the sky; together they produce large families and fertile valleys. These different types of creation necessarily entail a radical difference in point of view. In the show musical the camera is the man's eye, wandering across miles of female bodies, aiming at woman's most private parts, caressing the female anatomy like a lover. Man is by nature Pygmalion; he molds the woman into a work of art through the life-giving, form-giving energy which is synonymous with his very maleness. In the folk musical, quite to the contrary, woman is the source of life—the land, the mother, the one who attracts the seed, nourishes it, helps it grow, and brings the new fruit forth. We have the impression that woman alone, or nearly so, is responsible for the new creation. The center of gravity of the folk musical is nearly always the interior of a family dwelling place, a matriarchal space into which the energetic male must be drawn. In *Oklahoma!* we catch only a few short glimpses of Curly riding the range. *Meet Me in St. Louis* takes place almost entirely within the family mansion, as does *Summer Holiday*. When there are two basic sets, the film functions to draw the men away from theirs and into the women's (*The Harvey Girls, Centennial Summer, The Unsinkable Molly Brown*). When the plot is mobile it invariably ends with an archetypal return home (*Cabin in the Sky, State Fair, Living in a Big Way, This Time for Keeps, One Sunday Afternoon*). The female, civilizing viewpoint thus dominates throughout, converting male energy into social usefulness, making the folk musical into the matriarchal form *par excellence*. This emphasis on the family unit (paralleled by a similar emphasis on the civilized community) provides the folk musical with its characteristic *folk* thematics and emphasis on the constitution of a unified and homogeneous community.

The extent to which the folk musical stresses community can best be suggested by consideration of the audience's relationship to the folk musical. In the show musical a group of "kids," often previously unknown to each other, "get together and put on a show." During this process a certain coherence is reached, a certain community feeling characteristic of the musical genre as a whole. The internal audience in the show musical, however, is of necessity left out of this sense of community; this internal audience sympathizes with the performers, applauds them, and in general supports them, but it is by definition never destined to become part of the on-stage community. By extension, the film audience also maintains a certain distance from the film performers. Just as the internal audience is separated from the performers by a proscenium and the conventions it represents, so the external audience recognizes the framed film image as other. We identify to a certain extent with the performers, but we also must identify with the internal audience, and this dual identification prohibits us from achieving a full sense of belonging to the film's internal community. In the folk musical the handling of the audience changes radically. Instead of the permanent split between performers and spectators which characterizes the show musical (except for certain conventional devices borrowed from the folk tradition, such as singalongs), the folk musical posits a fundamental continuity between performers and audience. It does this by borrowing the interchangeability of role and space characteristic of folk (and especially square) dance:

1) *interchangeability of role*. In folk dance each member of the couple, each couple in the square, is alternately protagonist and spectator. When one couple is moving, the others are stationary, only shortly to take up the motion themselves.

The singalong—an island of folk entertainment in the show musical—led here by Jeanette MacDonald in *Broadway Serenade*.

The same interchangeability of role characterizes folk music and all other folk arts. The passed-along song, the song in which each verse is sung by someone different, the song-with-refrain sung antiphonally—all these are amply represented in the folk musical. When Bing Crosby sings in *Riding High* he is never on a stage but always in an informal place, singing as an elated individual and not as a performer; this naturalization of song permits him always to be joined in song by those around him: his groom, his friends, fellow race fans, and so forth. The *locus classicus* of this interchangeability of performer and spectator is undoubtedly the state fair, as two films (1945, 1962) clearly demonstrate; every member of the family alternates between producing his/her own spectacle and observing with pleasure the produce of his/her fellow family members. Producer and consumer are not separated by a proscenium, they are part of the same family.

2) *interchangeability of space*. The basic shot vocabulary and spatial creation of the show musical are defined by the performer/audience dichotomy. During a performance, the two primary cameras are placed in mirror-image positions

In the folk musical any place can become a stage. Here Bing Crosby and Coleen Gray draw the racetrack urchins into a song in Frank Capra's *Riding High*.

[BFI]

across the line of symmetry constituted by the proscenium, as in the following diagram:

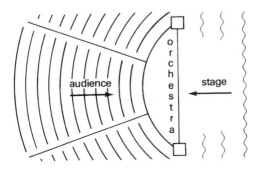

This conventional relationship serves to guarantee the separation of levels (art/life) only at the expense of a similar separation between audience and performers. Since any shot which would break down the barrier between spectators and performers (e.g., shots from the wings which make performers into spectators) would also tend to destroy the artistic illusion, such shots are reserved for purposefully ironic or disillusioning effects (as in the shots from the wings in the *Band Wagon's* Oedipus Rex production, or the famous shot parallel to the proscenium which reveals Debbie Reynolds singing for Jean Hagen in *Singin' in the Rain*).

Instead of resorting to staged productions, the folk musical typically relies on ritual or spontaneous entertainment in which everyone participates, thus creating a space which is more than two-dimensional. By using a series of different camera placements, each implicitly linked to the point of view of a different spectator, the typical folk musical production number creates a circular space, where each spectator/performer as well as each camera position is continuous with, rather than opposed to, every other. In the show musical there is only insignificant overlap between the coverage of the two basic shots, whereas the folk musical produces constant overlap, thus prohibiting permanent separation of performer space from spectator space. Let us visualize a group of characters—dancing, fighting, or simply standing and conversing. We first see *a* from *b*'s point of view, then *a* and *b* together as seen by *c*; all three are then included within *d*'s gaze, which further reveals the approaching *e*, from whose point of view we see the entire group:

When we first see *a* in the first shot of the sequence we as viewers are not part of the action but spectators. The second shot, however, makes our previous vantage point a part of the spectacle (i.e., it permits us to identify our point of view with that of *b*). Shot three compounds this effect: whereas shot two seemed to separate us from the action by placing us outside the *a-b* interchange, shot three attributes shot two to *c*'s point of view, thus creating a three-way interaction (*a-b-c*). When *e* enters the frame and we are given a shot from his point of view, the circle is closed, for we now see that even shot three emanated from within the action (i.e., from character *d*). Sequences of this type, which avoid identification with any single character or point of view, yet constantly place the spectator within the field of action, eventually make the spectator feel like a participant in that action, a resident of the world evoked on screen. The Bazinian sense that the screen is a window prevails: the external spectator is just off-screen, taking part in the folk celebration. Long before Cinerama and Sensurround the folk musical provided a wrap-around feeling, a sense that the spectator is surrounded by the space of the film.

The phenomenon of interchangeability has extremely important ramifications within the film itself, but its greatest effect derives from its ability to cement the external audience to the film, to give the external spectator the sense of actually being a part of the film. It should be clear from the diagrams above that the internal spectator in the backstage musical remains eternally separate, physically and functionally, from the internal performer. This configuration replicates that of the film theater, where the spectator sits in a single seat, permanently separated from the performers on the screen. The internal folk musical "spectator," however, may at any point be "on stage" (if these terms were still appropriate for a form whose very secret is its ability to break down the distinction between world and stage by treating the entire world as a stage). Nearly every important folk musical from *High, Wide and Handsome* to *Nashville* employs this technique (e.g., the party in the Smith house in *Meet Me in St. Louis*, the picnic in *Summer Holiday*, nearly the entirety of *State Fair* and *On the Town*, the "Horse Told Me" number in *Riding High*, the "Portland Fancy" dance in *Summer Stock*, and scores of others). Perhaps the most creative use of this "theater in the round" approach is to be found in the barn-raising scene of *Seven Brides for Seven Brothers*, in which a dance is followed by competitive acrobatics and a choreographed fight. Each of the seven brothers and each of the town's people is alternately spotlighted (indeed the lighting problems in a folk musical production number resemble those of theater in the round rather than the typical Hollywood stage paradigm). Constantly alternating between the role of each other's spectators and each other's spectacle, the men operate in a space which permits no stable differentiation between spectacle space and spectator space. The "interchangeable" space of the folk musical thus approximates that of the square dance, in which action and glances crisscross constantly, producing an interwoven space rather than the single set of paired glances characteristic of the proscenium stage.

Many other techniques contribute to this generalized breakdown of the barriers that separate spectator from performer, world from stage. Nearly every folk musical includes one or more songs already known to the audience, thus permitting them to hum along or even anticipate the words on the screen. The audience for *Hallelujah* recognized many of its old favorites—primarily Negro spirituals—permitting every showing to take on the nature of a singalong. With Broadway remakes the effect is taken still one step farther, for the recognition factor operates in this case not on true folk songs but on songs written for Broadway shows, popularized by radio and records, and known by heart by nearly every spectator of the Hollywood version. The first original cast recording of a Broadway show was made for *Oklahoma!*; after that virtually every important show was available in any neighborhood record store. In short, the Broadway-Hollywood relationship permits Hollywood to exploit Broadway as the source of modern folklore. Now *every* song in the Hollywood folk musical is a familiar one; the audience can hum along throughout the entire film. Just as Oscar Levant—in his dreams—can conduct and play all parts of Gershwin's "An American in Paris" (in the movie of the same name), so the spectator of a folk musical can now play not only a single role but all the roles in the musical enterprise. The technique of using familiar music is of course not limited to the folk musical, but it is in the folk musical that this method reaches its height, for the folk musical employs every possible device to create a link between each American and the past, the community, and the land.

In other words, the folk musical does its best to pass for what it is not, a true folk art. In general, *folk art* is a spontaneous creation of the people; it is characterized by the spectator's ability at any moment to become a performer, and vice-versa. In *popular art*, (or mass art), on the other hand, consumers are alienated from the producer; they consume without ever producing and thus risk being manipulated by a production system from which they are excluded. Hollywood products clearly belong to the second category (films are made not by the folk but by professional entertainers and technicians), but the folk musical disguises that fact.[9] Spectators project themselves into the community established during the film: the surroundings are familiar (even if they don't look like the America experienced daily, they resemble the image of America gained from pictures), the tunes are old favorites (borrowed from folk culture, Tin Pan Alley, or previous film musicals when they are not lifted from Broadway), the historical references are part of our own history. Under the influence of the folk musical, spectators have the illusion of belonging to a national folk, yet all the while they are in fact being manipulated by the mass media, by Hollywood and its production system.

The folk musical is thus built on a paradox. It speaks to a big city, blue-collar world in which values have been eroded, in which man and woman have been separated from their past, their community, their land. To this world it proclaims a message (and provides an experience) of a state in which we were not yet alienated from our partners in work, in love, in worship. In short, the folk musical preaches a gospel of folk values to an age of mass media. It creates a myth to dissemble the break between production and consumption, between capital and labor, between past and present. Yet paradoxically this folk message, this attempt to reconstitute a national folk, must be carried by the very mass media which represent its avowed enemy. The folk musical is thus open to two diametrically opposed readings: *either* it is a triumph of folk sentiment over Hollywood business (since Hollywood has consented to advertise the very virtues which it lacks), *or* conversely, it is Hollywood's ultimate triumph (since the folk musical succeeds better than any other genre in hiding Hollywood's status as big business and mass media). Whichever way we interpret the rhetoric, the folk musical remains structured by its paradoxical ability to make the folk arts (seem to) survive into the age of mass media.

Throughout the fifties and sixties this constitutive paradox remained submerged beneath the polished and picturesque surface of the Broadway remake. The few films which set about to parody the folk musical (e.g., *Red Garters*, 1954, a western in which the main event is a barbecue!) poke fun at the subgenre without exposing its paradoxical structure. *It's Always Fair Weather* goes farther in this direction, but it exposes the subgenre's folk logic only in order to reinforce it. Originally conceived as a remake of *On The Town*, with the original actors returning to the city to celebrate the tenth anniversary of their forties' shore leave, *It's Always Fair Weather* eventually had to be made with only one of the original trio (Gene Kelly), now joined by two talented dancers (Dan Dailey, Michael Kidd). The entire film plays on the opposition of spontaneous activity to planned activity: the reunion is sour as long as it progresses according to the fixed pattern of all other reunions; only when chance encounters produce spontaneous solutions or impromptu clowning do the three former buddies recover their youthful joy. Within the most developed of the individual stories, Gene Kelly is promoting a fight which he learns has been fixed; in order to avoid the shame (and dullness) of a fixed fight, he and Cyd Charisse delight in spontaneously mauling Kid Mariacchi, the fighter who was to have thrown the fight. The same configuration governs the television show which Cyd Charisse directs. All the staged spontaneity planned for the show (including fake commercial product endorsements) fall flat, but when Kelly is without warning attacked by the gangsters who sought to fix the fight, the television cameras are turned on them, producing not only an uproariously funny spontaneous spectacle, but also incriminating the hoods by inducing them to admit their guilt in front of the entire television audience. This basic spontaneity/fixity dichotomy is transferred into the film's primary couple as Kelly's inspiration and Charisse's photographic memory. For once in the folk musical the man and his energy are allowed to dominate, turning a reunion into recovered youth, a fixed fight into an impromptu brawl, and a rehearsed talk show into a live document. Far from un-

masking the folk musical's attempt to pass the mass media off as a folk art, however, *It's Always Fair Weather* actually expands the paradigm a step further to encompass television as well. Not only does Betty Comden and Adolph Green's witty script insist on the importance of spontaneity (the folk characteristic) over fixity (the mass media characteristic), but it suggests that both television and film have the power to provide such spontaneity. In so doing, *It's Always Fair Weather* simply returns us to the paradox with which we started, namely that the folk musical attempts to reproduce a folk experience through a medium which is by definition excluded from such experiences.

Not until Robert Altman's *Nashville* (1976) does a film fully exploit the folk musical's paradoxical folk art/mass art foundations, revealing every contradiction, every false assumption, every self-deception of the folk musical. In 1946 Fox delegated to Otto Preminger the task of making a musical about the Philadelphia World's Fair in 1876, America's *Centennial Summer*. In close imitation of the World's Fair plot in *Meet Me in St. Louis*, Preminger turned out an ode to the American extended family, to Yankee ingenuity, and to old-fashioned fidelity. America's birthday celebration is used in Preminger's film, as in the Independence Day setting of *Summer Holiday*, to reinforce a sense of national unity, a feeling of pride in a job well done. *Centennial Summer* is the joyful cry of a country victorious in war and looking forward to peace. *Nashville*, too, is a self-consciously conceived birthday celebration, but far from celebrating victory and unity it provides a bicentennial record of defeat in Vietnam and the commercially inspired disintegration of the American folk. *Nashville* is not just a film with music which fails to be a musical for lack of joy or appropriate staging; it is a calculated and brilliant point-by-point deconstruction of the folk musical. Nearly every basic principle of the folk musical subgenre is turned on its head by the multiple plots of this innovative and difficult film.

In its general outlines, *Nashville* would seem to have the makings of the ultimate folk musical. Set in America's heartland, in the very home of American folk music, *Nashville* makes a remarkable attempt to include the entire entertainment world, not only the performers, agents, technicians and their friends (as in *A Star Is Born* and many earlier musicals), but the audience as well. The entire film, with its multiple plots and intercut scenes, appears as an elaborate introduction to one final scene—the political rally at the Parthenon—which we are thus made to see from many different points of view. We know nearly every performer present, as well as many members of the audience: why they came, how they got there, and what they expect. With such elaborate preparations, this final rally might easily have been made into the type of unifying finale which has characterized the folk musical ever since *Oklahoma!* Instead, it is used to emphasize the disintegration of America. Barbara Jean is there only because she broke down during a previous concert; in order to save her from the raging crowd her agent had to promise she would sing at the rally. Haven Hamilton is present only because he believes that Hal Phillip Walker, the Replacement

party candidate, will support him in his bid for the governorship. Suleen Gay has been allowed to appear only in recompense for her strip-tease performance at the previous night's fund-raiser. The old man (Keenan Wynn) is there only because his wife was just buried nearby. The man with the violin case—the only major character whose motives have not been revealed to us—has come in order to assassinate Barbara Jean. *Nashville* is about the audience as well as the performers, all right, but what it has to say about entertainment in America is a devastating commentary on the shortcomings of bicentennial America and the folk musical alike.

As we have seen, the folk musical tries desperately to inject folk values and experiences into a world governed by the mass media. In order to achieve this goal, the folk musical must disguise its identity as a commercial, mass media product. *Nashville,* quite to the contrary, plays up the manufactured nature of the folk music experience. Instead of disguising the credits beneath a straightforward, conventional presentation, *Nashville's* credits are sold to the spectator like cheap records on late-night television. Imitating both the soundtrack and the garish visuals of these tasteless ads, *Nashville* identifies its own commercial nature from the start. As the credits continue we watch Haven Hamilton record a bicentennial song ("We must be doing something right to last 200 years") in a Nashville studio. Music is presented as a source of fame and fortune, lacking all spontaneity, largely fabricated by technicians (and unsavory musicians with names like Pig and Frog). No spectators are allowed; music

Undermining the folk musical's tradition of turning a song into a source of increased human contact, Robert Altman isolates his performers behind glass in *Nashville*.

[BFI]

is not for the audience, it exists only to contribute to the performer's reputation. The uninvited BBC reporter (Geraldine Chaplin) is thus unceremoniously ejected with instructions which more than any other single phrase sum up the film's message: "Let her buy the record," says Haven Hamilton, as if to say "I relate to the audience only through a plastic intermediary."

The relationship between performers and audience throughout the film is thus radically different from that of the classic folk musical. Instead of forming a single community, the performers are always physically separated from the audience, whether by armed guards, glass walls, elevated stages, or social barriers. When Barbara Jean loses her hold on reality during an Opryland performance, the audience is concerned not about her mental health but about their wasted dollars. It is hardly surprising that Barbara Jean's only free public performance should end with her being shot. The spontaneous singing and dancing chorus, so important to the folk musical's ritual sense of community, is replaced in *Nashville* by motifs of an entirely different order. Either the supporting chorus is hired (the Fisk Gospel Singers, once a proud expression of black religious feeling, now a commercial outfit made up of professional singers of various races), entirely inappropriate (the Tennessee Twirling Institute, which performs at the airport), or totally chaotic

In *Nashville* song is always a commercial enterprise. Even the Grand Ole Opry is just an oversized billboard for Goo Goo Clusters.

[BFI]

(the motorcade leaving the airport might have been turned into a parade, but instead becomes a multiple-car accident and mammoth traffic tie-up). The relationship between audience and performer is further destroyed by a clear demonstration that the two are not interchangeable: Suleen Gay's terrible voice proves that not just anyone can be a performer. To get up in front of a crowd with no voice is tantamount to psychological striptease.

In the syntactic folk musical, music is an expression of love for the land. In Nashville music is for pay, for political influence, for seduction of married women. As metaphor, music is presented as mental disease, as striptease, as weapon. The words have not changed—they are still tender, loving, patriotic—but the cause and manner of delivery make music into an ugly affair. Altman's characteristic multiple soundtrack masks most songs with a hyperrealistic accompaniment of traffic sounds, insignificant conversations, overamplified speeches, and myriad other ugly noises—the very sounds traditionally diminished in order to highlight the music itself. During the musical's golden years, we often hear a voice without seeing the singer; in *Nashville* we see singers without hearing their voices, to the point of having one performance entirely drowned out by the roar of race cars, each identified by a singer's name painted on its side. Solo performers are muffled by extraneous noises, people singing in unison are not together, the impromptu singalong is painfully off-key. It is hardly surprising to find that the man with a violin case uses it to carry a gun, for everyone uses music as a weapon at one time or another. The most beautiful sounds in the movie come, paradoxically, from Lily Tomlin's deaf children; they too are off-key, but they sing out of joy, and in that they are alone in the entire film.

Another era would have used male/female relationships to reflect a higher unity. *Nashville* maintains the connection between the couple and the community, but only inasmuch as the dissolution of family ties reflects a more generalized fragmentation of society. Sexual relationships occur in triangles, not pairs (including that of the folk trio modeled on Peter, Paul and Mary). Marriage partners typically run away from each other, not into each other's arms. All sex in the film is sensed as infidelity, with a carefully planned rhetoric convincing us that infidelity is often the best solution (especially in the case of the Lily Tomlin/Keith Carradine couple). The breakdown of the couple is replicated on every level. "Redneck music" is opposed to rock; a successful black musician is called a "white nigger" by a fellow black; the supposedly grassroots Replacement party is a sham. In the classic folk musical a permanent male/female bond civilizes the land, turn-

ing chaos into cosmos; in *Nashville* the final rally takes place at the "Parthenon" only to highlight the lack of culture and civilization which characterizes contemporary America.

Even the idols of the musical film itself have been broken. When Barbara Jean refers to the *Wizard of Oz* during her performance, it is a sign of her mental illness, and not of some childlike purity. She has become not the Judy Garland of Oz but the real Judy Garland, the one who couldn't handle the pressures of stardom and was forced to abandon her career and eventually her life. Thus when *Nashville* closes with a final vertical pan, from the Parthenon into the sky, it is not the blue sky of the *Wizard of Oz* that we are seeing, but a totally blank screen, a space fit only for the display of postcredits. It is with a certain amount of relief that we leave Nashville behind us, with its petty people and its manufactured music. "Come home America," was the motto of a recent president. If *Nashville* represents the America to which we might come home then few will bother. By exploding the very syntax on which the folk musical is based, Nashville provides a terrifyingly effective critique of the mythology which serves as a foundation for the entire enterprise of American life today.

Genre and Culture

IN THE OPENING CHAPTER OF THIS BOOK, I STRESSED THE IMPOR-
tance of the interpretive community in fixing textual meaning. In
developing a corpus and a definition of the musical, and in tracing
the musical's history, I have nevertheless devoted little attention to
the genre's interpretive community. In this final chapter I propose to
restore the notion of interpretive community to its rightful place within
the realm of genre study.

In chapter five I argued that the relationship between the semantic and the
syntactic constitutes the very site of negotiation between Hollywood and its
audience, and thus between ritual and ideological uses of genre. Implicit in this
argument is a set of interrelated claims regarding the effect of the interpretive community and the genre on each other. First, Hollywood's economic imperative man-
dates concerted attempts at economy of scale. Only by producing large quantities of
similar films can studios justify their enormous investment in real estate, personnel, publicity, and technology. Second, the process of locating formulas and structures capable of
attracting consistently large audiences is an interactive one, with audience response necessarily playing a role in the artistic and commercial decisions of studio heads. Third, the type of
formula and structure thus achieved is predetermined by the size of the group targeted: only material that is familiar and acceptable to a broad public will do, for only such "lowest common denominator" material has a chance of attracting the size public necessary to guarantee a return on
Hollywood's investment. (This effect of mass media distribution and economics of course differs enormously from the practices of previous centuries, where until the perfection in the nineteenth century of
inexpensive, high-speed printing nearly all representational forms targeted a specific group or class. Indeed,
it differs as well from the current post-mass media world, in which vast fortunes may be made on films which
are aimed at a limited slice of the overall audience. Whereas fifty-four percent of the 1984 movie audience was

under twenty-five, and eighty-five percent under forty, the audience of the three decades during which the musical flourished was far broader, thus guaranteeing semantic and syntactic elements attractive to the entire range of the public, and not just to the small group who by historical accident have become today's movie audience.) Fourth, Hollywood's economically motivated decision to seek structures acceptable to the entire audience has a unifying effect on that audience itself. Constantly defined in terms of a shared Western European or American past, and in terms of problems which they easily recognize as their own, the American genre film audience rarely has a chance to think of its separate national backgrounds, its radically divergent interests, or its class-defined needs. Instead, the numerous nationalities, traditions, and classes which together constitute these United States are leveled by successful appeal to a common denominator linking the various categories.

We are accustomed to using the term "identification" with regard to individuals: individual spectators recognize some parts of their own bodies, their own lives, their own psyche, in the film they are watching. This self-recognition leads to the identification on which most traditional representational forms depend. Such a personal version of the notion of identification remains inappropriate for genre films, however. While individuals no doubt do enter into such a process of personal identification, their total experience cannot be understood without reference to the parallel process of *community identification*. Just as, in the addition of

fractions, use of the lowest common denominator of twelve permits the otherwise unrelated thirds and fourths to be perceived as fundamentally similar, so the use of "lowest common denominator" themes and plot formulas permits Americans of radically different origin and class to see each other as sharing a fundamentally similar experience (with the notion of lowest common denominator now to be taken as a descriptive, not a judgmental term). In short, they not only see themselves reflected in the events and characters portrayed on the screen, but they thus more easily see themselves reflected in the other, quite different, individuals who make up the audience. Just as the seemingly qualitative difference between thirds and fourths becomes no more than a demonstrably quantitative difference when the two fractions are counted in twelfths, so city dweller and farmer, suburban doctor and factory worker, Southern gentleman and Irish immigrant are stripped of their qualitative differences as they laugh together at a screwball comedy, thrill together in the western wilderness, or leave a musical humming the same tune. In other words, the process of accommodation between ritual and ideological needs doubles as the process of establishing a firm and stable interpretive community, one built on shared factors of sufficient generality and breadth to permit broad assimilation. The relationship between the genre and the interpretive community is thus a symbiotic one: just as the audience supports Hollywood, guaranteeing a continued supply of films corresponding to the desired type, so the genre guarantees the coherence and continuity of the interpretive community. Generic structures do not replace the interpretive community, as the structuralists would have it, but they do assure a particular definition of that community, one which is simultaneously of service to Hollywood and—for whatever reasons—acceptable to the mass audience whose very community identity is constituted by those structures.

A new task thus appears on the genre critic's horizon: to identify the formulas and structures which explain a genre's popularity with so many groups of radically divergent characteristics. Why is it that this particular choice of semantic and syntactic material has the power to capture the imagination of such a broad spectrum of the public? By tracing the constitution of the interpretive community which gave a genre its original impetus and assured its continued life, the critic thus simultaneously delineates the genre's operation as a cultural phenomenon, for to explain why a particular set of semantic and syntactic choices has consistently been made is to step beyond the limits of film criticism proper and to enter, slowly and by stages, into the complex world of cultural criticism. The responsibility to engage in cultural criticism is not one that the genre critic can easily dodge, for the very choice of genre films as an object of criticism exposes the critic to texts which by definition transcend their artistic existence in the process of constituting a unified audience, thus entering fully into the world of cultural activity. Cultural criticism imposes itself on the genre critic, because the very constitution of a genre is

in and of itself a cultural activity of multiple ramifications.

The Fundamental Characteristics of Genre Film

Given Hollywood's economic imperative to establish and maintain the widest possible audience, it is not surprising that established genres regularly call on a rather limited range of proven techniques to attract a stable audience. Before we turn to careful consideration of the specific strategies chosen by the musical, it will be helpful to review seven attributes continually characterizing those films which contribute to and derive from a stable generic base. For proper coverage, each of these characteristics would need chapter-length treatment by itself. Nevertheless, abbreviated presentation must here suffice. Overall, genre films are:

1. *dualistic*. The dual-focus structures described in chapter two apropos of the musical are characteristic of genre films as a whole. Perhaps in response to the traditional attraction of the masses to dualistic structures, genre films regularly oppose cultural values to counter-cultural drives, with a consequent doubling of protagonists. In the archetypal western scene, the sheriff confronts an outlaw in a shoot-out; not one but two heroes occupy the screen, alternately receiving the viewer's attention. In like fashion, the ganster is doubled by a rival gang leader or FBI agent, the Army commander is matched by a German or Japanese counterpart, the human hero is pitted against a monster from outer

space, even Fred Astaire must share the billing with Ginger Rogers. Whenever a single individual manages to hold the spotlight throughout, it is usually because he is himself considered as a schizophrenic, divided like Fredric March in Mamoulian's *Dr. Jekyll and Mr. Hyde* into two radically separate and opposed beings.

2. *repetitive.* Both intratextually and intertextually, the genre film uses the same material over and over again. "If you've seen one you've seen 'em all" is a common complaint leveled against the western or the musical; in fact it is a very good description, at least in a limited sense. The same fundamental conflicts are resolved over and over again in similar fashion—the same shoot-out, the same sneak attack, the same love scene culminating in the same duet. Each new film varies the details but leaves the basic pattern undisturbed. The cavalry riding across the prairie, the chorus girls dancing across the stage, the monster lumbering toward the city—shots like these have a symbolic quality which permits them to be repeated again and again with little variation. Sometimes there is no variation at all. In John Ford's *Wagonmaster* the same footage of the wagons crossing the river is used repeatedly. In *Ride the Wild Surf* Tab Hunter appears to be surfing thanks to repeated use of the exact same back projection. The extras of adventure and war movies die a thousand deaths—once shot they must change costume or location in order to repeat the exercise. In some ways, the genre film seems to represent nothing more than the endless repetition of the same confrontation, the same two-shot, the same love scene.

3. *cumulative.* Since the genre film is repetitive, its effect depends not so much on the conclusion of its plot, conceived as a straight-line cause-and-effect sequence, but on accumulation of the film's often repeated situations, themes, or icons. Early critics of the gangster film were well aware of this fact; the deaths of Cagney, Robinson, and Muni at the end of *Public Enemy*, *Little Caesar*, and *Scarface* are insufficient to reverse the impression left by the rest of the film. In its totality, the gangster film glorifies the gangster by accumulating scenes in which he shows bravado, wit, good sense, fidelity to his friends, or just plain guts. If the musical constantly gives the impression that the world is a good place to be, overflowing with happy people ready to sing and dance at a moment's notice, it must be because the average musical takes every opportunity to turn a scene into a festival. Each sequence contributes to the desired overall effect, which is more important than any single dialogue, character, or action. The cumulative effect is even more important when we turn to an entire genre. Analyzing many films of the same genre, we might as well be collating the variations on a single myth, according to Lévi-Strauss's methodology for analyzing the Oedipus myth. Though no single film can present the entire myth, the system of generic variations creates a myth, a single coherent narrative mediating cultural contradictions which the culture can handle in no other way. When spectators go to a horror film or a

western they tend to see the film not as an isolated work of art but as another in a series; their viewing of the present film is highly colored by their knowledge of the tradition which the genre constitutes.

4. *predictable*. The fact that genre films are both repetitive and cumulative in their effect naturally makes them extremely predictable. A western fan can usually predict the ending before the second reel starts; a musical devotee often can foresee the plot before the credits have finished. Indeed, the star system contributes heavily to the predictability of the genre film in which it flourishes. Certain roles became associated with a given character to such an extent that the audience went to the theater expecting a certain type of film, with a definite plot and a predictable ending. Names like Errol Flynn, John Wayne, Jeanette MacDonald, Boris Karloff, and Gene Kelly designate more than just actors and actresses—they all but guarantee a certain style, a particular atmosphere, and a well known set of attitudes. The pleasure of the faithful genre film fan is thus not so much a question of novelty as it is one of reaffirmation. People go to genre films to renew contact with old friends, to hear old stories, to participate in events which somehow seem familiar. To be sure, they are looking for strong emotions, exciting scenes, and fresh dialogue, but like those who go to the amusement park in search of adventure they would rather have their excitement in an environment which they feel they can control. Genre film suspense is thus false suspense, like that of melodrama: in order to participate in the film's strong emotions we must pretend we don't know that the heroine will be rescued, the hero freed, and the couple reunited.

5. *nostalgic*. The very impulse that makes genre films predictable causes them to turn to our culture's earlier days for their subject matter. Not only is the same basic story repeated over and over again, but it is often set in a time and place which readily identify it as a segment of American history. The "backstage" musical retells the story of vaudeville, Broadway, or the Ziegfeld Follies; other musicals recall the turn-of-the-century Midwest, the antebellum South, or earlier days in Hollywood. (Even the musicals which take place outside of this country stress locations and activities which are transparently those of American vacations, American travelogues, and American daydreams.) The western portrays the settling of the West during the second half of the nineteenth century; the gangster movie continued to be set during Prohibition even after its repeal; the family melodrama often portrays the South during the Depression; war films usually center on the American war effort during one of the great wars. Even science fiction and horror films refer to a shared fund of fantasies popularized by previous texts. By attributing epic proportions to the past, as well as pure motives and larger-than-life reputations to its inhabitants, the genre film perpetuates the notion that the past was somehow more complete, more rewarding, more exciting than the present. Though it often concludes by resolving the past/present dichotomy, the musical seems to return the audience to that mythical moment before values were

eroded, before man was separated from the land, from women, from his God. Such overt praise of the "good old days" suggests that only a return to the past can make the present into what we want it to be.

6. *symbolic*. Had the genre film avoided the American landscape, American history, and typically American values, it might perhaps have succeeded in being "just" entertainment. At every point, however, the genre film fairly cries out for a wider interpretation. If we know what the railroad, the telegraph, and cavalry outposts meant for the settling of the West, how can we avoid treating the building of a railroad as a symbolic enterprise representing the spread of civilization? When the train sweeps across the screen at the beginning of *The Man Who Shot Liberty Valance*, how can we help but understand its larger meaning? The opening scene of *The Harvey Girls* puts it even more bluntly: "Wherever a Harvey House appears, civilization is not far behind." Just as the women of this western musical represent certain quite specific values, the fairer sex serves throughout the musical and western traditions as a figure of cultivated morality, of stability, of all that culture means to a new and sometimes savage land. During the Depression the musical constantly played up the values of togetherness, of joy-in-the-face-of-sorrow, of better times to come. "Inaugurating a NEW DEAL in ENTERTAINMENT!" proclaims an advertisement for *Forty-Second Street* which appeared simultaneously with Roosevelt's inauguration, implicitly recognizing that the President and Warner Brothers' films were trying to resolve the same problems.

During the war, musicals and war films made no bones about supporting the Allied cause through their emphasis on military service for men, war-related vocations for women, and War Bonds for all. Even the horror film relies on a more or less protracted use of psychological or cultural symbolism. Can King Kong be understood if we treat him simply as an oversized prehistoric gorilla? Would our film monsters spend so much time fondling women if they had no symbolic sexual meaning? The curious thing about genre film's symbolic discourse is that it operates even on the most unsuspecting viewers. You don't have to see too many westerns before the majesty of Monument Valley and the quiet courage of John Wayne and Walter Brennan become symbols of the American heritage.

7. *functional*. Attempting to demonstrate the function of an activity previously considered lacking in purpose, many of the major thinkers of this century have discovered logic and coherence where none had previously been expected: Malinowski and Radcliffe-Brown with regard to ritual, Langer and Cassirer in the case of myth, Huizinga with play, Freud for dreams. Each of these seminal thinkers explains a particular form of seemingly gratuitous behavior or wasted time in terms of individual needs and social equilibrium, viewing it as an adaptive and adjustive response to the social and physical environment. Among forms of entertainment, the American genre film cries out especially loud for such a functionalist approach. The symbolic qualities of genre films make them particularly able to play a fully functional role. If *The Music Man*'s Marian-the-Librarian is

River City's books, its music, and its manners rolled into one—in short, its culture—then the traveling salesman Harold Hill is a one-man committee devoted to subverting that culture and leading it down the primrose path—toward other, perhaps more exciting ends. The eventual compromise, whereby Marian ties Harold to her apron strings and Harold seems to have taught Marian some counter-cultural values, serves to reinforce our simultaneous belief in both sets of values, to solve the problem constituted for us by our society's seeming treatment of the two sets of values represented by Marian and Harold as mutually exclusive. Not only does genre film constantly underscore the categories which define us (sexual, national, moral, etc.), but it celebrates those categories even when they seem to be contradictory, thus contenting the audience with the status quo by reestablishing social equilibrium and balancing sexual, financial, or national insecurity. Nineteen-thirty was a rough year for everyone. Here is what the October, 1930, *Photoplay* magazine had to say about United Artists' recent musical, *Whoopee*: "This is the new type of screen musical. There is no attempt at realism. It's simply a rollicking, roistering, beautiful production that will make you forget Hoover's advice to sit tight because better times are coming. Heck! They are here!" To be sure, the function played by genre films is not always so simple and direct, so obviously a case of wish-fulfillment, but the pattern is always similar: the genre film asks questions and solves problems (or at least seems to) which society has thrust aside because it refuses or is unable to handle them. The first step in

understanding the functional role of a Hollywood genre is thus to isolate the problems for which the genre provides a symbolic solution.

The seven characteristics sketched out here apply to all Hollywood genres and not just to the musical. As such, they are perhaps misleading, for the reader could wrongly conclude that the only road to cultural understanding of the musical passes through this list of attributes. Instead, I would suggest that one of two major cultural functions of the musical may reasonably be approached through the above list of characteristics. This first function will be treated in the next section. A subsequent section will be reserved for an entirely different role played by the musical in American culture.

Symbolic Spectatorship

During the course of this century we have witnessed an extraordinary growth in the scope of entertainment forms. Instead of minuscule local competitions we now watch televised presentations of marathons featuring numerous thousands of runners. We once observed ice-skaters on the nearby pond a few months every year; now we have access to triple toe-loops and professional hockey nearly year-round. Dramatic presentations which once were limited to a backdrop of poorly painted flats are now showcased before the world's great monuments, thanks to the wonders of film and television. Daredevils used to impress audiences by jumping off high platforms into small pools; over the years the audiences have grown as the platforms got higher and the pools smaller. Even the neighbor's vacation pictures have become increasingly complex as they have turned first into slides, then movies, and now Instant Polarvision. Along with these increases in scale and speed has come a reduction of the audience's physical investment in the process of entertainment. Once largely an outdoor phenomenon, entertainment has moved increasingly indoors, and now, with the advent of twenty-four-hour cable television, into every individual home at every moment of the day. No longer must anyone freeze to watch ice skating or get drenched to view a football game. Looking for a parking space, finding the best available seat, craning for a better view—these are now activities of the past. Modern technology and the social structures that support it have assured us all a VIP ticket with a front-row seat. No doubt critics are right to speak of the increasingly passive role allotted to the spectator by American entertainment.

I have no quarrel with this familiar position (indeed I will push it a step further in a later section). There can be no doubt that American entertainment developments have served to reduce significantly the direct participation and active involvement of mass audiences. I submit, however, that this very process of passification has increasingly liberated American entertainment and its audience for another kind of participation, of a "symbolic" nature. The very process of recognizing a film (or any other text) as representational requires a specific investment on the part of the spectator. Representation can never be guaranteed by the text itself, but only by our willingness to match the phenomena generated by the

text with our perceptions of the world (or memories of other texts). A simple picture of a woman sitting in a living room chair is thus already an exhortation to audience participation, for in order to recognize the representational quality of the image, we must implicitly place ourselves in the image, accepting it as part of our own experience. This process of participation/identification is furthered by recognition of a narrative pattern within the text. Each time we (tacitly) agree to connect two events, we are calling on our own experiences (with other texts as well as with the world) and thus indirectly participating in the constitution of the text (which, by the same token, is indirectly participating in our adoption of a particular subject position, conditioned by the types of experience which the culture—our broadest interpretive community—lets us recognize as representational or narrative).

Now, this process of representational and narrative recognition might well already be termed "symbolic," for through it the spectator unconsciously reaffirms a commitment to certain ways of perceiving which have been learned from the society. In the following discussion, however, I shall reserve the term "symbolic" for the more topical and genre-specific activity induced by genre films. In the opening chapters of this book I stressed a methodology for interpreting the musical which involves the recognition of a thematic opposition represented by and through the musical's fundamental opposition of one sex to the other. In order to identify the operative thematic oppositions I often employed general terms, which, while having special meaning in American society, were nevertheless not present as such in the specific film in question. In educing such general categories from individual films, I was following a fundamental hypothesis, so fundamental to genre study as to be nearly constitutive of it. I refer to the assumption that variation over a genre's total production is in part subtracted out by the genre's tendency toward repetition of key shared elements. The operative metaphor here is not so much Wittgenstein's celebrated notion of "family resemblance,"[1] for the imprecision of that approach leads only to an indefinite, unstructured impression of shared elements, but the "lowest common denominator" metaphor advanced earlier in this chapter. Out of a large group of similar yet varied films there arises a small set of basic thematic oppositions which are only implicitly present in any given film, yet which appear clearly as the common denominator of a large number of films. The musical genre as a whole, as I have suggested previously, thus develops from a large number of related but separate thematic commitments into a single set of overarching concerns deriving from the traditional American opposition between business or work and entertainment.

Throughout the course of this study, I have insisted on the musical's tendency to use the mystical connotations of marriage (whereby two become one, adopt a single name, and gain the right to procreate) to bridge societal gaps dependent on principles which, like the male/female opposition, are conceived as diametrically opposed and mutually exclusive. While the specific analyses I have proposed have been somewhat schematic, the principle, I believe, is clear. Audiences are faced with

a familiar narrative which can be resolved only by a compromise of style and theme, culminating in a marriage of male and female and a marriage-like fusion of the thematic elements which the members of the couple introduce. Our present task is to discover how this narrative/thematic activity changes as it moves from the level of individual texts to the genre as a whole. The difference, I suggest, is caught up in the lowest common denominator process explained above, whereby text-specific thematic concerns are transformed by the context of the genre as a whole into questions of a broader societal nature. In viewing any specific film, therefore, the spectator must necessarily participate in two nearly identical but separable processes: 1) become engaged with a particular set of characters having their own specific problems calling for resolution within the limited context provided by the film at hand; 2) resolve a more general cultural problem which exists for the spectator thanks to tacit common-denominator processing involving numerous texts sharing properties with the one at hand (i.e., often—but not always—texts of the same genre).

The second type of audience participation is what I will call *symbolic spectatorship*, for it turns the immediate process of spectatorship (the identification/recognition model of number one above) into a different mode, a cultural process where particular objects and actions take on the new meaning provided by a broader cultural context. By creating a privileged connection between the notion of symbolic spectatorship and genre film, I in no way mean to suggest that symbolic spectatorship is limited to genre film, but only that the symbolic level is more readily reached with genre film than with less obviously aligned texts, for the unconscious common denominator processing which characterizes the genre film spectatorship experience guarantees symbolic activity, albeit tacit, on the part of the spectator. Genre films are often denigrated as lacking culture. The formula is half right. Genre films do not *flaunt* culture, for they are too busy promoting symbolic spectatorship, largely responsible for integrating individuals into the culture while assuring the culture's continued existence. It remains for us to see just how that process is effected in the case of the American film musical.

Work and Entertainment

As a form of entertainment, the musical inherits a well known tradition within American life. According to Max Weber's celebrated hypothesis on *The Protestant Ethic and the Spirit of Capitalism*,[2] the condemnation of entertainment so often practiced by American moralists derives from the Protestant tendency to transpose the notion of religious calling to secular life. All men and women, according to this religious approach to economic life, have a responsibility to devote themselves to mundane occupations just as if they were monks devoting themselves to prayer. People's capacity for work thus becomes a measure of their religious as well as worldly status, while unwillingness to work is symptomatic of the lack of grace. Reordering a time-honored hierarchy of capital sins, Puritan moralists thus identified waste of time as the first

and in principle the deadliest of sins: "Idle hands are the devil's playthings."

Now, the Weber thesis has by no means been uniformly accepted by cultural historians.[3] Indeed, few theories have engendered such violent quarrels and well researched debates. Nevertheless, certain relatively uncontested conclusions may be advanced here as a background for further deliberations about the musical. First, it seems quite clear—whether or not specific tenets of Protestant theology may be taken as the major cause for the rise of Western capitalism—that the traditionally low status of entertainment in American life derives from the combined and undifferentiated condemnation by business and religious interests alike. Entertainment is not just a waste of valuable time, thus offending canons of business value alone, for wasting time is itself defined as a specific religious failing.

Second, as numerous scholars since Weber have confirmed, business interests for centuries took advantage of convenient religious condemnation of leisure activities in order to serve their own needs. Weber himself spells out the criteria according to which non-work activities were evaluated by Puritan America. "Sport," he explains, "was accepted if it served a rational purpose, that of recreation necessary for physical efficiency. But as a means for the spontaneous expression of undisciplined impulses, it was under suspicion; and in so far as it became purely a means of enjoyment, or awakened pride, raw instincts or the irrational gambling instinct, it was of course strictly condemned" (167). Here we meet for the first time the definition of the term "recreation" that eventually consoles nineteenth-century industrialists to certain well chosen leisure activities: not recreation in the modern sense of a pause from work, an opportunity for activities totally unrelated to work, but re-creation, like sleep a necessary break in the interest of higher overall productivity. The worker must, like a battery, be recharged in order to deliver a full measure of work. Entertainment is thus allowable, but only because it fits into an overall scheme of guaranteeing a sufficient labor force for an increasingly industrialized world.[4] In other words, leisure activity in this country has always maintained a close connection to business concerns, in spite of the well known condemnation under which entertainment activities have always suffered, from Puritan strictures to the uncomplimentary identification of entertainment activities with "popular culture."

Third, though leisure activities of various sorts have regularly been condemned by religious figures, moral reformers, and business interests alike, numerous forms of entertainment have nevertheless thrived in American life. Early settlers had their Maypoles and turkey-shoots; the agrarian nineteenth century could indulge in square dances and corn-shucking, in singing-bees and play-parties; city-dwellers of the last century could count on melodrama and minstrels, vaudeville and burlesque, dime-novels and parades. Yesterday's State Fair, with its prizes for log-rolling or bronco-riding, yearling bulls or peach preserves, has become today's amusement park, with its roller coaster and house of mirrors, its Ferris wheel and bumper cars. Beauty pageants, cartoons, sporting events, the circus—all testify to a fundamental need to

shed excess energy, to exercise those feelings and desires for which the Protestant work ethic makes no provision. Constantly threatened by religious and societal strictures, entertainment has never faltered: far from vanishing, it continues to expand, spreading into ever new areas. Such an ability to resist criticism can derive only from a powerful force, an unspoken principle which justifies entertainment unto itself and protects it from the attacks of the work ethic.

Indeed, we may note that entertainment's location ouside the canon of prescribed activities undoubtedly liberates numerous forms of entertainment to evolve independently of society's avowed preferences and programs. In all periods, certain subjects or activities have been purposefully excluded from public exposure; it is precisely these areas that entertainment, given its marginal and unspecified nature, has concentrated on. Amorous interchange between the sexes, for example, was long excluded from the public arena. Young men and women of marriageable age had little opportunity to meet and get to know each other. Various forms of entertainment grew up in response to this vacuum: square dancing, play-parties, corn-shucking (where the one who finds the red ear gets to kiss the partner of his/her choice), and so forth. As America urbanized, opportunities for courting became less of a problem but the general prohibition on public display or discussion of sexuality remained, giving rise to such entertainment forms as burlesque, the peep-show, the musical revue, and the beauty pageant.

When society attempts to exclude such important concerns from its value structure, they are bound to take refuge elsewhere—usually in those activities to which the society ascribes no specific productive role. Entertainment is thus able to serve a function, to operate as a symbolic discourse, *precisely because* is has no prescribed role. In American society, where religious influence has created an especially wide gap between the asserted value of work and the presumed frivolity of entertainment, this process takes on a special importance. The more we emphasize the virtues of the work ethic as the only authentic values, the more we create a need for expression of natural emotions which lie outside society's avowed moral structure (but well within the range of human needs and desires). The more we identify entertainment as frivolous, worthless, and wasteful, the more we increase its capacity to take up the slack created by the work ethic.

Contained in this lengthy aside on the place ascribed to entertainment by the Protestant work ethic are two considerations which prove to be determining for the musical's symbolic spectatorship. On the one hand, we learn that entertainment is clearly conceived as the inverse of work and business, the very type of leisure activity that leads to dissolution rather than re-creation. Entertainment and work are thus not only conceived as paired, oppositional terms, but within our society they implicitly carry the power and prestige of a quasi-religious judgment. They thus constitute a thematic opposition essential to the constitution of our society, but one which rarely receives balanced treatment within the society. The entire culture speaks in favor of work, but there is no spokesperson within the culture to speak on behalf of entertainment (unless it is for entertainment conceived as re-creation

for work). On the other hand, the marginal position of leisure activities would seem to make entertainment itself the ideal defender of its own position. As repository for all those basic impulses for which the culture provides little or no space, entertainment forms might logically take on the defense of their own cause.

The musical's symbolic spectatorship is thus doubly conditioned by the musical's status as entertainment in a country where entertainment has for centuries been considered the devil's handmaiden. As I suggested earlier, however, the general thematic level at which symbolic spectatorship operates is not achieved within the individual text. In order to reach this symbolic level, spectators must fulfill two separate requirements. First, they must be sufficiently familiar with the genre to effect—even if only subconsciously—the common denominator processing which transforms text-specific themes into generic cultural concerns. Second, while the critic who consciously seeks to explain a genre's operation might reasonably depend on acquired knowledge in order to locate a genre's characteristic structures, the general public will fully enter into the process of symbolic spectatorship only when their daily experience provides them with an appropriate context and sufficient grounding for their perception of cultural themes across seemingly diverse generic texts. When American audiences watch the musical, they bring with them a rich store of inherited knowledge about American culture. Without having read Weber or Horatio Alger they understand the quasi-religious sanctions that weigh on individuals who squander their leisure time on frivolous pastimes. Without having read the sermons of moral reformers or the pronouncements of the rational recreation movements of the nineteenth century, they understand the seemingly natural (but actually quite cultural) animosity in our culture between work and entertainment. Without even knowing what the Sabbatarian movement was, they understand the fundamental fear underlying Blue Laws. In short, the American musical fan comes to the theater with the entire critical apparatus necessary to understand the genre's symbolic investment. It is hardly surprising that the musical as we know it has never really caught on in any other country (in spite of pockets of critical acclaim and the odd experiment in a variety of countries and periods), for even the most advanced critics or the most devoted public in other countries must necessarily lack the cultural background on which symbolic spectatorship depends (though, not surprisingly, England is the country which comes closest to sharing both our entertainment tradition and our evaluation of the musical as a genre).

What is it that is symbolic about symbolic spectatorship? The previous paragraph suggests that lack of knowledge of a cultural tradition inhibits only the recognition of the genre's fundamental cultural concerns. More, however, is at stake, for even though French academic critics may understand the context and meaning of *Singin' in the Rain*, they cannot have entered into the process of symbolic spectatorship. For symbolic spectatorship involves more than simple recognition of the presence of cultural material. It assumes that the spectator

serves as translator of the film's raw thematic material into the genre's—and the culture's—master themes. That is, the very locus of the genre as cultural practice is neither the text nor the culture, but the spectator, for only the spectator—familiar with the culture—can recognize the categories of the culture within the film. And only the spectator familiar with the cinema can recognize the clichés of the cinema within the culture. The culture's master themes are not actually *in* the text, yet the text is produced in such a way as to evoke them for a particular interpretive community. Perception of the relationship is a more important cultural phenomenon than any actual relationship that might exist. It is thus through the spectator's knowledge and perception that culture and cinema interact in a reciprocal relationship. Not only do the culture's concerns form the genre's themes, but through the spectator's participation in a symbolic working out of generic and cultural problems alike, the genre's formulations also produce their own effect on the cultural patterns out of which those formulations grow. We must not forget that the audience for a genre as widespread as the musical was through the fifties all but coterminous with the American public as a whole. Symbolic resolution of familiar problems within American culture, when repeated fifty million times a week, looks like nothing so much as actual resolution of those same problems.

Numerous specific strategies characterize the musical's handling of the work/entertainment dichotomy. Not surprisingly, the different strategies adopted correspond by and large to the musical's three familiar subgenres. As the subgenre most fully borrowed from non-American sources, the fairy tale musical displays a thematic structure somewhat different from its homegrown cousins. Taking up where Viennese operetta left off, the fairy tale musical commonly opposes a happy-go-lucky commoner to a proper aristocrat, a woman with duties to her country, to her family, and to her own pride. Within this rather formulaic context, visible in such well known fairy tale offerings as *Love Parade, Monte Carlo, Love Me Tonight, Flying Down to Rio, The Gay Divorcee, Roberta, Gold Diggers of 1935, The Merry Widow, Top Hat, Damsel in Distress, The Great Waltz, New Moon, Yolanda and the Thief, The Pirate, A Connecticut Yankee in King Arthur's Court, Call Me Madam, Brigadoon, Silk Stockings,* and *Hair,* an opposition is established between the joy and talent of the lower classes, as represented by the commoner (nearly always the man), and the stuffy, limiting tradition identified with the woman and her entourage. In a sense, then, there is little to identify the fairy tale musical as specifically American, for the thematic concerns which it tenders are clearly borrowed from the Old World. Even within this context, however, specifically American attributes surface through the character of the commoner. Often cast as an American abroad, the commoner clearly derives his most salient features (lack of concern with material goods, sense of humor, independence, devil-may-care attitude, song-and-dance talent) from a larger cultural myth opposing New World virtues to their Old World counterparts. In *The Sound of Music,* one of the few films where the sexual roles are reversed (*Royal Wedding, The King and I, Gigi,* and *My Fair Lady* are others), nowhere is it so much as implied that Julie Andrews is playing an American, yet the set of character traits and values that she represents make her identity as a "symbolic" American quite clear. Throughout the fairy tale musical tradition we find characters who, like Andrews, represent simultaneously the values of America and entertainment. Opposed to a European aristocratic strain (sensed as European even when it is transported onto American soil), these entertainment values eventually glorify the working class status of the characters who serve as vehicle for them. The American entertainment-minded commoner thus often provides a model not only of entertainment virtues but of the film's working class values as well. Thematically at least, the fairy tale musical often varies from the standard mystic marriage of diametrically opposed values, for the American commoner—Fred Astaire is the archetypal example—already provides a fully developed model of the combined work and entertainment virtues which will characterize the New World.

With the show musical comes a change of class—a generalization of the fairy tale musical's commoner role, we might say—along with an overt concern for cash. Growing out of indigenous American entertainment forms rather than from middle-European traditions, the show musical from its very beginnings opposes the show as a business transaction to the show as entertainment. Indeed, in the first of the show musical's many celebrated series (Warner's *Gold Diggers,* Paramount's *Big Broadcasts,* MGM's

Broadway Melody films), the combined virtues of a Broadway show are presented as a wholesome alternative to gold digging. Stressing the fact that work can be as pleasant as play when carried out in a communitarian atmosphere and spirit, the show musical regularly demonstrates that good entertainment *is* good business. Most overtly emphasized in *Dames, Little Miss Broadway, The Gang's All Here,* and *The Band Wagon,* the business value of entertainment underlies the large majority of show musicals, for the show musical nearly always portrays professional performers whose only income derives from their ability to entertain. As soon as entertainment's monetary value fades (as with MGM's prewar Garland-Rooney accounts of kids putting on a show, or with wartime troop shows, or even in the case of the genre's innumerable charity performances), then we begin to slide in the direction of the folk musical, with the cause behind the charity show taking precedence over the show musical's typical combination of business and entertainment. While the show musical commonly matches a brilliant, natural singer or dancer with a more workmanlike or highly trained performer (e.g., *Born to Dance, One Hundred Men and a Girl, Anchors Aweigh, The Barkleys of Broadway, The Band Wagon*), it must also often resort to New Comedy techniques in order to assure sufficient thematic weight to the business side of the balance. The subgenre thus offers a large selection of penny-pinching producers, money-grabbing impresarios, and old-fashioned fathers—all intent on turning a profit which, to their surprise,

they are able to do thanks to a show. Of all the subgenres, it is thus the show musical that takes most literally the need to reconcile entertainment with work and business, for the show musical alone regularly confronts directly the question of entertainment's monetary value.

Looked at from one point of view, the folk musical exactly reverses the show musical's strategy. Whereas the show musical starts with entertainers—members of a profession which has always been located on the fringes of the business community—and proves that their product is a perfectly acceptable business commodity, the folk musical typically begins with everyday Americans going about their business—a business which will eventually be transformed, with the help of rhythm and rhyme, into a source of entertainment. *High, Wide and Handsome* turns an oil pipeline into a circus, *Ride 'Em Cowboy* joins singing cowboy movies like *The Man from Music Mountain* and *Song of Texas* in disclosing the poetry of the range, *Cabin in the Sky* discovers heavenly music in the life of lower-class southern blacks, *Meet Me in St. Louis* makes trolleys sing, while *On the Town* makes a whole city dance, and *Summer Stock* turns a tractor into a song. From city to city and occupation to occupation, there is hardly an area of American life that is not set to music by the folk musical, which again and again derives its rhythms, melodies, and harmonies from the daily activities of everyday America (the cotton gin in *Hallelujah*, the barnyard in *High, Wide and Handsome,* mechanized transportation in *Meet Me in St. Louis, The Harvey Girls,* and *Summer Holiday,* New York traffic in *On the*

Town, nature itself in *Seven Brides for Seven Brothers*, the Wells Fargo Wagon in *The Music Man*). The folk musical advances an implicit critique of Saussure's notion of the unmotivated sign, for in the folk musical all music is given as onomatopoeic, as growing directly out of daily activities as naturally as song comes from a bird. Within the family-based universe typically constituted by the folk musical, the man is often a loner, oblivious to the family values which the folk musical systematically identifies with those of work. The woman, to the contrary, has no notion of the entertainment values normally associated with the wandering male. If she can sing or play the piano at all, it is often because she has been trained to do so for cultural reasons specifically excluded by the folk musical from the notion of entertainment (e.g., Rose and her organ-playing in *Hallelujah* or Marian's piano-teaching in *The Music Man*). The entire process of creating the couple and settling the land is caught up in the subgenre's habitual negotiation between entertainment values and their more traditional work/business counterparts. The resultant couple and society are thus opened to a salutary combination of order and freedom, of work and entertainment.

That the American film musical mediates the diametrically opposed categories of work and entertainment seems clear. Less obvious, however, is the function of this symbolic mediation. We owe our understanding of the mediatory value of ritual texts to Lévi-Strauss and the many others who, working with traditional texts, have discovered the function of those texts within the society as a whole.[5]

Assuming the texts in question to be addressed by the society to itself (that is, having no author separate from the audience), this now familiar methodology concentrates not on the discursive concerns deriving from author-audience relationships, but instead on the internal narrative concerns of structure. The conclusions of Lévi-Strauss and other ritual critics thus offer little insight into the specific motivation for the production of so-called ritual texts. Whether or not the methods of Lévi-Strauss and his followers are appropriate to each corpus of texts I am not in a position to say. In the case of the musical, however, it is quite clear that the ritual approach alone will not suffice, for musicals are clearly not in any meaningful sense simply addressed to the society by itself. They are instead the industrial products of business concerns located in Hollywood (and controlled by still larger corporations with branches all over the world), destined to be distributed for a profit to anyone with the price of an admission ticket. It may well be that certain spectators attend musicals for reasons that have come to be termed "ritual," but we can hardly expect Hollywood to share those reasons fully. Just what is Hollywood's investment in the work/entertainment thematic? Why should Hollywood care about this particular piece of American culture?

Why, indeed, should the world's largest entertainment business care about the status, within its own major market, of the concepts of entertainment and business? In a way, the answer seems obvious, yet even here there is perhaps more than meets the eye. Like any "mixed" enterprise, Hollywood reaps the benefits of its dual connections to commerce and the arts, simultaneously suffering the consequences of mixing activities which the society has defined as immiscible. In foregrounding the business/entertainment dichotomy, Hollywood is thus baring its own breast. Attacked from one side for commodifying activities which should be conceived as spontaneous expressions of pure joy or as disinterested artistic productions, attacked from the other side for the frivolousness of its commodities, Hollywood might well have looked to Madison Avenue to bolster its public image. But why bother with Madison Avenue when you have all Hollywood at your disposal? No doubt the world's most complex and expensive publicity scheme, the American film musical serves as Hollywood's own self-justification. Even before it became overtly reflexive, the musical was investigating its own status and championing publicly its own solutions. Because it is engineered as a genre in which spectator common-denominator processing foregrounds the business/entertainment dichotomy, the musical serves Hollywood's purposes, for it is at the very junction of business and entertainment that the Hollywood enterprise is founded.

The process of symbolic spectatorship thus proves by itself to be double. Through common-denominator processing, audiences unconsciously recognize the operation of the vaguely familiar work/entertainment thematic. As they become involved with the film's fictional plot, they are thus implicitly working through the problems of their culture as well. Symbolically resolving the culture's own quandaries, the spectator infuses the text with a symbolic meaning, one which it can gain only in the presence of this spectator, someone who brings to the genre the very background that the musical is about. At the same time, of course, and by the very same process, the spectator has been lured into doing Hollywood's bidding, for the resolution to which the film leads the spectator is chosen by the film establishment for its greater glory, prestige, and profit. Recognizing the discursive as well as the narrative component of this process, we once again see how the process of genre film spectatorship reaffirms both ritual and ideological values.

The Musical's Operational Role

While the process of symbolic spectatorship is hardly limited to the musical or to genre films, the repetitious nature of a Hollywood film genre guarantees a symbolic quality to the genre viewer's spectatorship (the "genre viewer" being a spectator sufficiently familiar with the genre and the culture to effect what I have called common-denominator processing). The role of semantic material weighs heavily in the spectator's accession to the level of symbolic spectatorship. If the audience were to seek common denominators between each film and the totality of their cultural or cinematic knowledge, then common-denominator processing would be an interminable process. Semantic similarities among films provide easily recognizable raw facts inducing the audience to limit the field of films appropriate for comparison. In addition, semantic givens set up expectation of particular syntactic patterns, because of the audience's experience with previous films in which those same semantic elements have been featured and accompanied by a specific syntax. Symbolic spectatorship is thus a process available to any film audience, but much more likely to take place in the case of the genre film audience.

Recognition of the musical's tendency to engage its audience in a symbolic manner, thus transferring the locus of meaningful structures from the text to the spectator (as meeting place of cultural competence and textual practice), corresponds to the general move of the last decade from text-based concerns of narrative structure to spectator-based concerns of reception and ideology. In spite of the evident advances of such an approach, however, it is surprisingly limiting in terms of overall scope. Whether we speak of narrative structure or symbolic spectatorship, of ritual value or ideological effect, we remain limited to a rather tight text/audience unit, with the culture beyond implied primarily by parallels between textual structures and cultural configurations. Now, this strategy, which might be termed metaphoric (in Jakobsonian terminology)[6] because of its attention to the similarity between structures in the text and in the culture, is nowhere matched by a corresponding metonymic thrust, an attempt to treat the societal practices directly influenced, enabled, or engendered by a particular genre. Genres have more than symbolic effect on the culture. They contribute expressions to the language, concepts to our thought patterns, toys and games to our children's repertory, as well as clothing

fashions, life-style preferences, and leisure-time activities to our own. These direct contributions which a film genre makes to the society together constitute what I shall call the genre's *operational* role.

Now, the operational aspect of a genre's cultural impact might well be approached in numerous different ways. In broadcasting studies, where public policy questions have mandated innumerable reports on the effects of violence, pornography, media over-exposure, and so forth, researchers have stressed quantitative analyses of the effects of particular content material on various subsets of the population (often children). Operational film analysis does not even have this quantitative tradition to look to. Since the Payne Fund studies in the thirties, few attempts have been made to analyze the effects of specifically filmic material on a major sector of the population. Even fewer attempts have been made to discover the effect on American life of film's spontaneous or carefully engineered direct contributions to our daily routine. In the current section, I propose to demonstrate the importance of the musical's most direct contribution to American culture—its championing of the exercise of song and dance in American life. In order to be set in the proper context, this analysis of the musical's operational role must begin with a review of the basic criticisms which cultural analysts have directed at the musical and at the popular forms of music which it develops and champions. In previous sections of this chapter, I have been concerned only to identify the type of cultural activity in which the musical is engaged. In the present section, however, my task will be to defend the musical against its numerous accusers, revealing a cultural contribution of significant and unrecognized proportions.

In *Music, the Arts, and Ideas: Patterns and Predictions in Twentieth-Century Culture*,[7] Leonard B. Meyer develops an implicit evolutionary metaphor to justify his debunking of popular music. Popular music is termed "primitive," while art music merits the adjective "sophisticated" (32). Playing on the stone-age connotations of his term "primitive," Meyer goes on to demonstrate that popular music is characterized by a need for immediate gratification (the very need which civilization labors hard to destroy). Continuing the organic, evolutionary metaphor as he explains the value of deferred gratification, Meyer asserts that "self-imposed tendency inhibition and the willingness to bear uncertainty are indications of maturity. They are signs, that is, that the animal is becoming a man. And this, I take it, is not without relevance to considerations of value" (33). Value, for Meyer, is easy to locate. It is inherent in the music itself (22ff) and in the auditor's understanding (295). Writing in an era dominated by the New Criticism and textual analysis, Meyer clearly conceives the musical text as pattern and correct response as a proper construing of that pattern. The more complex ("mature") the pattern, the better the text. *Ergo*, popular music is bad.

Similar arguments are advanced in numerous texts by the music expert of the Frankfurt School, Theodor W. Adorno. While Adorno's views are at times vehemently and needlessly overstated ("today—unlike a hundred years ago— popular music is bad, bound to be bad, without exception,")[8] his critique has the power of thoughtful formulation and careful elaboration. Concerned as much about the effect of what he deems bad music on the society at large as he is simply to chastise the plebes for their preferences, Adorno locates the demise of popular music with the Viennese composers instrumental in establishing fairy tale musical conventions. The popular music spawned by Strauss, Offenbach, and Lehar, he says, "constitutes the dregs of musical history" (*Sociology*, 29). But he also explains why. When we remember a hit song, Adorno claims, we tend to turn into the song's ideal subject; our isolation is eased by this identification and the consequent integration into a community of fans. We are thus deceived into believing 1) that the song is really for us, and 2) that popular music decreases isolation. Protesting that "the composition hears for the listener," that "popular music is 'pre-digested,' " and that "the fundamental characteristic of popular music [is] standardization," Adorno blames popular music's major deception on its tendency toward "pseudo-individualization,"[9] the process of bamboozling the public into believing that the song is addressed to each listener individually. Reflecting his own musical training, Adorno regularly champions the twelve-tone techniques of Arnold Schönberg, the only system which, according to Adorno, avoids the falsely totalizing effects of classical harmony, by freeing each of the notes in the tone row from the domination of the tonic. In popular music, on the other hand, the link between elements is pre-given, so recognition and understanding coincide. For Adorno, the characteristic quality of serious music is its refusal to deliver up prepackaged relationships between part and whole; in serious music, recognition leads through understanding to something fundamentally new.

Adorno's position here resembles that of Meyer: deferred gratification is preferable to immediate understanding, while value is ultimately to be located in the patterns of a composition and the audience's correct perception of them. To Meyer's text-centered view of musical value, Adorno uncontestedly adds a social concern. Recognizing the potential for passification inherent in certain kinds of popular music, Adorno extends the range of his analysis to include the sociology of music reception, concluding that "Entertainment music no longer does anything but confirm, repeat, and reinforce the psychological debasement ultimately wrought in people by the way society is set up. The masses are swamped with that music, and in it they unwittingly enjoy the depth of their debasement" (*Sociology*, 225). This broader vision, characteristic of Adorno and of the Frankfurt School in general, is a welcome addition to the narrow critique often leveled against popular music.

In spite of its admirable breadth, however, there remains an important consideration never broached by Adorno's work. Adorno's model of music production—like that of most culture critics—is restricted to the familiar trio of composer, professional performers, and listener. Rarely in his considerable writings on music does Adorno admit that music might have a final purpose other than that of providing new intellectual sensations for the attentive listener. Indeed, his very definition of the sociology of music ("knowledge of the relation between music and the socially organized individuals who listen to it"—*Sociology*, 1) indicates his prejudice toward listening, to the exclusion of all other activities related to music (many others come immediately to mind: composing music, playing or singing music, promoting music, making musical instruments).

It is instructive in this regard to ponder the history of American music. Most of the earliest American writings about music are not about composition or the music's innate qualities, but about public singing—how, where, and when it should be done. The emphasis in those early days was clearly on production of music (an active, physical, phenomenon in which the entire community shared) rather than on composition or listening to music (an intellectual affair reserved in later years for a few highly trained individuals).[10] Throughout the nineteenth century, the history of American music is tied to producers of music. Chapters on band music, for example, routinely deal with bandmasters rather than independent composers of band music.[11] As long as theater was conceived as a participatory affair, in which the text was always to a certain extent a collaborative endeavor, then the distinction between "author" and "actor" was a moot one at best (certainly this is the case of Italian Renaissance theater or the work of Molière and many another neo-classical playwright/actor). Likewise with music, where only during the course of the nineteenth century does the composer/performer distinction become a given, and then only with so-called "serious" music.

What are the forces that led to increased specialization within the musical marketplace, and thus to a significant reduction in the attention paid to amateur performance? The question is an important one, far too complex to receive adequate response here. Nevertheless, a preliminary hypothesis may not be unwarranted. Early settlers brought to this country a large repertory of popular musical forms, music meant for singing or dancing, music that was part of life. Often learned by convenient face-to-face methods (e.g., "lining"), this music was clearly conceived for public reproduction, as the hymn books and sheet music of the colonial period testify. Whether aimed at congregational singing or secular musicians, the published music of this period was not yet divided into the two categories that would arise during the course of the nineteenth century, amateur and professional. The development of this rift grows largely out of the spread of concertizing during the nineteenth century, and the resultant growth of virtuosity in performers. With the development of concert music as a major commercial form of music, performance style and virtuosity become commodified. The way to sell a concert (i.e. to make money from one's training) is no longer to establish a continuity between one's own musical gifts and the client's (as in the contemporary case of the music teacher), but to develop a style which the average spectator could not imagine possessing, or even imitating.

While the virtuoso attracted increasing attention to music—and particularly to European music, composed music, difficult music—it was by and large a new kind of attention. In the past, music heard had always been a blueprint for music to be played, but now the process of listening took on a life of its own, independent and aesthetic. From a situation where composition, listening, and performance remain interchangeable community activities, shared by many, we move to an increasing specialization, engendered by the potential economic returns of virtuosity. At first the virtuoso is his own composer, but as performance demands grow, the composition duties must be taken over by someone else. As concert attendance became an increasingly widespread and respected cultural activity, listening to music took on a societal role independent from the production of music. Paralleling increasing industrial specialization throughout the nineteenth century, we thus find a growing tendency toward musical specialization, along with a commodification of virtuoso performance that is fully the equivalent of the century's other, better known, tendencies toward commodification.

In the wake of the virtuoso performer came the professional orchestra, the professional singer, the professional organist, and the professional choir director. Throughout public life, the standards of musical quality changed. From the values of participation and expression, America moved to the professional values of the concert stage: musical training and talent. This emphasis on a new standard of quality in music led those responsible for the production of music in America to turn increasingly toward the world's primary source of quality music and musicians, Europe. Emphasis on classical, cultured, or "quality" music thus not only alienated American listeners from the process of production, it often alienated them from the productions, performers, and styles of their own country. Such a heavy emphasis was placed on proper training and quality of performance that nineteenth-century indigenous musicians had no more chance than amateur performers today. With the twentieth century this situation is compounded by the development of new European styles of still greater complexity and difficulty. The twelve-tone compositions introduced by Arnold Schönberg and championed by his pupil Theodor Adorno further discourage the amateur performer, completing (along with numerous other equally difficult modern schools) the split between "serious" music and "popular" music, along with the parallel separation between professional and amateur performers.

This somewhat lengthy sketch has been necessary to describe the background against which popular music, and particularly the musical, arises. According to Adorno, musical theater is responsible for the downfall of popular music. Yet, because Adorno is interested solely in music as an intellectual phenomenon and never as a physical production (in spite of the fact that he was himself an accomplished piano player), he misreads one key aspect of the music associated with popular theater. For Adorno, the simplicity of popular music is proof that it is pre-digested, that it hears for the listener, whereas in fact the simplicity of the musical's music is produced by design and at great pains,

in order to serve a specific purpose. The music of the musical differs from that of opera, *Lied*, and oratorio in that it is self-consciously written not to surpass the range and capabilities of the average amateur music lover. Musical music is thus *engineered* not to be passive music. It is "hummable" music, the kind of music that most easily gets carried home, the kind of music whose life will not end with the intellectual experience of listening. In short, it is music whose major purpose is to counter the specialization engendered by nineteenth-century aristocratic taste for "cultured" music (a taste which lives on in the preferences of this century's academic critics of popular culture). Treating the process of listening to music as a beginning rather than an ending, as a tool rather than a finished product, American popular music consciously presents an alternative to the specialized model afforded not just by classical music in this country, but by the more general tendency in America over the last half-century to substitute spectatorship and vicarious experiences for the process of production and participation.

Consider the Winter Olympics and typical American reaction to them. We often react to Soviet or East German successes in the lesser known events with a shrugging off of these sports as "minor," in comparison to the "major" sports in which "we" excel. But what is the difference between cross-country skiing and figure skating? Perhaps the most important difference is that which separates the participatory from the spectator sport. How does one watch a ten-kilometer cross-country race, even with multiple cameras? I can't watch it effectively, but I can easily identify with the racers, because I can certainly imagine myself cross-country skiing. Conversely, how can I imagine myself doing an ice dance or figure-skating routine like those featured at the Olympics? Yet I can easily imagine myself watching such a routine. We have reached the point in our sports broadcasting where the spectacular alone is emphasized (etymologically, spectacular means watchable). Whereas television might have been a medium aimed at facilitating my own sports participation, at feeding my own desire to produce sports activity, it has instead followed the model of classical music—with performers of increasing virtuosity (not to mention size and talent), and announcers who are trained increasingly to intellectualize the game—thus transforming the process of sports viewing into an independent phenomenon, entirely separate from the playing of sports. About the only sports left on network TV that are really accessible to the average man/woman are golf and bowling (but they are hardly considered front liners). Public television alone retains the how-to shows that might have characterized the medium. Like music, sports and television have gone the way of specialization, sacrificing their potential operational value to increasing professionalization and specialization.

The Practice of Music in the Age of Electronic Reproduction

What becomes apparent through the parallel example of American sports broadcasting is that popular music, at its best, corresponds not to a degraded form of serious music, but to a radically different notion of societal organization. The approach championed by Adorno assumes the value of uniquely intellectual consumption, just as American television feels fully justified in separating the "major" sports from their "minor" counterparts. While I am aware that it may be hard to see this point from the country and the time in which we live, *there is another alternative*, a solution periodically advocated by public figures throughout our history. Listen, for example, to the Depression era voice of Joseph Lee, President of the National Recreation Association:

> The purpose of community recreation is to liberate the power of expression of people and communities. What we are trying to do is to help the men, women and children of America to find their voice—to set forth in drama, art and music and in the hundred other forms of play what it is they have all along been trying to say which could not get itself expressed within the confines of their daily work. . . . We should not be drawn aside by the desire to make a showing or get things done. It is not the size of the thing that happens but its expressiveness that counts. If it does not come from the hearts of the people, it is of no use to them.[12]

As recently as the middle of this century, Lee's word "recreation" was the dominant term, implying physical participation; today that term has given way to "entertainment," with its connotations of passive finality. Clearly, as Daniel Gregory Mason pointed out over a half-century ago, one of the major signs of our culture's unwillingness to support a primarily recreational use of music is the overall allocation of funds within the society:

> If we spent half as many hundreds of dollars yearly on forming ourselves into amateur groups to produce music for the creative joy of it as we do thousands on hiring professionals and manufacturing machines to amuse us, we should become a music-enjoying and perhaps even a music-producing instead of a musically exploited people.[13]

The ideal here is clearly that of an integrated experience of music. Mason recognizes the pleasure that is to be gained from musical production—not just as an intellectual extension of the intellectual activity of careful listening, but also as a physical activity which brings together in harmony numerous bodily functions (the voice, hearing, the touch of the piano keys).

More recently, Ernst Roth has provided yet another important justification for the operational value of musical production:

> Music . . . is a very special art. Literature and the visual arts, as object of admiration or understanding, remain as it were outside the reader or observer, like the sun or the moon or a landscape which one knows and loves without being able to make it one's own. Music, on the other hand, not only allows but demands re-creation, appropriation. Only in its re-creation does music fulfill its mission entirely. The piece of music which I play myself is "mine" in a fundamentally different sense from the picture which hangs on my wall or the poem which I know by heart, because I participate in the musical work which I re-create. I do not participate in either the picture or the poem. While the picture and—in a somewhat less material sense—the poem *are* the works, the printed or manuscript sheet of music is no more than a guide or recipe for the re-creation of a work which has no real existence otherwise.[14]

Where has the harmonica gone, and where the jew's harp? Who among us can still play the ukulele, the auto-harp, or the washboard? Where is the old practice of singing at the work place alive today? Does anyone still sing rounds? When did you last hear someone whistling a tune? To be sure, we retain some formal singing groups—at school, at church, in singing clubs like S.P.E.B.S.Q.S.A. and the Sweet Adelines, but by and large we live in a society which attributes little value to musical production and thus has created few structures in support of amateur music (and by amateur music I mean everything from Barbershop Quartet concerts to Friday night chamber music groups to singing in the shower).

It is tempting to blame this situation on the mass media. This is, for example, the tack taken by Paul Carpenter: "Power complexes known as the radio industry, the motion-picture industry, and the recording industry are impoverishing the musical life of our regions by pre-empting the listening ear of every town, hamlet, and farm house in the nation . . . they have converted a great many of our potential performers and composers into passive listeners" (Carpenter, 13). I suggest, however, that it is shortsighted to blame the media for our communal willingness to accept a passive role in the music-making process. The entertainment industry does not do the job alone. The media passify only when there is no support mechanism actively turning consumers into producers. It is the lack of this support system—a cultural problem of a broad nature—that converts potential performers into passive listeners. (And this is fully as true of the concert hall as it is of popular radio. Just as heavily mixed, rerecorded, and manipulated rock music precludes copying by amateurs, so the choice of difficult intervals, rhythms, and harmonies makes concert music unlikely to be emulated by amateurs.) Criticized for leveling regional differences, treating the arts as a business concern, and making the audience into passive consumers, these very same media could just as well be used in support of regionalism, amateurism, and participation.

Yet, paradoxically, this country did have for half a century a powerful and well financed support system for amateur music, a system that led nearly everyone born in the first half of this century to a level of informal musical production that has now largely disappeared. This magical method was, quite simply, the musical itself, first as a Broadway phenomenon and then, for a far broader public, through the cinema. Economically speaking, the musical has always been a rather complex phenomenon, with admissions never constituting the entirety of revenues. Throughout the heyday of the musical (from the twenties to the fifties), ticket revenues were amply supplemented by sheet music sales, while since the war phonograph record rights and sales have formed a growing percentage of a production's overall revenues. For decades the musical—with its tendency to prefer "hummable" tunes—joined hands with

the sheet music industry to keep American pianos playing and American voices singing. Or, rather, I should reverse the formula: because the musical's music was destined for the sheet music industry and the family piano, it remained hummable, i.e. appropriate for the amateur musician. In short, for over a quarter-century the musical and the sheet music industry together combined to provide the nation's most powerful defense against mass-mediated passivity.

The film musical's overall history takes on new meaning when placed in this context. It is tempting to see in the development of the folk musical a simple reflection of the growth of folk motifs across American life under Roosevelt and during the war. Another explanation now offers itself, however, for the slow growth of fairy tale material into folk motifs and structures. In the fairy tale musical, singers' talents are normally justified by their class or training. In the folk musical, quite to the contrary, an overt effort is made to allot songs to the nonsingers within the cast. Now, singing, in the folk musical, is always conceived as a natural activity to begin with, one which we do by virtue of our joy in living: the casting of non-singers in singing roles guarantees that the audience will leave the theater convinced of their own ability to reproduce the film's songs at home. With the likes of Leon Ames, Walter Brennan, Walter Huston, Walter Matthau, and Steve Martin singing on camera, there is little likelihood that I will worry about my own voice.

Two recent films are particularly instructive here. The Neil Diamond remake of *The Jazz Singer* bends what

Increasingly, during the late thirties and forties, the musical foregrounded the sheet music which carried the musical's songs to pianos and voices across the land. Here, scenes from *Broadway Serenade*, *Meet Me in St. Louis*, and *It Happened in Brooklyn*.

[a & b = BFI, c = MOMA]

once was primarily a show musical toward the folk subgenre, turning Jolson's personal quest into a broader concern, culminating in an enormous singalong of "America." The question is no longer whether the son of a Jewish cantor may sing jazz, but whether the sons and daughters of America will sing at all. This same question provides the underlying motif of one of the great surprise films of recent years. *Pennies from Heaven* seems to have sensed the cultural problems to be posed by MTV and music videos years before the problems existed. With the first half of the film built around overtly post-synchronized songs, *Pennies from Heaven* suggests that Steve Martin's soul has been emptied out and replaced by the voices of others. In order to be ourselves we must learn to sing again with our own voice, we must regain the right to our own soundtrack, we must return our voices to their rightful place in synchronization with the rest of our body. The most beautiful song in this strangely haunting film is thus the last one, the only one

that Martin sings with his own voice. A similar paradox makes the (musically) least satisfying song of *Nashville* into the (humanly) most satisfying: the song sung from the heart by Lily Tomlin's deaf children. All other songs are sung by professionals and have nothing of the amateur, participatory joy which the folk musical stresses so consistently.

If the folk musical represents a last holdout against the demise of personal musical production, the decline of the musical as a whole in the late fifties is closely tied to a generalized change in the consumption/production configuration characteristic of the musical's operational role. With the rise of the original-cast recording in the late forties, along with the long-playing record, Hollywood rapidly abandoned the sheet music industry in favor of the disc industry, going so far as to bankroll Broadway shows in order to assure lucrative rights to title, plot, and music alike. At the same time, however, recording practices began a major change which still shows no sign of being re-

Ever since World War II, the show and fairy tale musicals have turned increasingly toward folk motifs and material. The show for which Bing Crosby tries out in *The Country Girl* is entitled "The Land Around Us" and features a familiar folk setting along with the communitarian values absent from the film's main story. Like the most recent remake of *The Jazz Singer*, the film version of *Hair* injects nationalistic concerns into quite unexpected places.

[MOMA]

At the conclusion of their recreation of a classic Astaire/Rogers dance, Steve Martin and Bernadette Peters find themselves imprisoned by a line of cane-wielding male dancers—a step on their way to learning *Pennies From Heaven*'s most important lesson, that true pleasure comes from singing in your own voice and dancing your own dances.

[MOMA]

versed. With electronic recording technology making it possible to doctor the originally recorded sound in numerous fashions, recordings have become more than simple records of a performance: they increasingly recreate a supposedly single and unique "performance" out of numerous takes and an infinite number of electronic enhancements. In the last thirty years music has thus developed to the point where even purportedly "live" music is in fact heavily doctored by sophisticated amplification and "enhancement" systems which treat the sound before it reaches the public. During the sixties, music starts to be *conceived* as canned, i.e., an increasing number of compositions call for electronic sound sources as primary production "instruments" and not just as post-production enhancements, the media of *reproduction* thus becoming increasingly inscribed within the process of *production*. Written for electric guitar, synthesizer, massive amplification, or other electronic devices, the new music can rarely be *recreated* by the listener in the home—it can only be *reproduced*. For music is no longer written with human re-creation in mind. We are simply not equipped with the necessary instruments, as we once were in the good old days of the musical, when music was written for the everpresent piano and the fundamental item of human standard-issue equipment, the voice.

In other words, the downfall of the musical corresponds to a change in American musical styles from music written for the voice and the piano (melody plus harmony, as in a fake book) to music written for a new apparatus, the loudspeaker. After decades of steadily increasing sales, the bottom finally dropped out of piano sales during the Depression. The American film musical thus begins at the very high point of piano sales in America, at a time when home music production was still in a position to rival music consumption through the home's newest toys, the radio and the phonograph. Singing was still a family and public habit; buttressed by hymn singing and the universal piano, the combination of ability and desire to sing was at an all-time high. Thirty years later, with the arrival of rock music and the electric guitar, the era of the piano was over. For decades the musical had managed, nearly single-handedly, to hold off the combined threat of the new mass media and American obliviousness to the importance of music production. When television joined with electronic music in the fifties, however, the menace proved overwhelming. The music once engineered for re-production now was refitted for pure consumption by Mantovani and his jillion and one strings, and then piped through every public building by a Muzak system. Where once American popular music had provided a liberating impulse working against the very media serving as its vehicle, now that same music fully deserved the criticisms leveled at it by Adorno.

For, as it should by now be clear, music can neither claim nor be stripped of value solely on the basis of internal patterns. Twelve-tone music is no more "better" than Irving Berlin than Gershwin is "better" than Albinoni. If our purpose is to discover how musical phenomena influence and are influenced by their society, then we must not limit ourselves to a model of musical value that stresses consumption to the exclusion of production, hearing at the expense of singing, the intellectual instead of the physical. In order to understand the functioning of music within a society, we must be willing to analyze the operational along with the symbolic, even when that analysis leads us to a paradox like the one I have presented here: that coupled with the closely related sheet-music industry, the Hollywood musical—certainly the most sophisticated form among the modern media—served for thirty years to stave off eventual complete capitulation to the consumption orientation of those same media. Constituting a privileged musical form which existed as a major genre only during the short period between the coming of sound to film and the coming of sound to the American home (in the form of hi-fi, stereo, and television), the film musical is the last bridge, the last holdout in the passage from live to mechanical and electronic reproduction, for the musical represents the last musical form sys-

With the growth of the record industry after the war, the musical's structure and Hollywood's financial returns increasingly diverged. Here, we see *Rhapsody in Blue*'s championing of sheet music as the avenue to live music, while the publicity regularly stressed recorded music, destined for listening rather than singing or playing.

[UW]

tematically to be produced for re-production.

Adorno was concerned that popular music does the *listening* for us. What he never seems to consider is that the alternative system he champions does the *playing* and *singing* for us. For thirty years—and perhaps even today, for some—the musical collaborated with the sheet music industry to defer the moment when all our playing, singing, and dancing would be done for us. Too exclusively dedicated to an intellectual definition of knowledge, Adorno never recognizes the fact that *making music is a form of knowing*. In order to achieve such body knowledge we must learn to refuse the last two

centuries' sole devotion to the intellect, and to the aural and visual senses which support it, turning instead to the mouth, the hands, and the feet. To sing, to play, to dance—these are the ancient forms of knowledge championed anew by the musical and the cultural practices which lend it an operational dimension.

It is important to recognize the anti-ideological role played by sheet music's operational complement to the musical. Throughout its history, the musical labors to erase the shameful spectre of its mediated status as well as its commercial function. While careful manipulation of the work/entertainment thematics solves the latter problem, the former is often re-

The show musical typically concludes with an ode to entertainment, as with this reprise of "That's Entertainment" at the end of *The Band Wagon*. Lurking behind this defense of entertainment, however, lies a potential problem: the people who are singing are the ones in the film, while we sit in the audience passively listening. Only when the audience too gets in on the singing does the show musical achieve its potential.

[MOMA]

solved by some form of *mise-en-abyme*; that is, the problem of the film medium's mediated status is projected into the film as a thematic concern, often appearing in displaced fashion apropos of another representational mode. In its most familiar form, this process uses an internal show to figure the film medium itself. Thus, in *The Band Wagon*, the values of the entire entertainment world are caught up in the "The Band Wagon" show that Astaire and Charisse bring to fruition, championing the values of participation, community, and song. The ideological component of this convenient solution lies in the fact that the external audience—the one that has just paid money to see the film—is excluded from participation, from the film's community, and from the songs that the film's characters sing. Structures which encourage the external audience to participate in their own community singing reverse the pattern, however. By giving the spectator the chance to identify physically with the film's characters—by singing the same songs—the sheet music industry combines with the musical's preference for singable music to undermine part of the film's seeming ideological project. While the sheet music industry is in one sense nothing but another industry, it nevertheless serves to unveil the film's attempt to hide cinema's mediating nature, thus reversing an ideological effect. The characters' attempts at song may be mediated, but ours are decidedly not.

Today, a quarter of a century after the decline of the Hollywood musical, it is difficult for us to imagine the extent to which the musical once engendered active modes of entertainment, of re-creation. Sheet music releases were awaited with the same urgency as new music video releases are today. Every new film initiated a run on the music stores, just as "Top 40" radio programs have done since the fifties. The only difference is that one purchase leads to music production, while the other feeds only our appetite for consumption. But music to play and sing is not all that the musical championed during its halcyon years. From the Depression through the Eisenhower years, America was still a dancing country, learning every year a new Astaire-Rogers dance during the thirties and a new Latin dance during the craze of the forties. People not only danced, thus increasing their capacity for identification with the dancing couples on the screen, they also paid money to learn to dance. Tied into the country's musical production through the sheet music industry, the film musical was tied into dance production through the nationwide dance school industry, from the chic of Fred Astaire and Arthur Murray to the downhome fun of classes in the local high school gymnasium.

It is of course tempting to think that the dance connection has never been broken, for from rock to break-dancing, the musical has continued to reflect and champion current dance modes. From *Rock Around the Clock* through *Saturday Night Fever* to *Flashdance*, the tradition appears unbroken. In fact, however, two important considerations belie such a simplistic attempt at maintaining at all costs the coherence of the musical genre over its entire history. First, the musical's audience changes radically in the late fifties. From family entertainment, the musical rapidly becomes the fief of the youth crowd. It may have an operational value for that section of the population, but the limiting of the audience clearly limits the overall effect. What's more, as we can see from the recent break-dancing craze, the tendency is toward increasingly idiosyncratic and spectacular dance forms. Where once every new dance was aimed at enticing more couples onto the dance floor, now the new dances simply multiply the number of spectators. If we sometimes feel that the soul has disappeared from the musical in recent years, it is surely in part because of the genre's revised relation to the process of music and dance production. As long as every musical spoke to us of our own capacity for and joy in the production of music and dance, then the musical was serving a social function which, alas, it no longer serves for the society as a whole.

Conclusion

ONE FINAL ASPECT OF THE MUSICAL'S ROLE IN AMERICAN SOCIety deserves attention here. Students of American culture have long recognized the extent to which American life is marked by a sense of absence, a sense of loss which is repeatedly assimilated to the Christian notion of the Fall. In consequence, much American imaginative endeavor is self-consciously redemptive in nature. Indeed, it might reasonably be claimed that the need for redemption, for recovery of lost values, is what energizes American creative production. It is this thirst for redemption that leads American literature, art, and music to a sort of secular religious feel, a sense of restoring Eden in a fallen society. The extent to which American cinema shares this redemptive aura has been insufficently recognized.

Hollywood's major genres might well all be redefined from the standpoint of the particular Eden that they set out to recover. The western constantly grapples with nature's lost purity, with the rape of the virgin land. Evincing an evident nostalgia for the wilderness and pioneer values, the western openly regrets—and to a limited degree recovers—the importance of the individual before modern society. With the melodrama, it is the newly mobile and fragmented nature of the family after World War II that is sensed as a loss in comparison to earlier, more stable days. Only overt reaffirmation of traditional values saves the melodrama family from the insecurity which implicitly haunts it. Screwball comedy grows out of a peculiarly thirties' version of the same threat: money increasingly replaces the couple, the family, and other homespun, human values. Redemption comes here only by insistence on the new-found (i.e., rediscovered) value of human feelings. The detective genre gives voice to the fall from rural communal security into the individuality and impersonality of the city. Here the only solution available is the detective's intelligence, itself so individual a process that it risks impersonality unless the detective figure possesses a personal touch and/or a sympathetic entourage (lacking which, the detective film shades into the *film noir* genre, whose very name designates it as the only Hollywood genre to display overt preference for the fallen state over redemption). In the war film a falling apart of men of differing nationalities is counterbalanced by a studied unification of men of differing backgrounds but of the same nationality. The list could go on. Revealing as beleaguered those values which contemporary society has in fact endangered, Hollywood genre films turn on the discovery of a redeeming hero or set of values, capable of restoring the lost Eden.

Read from this point of view, each of the musical's subgenres may be seen as taking on a particular redemptive function. The fairy tale musical begins with a vision of the Old World from the standpoint of America. Seen from the simplicity of the New World, European sophistication seems to glimmer in the distance like a star to be followed or a setting sun to be regretted. A world of royalty has given way to a nation of commoners; the aristocratic standard of value by birth has been degraded by increasing attention to monetary concerns; even the freedom of Old World attitudes toward sex has been lost in the repressed atmosphere of the New. Now, the reader will of course recognize in all these supposed losses the creation of the very values that Americans have defended for centuries, the very values that constitute the genius of American life. Yet, according to the characteristic American strategy, history must be seen as a fall requiring redemption. Only in this way can the text appear to carry a message of mythic proportions. The fairy tale musical fashions its myth around a commoner (often an American)

who can take European royalty by storm, thus establishing a new royalty through charm (*Prince* Charming), while replacing unattainable birth values by success in song and dance, and by displacing sex onto more familiar objects and activities. As the fairy tale musical develops, its attention slides from Europe to the haunts of the local aristocracy, but the pattern remains the same, thus dispelling any regret we might harbor that Europe was by necessity left behind in the creation of a new nation on the North American continent.

The show musical must constantly contend with the fall implied by the very term "media." In moving from live entertainment to film, we are condemned to banishment from the immediacy of the original event by an intermediary, by the mediation of the medium itself. No longer are we in the presence of real human beings, but of actors instead, of shadows rather than flesh and blood. Where once the space of the show was total space, participatory space, 360-degree space, now it is restricted to the field of the camera. Where once the time of the show was total time, continuous time, now the process of editing fragments time, imposing on the spectator the perceptions of another. In response to this fall from live entertainment into the media, the show musical imbeds live entertainment forms into the mediated film, choosing performers blessed with the capacity to exude presence even on film. By revealing the non-stage life of the actors (i.e., treating them like flesh-and-blood individuals rather than actors), the scandal of their celluloid existence is dissipated. Through systematic use of the high-angle shot, top

The king of the early musical, Al Jolson, had a unique ability to bestow his gift of presence, of liveness, on the film musical. Taking advantage of the runway which he insisted on adding to his stage numbers, Jolson brought his personable style right into the audience.

[MOMA]

shot, or traveling crane shot, the show musical breaks us free from our conventional horizontal gaze, at the same time liberating film of its debt to the theatrical proscenium, thus convincing us that we see even better through the cinematic eye. What might have been seen as a simple technological development—increased use of new representational media—is thus redefined in a peculiarly American fashion first as a fall into the media, then as redemption from that fall.

The folk musical follows up directly on the show musical's vision of recent history. Stressing not only the loss of live-

ness in mediated entertainment, but the demise of folk qualities as well, the folk musical puts special emphasis on the fall from singing as fun to singing as work, from singing as an amateur pastime to singing as a profession, from singing as expression to singing as the medium of someone else's thoughts, words, and emotions. At the same time, the folk musical implicitly mourns this century's move from small country towns to big city living, as well as the parallel historical progression from pioneer times (with the attendant virtues of the pioneer community) to a mobile society attentive to national and international rather than regional or local concerns. This perceived folk fall is redeemed by familiarizing, by "folkifying" the mass media, stressing improvisation, passed-along songs, community sings. This emphasis on the amateur, the unmediated, and the provincial (even in St. Louis or New York) blends with a settlement narrative and a studied dispelling of apocalyptic motifs in order to reaffirm the small town values of America even in a world which seemingly has surpassed them. The folk musical thus joins hands with the regional art movements of the thirties, the war-spawned chauvinism of the forties, the suburbanization of the fifties, the redevelopment projects of the sixties, and the ecology movement of the seventies and eighties in restoring to this country some of the pride and purpose which decades of industrialism, growth, and profit motives threatened to destroy.

Faced with a fall from music as royal, sacred, natural, and live, to the modern world's view of music as common, secular, manufactured, and mediated, the American film musical has systematically labored to reorder our attitudes toward music. Identifying music with love, with religion, with nature, and with the creation of community, the musical clears away a space for us commoners to experience the practice of music as a royal, sacred, natural, and live activity. Once concerned to defend live music and amateur music production against the multiple attacks of radio and the talkies, or to protect the piano against the onslaught of hi-fi, stereo, and television, the musical even today continues, albeit in a reduced and largely unsuccessful manner, to marshal its resources in support of the last

vestiges of personal and communal creativity in the face of the Walkman and MTV. From *Saturday Night Fever* to *Flashdance*, the musical has continued to champion new dance styles, while films like *Fame* and *Pennies from Heaven* have revealed anew the personal pleasures of song. If the musical of the future can continue in this vein, then it will succeed, like the musical of the past, in creating its own audience. For the audience will not be just a nation of young hearers, but a community of young performers as well, people who—like you and me—will grow up singing in the shower, humming along with the record, and loving to listen to music because we identify with it as performers.

If the musical is to survive very far into its second half-century, rather than succumb to its first cousins, MTV and the concert film (as in a monarchy, first cousins are always the most dangerous rivals), then it will have to look to its past—and to American musical tradition as a whole—in order to rediscover the symbiotic relationship which once tied the musical's canned entertainment to the audience's potential for live, personal production. The musical can regain its once lofty status only by supporting music production as well as music consumption, the practice of dance as well as admiration of others' skills, the pleasures of the mouth and the hands as well as those of the eyes. The musical may revive again, but it will do so only if we revive along with it.

This book too is marked by the American tendency to conceive history as a fall, and creative activity as redemption. If this book sends you back to the musical, then it will have fulfilled part of its role. Its full

From disco dancing to break dancing, the musical of the last decade has been most successful, as here with *Saturday Night Fever*, when it provides a dance style destined to be imitated by today's musical's young devotees. With current music largely unreproducible by the human voice alone, only dance has continued to provide the musical with an operational dimension.

[BFI]

mission will not be served, however, until you return to the piano and bang out one of your old favorites—missed notes and all—or until you find yourself once again beating time to the music on the radio, and then singing the tune the next day in the shower. If this is the book I mean it to be, then it too must help to break the ty-rannical cycle of spectatorial entertainment. It must enter into an economy of production with you, the reader. It must make you return to your piano, your clarinet, or simply your vocal chords. It must lead you to the kind of music that is truly re-creation, and not just entertainment.

Writing on the American film musical has been uneven at best, with most books on the subject notable by the quality of their illustrations, not their analyses. Among general studies, Jane Feuer's *The Hollywood Musical* (Bloomington: Indiana University Press, 1982) stands out from the standpoint of both the quality and the clarity of its arguments. For readers of French, Alain Masson's *Comédie musicale* (Paris: Stock, 1981) will prove insightful. John Kobal's *Gotta Sing, Gotta Dance: A Pictorial History of Film Musicals* (London: Hamlyn, 1971) provides useful production information and a unique chapter on the European "musical." Ethan Mordden has written a somewhat chatty book on *The Hollywood Musical* (New York: St. Martin's, 1981). Other general books offer less substance: John Springer's *All Talking! All Singing! All Dancing! A Pictorial History of the Movie Musical* (New York: Cadillac, 1966), Douglas McVay's *The Musical Film* (New York: Barnes, 1967), Lee Edward Stern's *The Movie Musical* (New York: Pyramid, 1974). Still other picture books may be found at local libraries and book stores. The best articles on the musical have been collected in *Genre: The Musical*, ed. Rick Altman (London and Boston: Routledge and Kegan Paul, 1981).

In addition to these general works, an increasing number of specialized books have become available in recent years. In addition to separate large format publications on nearly all the major figures (Chevalier, Berkeley, Disney, MacDonald and Eddy, Faye, Garland, Crosby, Astaire, Kelly, Presley, and others), a number of studies deserve special recognition. Miles Kreuger's *The Movie Musical from Vitaphone to Forty-Second Street* (New York: Dover, 1975) provides valuable information on the musical's early years from the pages of *Photoplay* magazine. Aljean Harmetz has done a masterful job of tracing *The Making of the Wizard of Oz* (New York: Knopf, 1981). Hugh Fordin's *The World of Entertainment! Hollywood's Greatest Musicals* (New York: Doubleday, 1975) chronicles two decades of musical productions by MGM's Freed unit. Leo Braudy's *The World in a Frame: What We See in Films* (New York: Anchor, 1976) includes a useful chapter on the musical. Arlene Croce's *The Fred Astaire and Ginger Rogers Book* (New York: Dutton, 1972) makes for entertaining and informative reading. On dancing in the musical, see also Jerome Delamater, *Dance in the Hollywood Musical* (Ann Arbor: UMI Press, 1981), and John Mueller, *Astaire Dancing: The Musical Films* (New York: Knopf, 1985).

Until recently, the best filmographies available were in Tom Vallance's *The American Musical* (New York: Barnes, 1970) and John Russell Taylor and Arthur Jackson's *The Hollywood Musical* (New York: McGraw-Hill, 1971). The publication of Clive Hirschhorn's *The Hollywood Musical* (New York: Crown, 1981), with a paragraph on every musical produced by Hollywood, now provides the most complete and reliable information, though it is usefully complemented for recent rock productions by David Ehrenstein and Bill Reed's *Rock on Film* (New York: Delilah/Putnam, 1982). Further bibliography (biographies, interviews, close analyses, etc.) will be found in *Genre: The Musical*, listed above.

1. An Introduction to the Theory of Genre Analysis

1. Fuller treatment of the traditional model may be found in Roman Jakobson, "Closing Statements: Linguistics and Poetics," in T.A. Sebeok, ed., *Style in Language* (Cambridge: M.I.T. Press, 1960). The revised model which I propose is inspired in part by the work of Stanley Fish, e.g., *Is there a Text in This Class?: The Authority of Interpretive Communities* (Cambridge: Harvard University Press, 1980), and Tony Bennett, e.g., "Texts, Readers, Reading Formations," *Bulletin of the Midwest MLA* 16, no. 1 (Spring 1983), 3-17; and "Texts in History: The Determinations of Readings and Their Texts," *Bulletin of the Midwest MLA* 18, no. 1 (Spring 1985), 1-16.

2. See my "Intratextual Rewriting: Textuality as Language Formation," in *The Sign in Music and Literature*, ed. Wendy Steiner (Austin: University of Texas Press, 1981), 39-51.

3. See Claude Lévi-Strauss, "The Structure of Myths" in *Structural Anthropology* (New York: Basic Books, 1963), and John Cawelti, *The Six-Gun Mystique* (Bowling Green: Bowling Green Popular Press, 1971), and *Adventure, Mystery and Romance* (Chicago: University of Chicago Press, 1976).

4. Stephen Neale's study on *Genre* (London: BFI, 1980) suggests one possible avenue toward a more discursively oriented theory of genre.

5. Tzvetan Todorov, *The Fantastic* (Ithaca: Cornell University Press, 1975).

6. For the discourse/disclosure model, see especially Christian Metz, "Story/Discourse (A Note on Two Voyeurisms)," in *The Imaginary Signifier: Psychoanalysis and the Cinema* (Bloomington: Indiana University Press, 1982).

7. See especially Thomas Kuhn, *The Structure of Scientific Revolutions* (Chicago: University of Chicago Press, 1962).

2. The American Film Musical as Dual-Focus Narrative

1. On the causal model of narrative structure, see Roland Barthes' influential introduction to *Communications 8* (1966), entitled "Introduction à l'analyse des récits," as well as any current manual of literary terms, e.g., Sylvan Barnet, Morton Berman, and William Burto, *The Study of Literature: A Handbook of Critical Essays and Terms* (Boston: Little, Brown, 1960). On the notion of "classical Hollywood narrative" and its adoption of this causal model, see my "Classical Narrative Revisited: *Grand Illusion*," *Purdue Film Studies Annual* 1 (1976), 87-98.

2. Further theoretical considerations regarding dual-focus narrative may be found, with medieval examples, in my "Medieval Narrative vs. Modern Assumptions: Revising Inadequate Typology," *Diacritics* 4 (1974), 12-19; "Two Types of Opposition and the Structure of Latin Saints' Lives," *Medievalia et Humanistica*, New Series 6 (1975), 1-11; "Interpreting Romanesque Narrative: Conques and the *Roland*," *Olifant* 5, no. 1 (Oct. 1977), 4-28.

3. Raymond Bellour, "Segmenting/Analysing," in *Genre: The Musical*, ed. Rick Altman (London and Boston: Routledge and Kegan Paul, 1981), 102-33.

3. The Structure of the American Film Musical

1. On the importance of repetition in popular texts, see Claude Lévi-Strauss, "The Structure of Myths," in *Structural Anthropology* (New York: Basic Books, 1963).

2. On Astaire's technique for shooting dance, see John Mueller, "The Filmed Dances of Fred Astaire," *Quarterly Review of Film Studies* 6, no. 2 (Spring 1981), 135-54.

4. The Style of the American Film Musical

1. The lyrics are from Ira Gershwin's "Blah, Blah, Blah."

2. Jane Feuer makes a similar point in *The Hollywood Musical*, pp. 72-73, a book which grew, along with this one, during years of enjoyable discussions at The University of Iowa.

5. The Problem of Genre History

1. Northrop Frye, *An Anatomy of Criticism* (Princeton: Princeton University Press, 1957).

2. Northrop Frye, "The Argument of Comedy," *English Institute Essays*, ed. Alan Downer (New York: Columbia University Press, 1949), 58-73.

3. Especially in Vladimir Propp, *Morphology of the Folktale* (Bloomington: Indiana Research Centre in Anthropology, 1958); Claude Lévi-Strauss, "The Structure of Myths" in *Structural Anthropology* (New York: Basic Books, 1963); Tzvetan Todorov, *Grammaire du Décameron* (The Hague: Mouton, 1969), and *The Fantastic* (Ithaca: Cornell University Press, 1975).

4. John Cawelti, *The Six-Gun Mystique* (Bowling Green: Bowling Green Popular Press, 1971) and *Adventure, Mystery and Romance* (Chicago: University of Chicago Press, 1976); Leo Braudy, *The World in a Frame*; Frank McConnell, *The Spoken Seen: Films and the Romantic Imagination* (Baltimore: Johns Hopkins University Press, 1975); Michael Wood, *America in the Movies, or Santa Maria, It Had Slipped My Mind* (New York: Delta, 1975); Will Wright, *Sixguns and Society: A Structural Study of the Western* (Berkeley: University of California Press, 1975); Thomas Schatz, *Hollywood Genres: Formulas, Filmmaking, and the Studio System* (New York: Random House, 1981).

5. See especially the collective text on "Young Mr. Lincoln de John Ford," *Cahiers du Cinéma* 223 (Aug. 1970), 29-47 (translated in *Screen* in Autumn 1972, pp. 5-44, and commented on by Ben Brewster in *Screen* in Autumn 1973, pp. 29-43); and Jean-Louis Comolli's six-part article on "Technique et Idéologie," *Cahiers du Cinéma* 229-41 (1971-72). The entire *Screen* project has been usefully summarized, with extensive bibliographical notes, by Philip Rosen, "*Screen* and the Marxist Project in Film Criticism," *Quarterly Review of Film Studies* 2, no. 3 (Aug. 1977), 273-87; on *Screen*'s approach to ideology, see also Stephen Heath, "On Screen, In Frame: Film and Ideology," *QRFS* 1, no. 3 (Aug. 1976), 251-65. The most important influence on all these positions is Louis Althusser, "Ideology and Ideological State Apparatuses," in *Lenin and Philosophy and Other Essays* (New York: Monthly Review Press, 1971), pp. 127-86.

6. Paul Hernadi, *Beyond Genre: New Directions in Literary Classification* (Ithaca: Cornell University Press, 1972).

7. Tzvetan Todorov, *The Fantastic* (Ithaca: Cornell University Press, 1975).

8. Fredric Jameson, "Magical Narratives: Romance as Genre," *New Literary History* 7 (1975), 135-63.

9. Jean Mitry, *Dictionnaire du cinéma* (Paris: Larousse, 1963), p. 276.

10. Marc Vernet, *Lectures du film* (Paris: Albatros, 1976), pp. 111-12.

11. Jim Kitses, *Horizons West* (Bloomington: Indiana University Press, 1969), pp. 10-14.

12. John Cawelti, *The Six-Gun Mystique* (Bowling Green: Bowling Green Popular Press, 1971).

13. See, for example, Christian Metz, *Language and Cinema* (The Hague: Mouton, 1974), pp. 148-61; and Will Wright, *Sixguns and Society* (Berkeley: University of California Press, 1975), *passim*.

14. This relationship is especially interesting in the work of Richard Dyer and Jane Feuer, both of whom attempt to confront the interdependence of ritual and ideological components. See in particular Richard Dyer, "Entertainment and Utopia," in *Genre: The Musical*, 175-89; and Jane Feuer, *The Hollywood Musical*, passim.

15. See my "Intratextual Rewriting: Textuality as Language Formation," in *The Sign in Music and Literature*, ed. Wendy Steiner (Austin: University of Texas Press, 1981), pp. 39-51.

16. Henri Focillon, *The Life of Forms in Art* (New York: George Wittenborn, 1942).

17. Leonard B. Meyer, *Music, The Arts, and Ideas: Patterns and Predictions in Twentieth-Century Culture* (Chicago: University of Chicago Press, 1967).

18. Christian Metz, *Language and Cinema* (New York: Praeger, 1975).

19. Will Wright, *Sixguns and Society* (Berkeley: University of California Press, 1975).

20. For a useful review of approaches to the question of integration, see John Mueller, "Fred Astaire and the Integrated Musical," *Cinema Journal* 24, no. 1 (Fall 1984), 28-40.

21. Jerome Delamater, "Performing Arts: The Musical," in Stuart Kaminsky, *American Film Genres* (Dayton: Pflaum, 1974), 130.

22. Vladimir Propp, *Morphology of the*

Folktale (Bloomington: Indiana Research Centre in Anthropology, 1958); and Tzvetan Todorov, "Narrative Transformations," in *Poetics of Prose* (Ithaca: Cornell University Press, 1977).

23. Claude Lévi-Strauss, "The Structure of Myths," in *Structural Anthropology* (New York: Basic Books, 1963).

6. The Fairy Tale Musical

1. See, for example, Michael B. Druxman, *The Musical from Broadway to Hollywood* (New York: Barnes, 1980).

2. On the development of American musical theater, see especially Gerald Bordman, *American Operetta* (New York: Oxford University Press, 1981). Other valuable books on this topic include David Ewen, *The Story of America's Musical Theater* (Philadelphia: Chilton, 1961), and Lehman Engel, *The American Musical Theater* (New York: Collier, 1967).

3. On the European tradition, see David Ewen, *European Light Opera* (New York: Holt, Rinehart & Winston, 1962).

4. John Kobal, *Gotta Sing, Gotta Dance*, pp. 174, 176.

5. On the Astaire/Rogers dances, see Croce, *The Fred Astaire and Ginger Rogers Book*, and Mueller, *Astaire Dancing*.

6. Leslie Halliwell, *The Filmgoer's Companion* (New York: Avon, 1974; fourth American edition) p.699.

7. The Show Musical

1. On vaudeville, see Eugene Elliott, *A History of Variety-Vaudeville from the Beginning to 1914* (Seattle: University of Washington Press, 1941); Joe Laurie, Jr., *Vaudeville: From the Honky Tonks to the Palace* (New York: Holt, 1953); Albert McLean, *American Vaudeville as Ritual* (Lexington: University of Kentucky Press, 1965); John E. DiMeglio, *Vaudeville U.S.A.* (Bowling Green: Bowling Green Popular Press, 1973).

2. On the minstrel show, see Robert Toll, *Blacking Up: The Minstrel Show in Nineteenth-Century America* (New York: Oxford University Press, 1974).

3. On burlesque, see Bernard Sobel, *A Pictorial History of Burlesque* (New York: Putnam, 1956).

4. Denis de Rougemont, *Love in the Western World* (New York: Harcourt, Brace, 1940).

5. While the phenomenon I am describing here bears a close relationship to that detailed by Laura Mulvey in "Visual Pleasure and Narrative Cinema," in *Women and the Cinema*, ed. Karyn Kay and Gerald Peary (New York: Dutton, 1977; original in *Screen* 16, no. 3 [1975]), it is important to note that I am not claiming a male/camera identification for the whole of the musical, but only for the show subgenre. In particular, I will later show how the folk subgenre develops a uniquely female point of view.

6. On the identification between spectator and apparatus, see Jean-Louis Baudry, "Ideological Effects of the Basic Cinematic Apparatus," *Film Quarterly* 28, no. 2 (1974-75), and Christian Metz, *The Imaginary Signifier: Psychoanalysis and the Cinema* (Bloomington: Indiana University Press, 1982).

7. On sexual positioning in Berkeley, see Lucy Fischer, "The Image of Woman as Image: The Optical Politics of *Dames*," in *Genre: The Musical*, 70-84.

8. The Folk Musical

1. Vincente Minnelli, *I Remember It Well* (Garden City: Doubleday, 1974), p. 135.

2. Hugh Fordin, *The World of Entertainment*, p. 181.

3. Matthew Baigell, *The American Scene: American Painting of the Thirties* (New York: Praeger, 1974), provides background information and ample illustration of the painting style which most affected the folk musical.

4. Agnes de Mille, *Dance to the Piper* (Boston: Little, Brown, 1952), pp. 307-08.

5. Miles Kreuger, *The Movie Musical from Vitaphone to Forty-Second Street*, p.19.

6. Tom Milne, *Mamoulian* (Bloomington: Indiana University Press, 1969), p.13.

7. Johan Huizinga, *Homo Ludens: A Study of the Play Element in Culture* (Boston: Beacon, 1950), pp. 158-59.

8. On *Show Boat*, see Miles Kreuger's extraordinarily complete production history, *Show Boat: The Story of a Classic American*

Musical (New York: Oxford University Press, 1977).

9. The following argument was developed in discussion with Jane Feuer. It thus bears a close resemblance to the argument put forward in the first chapter of Feuer's *The Hollywood Musical*.

9. Genre and Culture

1. For presentation of the family resemblance approach, see Ludwig Wittgenstein, *Philosophical Investigations* (New York: Macmillan, 1968), # 67.

2. Max Weber, *The Protestant Ethic and the Spirit of Capitalism* (New York: Scribner, 1958). See especially chapter five, "Asceticism and the spirit of Capitalism," pp. 155ff.

3. For a history of the debate surrounding the Weber thesis, see especially Robert W. Green, *Protestantism and Capitalism: The Weber Thesis and its Critics* (Boston : Heath, 1959); and Paul Seaver, "The Puritan Work Ethic Revisited," *Journal of British Studies* 19, no. 2 (Spring 1980), 35-53.

4. Hugh Cunningham provides an insightful look into the influence of the industrial revolution on the status and forms of recreation, in *Leisure in the Industrial Revolution, c.1780-c. 1880* (New York: St. Martin's, 1980).

5. Edmund Leach has provided an eloquent defense and explanation of Lévi-Strauss's position in *Claude Lévi-Strauss* (New York: Viking, 1970).

6. On the metonymic/metaphoric distinction, see Roman Jakobson and Morris Halle, "Two Aspects of Language and Two Types of Aphasic Disturbances," in *Fundamentals of Language* (The Hague: Mouton, 1956).

7. Leonard B. Meyer, *Music, the Arts, and Ideas: Patterns and Predictions in Twentieth-Century Culture* (Chicago: University of Chicago Press, 1967).

8. Theodor W. Adorno, *Introduction to the Sociology of Music* (New York: Seabury Press, 1976; original 1962), p.225.

9. T. W. Adorno, "On Popular Music," *Studies in Philosophy and Social Science* 9, no.1 (April 1941), 17-49.

10. On the nature of early American writings on music, see Gilbert Chase, *America's Music From the Pilgrims to the Present* (New York: McGraw-Hill, 1955), pp. 22ff.

11. On bandmasters as composers, see H. Wiley Hitchcock, *Music in the United States: A Historical Introduction* (Englewood Cliffs: Prentice-Hall, 1969), pp. 113ff.

12. Joseph Lee, quoted by Augustus Delafield Zanzig, *Music in American Life: Present and Future* (New York; Oxford University Press, 1932), pp. 12-13.

13. Daniel Gregory Mason, *The Dilemma of American Music* (New York: Macmillan, 1928), quoted in Paul S. Carpenter, *Music: An Art and a Business* (Norman: University of Oklahoma Press, 1950), p. 11.

14. Ernest Roth, *The Business of Music* (New York: Oxford University Press, 1969), p. 13.

The following table provides a convenient overview of the American film musical, divided by subgenre. Providing date, title, and studio for over three hundred musicals (approximately twenty percent of the total production), this table permits at a glance a chronological overview of the musical's subgenres. It should not be used, however, as a substitute for the more nuanced arguments presented in the text. In particular, it is important to recognize that no musical represents its category purely. A film like *Brigadoon* taken in its entirety, clearly operates according to principles outlined in the chapter on the fairy tale musical. Viewed solely from the view of the Scottish Highlands scenes, however, *Brigadoon* may be seen to share numerous traits with the folk musical. *It's Always Fair Weather* concludes with a scene that draws the film toward the show musical category, yet the film as a whole operates as an urban folk musical. In general, where films combine semantic traits deriving from one subgenre with the syntactic characteristics of another subgenre, I have classified them according to their syntactic affinities. Furthermore, subgeneric "sensitivity" differs according to period. During the forties, for example, there is relatively little crossover between subgenres, which appear well defined and self-contained (except in the folk/show troop entertainment films), whereas the period since the sixties is marked by a tendency toward mixing subgenres. The border between the folk and fairy tale subgenres is thus less clear before 1940 and after 1960 than it is during the forties and fifties. Major studios are identified for each film (with coproductions or merged company productions such as United Artist/Mirisch or Warner/First National listed under the more familiar name); productions by companies not dependent on one of the major studios are listed as independent productions. Director's names may be found in the index under the title of the film.

Date	The Fairy Tale Musical		The Show Musical		The Folk Musical	
1927			The Jazz Singer	War		
1928			The Singing Fool	War		
1929	The Desert Song	War	Applause	Para	Hallelujah	MGM
	The Love Parade	Para	Broadway	Univ		
	Rio Rita	Radio	Broadway Babies	War		
	The Vagabond Lover	RKO	The Broadway Melody	MGM		
			The Great Gabbo	Para		
			On with the Show	War		
1930	Dixiana	RKO	Free and Easy	MGM	Check and Double Check	RKO
	Golden Dawn	War	The King of Jazz	Univ	Song of the West	War
	Monte Carlo	Para	Show Girl in Hollywood	War		
	Paramount on Parade	Para				
	The Vagabond King	Para				
1931	The Hot Heiress	War				
	The Smiling Lieutenant	Para				
1932	Love Me Tonight	Para	The Big Broadcast	Para		
	One Hour with You	Para	Speak Easily	MGM		
1933	Flying Down to Rio	RKO	Dancing Lady	MGM	Hallelujah, I'm a Bum	UA
			Footlight Parade	War		
			Forty-Second Street	War		
			Gold Diggers of 1933	War		
1934	The Gay Divorcee	RKO	Dames	War	Flirtation Walk	War
	The Merry Widow	MGM	Twenty Million Sweethearts	War		
	Wonder Bar	War				

Date	The Fairy Tale Musical		The Show Musical		The Folk Musical	
1935	Folies Bergère Gold Diggers of 1935 In Caliente Naughty Marietta Roberta Top Hat	UA War War MGM RKO RKO	Go into Your Dance	War	The Little Colonel Mississippi Shipmates Forever	Fox Para War
1936	Follow the Fleet The King Steps Out Stowaway Swing Time	RKO Col Fox RKO	Anything Goes Born to Dance The Great Ziegfeld	Para MGM MGM	Pigskin Parade Rose Marie San Francisco Show Boat	Fox MGM MGM Univ
1937	Damsel in Distress The Firefly Maytime On the Avenue Shall We Dance	RKO MGM MGM Fox RKO	Broadway Melody of 1938 Gold Diggers of 1937 One Hundred Men and a Girl Varsity Show	MGM War Univ War	High, Wide and Handsome	Para
1938	Carefree Gold Diggers in Paris The Great Waltz Snow White and the 7 Dwarfs	RKO War MGM Disney	Little Miss Broadway Sweethearts	Fox MGM	The Girl of the Golden West In Old Chicago	MGM Fox
1939	The Wizard of Oz	MGM	Babes in Arms Broadway Serenade The Story of Vernon and Irene Castle	MGM MGM RKO		
1940	Argentine Nights New Moon	Univ MGM	Broadway Melody of 1940 Dance Girl Dance Strike Up the Band Tin Pan Alley	MGM RKO MGM Fox	Little Nelly Kelly	MGM

Date	The Fairy Tale Musical		The Show Musical		The Folk Musical	
1941	The Chocolate Soldier Moon Over Miami	MGM Fox	Blues in the Night Lady Be Good You'll Never Get Rich The Ziegfeld Girl	War MGM Col MGM	Sun Valley Serenade	Fox
1942	Holiday Inn Rio Rita Ship Ahoy You Were Never Lovelier	Para MGM MGM Col	Babes on Broadway For Me and My Gal Yankee Doodle Dandy	MGM MGM War	Cabin in the Sky Ride 'Em Cowboy	MGM Univ
1943	The Desert Song Dubarry Was a Lady I Dood It	War MGM MGM	The Gang's All Here Stage Door Canteen Stormy Weather Thousands Cheer	Fox UA Fox MGM	Girl Crazy Hello Frisco Hello	MGM Fox
1944	Bathing Beauty	MGM	Broadway Rhythm Cover Girl Lady in the Dark Music for Millions Sensations of 1945	MGM Col Para MGM UA	Can't Help Singing Going My Way Irish Eyes Are Smiling Meet Me in St. Louis	Univ Para Fox MGM
1945	The Thrill of a Romance Yolanda and the Thief	MGM MGM	Anchors Aweigh Rhapsody in Blue	MGM War	The Bells of St. Mary's State Fair	Para Fox
1946	Blue Skies Ziegfeld Follies	Para MGM	The Jolson Story Night and Day Swing Parade of 1946 Till the Clouds Roll By The Time, the Place, the Girl Two Sisters from Boston	Col War Ind MGM War MGM	Centennial Summer The Harvey Girls Margie	Fox MGM Fox

Date	The Fairy Tale Musical		The Show Musical		The Folk Musical	
1947	Fiesta On an Island with You The Pirate	MGM MGM MGM	Mother Wore Tights	Fox	Good News It Happened in Brooklyn Living in a Big Way The Shocking Miss Pilgrim This Time for Keeps	MGM MGM MGM Fox MGM
1948	The Emperor Waltz Romance on the High Sea	Para War	Easter Parade A Song Is Born Words and Music	MGM RKO MGM	One Sunday Afternoon Summer Holiday	War MGM
1949	A Connecticut Yankee in King Arthur's Court	Para	The Barkleys of Broadway Jolson Sings Again Look for the Silver Lining My Dream Is Yours Red, Hot and Blue Slightly French	MGM Col War War Para Col	In the Good Old Summer Time On the Town Take Me Out to the Ball Game	MGM MGM MGM
1950	Cinderella	Disney	Let's Dance	Para	Annie Get Your Gun Riding High Summer Stock Two Weeks with Love	MGM Para MGM MGM
1951	An American in Paris Royal Wedding	MGM MGM	Call Me Mister The Great Caruso	Fox MGM	Show Boat	MGM
1952	April in Paris Lovely to Look At	War MGM	Singin' in the Rain With a Song in My Heart	MGM Fox	The Belle of New York Meet Me at the Fair	MGM Univ
1953	Call Me Madam The Desert Song Gentlemen Prefer Blondes Scared Stiff	Fox War Fox Para	The Band Wagon Give the Girl a Break Kiss Me Kate Lili The Stooge Three Sailors and a Girl	MGM MGM MGM MGM Para War	Calamity Jane The Farmer Takes a Wife	War Fox

Date	The Fairy Tale Musical		The Show Musical		The Folk Musical	
1954	Brigadoon	MGM	The Country Girl	Para	Carmen Jones	Fox
	The French Line	RKO	Deep in My Heart	MGM	Red Garters	Para
	White Christmas	Para	The Glenn Miller Story	Univ	Seven Brides for Seven Brothers	MGM
			There's No Business like Show Business	Fox		
			A Star Is Born	War		
1955	Daddy Long Legs	Fox	The Benny Goodman Story	Univ	Guys and Dolls	MGM
	Kismet	MGM	The Seven Little Foys	Para	It's Always Fair Weather	MGM
					The Lady and the Tramp	Disney
					Oklahoma!	Ind
1956	High Society	MGM	Anything Goes	Para	Carousel	Fox
	An Invitation to the Dance	MGM	Rock around the Clock	Col	Love Me Tender	Fox
	The King and I	Fox				
	The Vagabond King	Para				
	You Can't Run from It	Col				
1957	The Pajama Game	War	Funny Face	Para	Beau James	Para
	Silk Stockings	MGM	Jailhouse Rock	MGM		
			The Joker Is Wild	Para		
			Les Girls	MGM		
			Pal Joey	Col		
1958	Damn Yankees	War			The Girl Most Likely	RKO
	Gigi	MGM			King Creole	Para
	Party Girl	MGM				
	South Pacific	Fox				
1959	Some Like It Hot	UA			Porgy and Bess	Col
1960	Bells Are Ringing	MGM	Can-Can	Fox		
1961					Flower Drum Song	Univ
					West Side Story	UA

Date	The Fairy Tale Musical		The Show Musical		The Folk Musical	
1962	Blue Hawaii	Para	Gypsy	War	Girls, Girls, Girls The Music Man State Fair	Para War Fox
1963			Bye-Bye Birdie	Col		
1964	Mary Poppins My Fair Lady	Disney War			Roustabout The Unsinkable Molly Brown	Para MGM
1965	The Sound of Music	Fox				
1966	A Funny Thing Happened on the Way to the Forum How to Succeed in Business without Really Trying	UA UA				
1967	Camelot Clambake Half a Sixpence	War UA Para				
1968	Sweet Charity	Univ	Funny Girl Give a Little Love a Little The Producers	Col MGM MGM	Finian's Rainbow	War
1969					Alice's Restaurant Change of Habit Hello Dolly Paint Your Wagon	UA Univ Fox Para
1970	On a Clear Day You Can See Forever	Para			Woodstock	War
1971			The Boy Friend	MGM		
1972	Alice's Adventures in Wonderland	Ind	Cabaret	Ind		

Date	The Fairy Tale Musical		The Show Musical		The Folk Musical	
1973	Jesus Christ Superstar	Univ				
1974	Mame	War	That's Entertainment	MGM		
1975	The Little Prince	Para	Funny Lady	War	Nashville	Para
1976			A Star Is Born	War		
1977			New York, New York Pete's Dragon	UA Disney	Saturday Night Fever	Para
1978	The Wiz	Univ			Grease	Para
1979	Hair	UA	The Muppet Movie The Rose	Ind Fox		
1980			All That Jazz Can't Stop the Music Fame A Perfect Couple	Col Ind MGM Ind		
1981					Pennies from Heaven	MGM
1982	Annie	Col			Grease II	Para
1983					Flashdance Wild Style Yentl	Para Ind MGM

In order to keep this index within manageable limits, I have not included titles of songs, plays, operettas, and non-musical films. I have also left out the names of artists, critics, band leaders, opera singers, and composers and performers mentioned solely as the subjects of biopics, as well as performers who are mentioned only in the legends for illustrations. For all musicals, I have identified director and date. In most cases, the Table of Musicals by Subgenre (pp. 372–78) provides studio information.

Broadway Melody of 1940 (Taurog, 1940), 33, 75, 209, 231, 234, 287
Broadway musical, 66, 120, 127, 129ff, 196ff, 199, 251, 285, 298ff, 321, 322, 352, 353
Broadway Rhythm (Del Ruth, 1944), 234
Broadway Serenade (Leonard, 1939), 212, 214i, 234, 318i, 353i
Broderick, Helen, 173
Brown, Herb Nacio, 121, 225i
Buchanan, Jack, 33, 137, 150, 160, 259, 260
Burlesque, 203–04, 211, 213, 214, 218ff, 338
Business and economic concerns, 21–22, 47, 49, 50, 153ff, 182, 187, 192, 232, 233, 258, 270–71, 288, 294, 300ff, 322, 325, 326, 328, 329, 330, 341–42, 343ff, 348, 352
Bye Bye Birdie (Sidney, 1963), 32, 209, 274

Cabaret (Fosse, 1972), 121, 223, 265, 268
Cabin in the Sky (Minnelli, 1942), 61, 78, 82, 109, 285, 289, 298i, 312, 317, 342
Cagney, James, 137, 231–32, 237i, 265, 331
Calamity Jane (Butler, 1953), 311
Call Me Madam (Lang, 1953), 149, 152, 197, 288, 341
Call Me Mister (Bacon, 1951), 86
Camelot (Logan, 1967), 86, 197, 268
Cameo Kirby (Cummings, 1930) 182
Can-Can (Lange, 1960), 61, 82
Cantor, Eddie, 138
Capra, Frank, 167, 319
Captain of the Guard (Fejos/Robertson, 1930), 182
Carefree (Sandrich, 1938), 162, 164, 165, 167
Carmen Jones (Preminger, 1954), 139
Carmichael, Hoagy, 138
Caron, Leslie, 21, 29–31, 44, 45, 54, 78, 157, 246, 309
Carousel (King, 1956), 33, 35, 37, 38, 48, 82, 85, 139, 198, 268, 274, 289, 307
Carradine, Keith, 327
Cartoons, 71, 104ff, 194, 198
Caulfield, Joan, 245
Causality, 16ff, 64ff, 68ff, 76ff, 211, 292
Cavendish, Milly, 216
Centennial Summer (Preminger, 1946), 77, 139, 275, 288i, 306, 308, 310, 311, 317, 323
Challenge dance, 163ff, 171
Change of Habit (Graham, 1969), 273, 277
Chaplin, Geraldine, 325
Characters, 21, 68, 81ff, 102ff, 110, 134, 142, 155, 190ff, 208; unsuited to romantic interest, 31, 49, 104, 108, 135
Charisse, Cyd, 33, 41i, 44, 46i, 47, 54, 55, 67, 75, 81, 242, 246, 259, 323, 358
Charm—*see* Prince Charming
Chasing Rainbows (Riesner, 1930), 211
Check and Double Check (Brown, 1930), 296
Chevalier, Maurice, 21, 26, 36, 37, 44, 52, 62, 80, 111, 131, 136, 138, 142, 145, 146, 147, 148, 150, 152, 153i, 154, 155, 157, 158, 159, 160, 168, 169, 171, 182, 185, 209, 270, 273
Children's musicals, 103ff, 107, 121, 270
Chocolate Soldier, The (Del Ruth, 1941), 33
Choreography and choreographers, 151, 188–89, 229, 234, 245, 246, 283ff, 305
Chorus, 66, 119, 133, 136, 227, 285, 305, 306, 309, 325
Cinderella (Sharpsteen, 1950), 104
Clambake (Nedel, 1967), 198
Clowning, 55ff, 193, 228, 268, 323, 236
Colbert, Claudette, 150, 167

Colette, 21
Color, 33, 186, 188, 277
Columbia (studio), 111
Comden, Betty, 50, 121, 248, 258, 323
Comedians, 138, 147, 184, 194, 201–02, 203
Comedy, 91, 140, 175, 201ff, 315–16
Comedy, romantic—*see* Romantic comedy
Comedy, screwball—*see* Screwball comedy
Community, 238, 240, 259, 274, 292, 294, 301, 305, 306, 307, 309ff, 311, 315, 317, 322, 325, 327, 329, 342, 347, 358, 363
Composers (*see also* Biopic), 65–66, 131, 133, 139, 184, 197, 198, 225, 235ff, 259–60, 285, 286; European, 133ff, 138, 139, 149
Concert film, 102–03, 104, 112, 121
Connecticut Yankee in King Arthur's Court, A (Garnett, 1949), 153, 341
Cook, Donald, 314
Corpus definition, 12ff, 90ff, 96–97, 102ff
Costumes and costumers, 33, 75, 133, 142, 166, 175, 176, 204, 216, 285, 304
Counterculture, 49, 136, 330, 334
Country Girl, The (Seaton, 1954), 112, 121, 209, 228, 264i, 265, 268, 354i
Couples, 31–32, 35, 126, 144, 158, 162ff, 167, 200, 211, 227, 307ff, 309ff, 315, 317, 323, 327; secondary, 31–32, 37, 147, 151, 274, 306, 307–08
Courtship (*see also* Post-marriage courtship), 51, 105, 108, 144ff, 153, 156, 159, 168ff, 262ff, 268, 310, 312
Cover Girl (C. Vidor, 1944), 54, 55, 61, 75, 76, 243
Coyne, Joe, 136, 137i
Crawford, Joan, 230, 234
Criticism, role of, 5, 7, 12, 330
Crosby, Bing, 32, 111, 120, 121, 138, 171, 230, 264i, 265, 318, 319i, 354i
Cuban Love Song, The (Van Dyke, 1931), 182, 183, 186
Cugat, Xavier, 186, 241
Cukor, George, 167
Curry, John, 277, 293i

Da Costa, Morton, 53
Daddy Long Legs (Negulesco, 1955), 247, 274, 288
Dailey, Dan, 137, 323
Dames (Berkeley, 1934), 71, 86, 215i, 217, 227, 232–34, 288, 342
Damn Yankees (Donen & Abbott, 1958), 198
Damsel in Distress (Stevens, 1937), 77, 86, 152, 161, 245, 288, 341
Dance (*see also* Ballet, Challenge dance, Choreography, Narrative dance, Waltz), 40ff, 52, 67, 68, 85, 106, 110, 135ff, 157, 163ff, 166, 168, 171, 173ff, 174, 190–91, 203, 218ff, 229ff, 245, 246, 247, 269, 276, 282ff, 292, 294, 305, 307, 309, 317, 355, 357, 359, 363, 364
Dance Girl Dance (Arzner, 1940), 204, 228
Dance of Life, The (Cromwell, 1929), 205
Dancing Lady, The (Leonard, 1933), 112, 113i, 234, 287
Dancing Pirate, The (Corrigan, 1936), 186
Daniels, Bebe, 227
Deep in My Heart (Donen, 1954), 243
De Haven, Gloria, 278
Del Rio, Dolores, 30i, 83i, 161
De Mille, Agnes, 283, 284i, 286, 305, 309
Depression, 140, 155, 232, 258, 313, 316, 333, 334
Desert Song, The (Del Ruth, 1929), 140, 179, 180, 181i, 182, 184, 187, 192, 196
Desert Song, The (Humberstone, 1953), 194

Rick Altman is Professor of French and Communication Studies at the University of Iowa. He has also held visiting appointments at the University of Paris X (Nanterre) and III (Censier). He has edited volumes on *Cinema/Sound* and *Genre: The Musical* and has published widely on cinema theory and history, including prize-winning articles in *The Journal of Popular Culture* and *Cinema Journal*, as well as numerous reprinted articles.

Editor: Susan Harlow

Book designer: Sharon L. Sklar

Jacket designer: Sharon L. Sklar

Production coordinator: Harriet Curry

Typeface: Sabon

Compositor: Alexander Typesetting, Inc.